In Adamless Eden

In Adamless Eden

The Community of Women Faculty at Wellesley

Patricia Ann Palmieri

Yale University Press   New Haven and London

Copyright © 1995 by Patricia Ann Palmieri.
All rights reserved.
This book may not be reproduced, in whole or in part,
including illustrations, in any form (beyond that
copying permitted by Sections 107 and 108 of the U.S.
Copyright Law and except by reviewers for the public
press), without written permission from the publishers.

Designed by Sonia L. Scanlon.
Set in Berkeley type by Marathon Typography Service,
Inc., Durham, North Carolina.
Printed in the United States of America by Edwards
Brothers, Inc., Ann Arbor, Michigan.

Library of Congress Cataloging-in-Publication Data
Palmieri, Patricia Ann.
In Adamless Eden : the community of women faculty at
Wellesley / Patricia Ann Palmieri.
p.   cm.
Includes index.
ISBN 0–300–05529–3 (alk. paper)
1. Wellesley College—Faculty—Biography.
2. Women college teachers—Massachusetts—
Wellesley—Biography.   I. Title.
LD7212.2.P35   1995
378.744'7—dc20
94–31662
CIP

A catalogue record for this book is available from the
British Library.

The paper in this book meets the guidelines for
permanence and durability of the Committee on
Production Guidelines for Book Longevity of the
Council on Library Resources.

10 9 8 7 6 5 4 3 2 1

To the memory of my mother
Mildred Bonagur Palmieri, 1917–1990
To my father, Patsy J. Palmieri

For my friend George H. Ropes,
And for three special professors
Michael Luther
Beatrice Fry Hyslop, 1899–1973
Arthur Mendel, 1927–1988

Yes! It is delightful . . . for a woman . . . to belong to a college faculty. . . . Best of all, there is the sense of intellectual fellowship. . . . What pleasure not only to follow a private line of study or research . . . but to listen to others when they come back from their summers or sabbaticals. . . . The life of the faculty among its own members is fascinating in variety and stimulus. Probably it is especially fascinating to women, to whom this sort of group activity is comparatively new.

—Vida Dutton Scudder, "A Pedagogic Sunset," 1929

Contents

Contents

Preface

When I began this research in 1977, I had no idea that such an extraordinary community of women existed at Wellesley College during its early years. Wilma Slaight, the archivist at Wellesley, doubted that there was enough material on academic women to write a doctorate, much less a book. To our astonishment, I discovered a subculture of women scholars who had lived out their lives and careers at Wellesley. In *Adamless Eden* I reconstruct that world and interpret its significance.

The story of the Wellesley College faculty between 1875 and 1930 is a compelling one that reverberates with calls for a renewed sense of community in our contemporary culture. Although I did not attend Wellesley, I was beguiled by the attractiveness of the community these women created. The individuals who made up this pioneering faculty were at the forefront of higher education for women, an issue that continued in various forms over the years without being resolved. I hope to demonstrate how the intellectual life of this group of women faculty sparked a creative climate for succeeding generations of students.

As a collective biographer I confronted the problem of how to shape a narrative from an uneven range of materials. There was less information on the science faculty, for example, than on the literary and social science faculty. As a result, some of these noted academic women figure more prominently in the text than others. Yet it is the multiplicity of personalities and intellects that shaped what came to be known as the Wellesley world.

Wellesley College has always been a major institution of higher education that allowed educated women to seek their place in the intellectual life of the nation. In studying these faculty members, and the backlash that resulted from their personal and educational ideals, I believe that we can appreciate the contributions women scholars made to our cultural life, contributions that are often undermined and devalued. To rediscover such powerful intellectuals as Vida Dutton Scudder, Katharine Lee Bates, Emily Greene Balch, and Mary Whiton Calkins is to be made aware that without women's history and a feminist consciousness, the achievements of women in public and professional life can easily be erased.

Introduction

In 1888, Vida Dutton Scudder, a shy, nervous English instructor, arrived at Wellesley College. Immediately the ebullient and witty head of the department, Katharine Lee Bates, took the novitiate under her wings. More like "naughty school girls rather than sober instructors," Scudder recalled, they would saunter down the corridors of College Hall, sometimes gossiping, sometimes discussing English literature or their plans for a college settlement house. Quickly thereafter they converted Emily Greene Balch and Katharine Coman, both professors of economics, to their social cause and successfully launched Denison House Settlement in Boston.[1]

Of all the secular women's colleges founded in the late nineteenth century, only Wellesley was committed to having a female faculty and president. Over the years, this talented group of women garnered many accolades and honors: Vida Dutton Scudder became a well-known literary critic and social radical; Katharine Coman published pioneering economic histories; Mary Whiton Calkins became president of both the American Psychological Association and the American Philosophical Association; Margaret Clay Ferguson assumed the presidency of the Botanical Society of America; Katharine Lee Bates acquired national renown as the author of "America the Beautiful"; and Emily Greene Balch was awarded the Nobel Prize for Peace.

These faculty women worked together, exchanging syllabi, developing courses, and discussing their vision of women's higher education. Nightly they continued their sprightly intellectual repartee at roundtables as they visited one another's homes. Conversations continued on shipboard during their trips abroad or in the summer colonies they founded communally. Sometimes their activities took the form of social protest, as in 1900, when they denounced Wellesley's accepting "tainted money" from the Rockefellers. At such times they discussed resigning but stayed on, because "short of fleeing into a hermitage," they could not find an academic community more hospitable to women scholars or more tolerant of their dissent.[2]

Observers likened Wellesley educationally to a female Harvard. Vice-President Calvin Coolidge branded Wellesley a political "hotbed of radicalism." The first generation of students was awed by a faculty that stirred them; the next generation of faculty saw the old crowd as dedicated "war horses."[3] The pioneers, united in the "bonds of Wellesley," created a community that endured well over forty years.[4] As Florence Converse, the group historian, wrote, "Here was fellowship."[5]

In this book I recover and analyze the academic community at Wellesley. Three themes dominate this analysis: these women scholars were genuine intellectuals, who in challenging the consensual ascription of domestic roles for females have enlarged our understanding of educated women in the United States; they created a cohesive community that incorporated selective aspects of women's culture with intellectualism, feminism, and reform; and their success—in the cultivation of disciples who renounced marriage and pursued careers—produced a tremendous backlash.[6]

Who were the first generation of women scholars at Wellesley? What factors affected their choice of profession? In this collective biography I identify family culture, class, educational opportunities, sponsors, and personal ambition as sources of influence. I also describe the sociocultural climate of late-Victorian America, which tolerated the academic advancement of a "select few" intellectual women, as exemplified by the Wellesley faculty. Their contributions to women's higher education—in the form of educational ideals, teaching styles, curricula, and administration—extended from the Gilded Age through World War I. This reading of the Wellesley faculty connects their educational ethos to the formation of a middle-class cadre of students imbued with a new consciousness and motivation for careers. Moreover, I see this furthering of women's higher education as a form of feminism. Because many Wellesley faculty were social activists, I also place them in the larger context of the Progressive Era. Indeed, many were in the vanguard of the various movements to temper the evils of rapid industrial-

ization and urbanization. Using the discourse of social bonds and social efficiency, they helped define the progressive creed of an organic society that
abhorred individualism and attacked privilege and the excesses of wealth.
They aimed to correct social injustice and to diminish class conflict.[7] Their
continuous commitment to reform society through their scholarship distin-
guishes them from male peers who eventually retreated from advocacy into
objectivity.[8]

In seeking to elucidate Wellesley College and the female world within it,
one is wise to heed Estelle Freedman's suggestion that female institutions in
the late nineteenth century were important parts of middle-class American
culture and were key to the development of American feminism. Indeed,
the private and professional networks of the Wellesley faculty form the para-
meters within which their ideas about women's education, scholarship,
reform, and feminism blossomed. The concept of community is therefore
vital to the understanding of the academic subculture created at Wellesley.[9]

Vida Scudder commented that conflicts as well as friendships animated
the group life at Wellesley. I have therefore evoked the feuds that broke out
among the warring giants.[10] In this community of single women scholars,
many bonded for life in partnerships they termed "Wellesley marriages."
Historians continue to debate how to treat women's relationships in late
nineteenth-century America. Should these intimate dyads be considered lesbian, romantic, or simply friendly? In the current historical debate, some
scholars maintain the distinction between women-committed women and
lesbians. In chapter 8 I explore the female bonding at Wellesley within the
terms of this debate and conclude that while some unions may have
included erotic content or sexual intimacy, the Wellesley faculty community
is best considered a community of women-committed women. I also reconstruct the communal context that allowed friendships to flourish among
established couples.[11]

Virginia Woolf observed that to be creative every woman needs "a room
of one's own."[12] The academic women at Wellesley had an institution of
their own. To understand how this group of talented women assumed such
powerful roles within the college and cemented their communal ties, it is
essential to look at Wellesley's origins. In 1870 Henry and Pauline Durant, a
pair of romantic, evangelical reformers who had lost two children, sought
to assuage this loss by beginning to lay the foundation at Wellesley for a
tightly knit women's community whose hallmark would be its female professoriat. At a time when higher education for women was rare and few

women held professorships, this visionary endeavor was considered remarkably daring.

Henry Durant reveled in the intellectual powers and competence of his hand-picked women faculty. Nonetheless, his genuine belief in women's intellectual capabilities clashed with his conviction that even highly educated college women should adhere to the ideals of piety, purity, and submissiveness expected of every "true woman" in the nineteenth century.[13] This contradiction in ideology prompted faculty and students to challenge Durant and to shatter his lofty if inconsistent vision of women and Wellesley.

Forced to confront this crisis, Durant began to search for a woman president whom he could trust to uphold his vision and to govern after his death. In 1881 that search culminated in the appointment of Alice Freeman, who assumed Wellesley's presidency at twenty-six years of age. The youthful Freeman transformed Wellesley from what many believed to be merely an academy for girls into a modern collegiate institution. Blessed with a charismatic personality, Freeman consolidated her power by using gender to identify with her faculty and students; as a result, she successfully inspired as well as manipulated the members of this college community. Freeman favored the appointment of women scholars who could both teach the elective curriculum gaining favor in the 1890s and conduct innovative research. In 1925, Katharine Lee Bates praised these "purposeful women who have reared the college from struggling babyhood to glorious womanhood." Now they are all but forgotten.[14]

One asks why such outstanding academic women are unknown today. Although time has certainly distanced them from us, the more obvious reason is that historians have not considered them worthy of study. Traditional scholarship in the history of higher education consists largely of institutional histories, biographies of a few outstanding presidents and scholars, usually men, and the academic disciplines. *In Adamless Eden* is the first scholarly work to analyze in depth the lives and careers of a single faculty. It is also the first collective portrait of women who originated the role of academic at the women's colleges.[15]

In overlooking and devaluing women scholars and women's colleges, educational historians have retained a traditional periodization. They contend that after the Civil War a "great retrogression" beset higher education; by the end of the nineteenth century the liberal arts college was moribund. For them, only the rise of the university, spurred by the innovations of the university builders, all men, rescued a flagging educational system. In the past decade, such Whiggism has come under increasing attack, but historians still rarely give credit to the academic women who pioneered the development of scientific research or shaped the social sciences in the women's colleges.[16]

Scholars in women's history have likewise overlooked the first generation of academic women. Analyses of college-educated women in the Progressive Era have generally centered on social reformers, such as Jane Addams, Alice Hamilton, and Florence Kelley. Recently, splendid biographies of Charlotte Perkins Gilman have appeared, but she did not attend college, nor was she a professor. Therefore, a dearth of studies on women scholars in America remains.[17]

Most historians insist that higher education supported rather than challenged the ideology that prescribed domesticity as women's only proper role.[18] Educated women were either channeled into genteel, enlightened motherhood and home economics or at best, by the 1880s and 1890s, into social service. Hence, Jill Conway asserts that the first generation of college-educated women did not seize hold of intellectual inquiry. Rather, because they were wed to a romantic image of women's special, intuitive nature, all that these bright women could do was to create the helping professions. Thus intellectual life and academe itself remained male-dominated.[19]

Scholars usually disparage the women's colleges as citadels of domesticity that enshrined female virtue rather than intellectualism. Bryn Mawr, whose staunchly feminist president, M. Carey Thomas, appointed many male Ph.D.'s to the faculty, is sometimes exempt from this negative assessment. The other women's colleges, and particularly Wellesley, with its all-female faculty, are denigrated for faculty appointments that "did not aim to promote intellectual achievement."[20]

Many writers conclude that the women's colleges were devoid of feminist spirit. Indeed, interpreting the Gilded Age as bereft of reform impulses causes many to miss the significance of women's colleges. Few have appreciated how a shared sense of intellectual power and mission promoted a form of feminism.[21]

To dismiss the women's colleges as genteel, anti-intellectual, and anti-feminist backwaters is to misread their purposes and impact. Gentility did not preclude the development of a feminist consciousness among the academic women of Wellesley; nor did it prevent them from ardently supporting women's autonomy, women's rights, and the power of women's institutions.

The movement for women's higher education and for women's entry into the professions was for Wellesley's faculty very much a part of the larger women's movement.[22]

Recently, revisionist studies have accorded more revolutionary power to education, arguing that it provided women with the opportunity to control their lives, to seek careers other than teaching, and to create a new discourse about women's intellectual abilities, professional roles, and social status. Building on this wave of research, I attempt to broaden our understanding of women's intellectual history in the post–Civil War era.[23]

This story of the Wellesley community is both a collective biography and a social and intellectual history of women's higher education. By overlooking or denigrating women scholars, historians have missed a key tension in that history: success triggered as many problems as would have failure. Women shaped the intellectual life of the college between 1875 and 1930, but their achievement is obscured by a massive cultural backlash from detractors who denounced Wellesley for promulgating spinsterhood and causing race suicide. The limitations inherent in the emphasis on the select few also created backsliding. The next generation of students, less an intellectual elite than a socioeconomic one, chose not to renounce marriage for careers. In such a rapidly changing social climate, the strongest of women's institutions—women's colleges—were actually quite fragile and vulnerable.

The devaluation of American women scholars at the women's colleges is sustained by the histories of professionalization. Historians of the Progressive Era conclude that amateur scholars who were rooted in their communities, served a public audience, and advocated reform were, by the late nineteenth century, displaced by professionals who had no loyalty to their local communities. Instead, these cosmopolitan men identified more with their new disciplines of sociology or economics than they did with their college or university. Afraid to jeopardize their jobs by taking unpopular positions on thorny social issues in the 1890s and early 1900s, these academics renounced reform, comforted by the scientific neutrality of the emerging research university.[24] Yet few of the works on this subject consider the experience of academic women. Indeed, communities are of no particular interest to students of professionalization, who associate them with amateurs. The rhetoric of professionalization, however, impedes an understanding of the mentality of women scholars whose supreme value was personal interaction.[25] Women faculty, excluded from the research universities and many

professional societies, of necessity flourished in precisely the local institutions given short shrift by the literature of professionalization.[26]

This reappraisal of the role of academic women at Wellesley need not be
a sentimental journey. Rayna Rapp rightly cautions that "as we excavate and
legitimize women's history, social organization, and cultural forms, we must
not allow our own need for models of strong female collectivities to blind us
to the 'dialectic of tradition' in which women are both supported and constrained."[27]

Being female weighed heavily upon the Wellesley women scholars; in
spite of numerous supports from family, class, and new educational and
career opportunities, many of them complained of depression or devalued
their own professional contributions. As pioneers, these women faced challenges on all fronts: they demanded access to institutions of higher education formerly reserved for men; they rejected the patriarchal model of the
family and the submergence of women's energies within a private women's
sphere; and they transcended some of the conventions of nineteenth-century womanhood. Yet their rebellion against sentimentality and the amateur
female tradition now seems ironic, for it was never total; they retained some
aspects of these traditions by compulsion and some by choice. Their discourse on women's public lives did not entirely repudiate the ideology of
separate spheres or special female values. Seizing on some "remnants" of
women's culture—in particular cooperation and caretaking—they
endorsed new careers for women. They defined a new psychology and sociology of women in professional life that did more than merely mimic a male
model. They espoused a critical feminist pedagogy that makes them precursors to contemporary practitioners of women's studies.[28]

The Wellesley academic women combined a progressive spirit that valued science, rationalism, and public achievement with a commitment to the
romantic, genteel life. Yet to be a professor at Wellesley during this period
entailed costs: individuals were made to feel guilty if they considered leaving; in a climate that both praised and plundered a person's achievement,
many gifted women succumbed to self-disparagement, unable to overcome
their ambivalence toward success; and too often, homes, gardens, and summer trips compensated for stalled careers. By 1920, the war horses barred a
younger generation of faculty women from assuming power in the college.
Charges of lesbianism served to discredit professional women and devalue
their institutions. To lessen the stigma of separatism, Wellesley, like other
women's colleges, recruited married men. Throughout the decades that fol-

lowed, however, the legacy of the pioneers lived on—in their disciples and in the enduring college.

The intellectual community at Wellesley, once referred to as an "Adamless Eden," represents no small achievement.[29] This community, cemented by shared purpose and meaning, comprehended the whole of life. In it, public and private merged; women faced the joys and sorrows of youth, maturity, and old age together. For these women intellectuality and community coexisted. In the words of Vida Scudder, Wellesley afforded them an "adventure in fellowship."[30]

Presidents of Wellesley College

Ada Howard	1875–1881
Alice Freeman Palmer	1881–1887
Helen Shafer	1887–1894
Julia Irvine	1894–1899
Caroline Hazard	1899–1910
Ellen Fitz Pendleton	1911–1936
Mildred McAfee Horton	1936–1949
Margaret Clapp	1949–1966
Ruth M. Adams	1966–1972
Barbara Newell	1972–1980
Nannerl Keohane	1981–1993
Diana Chapman Walsh	1993–

Part I

Putting Women in Professors' Chairs
1875–1899

1

Incipit Vita Nova

The New Life Begins

In late August 1875 Ernestine Giddings, a senior at Bangor High School in Maine, wrote to a friend: "Dear Mary, I am going away to school,—in two weeks now,—to Wellesley College, a new school opened for the first time on the eighth of September. Miss Hallowell has gone there, as a teacher of Natural History, and the best teachers in the country are thought to have been secured. There are about fourteen girls going from here, so of course we shall be company for each other."[1]

There was plenty of company. During the first week of September 1875, over three hundred young women, together with their families, congregated at Wellesley College. The majority (more than a thousand in all) had traveled via the Boston-Albany Railroad, which stopped in West Needham, the town that hosted Wellesley and would soon take its name. Along with trunks and valises they carried circulars announcing the opening of Wellesley for the "purpose of giving to young women a collegiate education, opportunities fully equivalent to those usually provided for young men."[2] The students and their entourages were met at the West Needham station by horse-drawn omnibuses with "Wellesley College" painted on the sides. This caravan slowly proceeded past elm trees and purple beeches on the one-mile drive from the depot to the gates of the college. From there it wound through the magnificent three-hundred-acre estate designed by Wellesley's founders, Henry and Pauline Durant. At length everyone disembarked at

College Hall and was greeted by Ada Howard, Wellesley's first president, who assigned rooms to the young women and assuaged anxious parents.[3]

Local and national newspapers made much of Wellesley's opening, and the many journalists among the throng were equally caught up in the excitement. One asserted that an institution such as Wellesley College measured "the century's progress."[4] A second reporter commented on the most radical feature of the Wellesley experiment: "President, professors and students are all women; only two men belong to the establishment, the chief cook and the chief baker." Another writer concluded wistfully: "It is the men who feel lonely on this college campus."[5]

On September 8, 1875, 314 young women began their new life. In looking back on the experience years later, Louise McCoy North recalled the sense of uniqueness and of mission: "We were pioneers in the adventure,— voyagers in the crusade for the higher education of women,—that perilous experiment of the '70s, which all the world was breathlessly watching and which the prophets were declaring to be so inevitably fatal to the American girl."[6]

North's reminiscence evokes one of the most profound paradoxes underlying women's higher education in the late nineteenth century. Originally excluded from higher education in the Colonial period, women had been attending seminaries since at least the 1820s. By the 1870s, women graduated from a host of institutions, such as the University of Michigan and Vassar. Nonetheless, as North noted, the American public viewed women's higher education as an experiment. As late as 1892, Thomas Wentworth Higginson, a supporter of women's rights and women's higher education, would comment about this curious phenomenon: "Why is it, that, whenever anything is done for women in the way of education it is called an 'experiment,'—something that is to be long considered, stoutly opposed, grudgingly yielded, and dubiously watched,—while if the same thing is done for men, its desirableness is assumed as a matter of course, and the thing is done?"[7]

The answer is that the history of women's higher education in America is inextricably mixed with cultural ideas about women. During the seventeenth century a woman's intellect was considered inferior to a man's, and extensive learning was deemed inexpedient and dangerous. In this Puritan culture, higher education was linked almost exclusively to religion and the ministry, from which women were barred.

In the eighteenth century, as evangelism spread, women flocked to revivals. Church going and religion itself became increasingly feminized. Women were no longer deemed evil. This new religious role for women was matched by changes in their secular status.[8]

The American Revolution opened up further possibilities for the education of women. Postrevolutionary society was permeated with a new optimism derived from two sources: liberal enlightenment and romanticism. The new ideology elevated and idealized women as pure and sentimental. By 1820, what Barbara Welter has termed the "cult of true womanhood" was enshrined. Women were expected to cultivate four virtues: piety, purity, domesticity, and submissiveness. Innocence and emotionalism reigned, to the detriment of intellect. Too much education was thought to threaten the virtuous female. This same romantic image, however, could work on woman's behalf by emphasizing perfectionism. Educational reformers stressed that learning would not masculinize women; indeed it would ensure a more developed social character.[9]

Although women were not expected to participate in the public domain, they were made responsible for the education of their sons. The new republic, earnestly seeking to produce a virtuous citizenry, assigned women roles as influential caretakers, or republican mothers.[10] The new romanticism operated on women's behalf in other ways. It equated genius with such qualities as intuition, emotional empathy, and insight—qualities preeminently associated with women. By laying claim to special emotional and moral traits, women could cultivate intellectual roles as teachers, translators, and reformers. Concomitant with these cultural changes, economic factors were also operating to provide a rationale for women's education. In the increasingly industrialized society, with factory work replacing family production, young women were less needed for farm chores or home crafts. As men moved into the urban economy or ventured West, the marriage age rose. Sensing these changes, New England families engaged in a "life-planning strategy" that promoted the education of daughters. A seminary education would allow young women to teach, thus increasing the family income and enabling them to support themselves until they married.[11]

The common school movement, which institutionalized public education and created a need for a cheap labor pool, dovetailed nicely with this new ideology. Woman, as the natural caretaker of the young and an inexpensive worker, could be assigned a place in the national teaching force.[12]

In the 1860s and 1870s, the putative excess of single women in New England prompted educational leaders to promote women's higher education. They argued that education would increase women's independence, prepare them for work, and allow them to serve their generation. John Raymond, the president of Vassar, astutely connected the movement for women's higher education during this period with the women's rights movement that had begun before the Civil War. Perceiving a restlessness among women, Raymond commented that the "whole world is astir with a sense of coming change." In 1868, the Reverend John Morton Greene, in encouraging Sophia Smith to endow a women's college, similarly stated, "The subject of woman's education, woman's rights and privileges, is to be the great step in the progress of our state."[13]

Other educators and commentators, however, viewed the impending change with fear. In 1873 Dr. Edward Clarke, of Harvard University, published *Sex in Education, or a Fair Chance for the Girls,* in which he argued that higher education would damage women's health and inhibit their reproductive capacity. The book sold out immediately and was reprinted twelve times. Clarke's ideas stimulated a debate that only heightened the already millennial-like quality of the struggle for women's higher education. But his dire predictions did not dampen Henry Durant's desire to open Wellesley. Nor did it derail the young women who sought to enter Wellesley's first class.[14]

Although Edward Clarke and Henry Durant had been classmates at Harvard, they had distinctly different attitudes about women's educability. This ideological disparity throws light on the complexity of the dialogue about higher education for women. Indeed, by the 1870s this debate had become, at least in middle-class American society, what the abolitionist and women's-rights debate had been before it—a large-scale social movement with different intellectual strands, involving the energies of many men and women.[15]

The idea that women were malleable and perfectable loomed large in Henry Durant's mind as he planned the Wellesley College experiment. The appointment of women as full professors was an act of defiance not only against the ideas of Clarke but against all who considered women second-class citizens because of their biology. Durant fused his romantic, even sentimental image of women with a more liberal belief culled from ideas presented by proponents of women's ability and their right to autonomy. Recognizing, as did John Raymond and John Greene, that women's higher education was the primary social movement of post–Civil War society, Durant wanted to take a leading role in the cause, with Wellesley at the forefront. He wished to give women the opportunity to put their intellectual stamp on this new movement. "Women can do the work," he stated, "and I give them the chance."[16]

Durant, who selected everything that went into the making of Wellesley College—from the bricks for College Hall to the wildflowers he planted on campus—chose a motto from Dante for the insignia to mark the opening of the college. It was an appropriate choice: "Incipit Vita Nova," the new life begins.[17] For Durant, Wellesley was an educational community that would transform the lives of middle-class New England women and dispel the cult of true womanhood. Wellesley students were to become "new women," to go out into the world, usually as teachers, to uplift the educational system. The most radical feature of this new community was the appointment of an all-women faculty. To outsiders this extraordinary proposal epitomized Durant's visionary utopianism, for few women held professorships in colleges. Charles Eliot, president of Harvard, warned that a teaching corps composed solely of women was a "grave evil" that would spoil the entire experiment of women's higher education. Even the liberal T. W. Higginson looked warily on such a decision.[18]

But Wellesley College was more than a radical innovation; it also reflected the ideals and lives of the Durants. Disillusioned with urban America and having lost their children, they hoped to re-create a new family of students and faculty who would become a "little world under one roof." Loyalty was the hallmark of this community. Ada Howard recalled that Durant was adamant that Wellesley "have a loyal Faculty and loyal students. Loyalty, or locked doors, must be our motto. United we stand, divided we fall."[19]

The founder of Wellesley College, Henry Fowle Durant, was born Henry Welles Smith in Hanover, New Hampshire, in 1822. He seems to have always been a misfit. Like many men of his century he found the conventional roles offered males repugnant. A succession of female mentors and a romantic philosophy concerning feminine values molded the critical contours of his life and career. The first influences on Smith were his mother, Harriet Fowle, "a passionate lover of books"; an aunt who graduated from Mount Holyoke; and an early teacher, Mrs. Sarah Ripley (the aunt of Ralph Waldo Emerson). The latter, who could, in Durant's words, be seen "holding the baby, shelling the peas, and listening to a recitation in Greek, all in the same moment," was the source of his ideal of educated women.[20]

Smith went to Harvard in 1837 but found little that appealed to him. After his graduation in 1841, he read law, as his father had wanted him to, and passed the bar in 1843. But he was deeply alienated and hoped instead to devote himself to poetry. In 1851, in one of the few poetic gestures of his life, Henry Welles Smith changed his name to Henry Fowle Durant, taking both new names from his mother's side of the family.[21]

Durant was an eminently successful lawyer whose prestige within Massachusetts approached that of Daniel Webster, his contemporary. Durant invested in several business ventures that soon made him wealthy. Although he prospered, he grew more contemptuous of the law and sought a change in vocation. Turning to his love of nature, he began delivering lectures on the virtues of rural life, the dangers of wealth and commerce, and the need to educate everyone—rich and poor—for a more democratic, harmonious community.[22]

Durant's pious wife, Pauline Adeline Cazenove Fowle Durant, served as an antidote to the crass, selfish men with whom he associated by day. Henry had met Pauline, who was his first cousin, while still in college. They married in 1854, when he was thirty-two, and she twenty-one. Pauline's evangelical fervor matched Henry's poetic and aesthetic nature. She had hoped to attend Mount Holyoke Seminary (founded in 1837), but several deaths in her family had prevented her from doing so. She nonetheless never gave up her faith in women's education.

Although the couple maintained a house in Boston because of Henry's law practice, the true center of their family life was a farm cottage, the "Homestead," in Needham, Massachusetts. Their two children, Harry and Pauline, were born on this farm. The death of their daughter within six weeks of birth deeply affected both Durants. In reaction, Pauline turned to Christianity, whereas Durant threw himself into more worldly pursuits. He enlarged his library and purchased three hundred acres of land on which he planned a grand estate for his son. Then in 1863 little Harry died. Durant was devastated. For Henry the death of his two children intensified his other losses—namely, his youth, the warmth and intellectuality of the Ripley household, and the dream of a life devoted to poetry. He now heeded his wife's pleas that they serve God by devoting themselves to a worthy cause. They sold their home and returned to Boston. Henry, influenced by Dwight Moody, became a lay itinerant minister; Pauline became founder and president of the Boston Young Women's Christian Association.[23]

Yet evangelism and good works provided only part of the answer. Choosing not to become an officially ordained minister, he instead explored education as a way to effect social reform. For him, the higher education of women was an area that evoked the ideals of his youth, which had been shaped by educated women.

To Henry Durant, women were especially fitted to counterbalance male roles, which he identified with crass commercialism, social isolation, and death. Women were to be his allies in the critique of social norms and values. Durant was not alone in espousing the power of women to transform the masculine world; his ideology was consistent with that of many other nineteenth-century reformers, both female and male, who conceived of women as morally superior beings capable of purifying culture. Rather than relegate women to a separate domestic sphere, he believed that women should participate in public life and that such activism would follow upon their access to institutions of higher education. Women's secondary status, he claimed, derived from social, not biological, causes—a stance that put him philosophically in league with those who asserted that women had been assigned second-class citizenship illegitimately. Indeed, just as proponents of women's rights in the 1840s and 1850s fervently focused upon the vote as a means for social change, Durant fixed upon the remedy of higher education.[24]

In 1867 Durant joined the Board of Trustees of Mount Holyoke Seminary to learn more about women's higher education. Impressed, he was quoted as saying: "There cannot be too many Mount Holyokes."[25] That same year, the Durants decided to found a college for women on their estate, to be called Wellesley, from an old family name. On Henry's part, the decision was inextricably mixed with a craving for community and the hope of ending the alienation that had long troubled him. That hope was realized. He was present every day, supervising the design and construction of College Hall. In the process he pronounced that he had "cured the poverty within himself." Similarly, since Wellesley was a joint venture, it brought a new sense of mutuality to the Durants' marriage. Through the college Henry also formed a lasting friendship with Eben Horsford, a chemistry professor at Harvard and a self-made millionaire who shared Durant's ideals for women's education. Horsford helped Durant select the first women science faculty and advised him on a curriculum and the construction of laboratories.[26]

The Durants derived many benefits from their social reform efforts. The opening of Wellesley College in 1875 represented not only the fulfillment of their dream to construct a community but the culmination of their attempt to remake their lives. Yet the private lives intersected with a wider social history. Wellesley College was very much a part of the larger romantic reform tradition and the quest for women's equality.[27]

Henry Durant mixed many social and educational ideals to formulate his radical experiment. An examination of the institutional setting, the curriculum, and the faculty reflects his unique vision.

For Durant, Wellesley College was a natural laboratory, an experimental community in which he could realize his social and educational ideals. In his Wellesley College plan of education, Durant called upon women to "revolt against the slavery in which women were held by the customs of society— the broken health, the aimless lives, the subordinate position, the helpless dependence."[28]

To this end he conceived of Wellesley as a hothouse of experimentation, a veritable testing ground for the latest schemes to transform women socially and physically. Through proper diet, exercise, and spiritual and intellectual study, women would slowly shed and ultimately disavow the ethos of frail and ornamental womanhood. He built the college on what he claimed was the state's healthiest piece of property and polished the natural scenery by importing a thousand rhododendrons and azaleas for the lawns. College Hall, which housed the faculty, students, and classrooms, looked more like a cathedral than a college. Durant decorated some rooms for didactic purposes. The Elizabeth Barrett Browning Room, for example, displayed a bust of the poet and the original manuscript of one of her poems to remind students of what a talented woman could accomplish.[29]

Durant tried to control the basics of women's lives. His experimentation included the creation of a "Wellesley diet," intended to counteract "the pernicious American habit of eating confectionery and sweetmeats at irregular hours." Dress reform was also a part of Durant's program for social change. Clothing was to be short enough for ease in walking and devoid of heavy or fancy trimming. The question of proper attire also related to the sense of community Durant was trying to foster. Expensive clothes, which were beyond the means of most students, would arouse sentiments erosive to the communal spirit. Durant's ideal woman dressed simply—she was a pioneer known for her health, vigor, and scholarship, not for the modishness of her dress.[30]

This fervor for reform led Durant to experiment with new curricular ideas, especially those emanating from German universities. In science this meant laboratories that encouraged a sense of independence and adventure in experiment and discovery. Educational specialists invited to inspect the new college reported that Wellesley was better equipped for individual laboratory work than any male college. Wellesley surpassed Harvard in its emphasis on independent scientific study, a situation that "produced skepticism and much shaking of the head by Harvard at the radicalism of the former institution."[31]

Although Wellesley's first curriculum retained many of the traditional subjects, such as Greek and Latin and mental and moral philosophy, it also introduced French and German, modern English literature, and a host of scientific studies, including botany, zoology, geology, chemistry, and physics. (See table 1.) One scientist remarked that Wellesley had a chair in botany when professors of botany were "scarcer than blue roses." Durant also advocated a strong mathematics curriculum for women. National newspapers noted that the library "has shelf-room for one hundred and twenty thousand volumes, nearly as many as the library of Harvard contains." Ten thousand volumes, including works in German and French, came from the Durants' private library. The entire collection was hailed as one of the best reference libraries in the country.[32]

But the most radical feature of the Wellesley College experiment was Durant's appointment of a professoriat made up entirely of women. This endorsement of women was also emblematic of Durant's propensity to flout tradition, of his constant urge to be in the advance guard. He once commented, "If we were like other colleges we should not be what we ought to be."[33]

Durant hired seven heads of departments with the rank of professor, and eleven other teachers of academic subjects were accorded the title of lecturer. All faculty were to live in College Hall. And because Durant still considered religious piety the hallmark of a virtuous woman, all were required to be members of evangelical churches.

Documentation on the first women professors is scarce, but we know that two, Sarah Glazier and Helen Storke, held bachelor's degrees from Vassar College, where they had studied with the famous astronomer and endorser of women's rights Maria Mitchell. Other women faculty were self-educated. Susan Hallowell and Sarah Frances Whiting were given the opportunity to spend their first year studying at the Massachusetts Institute of Technology. Although Durant elevated these women to faculty status and

Table 1
The First Curriculum of Wellesley College, 1875[a]

Year	Required Subjects[b]	Electives[c]
Freshman	Elocution Essay writing History Latin Mathematics Modern English literature	French German Greek
Sophomore	Chemistry Elocution Essay writing History of literature Latin Mathematics Medieval history	Analytical geometry Botany Calculus French German Greek
Junior	Elocution Essay writing History of literature Literacy and criticism Modern history Physics Rhetoric	Botany Chemistry French German Greek Latin Mathematics Zoology
Senior	Anglo-Saxon and early English literature Essay writing History of philosophy Mental and moral philosophy Modern history	Analytical chemistry Botany French Geology German Greek Latin Mathematics Physics Zoology

[a]This is the curriculum for the General College Course.

[b]Regular study of the Scriptures was also included in this curriculum, although there was no separate biblical department.

[c]Freshmen and sophomores were required to elect one subject; juniors and seniors, any two subjects.

had no doubts as to their mental abilities, he betrayed his concern about behavior by appointing an appropriate role model as president. Ada Howard, a Mount Holyoke graduate and an emblem of the submissive woman, was to be the keeper of his vigilant regulations.[34]

Amid cries from Dr. Clarke at Harvard that the rigors of college life would undermine women's health, the first Wellesley College students were keenly aware that national attention was focused upon them. They considered the college to be a "mother of women in a noble line" and identified the cause of the college—women's higher education—with their personal success or failure. This fierce loyalty to Wellesley was just what the Durants had expected. Yet conflicts developed in spite of this devotion to the community ethos, indeed because of it.[35]

Almost from the beginning everyone involved with the experiment experienced frustration. A major disappointment for the faculty and founders was the fact that of the more than three hundred students who enrolled at Wellesley, only thirty passed the entrance examination. As a result, a preparatory, semicollegiate class had to be established. Chagrined at the situation, Durant announced that the preparatory department was only temporary and would be abandoned as soon as possible.

Moreover, Durant's presumption that natural and spontaneous bonds of loyalty would regulate the community soon proved naive. Not all the students spontaneously exhibited the degree of moral and social perfection Durant expected from young ladies. He soon started drafting more formal rules and issued a "Grey Book" of regulations to govern the college home.[36]

Durant never lost his vision of Wellesley as a female Harvard equipped with the latest scientific apparatus, a fine library, and intellectually qualified female professors. At the same time, to the amazement and dismay of his student body, he became involved in converting souls with the same fervor he brought to educating women. Among students and faculty this religious zeal was a constant source of ridicule. One student noted: "I loved his poetic side but his fanaticism drove me out of the church and theology for all time."[37]

Durant advertised Wellesley as a college, but the students and faculty did not agree. They identified the proliferating regulations and the constant religious exhortation with life in a seminary and pressed Wellesley to transcend its seminary quality. The model most students had in mind was Mount Holyoke Seminary, which many had chosen not to attend precisely because it did not offer a true collegiate course. The student body at Wellesley self-consciously demanded that they be treated like college women. Mary Elizabeth Stilwell, of the class of 1879, complained: "Wellesley is not a college. The buildings are beautiful, perfect almost; the rooms and their appointments delightful, most of the professors are all that could be desired, . . . but all these delightful things are not the things that make a college. And Oh! the experiments! It is enough to try the patience of a Job. I am here to take a *college course* and not to dabble in a little of every insignificant thing that comes up." She claimed that professors and peers alike shared her feelings: "These very professors have *worked* to have things different and have expostulated and expostulated with Mr. Durant, but all to no avail." She summed up the situation by portraying Durant: "He is as hard as flint and his mind is made up of the most beautiful theories, but he is perfectly blind to facts. He rules the college, from the amount of Latin we shall read to the kind of meat we shall have for dinner."[38]

Nowhere was the tension more obvious than in the clash between the strong women faculty Durant had appointed and President Howard and her Mount Holyoke coterie. Durant seems to have expected this friction, for he noted when he appointed Howard that she would face "severe trials," adding, "She will be a target to be shot at." Kind students characterized Miss Howard as the "perfect Mid-Victorian gentlewoman." Others were not nearly so charitable. In a college where the healthy, vigorous, intellectual woman was the ideal, Ada Howard was an incongruous figure; she suffered continually from obscure illnesses that made her appear an invalid in the eyes of the community.[39] Hardly an intellectual, Miss Howard gave biblical instruction in an old-fashioned way that, according to Frances Robinson Johnson, class of 1879, "doesn't make it (Bible Class) interesting at all."[40]

A vigilant enforcer of Durant's growing list of regulations, President Howard tried to "press her somewhat narrow conception of discipline upon . . . a restive student body." She lectured students on "slamming doors, whistling, . . . running through halls and talking above a whisper after lights out."[41] To students, the regime she upheld was inappropriate in a college. A poem found in several student notebooks conveys their ridicule. It begins:

> Miss Howard stood up in Chapel
> With puffs all over her head
> "Young ladies keep your doors closed
> Lest gentlemen see your bed."[42]

It continues to mock Howard's concern for the stealing of crockery and use of bad language. It closed with the conviction that Howard valued rules over teaching and learning.

To the students, the Vassar-trained faculty represented the achievement of intellectual aims that critics thought experimental and visionary. They were "superwomen," feared and adored. Ada Howard, on the other hand, exemplified the "repressive Mount Holyoke tradition" that shrouded Wellesley in its first years. The faculty and students considered her evasive and longed for a leader who could make decisions for herself. For a time they found that leader in Sarah Glazier, who in spring of 1876 seriously challenged Durant's authority.[43]

Because Wellesley was yet not legally able to grant degrees, Durant had invited a group of visitors to evaluate the college. He expected the regular schedule of recitations to be interrupted for what students and faculty termed a performance. Sarah Glazier felt that this was demeaning and showed a lack of regard for women's intellectual independence. Further, the incident symbolized Durant's contradictory concerns: his desire to parade Wellesley before the larger educational community as a successful college while at the same time enforcing decorum and conformity within Wellesley. Glazier led a delegation of teachers to ask Durant to state whether Wellesley was a college or a seminary. He answered that "so far as the intellectual work was concerned, it was a college, but in its care for the students' health, morals, etcs. it was a seminary." Glazier tried to get Durant to alter his plans for the upcoming visit, but he was firm.[44]

A definite sisterhood had developed at Wellesley even in this brief time period. Faculty and students felt they were insiders and resented being evaluated by outside authorities—especially men. As college women they considered themselves to have established their equality with men. The incident provoked scorn among the faculty over the power and dominance of men, and they incited their students to be caustic in their criticism of the board. Frances Johnson described the scene when the visitors arrived: "We took them out rowing at five. . . . Both turned their backs on Miss Emerson (our teacher) and hardly spoke a word to her. The fat one was the 'Colonel.' I heard that the 'Col.' told one of the gentlemen(!) . . . who was remarking on the beauty of the college and surroundings that it was all nice but he should prefer a cottage with roses on the other side of the lake with two in it!!!! The whole crowd was certainly no gentlemen, as could be seen by the manner in which they acted in the classes."[45]

A week after the board's visit, Henry Durant dismissed Sarah Glazier and two other sympathetic teachers. Stunned by the decision, the students wrote home that Mr. Durant had dismissed the three leading teachers in the college. Frances Johnson wrote her parents that all Mr. Durant would give for a reason is that they conflicted with the government of the college: "Now I'll tell you what the real reasons are—Miss H and the underteachers have always been jealous of them. They the Profs have always stood up for us having privileges and have always been opposed to WC being a Seminary. . . . They have not bowed down and worshipped that woman; in fact I don't think they ever thought anything of her. . . . I never thought of H's knowing anything; always thought of her as the one to give permission—to refuse . . . and to order us around and be hateful—She is only a graduate from So. Hadley."[46] In another letter home, Johnson scornfully adds that Mr. Durant remarked: "He will have no Prof's next term—What a 'Harvard' that will be!" She thought it likely that Wellesley would become a "second M. Holyoke."[47]

This interpretation is confirmed by a letter written in 1876 by Bessie Capen, professor of chemistry, who resigned in indignation: "You know very well, that I have never had confidence in Miss Howard; certainly not in her ability. . . . I would not have a young girl in a school where her influence or that of women of similar character was to prevail. As for yourself . . . when you asked me to come to Wellesley, you entirely misrepresented to me the character that you intended to give the school. If you had told me the truth . . . I should have known at once that it was not the place for me."[48]

In the end, Sarah Glazier moved to temper the hostility and to heal the wounds of the community. At chapel she stated openly that if she had known that she was to be under seminary government she would not have reacted so hostilely. She asked Mr. Durant's forgiveness for all her wrongs and forgave him for all he had done. Loyal students took the dismissed teachers rowing on Lake Waban, crowning them with daisies and showing their love and respect.[49]

For Henry Durant this episode had lasting repercussions. By dismissing the professors who challenged his authority, he successfully contained the revolt; but student defiance of his and Ada Howard's dominion increased. Howard began to retreat into invalidism, and Durant was left daily to confront students who were far from his romantic ideal of noble womanhood. Some students flouted the dietary regulations; others damaged books. His vision tarnished, he began to withdraw from college life. To make matters worse, his health declined, and he suffered financial reversals that forced him to devote more time to his business enterprises in New York. Yet his dream for Wellesley was still intact, and he continued to appoint strong intellectual women to the highest academic posts. In 1877, when he began to cast about for a person to take his place, someone who could truly lead the college, he did not look to Mount Holyoke. Rather he turned to his friend James B. Angell, president of the University of Michigan. Angell, a staunch supporter of women's higher education, recommended that Durant select a graduate of Michigan named Alice Freeman. Young, vigorous, and intelligent, Alice Freeman embodied the type of woman with whom he had long been infatuated but whom he had been reluctant to install as president while he retained hope of controlling Wellesley's destiny. By choosing Freeman as his successor, Durant helped to ensure that Wellesley would transcend the seminary model.[50]

From 1879, when Freeman arrived at Wellesley, until Durant's death in 1881, they formed an "unofficial management team." Before he died, he left instructions that she be promoted to the presidency. Still it was not at all clear that this young woman of twenty-six would be accepted by the trustees and other senior professors. In the weeks following Durant's death students described the atmosphere at Wellesley as "living in a volcano [until] at last the eruption came." Everyone knew that "some change must come soon for Miss Howard without Mr. Durant is nothing."[51]

Finally, on November 14, 1881, the head of the trustees announced at chapel that because of Ada Howard's poor health, the board had recommended that she take a prolonged vacation and that Professor Freeman assume her duties. Although they were stunned that Freeman would be promoted over senior faculty like Whiting, Lord, Horton, and Hallowell, students were elated over Freeman's selection because she was a "woman of great energy and good business tact."[52] One student recalled: "It was a time never to be forgotten. We marched quietly from the chapel, but then our agitation overcame us, and we indulged in gymnastics both vocal and manual." That evening the class of 1882 visited the new president and "came away firmly convinced that our good ship would sail steadily and prosperously on under its new ruler."[53] There was "open tumultuous rejoicing at the change." Few took notice of the coach that on November 18, 1881, four days after the announcement at chapel, rolled away from College Hall with the furloughed President Howard. For the entire Wellesley community, the "age of iron" had ended and a "new regime" had begun.[54]

The women's community that emerged almost immediately at Wellesley stretched Henry Durant's prescribed definitions of a college, of collegiate women, and of community. He wanted to build a "perfect woman nobly planned," but this paragon was still burdened by mid-nineteenth-century ideals about women's moral position in the community, their piety, and their submissiveness. Hardly submissive, Wellesley College women students and faculty rejected those ideals in favor of independence and excellence. Their rebellion, although thwarted, was symptomatic of student and faculty initiatives in the late nineteenth century for an improved college community.

The Wellesley students and faculty were, like Henry Durant, tied to a moral definition of women's superiority. In Sarah Glazier and then in Alice Freeman they found their vision of the noble woman. Their loyalty to Wellesley matched Durant's, but for them the bonds of Wellesley were wrought not merely from devotion to an institution or an idea but from all they shared as collegiate women. As an exclusively female community, Wellesley became a source of identity for these women.

2

Alice Freeman and Young Wellesley

The new president of Wellesley, Alice Freeman, was hardly older than most students and younger in fact than many of the professors. Only twenty-six years of age, Freeman wore her youth like a badge and manipulated it so that both she and the college benefited. After Wellesley's difficult founding years, her ability to underscore and ennoble youth was crucial to the institutional development of the college. Freeman reversed the growing invisibility of the internal power structure caused by Ada Howard's and Henry Durant's illnesses and their psychological and intellectual distance from students and faculty. Her presidency was doubly visible because of her extraordinary youth and her status as a graduate of the University of Michigan. Freeman's elevation to the presidency regenerated a feeling of pioneering adventure and zest within the college community: "It was not only that *we* were young; the college was young, too, and so was our president."[1] While other women's colleges founded in the late 1860s and 1870s were subject to second-generation retrenchment in the 1880s, Wellesley under Alice Freeman experienced a reinvigoration.[2]

Between 1881 and 1887, the years of Freeman's presidency, a virtual cult of Freeman followers developed at Wellesley College. Alice Freeman was what sociologists would later call a charismatic leader; her powers as a teacher and administrator enabled her to turn Wellesley's crisis to her own advantage and to that of other women. The college itself may have gained the most from the enormous strength that Freeman wielded so skillfully. This outcome, however, was not inevitable. An alumna recognized that the whole college depended on Freeman: "It would have been dangerous for one person to have so much power had not that person been Miss Freeman."[3]

Far from being considered an authoritarian, Freeman was seen as an "emancipator of women"—a phrase that conjures up mythic qualities. Much of Freeman's singular power depended—as in the case of every great leader—on her personality, her leadership style, and the alchemy of her interaction with students, faculty, and trustees. As Leila S. McKee, an alumna who herself became the president of a woman's college put it, "The secret of Miss Freeman's power lay in herself."[4] It is thus important to know something of the woman, her formative influences, and her experiences prior to Wellesley, for these shed light on the style and substance of her presidency.

The portrait of Alice Freeman that hangs in the Wellesley pantheon of presidents conveys a "charmingly idealized, modern young woman, dressed in virginal robes with a childlike expression, dreaming of the future of Wellesley," according to George Herbert Palmer, Freeman's biographer and husband. Yet he also notes that the portrait hardly does her justice. The only qualities the painting captures are those quintessential features of nineteenth-century womanhood—youth, womanliness, and charm—which Freeman consciously cultivated in her public self.[5]

Concealed in the portrait, as they were in life, are traits that were less acceptable in a woman: driving ambition, scorn for lesser intellects, and imperviousness to insult. Freeman, however, was able to harmonize these conflicting qualities. She infused the genteel womanly style of behavior with a forceful, almost despotic will. Caroline Hazard, Wellesley's fifth president, noted that Freeman "reconciled the new and the old conceptions of women; . . . she combined in a very remarkable degree the traditional feminine virtues and the wider activities of women for the ideals of life, for freedom, for truth, for the highest development of the individual." This fusion of opposites was the basis of her personality and ultimately of her enigmatic power.[6]

The components of Freeman's complex character can be traced to early childhood. Born on February 21, 1855, in Colesville, New York, a farming community near Binghamton, Alice Freeman was the first child of Elizabeth and James Freeman. Elizabeth Freeman was only seventeen when Alice was born, and Alice later reflected that mother and daughter matured together. Treated more like a sister or companion than a daughter, Alice came to share her mother's sense of social responsibility; the Freeman home was a way station for the "poor, the aged and the sick."[7]

When Alice was five, her father gave up farming to study medicine, apprenticing himself to a physician in a neighboring town. It fell to Alice to share the burden of caring for the three younger Freeman children who had followed her in rapid succession. She tried hard to live up to parental expectations: after one sibling outburst disturbed her mother, for example, Alice resolved to curb her own volatile temper. Rigid control over her emotions, first mustered at the age of seven, became a key element of her character.[8]

Alice grew up particularly attached to her younger sister Stella, who wrote poetry and painted. Younger sister to her mother, elder sister to Stella and the other Freeman children, Alice was at an early age used to being central to networks of association. Sisterhood was something she understood and valued.

When Alice was seven, James Freeman enrolled in Albany Medical College. The rest of the Freeman family remained in Colesville, which was so isolated that the "family itself was a community." That female-dominated household was the model for Alice's personal life until she married at age thirty, and even thereafter; it also guided her administration at Wellesley.[9]

In 1865 Dr. Freeman moved his family to Windsor, New York, to establish his medical practice. At ten years of age, Alice had already begun to display publicly the dual identity that would characterize her life. On the surface a charming and precocious girl, she nevertheless manifested the inner authority of one who had been stripped of her childhood and called upon to bear adult burdens. Her teachers at Windsor Academy recognized her unusual composure and talents. Chosen to represent the academy at an annual county debate, Alice won first prize, although she was only twelve at the time and all her opponents were teachers.[10]

At Windsor, a sympathetic teacher created a college preparatory course for Alice. He also proposed marriage. She accepted and became engaged at fourteen. Soon after, she underwent a crisis that, according to Barbara Welter, often occurred at puberty among American women in the mid-nineteenth century. Many girls, by converting their sexual awakening into a religious experience, avoided the risks of childbirth and the anxieties of leaving the family and assuming an adult identity.[11] Such a religious conversion caused Alice to break the engagement, but it also gave her a sense of personal identity and empowerment. Thereafter, she hinged her destiny on

God's will: "If our Father wants me to go through College, I know I shall go; and if He doesn't I don't want to. That is the end of it. Meanwhile I am planning and thinking. If it comes to anything, I will report."[12]

Alice Freeman, who accurately assessed her special worth and competence, concluded that she should have the "power that comes from knowledge." She chose to become one of the first women undergraduates at the University of Michigan, dismissing Vassar and Elmira as merely female academies. Years later Freeman revealed some of the considerations that went into that decision. She wrote that an attractive girl in her teens had to contend with "the gallantry of men glad ever to accept the hard things and leave to her the easy." Nevertheless, Freeman argued, a woman is "a person . . . who has her own way in the world to make. . . . In a large tract of her character—is it the largest tract?—her own needs and those of the young man are identical." At sixteen, Alice Freeman understood that, for her, the stereotypical female role was incongruent.[13]

Alice's parents initially opposed her decision to attend college. Hardly well off, the Freemans were planning to invest instead in their son's education. Alice countered that if she were allowed to attend Michigan, she would ensure that all her siblings received adequate educations. Her family's economic straits thus provided Alice with a socially acceptable reason to pursue a career and cast her ambition within the pale of female virtue.[14]

In the summer of 1872, James Freeman drove Alice by horse and carriage the six hundred miles to the University of Michigan campus at Ann Arbor, which had admitted the first woman student only two years earlier. Although Alice's academy training had not prepared her well enough to pass the Michigan entrance examination, President James Angell noted Alice's maturity and determination and allowed her to enter the university. It was not the first time an older man had been captivated by Alice Freeman, nor was it to be the last. Part of her success throughout life stemmed from her ability to secure the aid of older men.[15]

At Michigan Alice was relatively free of what Jane Addams termed the "family claim," as her parents honored their part of the contract, supporting her financially and emotionally.[16] Nevertheless, she was hardly a carefree coed. Not only did she have to compensate for her inadequate academic preparation, but she was also part of a "dangerous experiment," namely, one of twelve women among sixty men in the class of 1876. She suffered other impediments, such as finding a rooming house that would accept women and having her performance constantly monitored. Although women were integrated into classes, theirs was a distinctly separate experience from that of men. Observing that women students were constantly scrutinized, President Angell portrayed the texture of their lives with sensitivity: "Being pioneers and representatives of many who would come afterwards, they were burdened with a sense of responsibility. . . . Such conscious conditions insure uprightness, but are hardly so favorable for ease and the graces." Alice merely made as much as possible of each day in college, as if it were her last.[17]

Alice's gender consciousness, fostered by her family status as sister and daughter, was fanned by the vicissitudes of her college experience. Close ties developed between women students who felt that the "fate of our sex hung upon proving that 'lady Greek' involved the accents, and that women's minds were particularly absorptive of the calculus and metaphysics."[18] Freeman observed a strong comradeship among these highly motivated young women. President Angell called her a natural leader, "the radiant center of a considerable group whose tastes were congenial with her own."[19] She was instrumental in forming the first women's debating club on campus, the QCs, several of whom became college teachers. The club aimed to "provide women with a sense of their worth." One question debated was whether higher education was as well adapted to women as to men; another was how to overcome the limitations put by society on women's professional roles. Freeman also helped to organize the Ladies Literary Society and revolutionized the all-male Young Men's Christian Association, converting it into a Student Christian Association.[20]

In 1876 founders and board members of the Ladies Library Association of Ann Arbor celebrated their tenth anniversary by calling on the women in the Michigan class of 1876 to draw up the following centennial message, which was opened in 1976, per their instructions. The message reads:

> The worst of miseries
> Is when a nature framed for noblest things
> Condemns itself in youth to petty joys,
> And sore athirst for air, breathes scanty life
> Gasping from out the shallows. You are saved
> From such poor doubleness. The life we choose
> Breathes high and sees a full-arched firmament.
> Our deeds shall speak like rock-hewn messages
> Teaching great purpose to the distant time.[21]

Although the authorship is unknown, Alice Freeman may have drafted the message, for she keenly felt the dilemma it addresses and struggled to emancipate herself from the "enfeebling indulgences" that surrounded a pretty girl.[22]

At Michigan Freeman laid the foundation of her educational empire. There she caught the attention of James Angell, who later recommended her for the presidency of Wellesley, and she established the professional network that would serve her so well. Later in life she reflected that "all round the world there are men and women at work, my intimates of college days, who have made the wide earth a friendly place to me."[23] The friendships she made with women in every department of the university had professional implications, too. Although most of the women in the literary department shunned the women in the medical department, Freeman made lasting friendships with the "hen medics."[24] She never forgot such acquaintances. As president of Wellesley, she invited one of these doctors, Eliza Mosher, to lecture on physiology; she appointed her friend Lucy Andrews to lecture on ethics; and she tried to hire Lucy Salmon, another QC member, who then taught at Vassar, as a professor of history. In all, six "Ann Arbor comrades" held professorships at Wellesley during Alice Freeman's presidency, enough for the 1880s to be known as the Michigan era. The separate female experience at Michigan created a group ethos and a vision of the ideal undergraduate milieu for women. Alice Freeman re-created both at Wellesley.[25]

To earn enough money to finish college, in her junior year Freeman took a job as a high-school principal in Ottawa, Illinois. With eight lessons to prepare, Freeman got her first glimpse of the hard life of the schoolteacher. Typically, however, she looked at the positive aspects of the experience. Shackled with an exhausting schedule, Alice wrote a friend that she had "cured herself of [her] abominable habit of wasting time" and had sharpened her powers of concentration, which later proved useful in her executive tasks at Wellesley. During this period, she avoided several detours—such as another marriage proposal from an older man and an offer to become the permanent principal at Ottawa. Freeman declined both and returned to Michigan, intent upon completing her bachelor's degree and beginning a doctoral program in history.[26]

After receiving her B.A. from Michigan in 1876, Alice took a teaching job at a girls' seminary in Lake Geneva, Wisconsin; part of her salary paid the tuition for her sister Ella. Although she found "being 'slave to a bell and a vassal to an hour' irksome," she began to evolve a distinctive educational philosophy. She gained influence among her students by being a "friend to them *all*" and by practicing an educational philosophy she termed "heart culture." Freeman encouraged her students to come to her for advice in "happy and sad times, in restless moments, or homesick and tired hours."[27]

In summer of 1877, Alice Freeman rejected an instructorship in mathematics at Wellesley College, accepting instead a better-paying offer as principal of the Saginaw High School in Michigan. Freeman felt compelled to make this decision because her beloved sister Stella was ill with tuberculosis and her father was in financial straits. She secured a teaching post for her sister Ella, and together they rented a local house for the family. This was a difficult period in Freeman's life. Because of her long workdays, her own health began to suffer. She became disheartened as she watched Stella deteriorate daily. Guilt, anxiety, and fear plagued her as she ministered "helpless help" to her dying sister. Stella's decline precipitated Alice Freeman's second identity crisis, one in which she felt the "solid earth giving way," as if she too were dying and her "present and future slipping out of control."[28] As Stella's condition worsened, Alice confronted not only the imminent loss of her sister but the impending dissolution of her role as family caretaker. She had to assume an interest in her career and come to terms with her own ambitions. Although later in 1878 she rejected two subsequent offers to teach mathematics and Greek at Wellesley, she finally accepted Durant's fourth offer, this time in the history department. She made preparations to begin teaching the fall semester of 1879, but her aspiration was shrouded by the loss of Stella. The twenty-four-year-old woman who was to become the fountainhead of Wellesley College, the charismatic leader of its community, initially shrank from assuming a prominent role there. She was determined to remain distant from her students and not to let them waste her time. She reflected: "Unless you are careful in this great family, all your time goes uselessly. . . . I think Mr. Durant expects his teachers to give themselves boundlessly to the girls; but I can't do that this year even if I don't 'make them adore me,' as he says I must. It is a good thing for my health to be unpopular enough to be let alone, and I shan't try to be anything else."[29]

Freeman's resistance to becoming embroiled in the life of the college, to adopting the family ethos at Wellesley as her own, took time to overcome. Gradually life at the college drew her in and succored her, as had her biological family. Alice Freeman ultimately gave much to Wellesley; and it gave back in good measure, rescuing her from her family problems and providing a clear career path.[30]

In her first term, Freeman taught a heavy schedule, gave a daily Bible class, and supervised domestic work. She also advised the senior class, which collectively rebelled against her out of loyalty to Mary Sheldon, who had resigned the previous year, a victim of Durant's autocratic control.[31] Everything seemed to be going wrong; she felt "full of disappointments and downright badness." Freeman's high standards initially earned her enmity: "They hated me when I first came to Wellesley. I had charge of the work in the dining room and I made the girls attend to it. They had fallen into slack ways and resisted." Freeman in time won the girls over. In the classroom too she soon gained a following; students found her to be an inspiring history teacher, one who showed more reverence for her subject than to expect mere rote mastery.[32]

By Freeman's second term, she was so fatigued that she suffered a hemorrhage in her lungs. Yet she was beginning to feel that Wellesley needed her. After three months leave at home in Saginaw, she was back at Wellesley in April 1881, her lesions healed. Freeman's change in attitude was remarkable; although she expressed annoyance with the domestic work, corridor care, and section meetings, she declared with a newfound sense of purpose that "there is so much of everything to be done here before things are as they ought to be!"[33]

Skillfully, almost artistically, Alice Freeman carved a position of influence within the Wellesley community. She won the admiration and respect of her students, restructured the history department to better suit her faculty, and as an unofficial dean challenged all students to do better academically. Moreover, she became a symbol of the community; the Durants designated her to "entertain and see all the fine company that came to Wellesley." By 1881, when Henry Durant died and Wellesley was pushed to the brink of crisis, Alice Freeman was ready for the leadership role that she had first eschewed.[34]

In contrast to stodgy Ada Howard, Freeman seemed like a sister to most students. One young woman gushed: "You have no idea what an enthusiasm the girls have for Miss Freeman—I feel O so proud of her—as if she were something I owned myself—that is the spirit which ought to be to make matters work. She is so fascinating and winning."[35]

Alice Freeman identified no less with the students than they did with her. Adroitly she played this trump card in her only major confrontation with Henry Durant, who had demanded that she counsel a student on religious matters. Freeman parried by saying that she could not discuss religion with a girl she barely knew. Durant exploded with anger, ordering Freeman to convert the young woman at once, because "now" was the day of salvation. Freeman answered that Durant knew nothing about girls, because he had never been a girl himself. Durant ended this conference, and others thereafter, by grudgingly capitulating: "Well, I suppose I don't understand girls; I've never been a girl myself." Freeman could just as cleverly manipulate students by mocking the striking similarity in their ages. One beguiled student recalled an incident in which Freeman told a group of girls who had been talking foolishly to stop, adding, "I'm glad I never was a girl."[36]

Some saw Freeman's empathetic understanding of other women—bordering on divination—as her preeminent quality. Yet Freeman commanded her loyal following not through magic but by the artful wielding of her gender-based power, combining her firsthand knowledge of women and college life with a discrete concern for each woman. In keeping with her theory of heart culture, she made each student feel her warm personal interest and encouraged "each woman to do her own thinking and to have respect for the process."[37] Such individualized treatment required constant attention to details. Freeman achieved an intimate relationship with the more than three hundred Wellesley students by keeping a memorandum book by her bedside in which all the names of the freshman class were listed. She annotated it every night with information acquired about each student and studied these notes as assiduously as her students were expected to study their lecture notes. To an associate who learned of this practice she declared, "Whatever we have to do, we can always do."[38]

Freeman applied the knowledge thus gained sympathetically and supportively. By making each woman feel more competent and secure, she exercised a subtle form of control over all of them. Because Freeman expected much from her girls and was blind to their shortcomings, few could let her down. She exerted her authority by enlisting the students' cooperation. On the day in 1881 that she learned of her appointment to the presidency, Freeman assembled the senior class and told them she had called them together because she needed their advice. She had been asked to become president of Wellesley, but she was too young for the office, and the duties were too heavy. If she had to meet them alone, she would have to decline. But if they were willing to look after the order of the college themselves, leaving her free for general administration, she might accept. The response was of course overwhelming.[39]

Cooperation sometimes faded into co-optation. Freeman seemed to let students—individually and collectively—choose among viable courses of action, yet to avoid disappointing her they ended by upholding her vision of their interest. Girls who intended to demand special privileges came out from appointments with her "subdued and chastened, agreeable to her wishes, still loyal to the hand that smote them."[40] Students delighted in, even admired, Freeman's subtle control of them: "One year many of us grew lazy and fell into the habit of sitting during the hymn. One morning Miss Freeman said quietly, but with her own look of humorous determination, 'We will *rise* and sing the 23rd hymn—"Stand up, stand up for Jesus."' Of course we rose, and kept on rising. Equally of course we were diverted by the cleverness which made any chiding word unnecessary."[41]

Alice Freeman knew she could count on the students' allegiance to her and to Wellesley, for in addition to their identification with her they shared the ethos that a true women's college had special implications. Durant had constrained the emergence of this ethos, fearing a female community, but Freeman could afford to liberalize some of the social restrictions so despised by Wellesley students and treat them as collegiate women, not as boarding-school girls.

Thus Freeman thoroughly broke the stern Mount Holyoke tradition that had oppressed Wellesley. She could shift easily from greeting the great lions of educational administration to mixing informally, even playfully, with the students, who delighted at her temporary abandonment of presidential dignity. But this carefree spirit coexisted with rigid self-control. In spite of a fiery temper, Freeman never showed overt anger. Rather than admonish students openly, she instead rebuked them with a glance.

During her presidency of Wellesley Freeman's personal life merged with that of the college. She lived in College Hall with her students and, serving as her own dean, held office hours for them every morning. A student recollected how "very slowly did the idea dawn upon me that there was a faculty back of all these very pleasant personal relations."[42]

Faculty reactions to the elevation of Alice Freeman to the presidency triggered responses that ranged from wildly enthusiastic to coldly disapproving. Freeman's most ardent supporters were the six other alumnae of the University of Michigan on the faculty. The Michigan women were "radiant companions" whose friendship had been forged during their difficult undergraduate days and furthered by living on the same corridor at Wellesley as faculty members.[43] They were immensely proud of Freeman and vowed to help make a warm home for her. Freeman's detractors, mainly among the senior faculty, doubted "whether this young girl of the prairies had wisely been entrusted with the leadership of Wellesley." Because this faction considered Freeman's youth a liability, she did her best to camouflage it by upgrading her wardrobe "to compensate for my undignified appearance."[44] In spite of her attempts to mollify the senior professors, at least one actively caballed against her. Susan Hallowell, head of the botany department, wooed Mary Alice Willcox, who joined the faculty in 1883. Willcox reported: "When I came to Wellesley Mr. Durant had been dead about a year. His death meant the replacing of Miss Howard, a dignified figurehead, with a real President—the young and brilliant Alice Freeman. I have never known why Miss Hallowell so disbelieved in her. She had built up a small group of opponents and hoped to add me to their number. She used to call upon me early in the morning before classes began and point out Miss Freeman's machinations and intentions." Unpersuaded, Willcox allied herself "heart and soul with the new president and the majority of the faculty." Thereafter her relations with Hallowell were never cordial. Willcox succumbed, as did most of the faculty, to many of the same traits and tactics that endeared Freeman to the students: hard work, personal concern, and shared ideals.[45]

Over the next few years Freeman added to her nucleus of support by making ten judicious appointments. One, Katharine Lee Bates, had been an undergraduate at Wellesley, but Durant's religious fanaticism had made her reluctant to return there to teach. Another appointee, Vida Dutton Scudder, attributed her self-discovery to the privilege of sharing in the "organic life of the growing College." A third, Carla Wenckebach, wrote glowingly: "What a splendid, independent, highly respected position I have here; what unlimited possibilities for educating myself and for exerting a noble influence on others."[46]

Freeman applied the personal touch to the faculty, just as she did to students. Wenckebach was particularly impressed by this trait, marveling that Freeman "in her overcrowded life of administrator, lecturer, housekeeper, [and] mother confessor" expressed personal feelings each time she saw a person or wrote a letter. A few faculty members nonetheless found fault with their young president, criticizing Freeman for "vanity and insincerity," bickering over what she ought to be, and claiming that her overwhelming charismatic power made her a benevolent despot, "born to govern a king-dom by the motion of her little finger." Nevertheless, Freeman did endear herself to the majority of the faculty by her concern for the development of Wellesley as a first-rate collegiate institution and for the advancement of women's careers. The opportunities she afforded academic women for inter-departmental transfer reinforced the loyalty of some and won that of others. Katharine Coman, whom she permitted to switch from English to history, teamed with Freeman, who continued to teach for the first two years of her presidency, to build a strong history department.[47]

Freeman provided the academic women with precisely the blend of free-dom and responsibility necessary to convert their intellectualism into sig-nificant, productive work. Sarah Frances Whiting, a Durant appointee, felt that Freeman's labors and commitment instilled a sense of purpose in the faculty. "No wonder," commented Whiting, "that professors often left their lectures to be written in the wee small hours, to help in uncongenial admin-istrative work, which was not in the scope of their recognized duties."[48] In the classroom Freeman allowed her faculty complete freedom, giving them carte blanche in matters of curriculum and pedagogy and supporting exper-imentation and innovation in both. This disposition may be traced to Michigan, where Freeman had studied history under Charles Kendall Adams, who required his students to examine primary sources, then a novel method. Indeed, by spreading this practice to Wellesley, Freeman helped to revolutionize the teaching of history. She also backed Carla Wenckebach's innovative methods for teaching German, even though these aroused much criticism. Ten years later Wenckebach was honored for those methods at the World's Columbian Exposition of 1893, held in Chicago. Freeman's timely support made Wenckebach fiercely loyal to her. To Wenckebach's profuse expressions of gratitude Freeman responded simply: "We will all help each other, will we not?" This spirit of mutual allegiance made Free-man seem a part of the faculty, not set above or apart from them.[49]

Busy with other matters, Freeman left the general management of the college to the faculty. Whereas Henry Durant had held tightly to his author-ity, Freeman's style was to delegate. She organized the faculty into twelve departments and then consulted regularly with the heads of these depart-ments, expecting that they would do likewise with one another. Freeman also depended upon the departmental heads to set appointment policies and left hiring decisions mainly to the senior staff. In her most significant administrative act, she empowered the faculty to form the Academic Council, which as the chief legislative body of Wellesley gave the faculty a framework for participation in the affairs of the college. The mandate of Council was to govern the academic life of the college, which meant determining admission requirements, planning courses, and setting rules of conduct. Durant had imposed his ideas about curriculum and discipline on the faculty; Freeman, in contrast, let the faculty decide these vital matters.[50]

An Educational Empire

Although Alice Freeman had an extraordinary impact on students and faculty, she considered her chief contribution to be the development of Wellesley as a liberal arts college. Upon assuming the presidency of Wellesley in 1881, Freeman upheld Henry Durant's wish and dropped the college's preparatory course. This action entailed grave risks, because few secondary schools prepared women adequately for college work. Freeman therefore set about to establish satellite secondary schools that would properly train young women for entrance to Wellesley. The difficulties she herself had experienced because of inadequate secondary preparation give a personal dimension to this mission. Freeman began by strengthening the ties with Dana Hall, the original Wellesley preparatory school, which had opened with the Durants' sponsorship in 1881. In 1883, Freeman directed the opening of the Park Institute in Chicago. By 1885, she had convinced business and educational leaders to open high-quality secondary schools for women in Auburndale, Massachusetts, New York City, Kansas City, and Philadelphia.[51]

Once having established the schools necessary to ensure that Wellesley could raise its entrance requirements and function less like a seminary, Freeman turned her attention to staffing the schools with Wellesley alumnae. Like Catharine Beecher, Mary Lyon, and Emma Willard, who earlier in the nineteenth century had campaigned for more women teachers, Alice Freeman believed that women could play an important societal function as teachers by forming the core of a new womanhood that would "counteract rich materialism," cure the jealousy between classes and "dispel the restlessness, ennui and discontent" she believed plagued middle-class women of the day.[52]

Freeman, however, moved beyond Beecher's and Lyon's concept of the woman teacher. Rather than limit such a teaching force to the classroom, she envisioned the active involvement of women teachers in moral and social reform causes. She saw them as important to public life and in the 1880s advanced the belief that college-trained women teachers were significant factors in the progressive civilization of America. These positions made Freeman a transitional figure whose educational philosophy links the intellectual frameworks developed by educational reformers like Beecher and Lyon to late nineteenth-century social reformers like Jane Addams and Vida Scudder, who a decade later would designate college women who went into social settlement work as "new factors in social order."[53]

Because of her great influence on students, Freeman was able to channel women into teaching careers. Her impact on Wellesley students is clear: in 1885 close to three-quarters of the senior class entered the teaching profession. (See table 2.)

That year, when an extraordinary 71 percent became teachers, marked a watershed in the career patterns of Wellesley College graduates. In the six preceding years just under 30 percent of Wellesley graduates had entered teaching; over the next fifteen years 43 percent of all Wellesley graduates did so. Concomitant with the jump in percentages of women entering teaching was a sharp decrease in marriage rates. In an era when many women had to choose between career or marriage, choosing to teach often meant remaining single. The same class of 1885 had a marriage rate of only 35 percent, compared to an average 51 percent for the six preceding years, a rate far below the national average. Alice Freeman thus remained true to Henry Durant's founding purpose of training a national corps of teachers who would effect the social reform of society. Whereas other women's colleges downplayed their role in preparing women for careers in education, Wellesley took pride in its mission of teacher training and put its stamp on hundreds of schools throughout the country.

Alice Freeman envisioned Wellesley as an "educational empire" no less broad or powerful than the Queen of England's.[54] She fulfilled that vision by converting Wellesley into a college with a national, and even international, reputation for elevating the condition of women's higher education in America. Freeman became known as one of the country's leading specialists and reformers of secondary education. Her penchant for collective association made her one of the founders of the Association of Collegiate Alumnae, which was dedicated to the promotion of college women's educational interests. Extending her passion for women's education beyond the United States, she served as the first president of the Board of Directors of the Institute for Girls in Madrid.[55]

Table 2

Students' Choices Following Graduation from Wellesley College, 1879–99

Class	No. in Class	No. Who Chose to Teach	% Who Chose to Become Teachers	No. Who Married	% Who Married[a]	Average No. of Children from These Marriages
1879	18	7	39	7	39	1.57
1880	41	9	22	19	46	2.68
1881	23	6	26	10	43	1.80
1882	28	9	32	15	54	1.87
1883	49	14	29	31	63	1.74
1884	48	16	33	30	63	1.33
1885	51	36	71	18	35	1.28
1886	51	25	49	24	47	1.42
1887	68	35	51	25	37	1.68
1888	60	20	33	27	45	1.22
1889	74	33	45	28	38	1.36
1890	111	45	41	37	33	1.24
1891	112	55	49	30	27	0.47
1892	113	44	39	32	28	0.97
1893	110	45	41	38	35	0.61
1894	109	47	43	21	19	0.57
1895	118	47	40	25	21	0.88
1896	120	48	40	17	14	0.18
1897	146	65	45	17	12	0.12
1898	146	64	44	5	3	—[b]
1899	131	55	42	1	1	—
Total / Avg.	1,727	725	42%	—[c]	—	—

Source: Percentages calculated from statistics of June 1900, compiled by Mary Caswell, Historical Address, Alumnae Day, June 27, 1900, Unprocessed LMN Papers, WCA.
[a]The average of marriage rates nationally for the years 1879–99 was approximately 90 percent. Daniel Scott Smith, "Family Limitation, Sexual Control, and Domestic Feminism in Victorian America," in *Clio's Consciousness Raised: New Perspectives on the History of Women,* ed. Mary Hartman and Lois W. Banner (New York: Harper and Row, 1974), 121, table 1.
[b]Fertility rates have been omitted for 1898 and 1899 because these classes had just graduated.
[c]A total or average for the remaining categories would be misleading, because those who graduated during the later years might have married and had children after the statistics were compiled.

During her six-year tenure, Alice Freeman endowed Wellesley with a new visibility and made it a public showcase of academic leadership by women. Unlike Henry Durant, who shunned publicity and ceremonies, she well knew the value of public relations. Realizing that alumnae were delighted with Wellesley's new prominence in the educational establishment, she scoffed at the attitude of some of the old-line trustees who worried lest Wellesley become too popular. Freeman's accomplishments made those associated with Wellesley "no longer sufficient to ourselves, shut away from the larger life at our doors, narrow, constrained, dogmatic, exclusive. At a bound our infancy was left behind."[56]

Freeman achieved this leap by wielding extraordinary power, manipulating forces within and outside of Wellesley, and overshadowing not only students, faculty, and trustees but also conservative clergymen. Professor Sarah Whiting recalled that well-known ministers delivered "what we used to call a woman-sermon—to tell us what we might and might not do. Finally President Freeman requested that some other subject be selected."[57]

Alice Freeman's forceful personality held at bay those factions within the college not completely happy with her administration. Above all, the Freeman presidency, though brief, promoted a vision of Wellesley as a modern liberal arts college. She helped solidify the success of this ideal by maintaining a controlling hand in the destiny of the college even after her official resignation. Her invisible authority as trustee and shadow president, along with the attendant clashes between an old and new guard among the faculty, is vital to our understanding of that "perilous transition."[58]

3

The Perilous Transition within
Wellesley's Academic Life

In May 1886, at the home of Eben Horsford, Alice Freeman met George Herbert Palmer, a professor of philosophy at Harvard. Palmer began courting Freeman and that fall proposed marriage. Freeman was favorably disposed to the offer but would not marry and resign the presidency until she had secured fundamental changes in Wellesley's administrative structure. Her courtship correspondence with Palmer is notable because it reveals Freeman's vision of Wellesley. She wished to see the hybrid institution—a college with many of the trappings of a seminary—develop fully into a liberal arts college.

To effect this transformation Freeman formulated a grand strategy that entailed eliminating such seminary vestiges as religious prescription for faculty, domestic work for students, and a non-elective curriculum; it also meant purging so-called incompetent faculty. Her first move before leaving the presidency was to liberalize the Board of Trustees, who controlled the fundamental character of the college through their selection of the president. Freeman enlisted Palmer in her attempt to reorganize the board. He concurred with her that a liberal board would be needed to prevent the nomination of a "goody-goody President" in the crisis following Freeman's resignation and committed himself to finding possible candidates for the board. He suggested Vida Scudder's mother, citing qualifications that demonstrate the aims he and Freeman pursued. Mrs. Scudder, he wrote, "will not be caught with the religious chaff. She is very devout but she sees that lack of intelligence is no fit companion to piety." Freeman wanted to eliminate those board members appointed by Henry Durant whose religiosity constricted their view of the college and restricted the types of women they sanctioned for academic appointments. She finally named two liberal trustees, Horace Scudder (Vida Scudder's uncle) and Lillian Horsford (Eben Horsford's daughter), whom she could trust to support her campaign to complete Wellesley's transformation into a modern college. Freeman herself became the most prominent and powerful board member upon her retirement.[1]

Next Freeman turned her attention to finding a worthy successor. She sought a strong woman who would be "disposed to join hands with [her] in Wellesley's work!" She felt satisfied that a Miss Evans, Dean of Carleton College in Minnesota, was the right woman, only to learn that she could not come to Wellesley. Thwarted, Freeman wrote, "Oh! For the woman created unto this work!" She outlined what the job would entail in her correspondence with Palmer. Because Freeman felt the principal defect of Wellesley was the "division of authority between the President and the Treasurer," one of the tasks was to remove Pauline Durant as treasurer. Although Pauline favored preserving the tradition of female presidents, she also remained loyal to the notions of religious piety, low tuition, and domestic work that her husband had created. Another task confronting Freeman's replacement was the ouster of some of the Durant faculty. She wanted to replace teachers of the old, classical curriculum with young, scholarly types. Palmer warned Freeman that she had best not be too critical of her present teachers, convinced that the religious requirements and low salaries would prevent Wellesley from attracting a superior faculty.[2]

In seeking a successor who was like her, Freeman hoped to minimize the trauma of her departure and to maximize the chances for realizing her grand scheme. But, as Palmer pointed out, her equal did not exist. Her resignation would jolt the college, but, he argued, "there must be a revolution at Wellesley, and it is just as well the Trustees should be obliged to face it squarely."[3]

Viewed from one perspective, Alice Freeman's resignation did indeed precipitate a perilous transition at Wellesley. After Freeman, the spirit of the institution was no longer embodied in a single charismatic leader; instead Academic Council, composed of all senior faculty, became the crucial center of the college. Freeman's successors had to contend with Council, which often overshadowed them. Within Council itself there was much jockeying for power. The old guard—Durant appointees who were loyal to the original religious purposes of the college and trained in the classical subjects and methods of instruction—vied with a new guard, a more secular band of academic women specifically recruited to establish a more vibrant liberal arts college.

Yet Freeman also helped smooth that transition: she handpicked the next three presidents, and as a powerful member of the board of trustees, her executive decisions were continually upheld. Standard accounts of Wellesley's history ignore the pivotal role that Freeman continued to play in the college even after her marriage to Palmer and her departure from Wellesley. Such interpretations overlook the fact that Alice Freeman Palmer remained extremely active at Wellesley. From 1887 until 1895, when she became dean of women at the University of Chicago, she commuted to Wellesley once a week, voted at board meetings, and guided her successor toward the fulfillment of her ideals.[4]

Despairing of finding a replacement who matched her talents, Freeman adopted a different strategy. She chose from within the ranks of the Wellesley faculty a temporary, caretaker president, Helen Almira Shafer. Shafer was forty-eight years old when she assumed the presidency in 1887; she was known to be ill with tuberculosis and died in 1894 while still in office. Shafer's personality was antithetical to Freeman's. Florence Converse described Shafer as self-abnegating, with a dry sense of humor. The class of 1888 commented that Freeman and Shafer were women so unlike as to afford almost no grounds for comparison. Shafer had graduated from Oberlin in 1863 and achieved acclaim for her innovative methods of teaching mathematics in the St. Louis public schools. As a highly respected faculty member at Wellesley, she raised the entrance requirements in mathematics as high as those of any college in the country.[5]

Nevertheless, Shafer's selection surprised and alarmed the Wellesley community. According to Marion Pelton Guild, an alumna trustee, Shafer had been "heartily wedded to her own specialty, and mainly engrossed in that." She was not well-schooled in the policies of the college.[6] Because of Shafer's unobtrusive career many expressed doubt about her ability to follow Freeman. Yet Alice Freeman, unable to get the outsider she wanted, needed an insider of precisely Shafer's demeanor and stature to execute the revolutionary policies she contemplated. She picked Shafer because she was a neutral figure who had neither strong detractors nor proponents among the faculty. As Mary Alice Willcox, professor of zoology, noted, Shafer was older and more conservative in her nature and training than Freeman and eventually became a capable administrator who "put foundations under some of the beautiful air castles which Miss Freeman had left."[7]

Shafer continued the Freeman policy of hiring young faculty. In fact, Shafer made more new appointments than any of the other presidents who served between 1875 to 1910. She appointed seventeen women, at least three of whom were chosen by Alice Freeman Palmer.[8]

Katharine Lee Bates, a respected professor of English, described the early portion of the Shafer presidency as a period in which Oberlin graduates dominated the college.[9] Just as Alice Freeman Palmer had been close to the Michigan alumnae who had been her undergraduate friends, Helen Shafer's strongest affinity was to her Oberlin colleagues: Ellen Hayes, Anne Morgan, Adeline Hawes, and Margaret Stratton. Wellesley under Shafer took on something of the radical, experimental spirit characteristic of Oberlin College in the 1860s and 1870s. In September 1888, for example, publication of the Wellesley College edition of the *Courant* began. No longer were college items sent to be printed in the local town paper. The advent of its own newspaper signified recognition of the college as a community, with a unique history, composition, and character. The *Courant* published alumnae reports from universities in England, France, Germany, and Greece, as well as from "mission fields at home and abroad, studios, nurseries, the doctor's office and the teacher's chair." Within the college, it recorded the activities of the Shakespeare Society, the Christian Association, the Temperance Association, and groups working for Indian rights and women's rights.[10]

The *Courant* gave the faculty a forum in which to disseminate their views, debate educational policy, and increase their influence within the community. Katharine Lee Bates edited the *Courant* and was a frequent contributor. Other contributors included Mary Case, Vida Scudder, Anne Morgan, and Katharine Coman, all liberal faculty members who wanted the college to become more involved in social and political causes.

In a weekly column entitled "Our Outlook" Ellen Amanda Hayes, professor of mathematics, commented on women's educational and occupational progress. Henry Durant had appointed Hayes in 1879, and on his deathbed in 1881 he directed his wife to "put forward Miss Freeman and Miss Hayes."[11] Hayes was a pivotal faculty member in the 1880s but rapidly became too radical to be considered seriously for the Wellesley presidency. To many on campus she personified feminism. She was an ardent follower of Frances Willard and reported frequently on the progress of the temper-

ance movement in her column. An enthusiastic supporter of women's suffrage, Hayes kept women apprised of the activities of the National Women's
Suffrage Association and the American Women's Suffrage Association. She
reported as well on women's admission to law schools and other university
programs and their status in diverse occupations. To show her students an
ideal feminist marriage, she took them to the home of Lucy Stone and
Henry Blackwell in Dorchester.[12] In the late 1880s, Hayes became an advocate of dress reform and began designing her own mannish suits. Beginning
in 1889, she wrote several articles for the *Courant* that challenged the pre-
vailing notion that mental traits were associated with gender. Dissenting
from Darwinian theories that women's roles were biologically determined,
she advanced the proposition that women were socialized into sex roles.
Her position was to gain currency in academic circles only after the turn of
the century. In a period often seen as the doldrums of the feminist movement, Ellen Hayes kept the beacon of feminism alive for Wellesley college
students.[13]

Ellen Hayes was not alone in this feminist spirit. Anne Eugenia Morgan,
professor of mental and moral philosophy, also carried the torch for
women's rights. The daughter of Oberlin philosophy professor John Morgan, an abolitionist who welcomed fugitive slaves into his home, Anne Morgan grew up at Oberlin and earned her B.A. and M.A. there. She was active
at Wellesley in temperance and women's rights. In 1891 she represented
Wellesley at the fortieth anniversary of the National Women's Rights Convention. On campus her feminist philosophy informed her teachings.[14]

Nor were the Oberlin group the only faculty to adopt a liberal spirit and
style. Carla Wenckebach, for example, cut off her long beautiful tresses in
an effort to feel free. She justified her action to a horrified friend by commenting, "What is the use of beauty if it causes continual annoyance?"[15]
Alice Freeman, in Europe at the time, recognized that Wellesley's social and
intellectual climate was changing. She wrote to Wenckebach in 1889, perhaps somewhat apprehensively: "I heard you cut off your hair, but I would
not believe it! When Miss Hayes gets the college as wide a reputation for
Women's Rights enthusiasm as the *Courant* can make, you will look a perfect specimen to send to the big conventions, to sit on the stage and represent Wellesley, I am afraid. But I won't scold you, and I will go on hoping
even yet that the teachers will keep their heads at least."[16]

If the faculty had gained a voice and were beginning to exercise it, they
were still constrained by various rules that restricted their intellectual free-

dom. An increasingly secularized faculty bristled at the requirement that teachers belong to some evangelical church. When the trustees attempted to tighten the regulation by requiring members of the faculty to be Trinitarians, tension mounted. After returning from Europe in 1889, Alice Freeman Palmer became the spokeswoman of the faculty; together they pressed the trustees to abandon the religious prescription. Freeman proposed the change to the board in 1890 and was "warmly seconded, as usual," by Horace Scudder, whose appointment to the board she had secured.[17] Her position was succinct; the college would lose talented academic women if the requirement were not relaxed. One faculty member affected by the requirement, Katharine Lee Bates, had always disapproved of the college's insistence on Christian opinion rather than character. She thought the trustees were wrong to make religious affiliation a criterion for employment in the college.

These views had been tolerated to date, but when the English department headship was offered to her in the midst of this religious controversy, she felt pressure to comply. She informed Louise Manning Hodgkins, the retiring head of the department, that she would not buy the position offered to her with "theological pledges" and that she would rather resign than take the religious oath. Cases like that of Bates persuaded the trustees to eliminate the religious oath for teachers. At the decisive trustee meeting, Mrs. Durant, who upheld steadfastly her husband's vision of the college, "hurled . . . her burning indignation" upon the board members, branding them traitors. Nonetheless, the Board, by a large majority, voted down the requirement. Katharine Lee Bates was among the happy and victorious faculty who welcomed the news that the faculty would henceforth be required only to be of Christian character.[18]

Palmer, in alliance with Shafer and the liberal faculty, next turned her attention to curriculum reform. Shafer had organized the faculty into twelve committees for that purpose, but in the winter of 1890 an attack of tuberculosis forced her to go to a sanatorium in Georgia to recover. Palmer prudently began discussing the leadership of the college with Horace Scudder. In her search for a potential successor, Palmer sought a strong woman to guide Academic Council through curriculum reform.[19]

Only senior and associate professors made up Academic Council. In 1890 there were twenty members who fell into two loose but discernible factions. (See table 3.) One, known as the old guard, consisted principally of Durant appointees who remained loyal to his vision. As early as 1884,

Table 3

Composition of Academic Council, Wellesley College, 1890

Faculty	Dept.	Appt'd by	Year of Joining Faculty	Age in 1890	Faction
Full Professors					
Angie Chapin	Greek	Durant	1879	35	Old guard
Katharine Coman	History	Durant	1880	33	New guard
Elizabeth Denio	German/Art	Durant	1876	46	Old guard
Susan Maria Hallowell	Botany	Durant	1875	55	Old guard
Ellen Hayes	Math	Durant	1879	39	Old guard
Louise Hodgkins	English	Durant	1877	45	Old guard
Julia Irvine	Greek	Shafer	1890	42	New guard
Frances Ellen Lord	Latin	Durant	1876	55	Old guard
Anne Eugenia Morgan	Philosophy	Durant	1878	45	Old guard
Margaret Stratton	Rhetoric	Durant	1881	46	New guard
Helen Webster	Comparative Philology	Shafer	1890	?	New guard
Carla Wenckebach	German	Freeman	1883	37	New guard
Sarah Frances Whiting	Physics	Durant	1876	44	Old guard
Mary Alice Willcox	Zoology	Freeman	1883	34	New guard
Associate Professors					
Katharine Lee Bates	English	Freeman	1886	31	New guard
Mary Sophia Case	Philosophy	Freeman	1884	36	New guard
Eva Chandler	Math	Durant	1879	35	Old guard
Clara Eaton Cummings	Botany	Durant	1879	35	Old guard
Sara Anna Emerson	Latin/Bibl. Hist.	Durant	1877	35	Old guard
Charlotte Fitch Roberts	Chemistry	Durant	1881	31	New guard

Alice Freeman had attempted to force some members of the old guard to strengthen the liberal arts components of their curriculum. The new guard, for the most part appointed by Freeman and Shafer, were less wedded to the old vision; they sought to deemphasize religion and favored an elective curriculum. Some members of Council, of course, were fiercely individualistic and not easily typed. Ellen Hayes, for example, was against maintaining the religious orientation but resisted the adoption of a new elective curriculum. Nonetheless, with a few exceptions Council divided into two camps.[20]

To bolster the power of the liberal faction that wished to reform the curriculum, Alice Freeman Palmer secured by "very special arrangement" the appointment of Julia Thomas Irvine as a junior professor of Greek. The Greek department already had one full professor, Angie Chapin. Eben Horsford, Wellesley's habitual benefactor, generously volunteered to pay the differential in salary that would allow Palmer to appoint Irvine as a second full professor.[21]

Palmer considered Julia Irvine's appointment crucial because she knew she could rely on Irvine to sponsor curriculum reform. Irvine's parents were both doctors, and her mother was an active supporter of the women's rights movement. Julia Thomas graduated with highest honors from Cornell in 1875; that same year she won an intercollegiate scholarship competition in Greek and in 1876 earned a master's degree from Cornell. In 1875 she married Charles Irvine, who taught Greek at several schools for girls, including Anna Brackett's progressive school. The innovative curriculum offered there allowed many graduates to enter Vassar College with advanced standing. Irvine's association with this school made her familiar with collegiate work. After Charles Irvine's death in 1886, Julia studied in Germany. She returned to teach literature at Pauline Shaw's school in Boston. Palmer probably met Irvine at Shaw's school in 1889; in 1890 she decided that Irvine, a woman known for scholarship, administrative experience, and strength of character, was precisely the person to execute her plan for modernizing Wellesley.[22]

Irvine's appointment caused problems within the Greek department by diminishing the power of Palmer's old colleague, Angie Chapin. In November 1890, a special executive committee of the trustees met to decide a question of jurisdiction between the senior and junior Greek professors. The committee decided that Chapin should maintain control of the work of instructors in Greek but that Irvine was responsible for her own course work. This decision, rendered with the approval of Alice Freeman Palmer, solidified Irvine's position in Council. Palmer tried to mollify Chapin, yet the conflict within the Greek department created an "unhappy condition of things at Wellesley."[23]

With Irvine's power assured, she could now prompt Council to take up the issue of curriculum reform. When the Council was through, the separate scientific and classical courses created in 1875 by Henry Durant were dropped in favor of one course of study that culminated in the B.A. There was a general reduction of Bible studies and work in the classics such as Latin and Greek. Latin was still required for admission, but neither Latin nor Greek was required in college. Of the fifty-nine hours of course work required for graduation under the new curriculum, one-third was devoted to required subjects, one-third to electives that had to meet major and minor subject areas, and one-third to free electives. Sixty-seven new courses were introduced.[24]

Many of the new courses represented the interests and training of the junior faculty. Mary Calkins, for example, created the first psychological laboratory in a woman's college in the United States. Elizabeth Kendall gave a course in constitutional law, and Katharine Coman one in advanced economics. For many of the faculty, the most significant change was liberation from what they considered an onerous duty, the teaching of Bible classes. A separate biblical history department, organized under Sara Anna Emerson, freed them from that irksome obligation.[25]

With the trustees liberalized, religious requirements abolished, and curriculum reform under way, Alice Freeman Palmer's grand scheme was well launched, but the transition to a secular liberal arts college still faced uncertainties. When Helen Shafer went on sick leave in September 1890, Council came under the control of the senior professor, Frances Ellen Lord, a "lady of the old school," old-fashioned in manners, theology, and educational ideals.[26] Lord governed Wellesley in Shafer's absence—and did so, in Horace Scudder's opinion, without distinction. On February 23, 1891, Scudder noted in his diary: "Lunched with Vida, and she talked most earnestly of the condition of affairs at Wellesley College. Her life is full of intellectual excitement and it is a pity that she should be thrown into this Wellesley cauldron where there is such seething and bubbling and such an absence of a chief cook who can bring something definite to pass." Besides having lackluster leadership, Academic Council was still in the hands of the old-guard senior faculty. Scudder's diary entry for February 25, two days later, recorded that Alice Freeman Palmer wanted to replace the "incompetent old teachers" with more highly trained women. He discussed the possibility of wholesale faculty dismissals with Palmer, emphasizing, however, that "personal considerations weighted more in a woman's college." Scudder felt that "we ought to take this into consideration and not use for example the same drastic methods as would hold in men's colleges." Although he was familiar with "President Eliot's summary mode of dealing with such matters," he maintained: "I doubt if such methods would be wise at Wellesley." This advice temporarily dissuaded Palmer from a faculty housecleaning.[27]

Helen Shafer's death in 1894 precipitated an internal power struggle. The conservative faction of the faculty sponsored Frances Ellen Lord for president, giving her their unqualified approval. Lord represented the "Old Wellesley," having helped shape the college since 1876. She was, in a sense, the last, best hope of the conservative old guard. They had opposed the appointment of Alice Freeman in 1881, only partly because members of their faction had been passed over; more important, Freeman was too progressive for them. Freeman eventually won over some of the senior professors, but others were unswayed. The senior faculty had viewed the appointment of Helen Shafer favorably and were assuaged by her conservatism, in spite of her concern for curriculum reform. In sanctioning Lord for president, the old guard sought to preserve their view of Wellesley.

Their attempt failed, however. The trustees, favoring Alice Freeman Palmer's candidate, announced that Julia Irvine would be Wellesley's fourth president. They also, at Palmer's request, significantly altered the role of the president by appointing a dean to handle matters of student discipline so that Irvine might concentrate on academic issues. They approved Irvine's choice of Margaret Stratton, professor of English language and rhetoric, as dean. Frances Ellen Lord was given no position in the Irvine administration. These appointments signaled the end of evangelical orthodoxy at Wellesley.[28]

Julia Irvine, acutely aware of the tensions surrounding her appointment, requested that her term be limited. It was. Irvine's tenure lasted only five years. Given her nature—Professor Katharine Lee Bates described Irvine as feeling "genuine disgust" for administrative work—and the nature of her presidency, five years was enough.[29] Irvine shared Alice Freeman Palmer's dream of a university at Wellesley and suggested that Wellesley strengthen its academic standing by offering a Ph.D. degree.[30]

Irvine was brilliant but formidable. Instructor Florence Converse wrote an early college history in which she observed that Irvine's "criticism, both constructive and destructive, was peculiarly stimulating and valuable; and even those who resented her intrusion could not but recognize the noble disinterestedness of her ideal for Wellesley." To Converse, Irvine had not "Mrs. Palmer's skill in conveying unwelcome fact into a resisting mind without irritation; neither had she Miss Shafer's self-effacing, sympathetic patience." The contrast between Alice Freeman Palmer's vibrant personality and Julia Irvine's cold demeanor was sharp indeed.[31]

Julia Irvine faced the unenviable task of ending traditions that had "worn themselves out into annoyances or insincerities." These reforms generated, predictably if not inevitably, acrimonious clashes between the entrenched "timid tradition" and the new Wellesley. One of Irvine's first actions was to abolish the domestic work required of students. In reality, students had not done domestic work for many years, serving instead as clerical workers and laboratory assistants. Still, abolition of the requirement symbolized modernization. Irvine granted students Sunday library privileges, ending a longstanding dispute within the college. She also pressured Mrs. Durant into resigning her post as treasurer; in her stead she appointed a professional. Severing this link to Wellesley's origins caused surprisingly little outcry, because it placed Wellesley on firmer financial ground.[32]

These measures were mild compared to Irvine's actions regarding the faculty. With full support from Alice Freeman Palmer—and sometimes at her direction—Irvine instituted a purge of the Wellesley faculty. According to Mary Case, professor of philosophy, Irvine "unflinchingly eliminated from the faculty, as far as she could, those who were superannuated and incompetent." Some women held their positions under terms of unofficial tenure that put them beyond Irvine's reach, but with the rest she was "inexorable."[33] This rolling of faculty heads created severe tensions on campus yet served educational, financial, and political ends. Irvine wished to apportion the senior professors' salaries among an enlarged junior staff; she also wanted to create openings to which women qualified to teach the new curriculum adopted under Shafer could be appointed. Furthermore, she sought to alter permanently the balance of power in Council.[34]

Some senior faculty, cognizant of their precarious position, left quietly of their own accord. Frances Lord, recognizing that her classes under the new curriculum would be small and that Irvine had usurped most of her power, voluntarily withdrew in 1897. Accepting an appointment as professor emeritus, Lord declined a specially voted retirement allowance, stating:

"What I would carry away from Wellesley is the remembrance of Christian affection. This I covet, and this alone."[35]

Other women departed with far less grace and with much pain. The failure to reappoint Sara Anna Emerson to the biblical history department caused considerable ill feeling. Eliza Kendrick, an instructor at the time, lamented Irvine's and Palmer's sacrifice of Emerson, who had the unqualified respect of her students and colleagues. Kendrick did not think that the scholarly interests of the department would be served by replacing Emerson with someone more prestigious. In spite of such support, Emerson's contract was not renewed; her dismissal came after twenty-two years of teaching at Wellesley. Although she went on to obtain a Ph.D. from Yale in 1903, she never fully recovered from her dismissal. Irvine offered Kendrick the position of head of the biblical history department in 1895, but, loyal to Emerson, she declined. For this gesture, she also was not reappointed and returned only to teach at the college in 1910—after Julia Irvine had resigned.[36]

Other changes in the faculty can be charted through Julia Irvine's presidential reports. Between 1894 and 1896 she reported that forty-seven women had "withdrawn from service."[37] Irvine's euphemism is ironic, for she and Palmer precipitated most of these withdrawals. Indeed, had the trustees given Irvine a free hand, there would have been even more dismissals. In 1899, for example, Irvine tried to persuade the trustees to terminate the contracts of two of the most powerful science professors at Wellesley, Susan Hallowell and Sarah Frances Whiting, both appointed by Durant. She wanted to advance Margaret Maltby, an associate professor and promising young physicist, but the trustees balked at the idea of ousting Whiting to make this possible. Whiting kept her post, while Maltby moved on to a full professorship at Barnard and a distinguished career.[38]

Even without the firing of Hallowell and Whiting, the housecleaning Irvine engineered was of significant proportions. Seven senior and associate professors were purged or induced to leave voluntarily; another, Margaret Stratton, was Irvine's dean, and resigned when Irvine left. Five of these women—Elizabeth Denio (art), Sara Anna Emerson (biblical history), Frances Lord (Latin), Anne Eugenia Morgan (philosophy), and Stratton— were Durant appointees. Mary Alice Knox (history) was appointed by Freeman; Helen Shafer appointed Eliza Ritchie (philosophy) and Helen Webster (comparative philology). Among those forced to leave were four departmental heads—Denio, Emerson, Lord, and Morgan—all Durant appointees. Interestingly, all of Alice Freeman Palmer's old friends from Michigan were spared.

To appreciate the magnitude of the change in senior staff, one need only consider that of the thirteen full professors at Wellesley in 1890, only six remained in 1900. Four had been swept out in Irvine's housecleaning; Stratton and Irvine herself had resigned. Had Irvine carried out her intentions to eliminate Susan Hallowell and Sarah Frances Whiting, the turnover among senior professors would have been even more complete.[39]

Palmer and Irvine characterized the faculty who were terminated as belonging to the incompetent old guard. Other faculty, including Mary Case, shared this perception. Although the term is useful, it may also cloud the issue. The case of Helen Webster is illustrative. Webster had been appointed by Helen Shafer in 1890, and the trustees considered her a "teacher of excellent and rare ability and an advanced student of comparative philology." They were pleased that she held a Ph.D. from Zurich and felt that her appointment brought "honor and strength to the Faculty." The trustees considered it so important to secure her services that they met her contract demands and made her a full professor at a high salary. Webster can hardly be termed old guard, but she was terminated in 1898 because of deficiencies in her department. Trustee reports indicate that they were critical of Webster's teaching and her politics. Her request to use Wellesley property as a summer school for working girls earned her the trustees' fierce disapproval.[40]

The results of the Irvine purge were not uniform. The mean age of the eight women who left during the Irvine era was 49, hardly old enough to be considered superannuated. The purged women were not decidedly older than the senior faculty who remained. Yet, the faculty appointed by Irvine averaged only 31.5 years of age. As a result, the mean age of the senior and associate professors, which was 40 in 1890, rose to only 42 in 1900. In terms of educational attainment, the purged faculty differed somewhat from those newly appointed. Of the eight women who left, 25 percent had Ph.D.'s, as opposed to 23 percent of the incoming faculty. In 1890, 5 percent of the senior faculty had Ph.D.'s; by 1900 that figure had reached 17 percent. Part of this increase is due to policies that obliged some faculty to upgrade their academic credentials. Mary Alice Willcox wrote that she had a cordial relationship with both Alice Freeman and Helen Shafer. She emphasized, however, that Irvine's "temperamental interference in department affairs was such that I made preparations for resigning." Realizing the need for a Ph.D., she went on leave and gained the degree from the University of Zurich. Serendipitously, she recalled, "when I returned in 1898, Miss Irvine's tenure was obviously near its end. So I remained in my old position."[41] It is worth noting that two of the women purged, Elizabeth Denio and Sara Anna Emerson, also earned doctorates after leaving Wellesley. After the Irvine shake-up the faculty did reach higher levels of distinction. Of the eight women who left, only two, Morgan and Webster, were cited for distinguished achievement in six compendiums. By comparison, 46 percent of Irvine's appointees were so cited. Also, 55 percent of the senior and associate faculty at Wellesley in 1900 were recognized for distinguished achievement. (See table 4.)[42]

In the final analysis, the faculty revolution instigated by Julia Irvine had mixed consequences. The Wellesley faculty was upgraded to some degree, and, more significantly, pedagogical changes took place within the college. Alice Van Vechten Brown, for example, reorganized the art department, introducing laboratory methods to replace the rote memorization of Elizabeth Denio's courses in the history of art. Eleanor Gamble strengthened the offerings in laboratory psychology. Mary Woolley brought a more scholarly approach to biblical history than had Sara Anna Emerson, for whom it was a second field at Wellesley, after Latin.

In spite of these improvements, the upheaval met with opposition from the junior as well as the senior faculty. Although many of them approved Irvine's efforts to emancipate Wellesley from rigid theological and curricular requirements, they still felt threatened by her monolithic emphasis on scholarship. Several professors, including Katharine Lee Bates, Vida Scudder, Katharine Coman, Emily Balch, Marian Hubbard, and Mary Case, lacked the formal scholarly credentials that Irvine demanded. Mary Alice Willcox, who was sympathetic to Irvine's attempts to modernize the college, expressed the fears of many faculty women: "Where should I look for a position even approaching that which I should leave?"[43] Their poor prospects for comparable employment elsewhere exacerbated their anxiety. An important group of Wellesley faculty valued social-reform activism as highly as scholarship. Vida Scudder, although she rued never getting a Ph.D., was committed to reform as much as to scholarly investigations. Julia Irvine did not share this outlook, warning Scudder that she was a "detriment to the institution."[44]

Scudder praised Irvine as a "brilliant and original spirit" with a "passionate intellectual quality" who unfortunately "startled many of her colleagues in one way or another."[45] Irvine did indeed alienate many Wellesley faculty. Unhappy with the curriculum in mathematics, Irvine divided the course work into two departments—pure and applied. She appointed Ellen Hayes head of applied mathematics, an action that stripped Hayes of her power and isolated her within a department that had no other members and only a few students. Irvine passed over Eva Chandler for the head of pure mathematics because Chandler was of the old school. Instead she elevated a friend, Ellen Burrell, but named her only as acting head of the department. Burrell furiously declared that she "never swallowed anything so hard."[46]

Irvine was, of course, aware of the tensions her policies produced and in 1897 expressed the opinion that she was "not the right person for the place." She wanted to resign, but the trustees pressed her to stay on.[47] Horace Scudder recorded, however, that there was "hopeless estrangement between her and the faculty." This strained atmosphere finally made Irvine's continuance in office impossible, and in 1899 she gladly retired in France.[48]

In 1898, for a third and final time, Alice Freeman Palmer personally selected the candidate ratified by the trustees as president of Wellesley College. Palmer herself was among the first to be nominated for the position. Mrs. Durant and several other trustees expressed the hope that Palmer would reassume the presidency in order to soothe the tensions left by Julia Irvine.[49] Palmer declined, saying she had no desire for the office. Instead, she advanced the candidacy of a member of Wellesley's Board of Visitors, Caroline Hazard, a move suggested by Horace Scudder and James B. Angell. Three successive presidents had been promoted from among the faculty; Hazard was attractive in part because she was an outsider who could bring to the college a new outlook and new connections.[50]

Caroline Hazard belonged to a prominent Rhode Island family, members of which had founded Newport in 1639. Following a private-school education, she attended classes at Brown University. After completing her studies, she lived at home in Peace Dale, Rhode Island, the planned community organized by her father. Rowland Hazard patterned Peace Dale after an English cooperative town and shared the profits of the woolen mills he built there with his workers. Caroline concerned herself with the social welfare of the children who worked in her father's mills but also earned a regional reputation as a poet and essayist. She possessed the genteel social graces of the elite, a practical understanding of business, a fondness for reform causes, and some collegiate education. What made her most attractive as a candidate, however, was that, as a prominent member of New England society,

Table 4

Comparison of Senior and Associate Faculty with Purged Faculty and Irvine Appointees, 1900

Faculty	Dept.	Age in 1900	Degree in 1900	Recognized for Distinguished Achievement[a]
Remaining				
Full Professors				
Katharine Lee Bates	English	41	M.A.	yes
Alice Van Vechten Brown	Art	38	Secondary	yes
Ellen Burrell	Math	50	B.A.	no
Mary Whiton Calkins	Psychology	37	Ph.D. (equiv.)[b]	yes
Angie Chapin	Greek	45	M.A.	no
Katharine Coman	Economics	43	B.A.	yes
Susan Maria Hallowell	Botany	65	B.A	.yes
Ellen Amanda Hayes	Math	49	B.A.	yes
Charlotte Fitch Roberts	Chemistry	41	Ph.D.	yes
Sarah Frances Whiting	Physics	54	B.A.	yes
Mary Alice Willcox	Botany	44	Ph.D.	yes
Associate Professors				
Charlotte Almira Bragg	Chemistry	37	B.A.	no
Caroline Breyfogle	Biblical History	?	B.A.	no
Ellor Carlisle	Pedagogy	?	Secondary	no
Mary Sophia Case	Philosophy	46	B.A.	yes
Eva Chandler	Math	45	B.A.	no
Grace Cooley	Physics	37	M.A.	no
Clara Eaton Cummings	Botany	45	B.A.	yes
Katharine May Edwards	Greek	38	Ph.D.	no
Margaret Clay Ferguson	Botany	37	B.A.	yes
Sophie Chantal Hart	English	32	M.A.	no
Adeline Hawes	Latin	43	M.A.	no
Sophie Jewett	English	39	Secondary	yes
Elizabeth Kimball Kendall	History	45	M.A.	yes
Adelaide Imogene Locke	Biblical History	31	B.A.	no
Annie Sybil Montague	Greek	46	M.A.	no

Table 4 (continued)

Faculty	Dept.	Age in 1900	Degree in 1900	Recognized for Distinguished Achievement[a]
Margarethe Müller	German	38	Secondary	no
Vida Dutton Scudder	English	39	M.A.	yes
Margaret Pollock Sherwood	English	36	Ph.D.	yes
Purged				
Elizabeth Denio	German	56	B.A.*	no
Sara Anna Emerson	Biblical History	45	B.A.*	no
Mary Alice Knox	History	49	B.A.	no
Frances Ellen Lord	Latin	65	Secondary	no
Anne Eugenia Morgan	Philosophy	55	M.A.	yes
Eliza Ritchie	Philosophy	35	Ph.D.	no
Margaret Stratton	English	56	M.A.	no
Helen Webster	Comparative Philology	?	Ph.D.	yes
Appointed by Irvine				
Emily Greene Balch	Economics	33	B.A.	yes
Malvina Bennett	Elocution	43	B.A.	no
Alice Van Vechten Brown	Art	38	Secondary	yes
Ellor Carlisle	Pedagogy	?	Secondary	no
Grace Davis	Physics	30	B.A.	no
Caroline Rebecca Fletcher	Latin	33	M.A.	no
Eleanor Acheson McCulloch Gamble	Psychology	32	Ph.D.	yes
Adelaide Imogene Locke	Biblical History	31	B.A.	no
Laura Emma Lockwood	English	37	Ph.D.	yes
Julia Orvis	History	28	B.A.	no
Alice Vincent Waite	English	36	M.A.	yes
Alice Walton	Archaeology	35	Ph.D.	no
Mary Emma Woolley	Biblical History	37	M.A.	yes

[a]The compendia used to determine distinguished achievement are: *American Men of Science* (1906, 1910, 1920, 1927, 1933); *Dictionary of American Biography* (20 vols., 6 suppls.); *Notable American Women* (1971–1980); *The Part Taken by Women in American History* (1912, rpt 1972); *Principal Women of America; Who Was Who in America* (vols. 1–3, 1943).

[b]Satisfied all requirements for Ph.D. at Harvard, but Harvard refused to grant official degree.

she would be able to attract philanthropic contributions to the college. Wellesley sorely needed someone with that capacity, for in 1899 the college was nearly bankrupt, with a debt of $100,000 and no general endowment.[51]

Caroline Hazard agreed only reluctantly to have her name submitted for nomination. Alice Freeman Palmer suggested to Hazard that she might play a memorable philanthropic role in higher education, but Hazard objected that she had "no fortune to devote to what might interest me." The money actually at her disposal, she claimed, was not large. After frank discussions with Julia Irvine about the president's role at Wellesley, Hazard came away convinced that she was ill-suited for the position and asked Palmer to withdraw her name: "I do not feel that it is in line with my previous training and achievement—such as it is."[52] In a letter to Horace Scudder she elaborated: "I have not a gift for people, and I am not sure that I should have the requisite firmness and independence to maintain a position of fairness and justice between opposing factions."[53] Palmer and Scudder would not comply with her request and persisted in encouraging Hazard to meet with the trustees. Scudder assured Hazard that she would have the advice and support of a sympathetic board, and he expressed confidence that she could bring "a fresh and independent judgment, and . . . escape the two perils, the one of regarding the college as a big boarding-school, the other of attributing some mystic virtue to the *collegiate education* of women."[54]

Hazard agreed to meet with the board, which responded to her so favorably that Palmer wrote her that she felt as if she had been given a great gift. At that meeting and in the weeks that followed Hazard exacted assurances from the Board that she would not have chief responsibility for fund raising; that a dean would assist with internal administration; and that her brother Rowland, an astute businessman, would join the board. In March 1899, after these concessions had been made, Caroline Hazard accepted the presidency, though still doubtful of her ability to meet its challenges; she wondered "at the confidence shown in me by the action of the Board. But I feel a strong response to the call, 'A Man's reach should exceed his grasp.'"[55]

In September 1899, Hazard became the fifth president of Wellesley in the first official inaugural of the college. The ceremony bespeaks Wellesley's increasing eminence among institutions of higher learning. In attendance were representatives from other colleges, state and federal educational authorities, and two former presidents, Alice Freeman Palmer and Ada Howard. Hazard delivered an address on collegiate ideals for women which argued that because men and women were equal in the eyes of God women should therefore receive an education equal to that of men. She also spoke of woman's "eternal feminine" spirit that prescribed involvement in social benevolence.[56]

With Hazard's appointment Wellesley's golden age began. The coldness and hostility that had marked relations between Julia Irvine and her faculty gave way to a growing sense of camaraderie and mutual trust. Whereas Julia Irvine had been a stern authoritarian, Caroline Hazard epitomized the genteel, wealthy, noble lady. Hazard modeled her role at Wellesley after that of Lady Margaret Beaufort, who as a patron of Christ's College, Cambridge, England, contributed much to British higher education. Beaufort, she wrote, was

> That noble foundress of a noble line
> Of scholars who have moved the world,
>
> . . . .
>
> And through that woman's thought we stand to-day
> A company of women.[57]

Interweaving this theme of the bountiful Lady Beaufort with the democratic impulses of her Hazard forebears, Hazard sought to create at Wellesley the milieu of a British women's university.

Hazard soon became a generous benefactor, having overcome her initial disinclination to tap her own resources for the college. Her first official donation was for a building to lodge domestic servants on campus. She also drew on her wealthy contacts, and by 1900 she and her brother had secured a gift of one hundred thousand dollars to the college from John D. Rockefeller. Before her term of office was over, Wellesley had added five dormitories, five academic buildings, a library, and a central heating plant. Under Hazard four new academic departments were endowed—astronomy, economics, English language, and hygiene and physical education. She made eleven new faculty appointments.[58]

Hazard espoused a moral and social philosophy that harmonized well with the social-reform ethos of the liberal academic women at Wellesley. Julia Irvine had upheld scholarship and made it the preeminent quality for faculty members. Hazard lauded scholarship but placed it within the context of gentility and the social gospel. This allowed her to bridge the old Wellesley of Henry Durant's evangelical fervor and the new Wellesley in which social activism flourished. Hazard pronounced: "The day of cloistered learning has gone by; knowledge for service is what we seek."[59] The new ethos of social reform activism already emerging at Wellesley blossomed under her "winning encouragement."[60] Almost to a woman the faculty revered her and welcomed her influence. Katharine Coman applauded Hazard's contribution to a college "in danger of being obscured by the merely academic."[61] Elizabeth Kendall praised Hazard for bringing a "liberal interpretation of womanhood" to the college. According to Kendall, Hazard gave "so much of what a woman's college specifically needs and rarely gets, a vision of public service combined with gracious and gentle womanhood."[62]

By the time Hazard resigned in 1910 she was praised for "diffus[ing] a warmth of goodwill which . . . made of the [faculty] a different body." Insecure about academic affairs, she allowed senior and associate professors to direct their departments and formulate educational policy with almost complete freedom. This state of affairs laid the groundwork for the exciting intellectual and social milieu of Wellesley's golden age.[63]

Henry Fowle Durant and Pauline Fowle Durant, founders of
Wellesley College.

College Hall, the main building on the Wellesley campus prior to 1881. At that time it
housed the entire community.

The Browning Room, furnished by Henry Durant, contained Elizabeth Barrett Browning's *Aurora Leigh* and other first editions. Appointments included busts of the Brownings, carved teak furniture, and ornamental stained-glass windows.

Alice Freeman Palmer, the youthful president
of Wellesley, in 1885.

Alice Freeman Palmer and George Herbert Palmer, ca. 1894, in the library of their
house in Cambridge.

President Caroline Hazard in the chapel doorway, 1910.

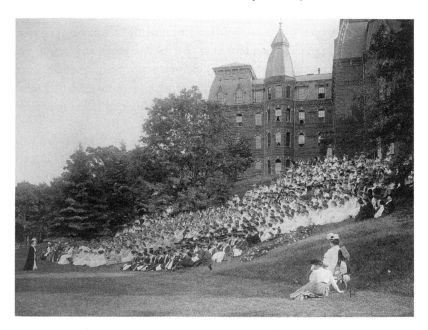

A senior in cap and gown gives an oration to the academic community on Tree Day, ca. 1902, then an annual spring ceremony at which the freshman class planted a tree. Currently, the sophomore class dedicates a tree in the fall.

Pioneer members of the English department: Katharine Lee Bates (*upper left*),
Vida Dutton Scudder (*upper right*), and Sophie Chantal Hart.

Three members of the English department: Martha Hale Shackford, ca. 1890 (*bottom right*); Margaret Pollack Sherwood, ca. 1890 (*top*) and Sophie Jewett, ca. 1895. Students gossiped that Miss Shackford stole Miss Sherwood from Miss Jewett.

Mary Sophia Case (*top*) encouraged Mary Whiton Calkins (*bottom left*), a young instructor of Greek, to study and teach philosophy. Case also inspired Eleanor Acheson McCulloch Gamble, one of her students, to become a member of the faculty. Both Calkins and Gamble eventually taught psychology as well.

Economics professor Emily Greene Balch (*top left*), a socialist and ardent pacifist, lost her job because of her pacifism during World War I. Katharine Coman (*top right*), professor of political and social science, combined teaching economics with social activism. Vida Dutton Scudder (*bottom left*), Wellesley's premier lecturer and a social reformer, co-founded Denison House, a social settlement in Boston, with Balch and Coman. Elizabeth Kimball Kendall taught British history as well as courses on the British Empire and international politics, with a focus on Asia. After earning a law degree, she also gave classes in constitutional law. An intrepid traveler, Kendall crossed both central China and the Gobi Desert alone, feats for which she was named a Fellow of the Royal Geographic Society of Great Britain.

A community of immigrants at Denison House, 1915. During the Progressive Era, Wellesley's activist faculty recruited a record number of students to volunteer at this social settlement.

Wellesley had several distinguished women scientists on its faculty, among them Sarah Frances Whiting (*top left*), professor of physics and astronomy; Margaret Clay Ferguson (*top right*), the first woman president of the Botanical Society of America; and Caroline Rebecca Thompson, professor of zoology.

The mathematics department included Ellen Hayes (*top*), a feminist and social radical, and Helen Merrill (*bottom left*), who held a Ph.D. from Yale and became the chronicler of the department. Ellen Fitz Pendleton, who graduated in 1886, became the sixth president of Wellesley in 1911.

Eben Horsford, a chemist and benefactor, donated the luxurious faculty parlor, the site of many social gatherings and committee meetings. His portrait is displayed in the middle of the room.

Part II
Women Scholars and Their Wellesley World
A Social Portrait

4

The Family Culture of the Faculty

It is not too sweeping to assert that Wellesley's development and academic standing are due to the cooperative wisdom and devoted scholarship of her faculty. The initiative has been theirs. They have proved that a college for women can be successfully taught and administered by women. To them Wellesley owes her academic status.

—Florence Converse, *Wellesley College*

In 1900, the academic women of Wellesley assumed genuine ascendancy within the college. Among the extraordinary women who dominated the college during this era were Mary Calkins, philosopher; Katharine Coman, economic historian; Margaret Ferguson, botanist; Ellen Hayes, mathematician and social radical; Vida Dutton Scudder, literary critic and social radical; Emily Greene Balch, economist and winner of the Nobel Prize for Peace; and Katharine Lee Bates, poet and author of "America the Beautiful."

The fifty-three senior and associate women professors who composed the faculty between 1900 and 1910 were a strikingly homogeneous group in terms of social and geographic origins, upbringing, and values. What they shared enabled them to forge a sense of collective identity, a so-called Wellesley world. They are significant not only as individuals but as a discernible social group that built a cohesive intellectual and social community in a largely male academic world.[1]

Unlike other women's colleges, Wellesley had very few academic men. Only two, William Niles, professor of geology, and Hamilton C. Macdougall, professor of music and director of Wellesley's choir, were in the senior ranks. Occasionally, junior men were appointed, but they had no voice in college policy.[2] Hence senior women dominated Wellesley's educational ideology and articulated its social and political philosophy. Their regime lasted well beyond the Hazard era (1899–1910) into the late 1930s. As late as 1935, fourteen professors emeriti lived in a colony in the village of Wellesley and continued to influence the college's intellectual life.[3]

Learnedness in women was scorned from the Colonial era well into the nineteenth century. In her study of women's intellect in the early republic, Linda Kerber concludes that the nation "inherited the image of the learned woman as an unenviable anomaly and kept alive the notion that the woman who developed her mind did so at her own risk." There were exceptional women whose families or spouses encouraged them to read and write, but in general the literacy of white middle-class women trailed that of men until sometime between 1780 and 1840.[4]

Prior to the Civil War selected intellectual women achieved levels of learning that placed them outside the accepted norms of womanhood. Domesticity may have been women's common fate, but by the 1840s the learned lady had emerged as a recognizable social type. Because of family background and class, women like Margaret Fuller and Elizabeth Palmer Peabody succeeded in defining themselves, and in being defined by their society, as intellectuals. Yet these women operated for the most part independently of the male-dominated clubs, societies, and colleges that comprised the formal organizational structure of antebellum intellectual life. They were thus unable to establish an ongoing female intellectual tradition.[5]

The "scribblers," as Nathaniel Hawthorne labeled the sentimental novelists who dictated the literary tastes of nineteenth-century America, constituted another set of intellectual women. The academic women of Wellesley, however, viewed the scribblers as too concerned with the private sphere of women. Katharine Coman criticized their writings for being filled with "self-seeking and vanity."[6]

A third group of intellectual women in the period between the American Revolution and the Civil War were the scientists whom Sally Kohlstedt labels the "private achievers." These privately educated women, many of whom were single, catalogued, drew, and collected specimens for male scientists. Some wrote popular scientific books for a female audience. In spite of these activities, most remained amateur scholars whose primary orientation was domestic.[7]

Although the faculty women of Wellesley recognized the women who had gone before them, they nonetheless prided themselves on being the first generation of college-educated public achievers, for whom, in Vida Scudder's words, "the mere exercise of thinking" defined their lives. They understood that they were among the few women at that time who were allowed to express and fulfill their intellectual aims and ambitions within institutions of higher learning. As Mary Augusta Jordan, a peer at Smith College, explained, for the first time in American history superfluous middle-class daughters could "dispose of the best years of their lives to . . . the choice of scholarship."[8]

A portrait of the faculty women at Wellesley reveals that they identified with the intellectual life throughout their lives. Moreover, one can discern in their accounts characteristics of intellectuals previously equated solely with men. Still, their intellectualism did at times clash with societal norms of femininity; how these women coped with this conflict reveals much about the role of the woman scholar.[9]

A Reading Childhood

In childhood these women were precocious and were recognized as such by their parents. Books occupied a central place in their youths and became their "special companions." Several learned to read before they were five, and many described themselves as bookworms. Mary Alice Willcox's home overflowed with books. Her grandmother's library, which included complete sets of Sir Walter Scott, Washington Irving, and Shakespeare, lined one wall in her house; another room was filled with her own books. "For years all of my small savings and money presents went to swelling this set." Yet the most alluring place in the house was the attic, where she thrilled to tales in *Harper's Monthly*. Given this environment, one tends to believe Willcox's claim that she had taught herself to read fluently by the age of five.[10]

Vida Dutton Scudder was also a self-described reader who exasperated her relatives with her inquiring mind. Before the age of ten, she had "devoured a miscellaneous diet" ranging from the children's series of Rollo Books to the Bhagavad Gita and Ralph Waldo Emerson's essays. She was attracted to mythology and claimed to have read at an early age Bulfinch's *Age of Fable* and the entire dictionary of classical mythology.[11]

The list of books that seven-year-old Katharine Lee Bates had read is most impressive: Scott's *Kenilworth, Waverly, Ivanhoe, The Talisman,* and *The Heart of Midlothian*; Louisa May Alcott's *Little Women*, its sequel, *An Old Fashioned Girl*, and *Hospital Sketches*; and Longfellow's *The Song of Hiawatha*. Bates filled her childhood diary with poems and stories, finding a "charm in bright clean unfilled pages which I, for one, cannot resist." The determined heroine of one of her stories speaks for many of the women in this study when she exclaims: "I would study and study. . . . I would know how the earth came to be, and all about the stars, and I would read the thoughts men wrote hundreds of years ago in strange letters and queer-sounding languages. I would find out why some poetry is poetry and some poetry isn't, and where the Garden of Eden was, and how my head thinks. I would study and study and study, and know and know and know."[12]

Ellen Hayes shared this temperament. Growing up on a farm in Ohio where books were few, she did extra chores to earn money to buy them. She recalled that in her childhood, while other girls sewed sheets, she discovered her "oasis in the desert"—*Harper's Monthly*. Throughout her life Hayes spent little on anything but books and social causes; she was shocked to learn that some people preferred an elaborate menu to books.[13]

Once describing her entire life as one of "desk and book," Margaret Sherwood read incessantly in her girlhood. As a Vassar College student she would sit "cross-legged on the floor [of the library] Sunday afternoons, discovering new worlds." Mary Calkins remembered that she and Sophie Jewett would sit for hours in her father's study "discussing grave mysteries" of books in foreign languages.[14]

Because of their intellectual gifts, these girls found adolescence painful. Having decided as children that they were not good looking, they found social functions and the need to display social graces painful. Dancing lessons, parties, and mixing socially with young men caused them torment. Katharine Lee Bates characterized herself as a "shy near-sighted child always hiding away in a book." Similarly Emily Balch felt unattractive, danced enthusiastically but awkwardly, and "was prone to talk too much on bookish topics or to run embarrassingly short of small talk." During her adolescence she experienced "a number of small agonies of shyness, mortification and disappointment." After these incidents, Balch gave up desiring the attention of young men. Any courtship was about as "imminent as the *judgment day* millennium."[15]

Vida Scudder was frightfully alarmed at human beings and pathologically shy. After one disastrous dancing class, she "went home and wept, utterly miserable." This sense of inadequacy abated somewhat after adolescence, but traces remained many years later.[16]

Sometimes their intellectualism culminated in a sense of detachment. Emily Balch saw herself as "a rather impersonal person, quite able to live on what is offered by books, nature and . . . religion." As adults "the inexhaustible pleasure of contact with the opulence and energy of human thinking" claimed them. Vida Scudder expressed the enjoyment she found in intellectual play: "My mind! 'A poor thing, but mine own.' I never cease to marvel at it. . . . To toy with ideas, dissecting them, chasing them through the wilderness within; weighing, analyzing . . . is there any fun so great?" She could not understand being lonely when books offered companionship, attesting that "many of my best friends live within the covers of books." The comment made about Ethel Puffer—that her mind "never took a vacation"— could apply to most of those who joined the Wellesley faculty.[17]

If these gifted women were predisposed from a young age to the intellectual life, they still had to make careers—a difficult task historically for American women. Motivation for and legitimation of careers came first and foremost from families.

Family Culture

Striking similarities characterize the Wellesley faculty. Nearly 50 percent came from New England; 22 percent were from the Midwest, and 20 percent from the mid-Atlantic region. Only one was a Southerner, and four women were born in Europe. Fifty-two percent of the group were born between 1855 and 1865, and 33 percent between 1865 and 1875. None of the professors married while on the faculty.[18]

There are other parallels. Perhaps the most crucial is the type of family setting they experienced as children. The academic women of Wellesley came predominantly from close-knit, middle-class families noted for the love and support they gave their bright daughters. As children, most of the women were a constant source of delight and pleasure to parents. Moreover, the family environments in which these women were reared included more than just attentive fathers and mothers: aunts and uncles, cousins and grandparents, were part of the wider family circle that counseled, taught, and comforted these women.

In fact, families provided the path to achievement for the Wellesley faculty. These women escaped many traditional expectations and were reared in an environment that encouraged education and preparation for careers and nourished a spirit of activism and creativity. The daughter's eventual achievement in the academic world is best explained as an effort of the entire family rather than as a successful revolt against the family claim.[19]

The women in this study shared a family style characterized by emotional warmth, expressiveness, intimacy, and connectedness. In these privileged families genteel and professional values mixed freely. Work and play were balanced; communing with nature was especially valued. Fathers and mothers alike endorsed intellectual life and took pride in the precocity of their children. Bright girls were allowed to be almost as active as their brothers; they were not schooled in submissiveness or passivity. Indeed, domestic duties were waived for bright daughters. Instead, from a young age, the future women faculty were expected to share adult social and political concerns with their parents.

Fathers

The Victorian world was marked by extreme cultural polarities between masculine and feminine, tough and tender. The fathers of this group of Wellesley women were men capable of both. Most were upper-middle-class professionals: ministers, lawyers, doctors, and educators. The rest were middle-class merchants, civil servants, and businessmen.[20]

During their youths and adulthoods many of these politically liberal men had actively agitated for abolitionism, temperance, and prison reform. They passed on to their daughters their zeal for social reform, their respect for learning, and their inclination for a life of service rather than financial success. Daughters remember fathers who appreciated beauty and were unafraid to express the feminine sides of their natures in their cultural sensitivity and their espousal of aesthetic, intellectual, and moral values.

Such gentlemen exhibited the traits of genteel liberal reformers and northern intellectuals who espoused English economic liberalism and a Protestant moral code. They also lived by a democratic social philosophy that idealized mutual kindliness and good will among social equals. Almost to a man these fathers were characterized as kind, moral, and reluctant to indulge in competition. These men were not so committed to their careers that they had little time for their daughters and, in fact, often appear alienated from or detached from their careers, as if ill at ease with their choices.

A few even gave up their first careers, often dictated by strong family traditions, because they craved more noble pursuits or greater self-realization.[21]

One such moral idealist was Samuel Gilman Brown, father of Alice Van Vechten Brown, professor of art. Following in his father's footsteps, he became president of Hamilton College but was dissatisfied with the job. Known more for his gentleness of character than for his executive talents, he abhorred the conflict and bitterness that came with the presidency and soon resigned to return to teaching. Having broken with family traditions himself, Samuel Brown approved his daughter's request to go to art school in New York.[22]

Many fathers were highly principled men. Francis V. Balch, father of Emily Greene Balch, professor of economics, was a clerk for Senator Charles Sumner and, like Sumner, worked as an abolitionist and civil service reformer. One colleague assessed Balch as excessively unselfish, another as a peacemaker. Someone once characterized Balch as a "combination of Abraham Lincoln, Santa Claus and Jesus Christ." To Emily Balch, her father set a constant standard of high moral principles: "He was . . . the most selfless person I have ever known."[23]

For these fathers, post–Civil War politics, business, and law became sullied. As the conservative politics of Reconstruction signaled the failure of abolitionism, such men withdrew from public life. They opted instead for private domestic lives, upholding within their families the gospel of idealism they had espoused publicly before the war. Thomas Sherwood, father of Margaret Pollock Sherwood, for example, soured on the law. Convinced that one could not be an honest man and a lawyer, Sherwood gave up the profession to work on his father's farm.[24]

Having once been concerned with the fate of mankind, such men chose instead to focus their energies on their families, nurturing in particular their bright daughters, who might succeed where they had failed. It is therefore not altogether surprising that more than a trace of millenarianism appeared in the movement for women's higher education, as it had in the pre–Civil War reform movements. This was one legacy of fathers to daughters.[25]

Many of the fathers of Wellesley women set extraordinarily high intellectual standards for their daughters. Francis Balch, who had unusual powers of concentration, read inexhaustibly for hours, keeping abreast of all the new social philosophy and literature and reviewing it for his daughter; he continued to guide her reading until well after Emily's graduation from Bryn Mawr. It is little wonder that Emily shared her father's intense intellectualism. Similarly, Thomas Sherwood had a suppressed creativity and would tolerate no vagueness in conversation or in the logic his daughter used in her homework essays.[26]

The involvement of these fathers in the intellectual development of their daughters went beyond setting high standards: many directly supervised their daughters' educations. Levi Coman, a lawyer-turned-farmer and collector of rare ferns and fossils, often took his children for long rides, pointing out trees and birds and later testing the children's knowledge of what they had seen. When Katharine, his first daughter, was born following three sons, Coman announced: "Now I will show them how a girl should be educated." He included Katharine in the Latin and mathematics lessons he gave his sons. Later, when Coman realized that Katharine was learning little at the seminary she attended, he directed the principal to give her more work. The principal refused because "he did not think the female mind capable of comprehending anything more difficult." Coman thereupon transferred Katharine to a public high school, scorning the dire predictions of what would happen to his daughter's manners and morals in a coeducational environment.[27]

Mary Whiton Calkins, professor of philosophy, also grew up under the intellectual tutelage of her father, Wolcott Calkins, a Congregationalist minister. Calkins wanted his children to learn foreign languages and for five or six years after Mary's birth permitted only German to be spoken in the home. Like other fathers in this study he had a voracious literary appetite. His second daughter, Maud, reported once that as light reading he had given Mary and herself some stories in German. "Light reading indeed," Maud commented.[28]

These fathers gave their daughters emotional as well as intellectual support, often at critical moments in their lives. Convinced that his freshman daughter was ill prepared for her first year at Wellesley Eliza Kendrick's father called her depressions "nothing more than a temporary blue spell." Benjamin Kendrick assured her that she was eminently qualified to distinguish herself and that she should "dismiss all doubts from her mind" by thinking of her family, who hoped that she would "dream good things and awake with new vigor for the battle." Under her father's wise aegis, Eliza Kendrick gradually became more confident of her intellectual powers and by senior year she had shifted her sights from secondary school to college teaching.[29]

Intelligent, caring fathers had enormous influence on their daughters' intellectual growth and career choices. Francis Balch not only consoled

Emily when she had self-doubts, he counseled her against entering law since he believed her true worth lay in social science research and reform activism. He wrote her that it was a mistake to give up that work: "I believe you can do a great deal of good. You have a very sound mind on all social questions, a high order of ability and a kindly and equable spirit. I believe that you will always have many loving friends and be a strong influence." This was fruitful advice, for Emily Balch went on to become an outstanding academic at Wellesley and a leading social reformer who was awarded the Nobel Peace Prize in 1946.[30]

As career mentors, these fathers exploited their class and community positions, arranged for special educational opportunities, and actively interceded to secure their daughters' professional placement. William Willcox helped his daughter Mary Alice Willcox obtain an appointment in the zoology department. Mary noted that her father approved of her career plans, though her mother "regretted my decision because it would mean giving up all possibilities of marrying." Wolcott Calkins arranged for Mary Calkins to have an interview with President Freeman, who invited her to join the faculty. Later, when Mary sought a Ph.D. in psychology from Harvard, which did not admit women, Wolcott petitioned the Harvard Corporation to admit his daughter as a special visitor. These fathers acted as career brokers rather than as marriage brokers.[31]

Vida Scudder's astute remark about Emily Balch could hold for many of the women in this study: "Her behavior conformed to her family tradition." These academic women were imbued with the intellectual or moral ideals of their fathers and strove to attain the goals set by them. Their reverence could be extreme: Mary Alice Willcox extolled her "earthly father" as a revelation of what "a God must be." She felt empowered by his social influence and proudly recalled his being stopped by people in the community who wanted to discuss his sermons. That enviable contact with other minds defined Mary Alice's identity and life purpose.[32]

Emily Greene Balch also was conscious of her father's status in the Boston Brahman community. On any given night she might sit down to dinner with twenty distinguished guests for an evening of cultured conversation. Not surprisingly, she admired her father, but she also worried that she might fall short of his expectations. Viewed as goodness personified, Emily nonetheless berated herself for not being as selfless as her father. Balch was not alone in her anxiety; many women in this group were ambivalent about emulating their fathers.[33]

Clearly, the burden of fatherly and family expectations weighed on these women. Daughters who perceived their fathers as paragons, who revered them as idols, and who pursued careers with parental endorsement found it psychologically difficult to rival or surpass them. Perhaps this is why so many talented and assertive women avoided issues of hierarchy, status, and power by adopting the persona of the pioneer, a person who does not supplant another because she is *first*.

Conversely, fathers who were so intimate with their daughters as to consider them soul mates were reluctant to rupture those ties. Although Francis Balch encouraged Emily's commitment to a career, he kept wishing she would live at home. When she traveled abroad, he praised her work but longed to "catch a glimpse of her." He both pushed her out into the world and pulled her home—a tug of war that may have been the Wellesley group's particular version of Jane Addams's battle against the family claim. These women paid the price for the support they got. Emily Balch was expected to carve a career of distinction for herself and to remain faithful, intimate, and useful to her family. Unable to disappoint her family on either front, she lived at home well into her thirties. Weighing the cost in later life, she concluded, "I do not regret it." Her father's inspiration and support were indeed essential to her achievement. Without such fathers, few of these women would have achieved all that they did.[34]

Mothers

Also supportive of a warm family culture, the mothers of these Wellesley women provided love, inspiration, guidance, and companionship, often for life. Information on the mothers is limited and hardly unbiased. One must often rely on a daughter's autobiography or assume that a fictional account of a mother-daughter relationship is drawn from life. Whatever the source, it is clear that most mothers in the nineteenth century were seen through the romantic lens of a sentimental era. Yet, even after allowing for the Victorian idealization of motherhood, it is significant that these Wellesley women described their mothers as nurturing, tolerant, learned, self-sacrificing, and stalwart; almost all earned praise for responding to their daughters' intellectual gifts. In some families the mother supplied the worldly competence and spirited activism to counterbalance a passive, almost ethereal father.

Educational information on mothers is much scantier than for fathers.

Evidence suggests that those who attended seminaries often regretted that they had not been able to attend college and were eager to have their daughters embrace the new opportunity.[35] Martha Seymour Coman fervently endorsed women's education, especially that of her daughter Katharine. Mrs. Coman, who trained at Putnam Female Seminary, an Ohio offshoot of Mount Holyoke, told her daughter that her own father had expected her to complete the course of study at Putnam, "even if I should be forty years old before it was done!"[36]

Lucretia Kimball Kendall, also a seminary graduate and a firm believer in higher education for women, taught with her daughters in a mid-western academy. An advocate of abolition and black education, Mrs. Kendall infused her daughter Elizabeth with a reformist spirit. Such teams of mother-daughter social visionaries were common. With her daughter Mary, Charlotte Whiton Calkins formed the Social Science Club of Newton, which dealt with issues of prison reform and temperance.[37]

The mother-daughter relationships in the Wellesley group entailed few of the preordained rituals of nineteenth-century womanhood. Indeed, they shunned domestic activities identified as stereotypically feminine, such as sewing.[38] Instead, mothers and daughters shared bonds springing from intellectual companionship and heightened expectations for daughters. Many of the mothers of the women in this study had already widened their sphere beyond the limitations of a private world. Their revised definition of womanhood stressed women's educability, intellectual equality, and physical strengths. The new woman was destined to have an occupation and, ideally, to dedicate herself to some form of social service.[39]

Renouncing passivity, submissiveness, or mindless duty, these mothers endorsed their daughters' inquisitive, adventuresome, and even rebellious natures. Ellen Hayes noted, "Mother never rebuked me for spatterings or stains. . . . She let me live." Ruth Wolcott Hayes gave in to five-year-old Ellen's urgings and "bent the first pin into hook shape that outfitted [her] to go fishing." Ellen Hayes appreciated how lucky she was, for "really proper girls of 1860 stayed indoors, wore their hair tightly braided and sewed sheet-seams over and over."[40]

Mothers such as Ruth Hayes might have been rejected by their daughters for their compliance with domesticity; they were not. Instead, daughters saw their mothers as models of industry and self-reliance.

Most of these mothers belonged to a cohort of American women for whom the hard labor of child rearing and household duties was a daily reality. For women in this study, their hardy and ingenious mothers performed heroic feats. As a child Mary Case moved with her family to Pikes Peak, Colorado, during the gold rush. En route they slept in the open under buffalo rugs and suffered many privations, but her mother's genius for improvisation overcame all. Even on the frontier, Mrs. Case always instructed Mary and saw to it that she studied. So fine was her home training that Mary Case entered high school two years early. Mrs. Case's achievement is especially remarkable in that her daughter had fallen from a crib in infancy and was confined to a wheelchair for life. Assisting Mary throughout her childhood and adolescence, Mrs. Case became a model of stalwart endurance, which Mary internalized and followed until her own death at ninety-nine.[41]

Another exalted mother is Ellen Noyes Balch, who encouraged Emily to take up languages at nine, letting a German book fall her way "not wholly by accident." Equally important, she tolerated, even sparked, her daughter's rambunctious behavior, allowing Emily to soil her dresses by climbing trees, sliding down mountains, and playing in dirt. When this active play resulted in scrapes or bruises, Emily noted, "She did not spoil us. A tumble was met not with sympathy, but 'Jump and take another dear.'"[42]

Mothers formulated careers for their daughters no less than did fathers. Margaret Hastings Jackson owed her career largely to her mother's influence. Mrs. Jackson, who lived with her artist-husband in Italy, had three daughters die prior to Margaret's birth. Fearing that Margaret too might contract a fatal disease, Mrs. Jackson would not allow her to attend school. Yet she did not stifle her daughter's intellectual growth and began to hire tutors for her once she recognized the girl's precocity. As cultural stimulation, she often took Margaret to the Uffizi to study paintings and encouraged her daughter's fondness for languages—Latin as well as Italian. Later, she arranged for Margaret's appointment at Wellesley.[43]

Mother-daughter relationships colored the atmosphere at Wellesley, because six mothers lived with their daughters on campus: Mrs. Cornelia Bates, Mrs. Jackson, Mrs. Kendall, Mrs. Coman, Mrs. Locke, and Mrs. Scudder; others lived close enough to visit their daughters regularly. In nineteenth-century America the unmarried daughter had, in Mary Calkins's words, "peculiar obligations" to her family and in particular to her mother. With such obligations came special compensations.[44]

The Calkins's mother-daughter relationship illustrates well how the claims of family could benefit a young woman as well as inhibit autonomy and vocation. During her childhood, Mary was not particularly close to her mother, whose delicate health kept her away from home for long periods. Mary's younger sister Maud felt the absences deeply, Mary less so, being immersed more in her studies than in the family. Maud died when Mary was twenty, and from that time on Mary and her mother were inseparable, so close that "you couldn't fit a knife between them." Calkins reflected that her life would have been extremely unhappy if it hadn't been for "philosophy and my parents, particularly my mother." Thomas Procter, her colleague in philosophy at Wellesley, found Calkins's relationship with her mother interesting: "Part of the time she was her mother's daughter; part of the time her mother was her daughter—a good deal of time."[45]

Another mother-daughter relationship that exhibited the duality of claim and compensation was that of Vida Dutton Scudder and her mother, Harriet Scudder. Vida, whose father died when she was a baby, was reared by her mother, who took the seven-year-old Vida to Europe and introduced her to a world of art and culture that became a permanent part of her life. Vida and her mother were emotional as well as intellectual companions until Vida left home to attend college. Unbeknownst to Vida, her mother had initiated this move by registering her at Smith College. Vida gladly acquiesced to her mother's action. In a thinly disguised autobiographical novel, *Listener in Babel,* Vida Scudder as Hilda Lathrop tries to become an artist like her mother. Yet she ultimately rejects the "phantom world of charming art because appreciation is valued over achievement." She nevertheless struggles to remain close to her mother, asserting that "Mrs. Lathrop never knew a more ardent lover than her daughter."[46]

In her autobiography, Vida Scudder attributes her choice of a more conventional career—it was hardly that—in academia over full-time social settlement work to her mother's displeasure with the latter; as an academic her mother could live with her, as both desired. Harriet Scudder's claims on her daughter, particularly her opposition to a career in social reform for her, should not be dismissed. Still she gave Vida support and in the end always "yielded to the fatality of her daughter's temperament." Like other women in this group, Vida Scudder was able to pioneer a new social role precisely because of the sense of security and competence she derived from her mother. Harriet's death when Vida was past middle age was a great tragedy in Scudder's life, one that required her to "steel herself to dispense" with her mother's companionship. Even as an old woman Vida Scudder awoke with bad dreams, "craving her mother's comforting arm."[47]

One aspect of the family claim too rarely discussed is how daughters coped with the demands made of them or how they distanced themselves from their families. Bright and independent women did not always succumb meekly to parental expectations. Although Vida Scudder argued with her mother over a career choice, she finally won out and divided her time between teaching and settlement reform. Elizabeth Kendall told her mother curtly that she could not escort her on an upcoming trip to England because she would be busy seeing friends. As a freshman in college, Eliza Kendrick, known as Lida, wrote her mother that she was astonished that her mother wanted her at home as a helpmate, adding that she was "utterly useless" at housework. If she were not suited to study, she would "perhaps discover it in a few more years. At any rate, it is well known, in the family certainly, that I am not of much account for anything else." Lida Kendrick remained at Wellesley.[48]

Mothers like fathers were close allies and contributed to their daughter's education and careers. Although the bonds between the generations were strong, they were not smothering.

Siblings and Sex Roles

Male siblings often provided alternate role models for the academic women of Wellesley. A review of the family histories demonstrates that the upbringing of these women differed little from their brothers'. Indeed, where differences exist, there seems to be greater divergence between how different sisters in the same family were raised than between bright brothers and sisters. In a family with more than one daughter, these intellectual women were often designated as bright, treated as predestined individuals, and exempted from the female behavior expected of their sisters.[49]

In the Willcox family, Mary Alice and Walter, both precocious children, were brought up together. Mary loved trying to match him in feats of daring. She, in turn, enlisted him in her dramatizations of Shakespeare. Both shared a love of reading and collecting books that lasted throughout their lives. Mary Alice remained Walter's intellectual companion even after his marriage, attending statistical conferences with him in Europe. There are many examples of such close brother-sister relationships in the group.[50]

Raised to be assertive and inquisitive, the Wellesley women were sensitive to differential treatment of themselves and their brothers and resented anything separating their worlds. Mary Alice objected that her brothers

were allowed to go barefoot in summer and asked her parents why girls
were not allowed to do so.[51]

A sense of naughtiness also characterized these women as youngsters.
An inveterate tomboy, Katharine Lee Bates liked to invent interesting games
to play outdoors. At a favorite retreat, an old burial ground near her home,
she organized battles using tree branches for swords and enlisted chums to
hunt turtles in the swamp. On one occasion she persuaded her reluctant
sister Jennie to watch her drop their cat from an upstairs window to see if it
would land on its feet. At the age of seven, Bates was able to perceptively
analyze the roots of such behavior in the following poem, complete with
charming errors:

> Girls are a very neccesary
> portion of creation. They
> are full as neccesary
> as boys. Girls (xcepting
> a spechies called Tomboys)
> play with dolls, when
> young. Afterwards
> croquet, games, etc. take
> up their spare time.
> Sewing is always ex-
> pected of girls. Why
> not of boys. Boys
> don't do much but out
> dore work. Girls work
> is most all in doors.
> It isn't fair.

Other entries in Kitty Lee's diary show her luxuriating in her badness.
Tempting and taunting a school chum leave her with some qualms of conscience, but she concludes, "I don't think much of doing penance for my
sins." After another series of pranks she wrote a poem, "Revenge Is Sweet."[52]

Nurtured as they were on literary diets that included Sir Walter Scott,
Gothic stories, and horror tales, many of the women wanted to assume
heroic roles. They longed to contest, subvert, or openly defy conventional
feminine behavior. At ten years of age, Scudder shocked her teacher by
memorizing and reciting with gusto lines from the "Ancient Mariner":

> The very deep did rot: O Christ!
> That ever this should be!
> Yea, slimy things did crawl with legs
> Upon the slimy sea.

When her appalled teacher would not let her continue, Scudder was crushed but "persevered for some time by myself."[53]

Mary Alice Willcox is another who remembered being naughty. Her mother noted that when Mary broke rules, "her conscience did not prick her at all." Unlike her sister Nellie, Mary was a "confirmed little liar." Nellie would beg Mary Alice to stop lying and to ask God's forgiveness, but Mary would do so only temporarily and then return immediately to her old ways. Not even her father's dire predictions that liars were punished by confinement to a lake that burned with fire deterred Mary Alice.[54]

As adolescents and young adults, these spirited individuals translated their naughtiness into an overt feminist critique. Upon graduation from Newton High School Mary Calkins wrote an essay entitled "The Apology Which Plato Should Have Written—a Vindication of the Character of Xantippe." Katharine Lee Bates's poem "The Ivy and the Oak," written in 1880 when she was twenty, clearly underscores her feminism. The poem caustically chastises women for being beautiful but dependent. The ivy's beauty is to be despised because it merely adorns the solid oak. Bates concludes that she would rather be an "upright, prickly shrub" than a dependent ivy.[55]

Sometimes this adolescent feminism was the result of following the lead of a bright, independent elder sister. Sophie Jewett was influenced by her elder sister Louise. When Louise started to study geography, Sophie followed suit, "mapping out the entire universe according to Louise's instructions." Louise led her siblings on expeditions over the hedges that shut in their family estate in order to attempt a journey that would lead them across the globe. Margaret Sherwood literally followed her elder sister Mary—first to Vassar, then to Europe, where she stationed herself in Zurich to study English literature while her sister began medical training.[56]

More often, however, the academic women of Wellesley were clearly the leaders in the family and overshadowed their sisters, not only in intellect but in their risk taking and rejection of stereotypical female behavior. Ellen Hayes recalled that of her family, "I was the eldest and naturally the leader." She explained that Anna, the next in line, was unselfish and obliging in their carryings-on. The youngest, Orlena, was "a genuine pal in devising and executing schemes" and always submitted to her sisters' will.[57]

Within the Balch family circle there was a similar separation of roles. The eldest, Annie, took over the maternal role when their mother died in 1884, but Emily Balch never engaged in domesticity. Unlike Annie, Emily "hated sewing and believed that grown up people favored dolls because they led to making doll clothes and ultimately learning to sew." Instead, Emily organized troops of her friends, climbed mountains, and played games in the cellars of nearby houses. Balch, unlike her sisters, attended college and was in the first graduating class at Bryn Mawr. When awarded the first European fellowship for a year of graduate study abroad, Emily wished to renounce the prize. Annie, however, advised her to put aside her Puritan scruples and accept the award. She rejoiced at Emily's success and suggested that "bells should be rung in default of the town crier" to announce Emily's honor.[58]

As adults submissive sisters sponsored their career-oriented sisters, subordinating themselves and even sacrificing their own career aims in order that their bright sisters achieve. Approximately one-quarter of the women in this study had sisters who lived with them at Wellesley or nearby and served as wives. These domestic, dutiful sisters administered the home and looked after the professional sister, often serving as social companions. At times, the academics felt uncomfortable, even guilty, about this situation. Katharine Lee Bates realized that her sister Jennie's life had been narrowed by her domestic role. Nevertheless, Bates carved out a career, leaving Jennie to serve as her secretary and typist and to care for their mother.[59]

Many of the self-sacrificing sisters were plagued by the problems associated with middle-class women in the nineteenth century—nervous breakdowns, depression, and physical ailments. Many of the sisters were frail and sickly; some died quite young. Emily Balch's older sister Annie and younger sister Betsy were plagued by ill health and nervous breakdown. Emily periodically suffered "the blues" but was able for most of her life to channel her depression or conquer it with work. For the Wellesley faculty, careers and supportive networks alleviated the damaging psychological ailments that drained the talents and health of their sisters.[60]

These primary bonds existed within a wider matrix of family ties. The Wellesley faculty women grew up amid other mediators and models—aunts and uncles, grandfathers and grandmothers, brothers and sisters and cousins. Large extended families meant involvement in the lives of numerous relatives who represented many different stages and styles of life.

Vida Dutton Scudder grew up in a large, stimulating family. Grandmother Scudder, aggrieved over the death of her son David, devoted much attention to his only child, whose name was a feminine form of David. Vida recalled how her grandmother picked blueberries with her on Cape Cod and fed her roast oysters: "She and I were the greatest chums." Scudder had other female models as well. Aunt Narnie, her mother's sister, was a physician who lived and traveled with Vida and her mother. Vida also relished being with her father's only sister, Aunt Jeanie, because she was selfish, a trait she admired in a family where "all my other elders had a disconcerting and exasperating habit of sacrificing or effacing themselves." Two other relatives were important to her: her cousin Eliza Scudder, who was "storm-tossed and passionate," and her uncle Horace Scudder, whom the fatherless Vida cherished. Horace was a man of letters, editor of the *Atlantic Monthly*, and a Wellesley trustee. The black sheep of the family, he possessed a social conscience much like the one Vida was to develop and devoted himself happily to city mission work. She remembered his firm habit of bringing his beloved vagrants home to dinner. Such behavior shocked the other members of the Scudder household but endeared him to his niece.[61]

When Emily Balch was growing up, both sets of grandparents and several aunts and uncles lived in or near the Balches' ancestral home. One aunt, Catherine Porter Noyes, her mother's sister, who taught black children in the South after the Civil War, taught Emily how to read before she went to school. Emily's Aunt Nannie (her father's sister) taught Emily enough Italian to read Dante. Nannie enjoyed books and her garden, pleasures that Emily learned to share. Emily's cousin Agnes was more like a sister than a cousin; together they went to Miss Ireland's School and then on to Bryn Mawr. They maintained a lifelong closeness: Agnes telegraphed Emily from Spain when her cousin won the Nobel Peace Prize: "This is Emily's day, Viva-a-a-a-a. . . . We are all proud of her and of being her friends."[62]

Religion

Rebellion against the limitations of women's roles was in many cases coupled with a rejection of narrow religious teachings. Several of the women in this group rejected official doctrines that either conflicted with their intellectual approach to life or limited their behavior as women.

Mary Alice Willcox, the daughter of a minister, was "full of infantile theological struggles." As a child she lay in bed, conjuring up a burning finger as an "introduction to the anguish of the horrors of hell." Yet even after imagining "burning and burning and not being any nearer the end of her eternal punishment," she defiantly declared that she "wouldn't give up my own way even if hell was to be the result." Willcox attended Sunday School, but without the intended effect: "As little children we were allowed to play with Noah's ark—in reality more edifying from a biological than from a devotional standpoint." For Willcox, no less than other women in this group, Sunday School was tolerated because it provided an opportunity to read. As an adult, the more Willcox pursued her scientific studies, the more her religious faith was undermined.[63]

Several Wellesley women were unconventional in their religious creeds. Alice Van Vechten Brown built a small sanctuary in the basement of College Hall so that faculty women could pray in private. Ellen Hayes, considered an unbeliever, once shocked those assembled at chapel by saying, "God himself cannot change the laws of mathematics."[64] Katharine Lee Bates also came to espouse a personal religion. As a child she wrote in her diary that she disliked Sunday because she had to dress in her best clothes and listen to a long sermon. She preferred to play. Throughout her life she never felt any particular attraction to organized religion. "I trust myself," she declared, "and believe in the poor dumb hidden self which dwells in solitude and looks to God."[65]

Although few adhered to formal religious doctrines, most were imbued with the Social Gospel impulse, a reform movement that inspired the devout to concentrate on secular social ends, particularly the problems of cities. Like other Progressives, the Wellesley women felt driven to do something with their lives. Emily Balch was deeply impressed by her minister's call for leaders to serve society without limitations and pledged herself to a life of service.[66]

For women who could not admit to the egotism of their ambitions, service was often, in the words of Vida Scudder, "a subtle form of ambition." At age twenty-two Emily Balch recorded that she had tried to slay her inner dragon—egotism—yet "the monster made his home within me." Struggling with ambition, which she believed to be a form of vanity, Balch admitted in her journal: "It has always been my desire to be known, a truly vulgar ambition." From childhood, she kept a mental record of all her accomplishments, a kind of hagiography. She found it difficult to break this pernicious habit. High motivations were often accompanied with a sense of conflict and guilt about achievement. Katharine Lee Bates, who considered quitting her Wellesley post to become a full-time writer, rejected this desire as an "egotistical prosing." For women with such ambitions, yet feelings of conflict over motivations, higher education was a legitimate sphere in which to pursue lofty goals. The intellectual life was endorsed by family culture; academe offered bright women a new frontier replete with rewards and adventure.[67]

5

From Cinderella to Woman Scholar
The Education and Career Paths of the Faculty

In the words of Margaret Sherwood, the Wellesley faculty had a sense of "great doors suddenly opening wide. Such privileges as women had never known before had come to [us]." Aware that women were traditionally denied access to the scholarly life, they felt fortunate to pursue higher educations. Formal education provided these women an entree into careers and accorded them a "feeling of power and privilege."[1]

At a time when about 1 percent of the eligible population attended college, only five of the fifty-three women in this study did not earn bachelor degrees. An even more impressive statistic is that 40 percent held doctorates. (See table 5.) The fact that over 80 percent studied in nondegree courses during summers or on leaves, both in this country and in Europe, suggests that love of learning, not credentials, motivated these women.[2]

Of course the older academic women in this study, those who joined the Wellesley faculty in the 1870s and 1880s, had fewer formal degrees than those who came later. Illustrative of the first generation of amateur women scientists is Susan Hallowell, a self-educated botanist who, prior to the opening of Wellesley, spent fourteen years teaching at Bangor High School in Maine. When she was appointed professor of botany in 1876, her sole formal training had been in various summer programs.[3]

Mary Alice Willcox began her scientific education by reading books on evolution that her sister Nellie brought home from

Table 5
Senior and Associate Faculty of Wellesley College, 1900–10

Name	Year of Birth	Bachelor's	Year Earned	M.A.	Year Earned	Ph.D.	Year Earned	Year of Appt.	Principal Dept.	Yrs. on Faculty
Edith Rose Abbot	1876	none	—	none	—	none	—	1905	Art	10
Emily Greene Balch	1867	Bryn Mawr	1889	none	—	none	—	1896	Economics	22
Katharine Lee Bates	1859	Wellesley	1880	Wellesley	1891	none	—	1886	English	39
Malvina Bennett	1857	Boston U.	1878	none	—	none	—	1896	Elocution	27
Charlotte Almira Bragg	1863	MIT	1890	none	—	none	—	1890	Chemistry	40
Caroline Breyfogle	1874	U. of Chicago	1896	none	—	U. of Chicago	1912	1900	Latin	6
Alice Van Vechten Brown	1862	Art Students League of N.Y.	1885	none	—	none	—	1897	Art	33
Ellen Burrell	1850	Wellesley	1880	none	—	none	—	1886	Mathematics	30
Mary Whiton Calkins	1863	Smith	1885	none	—	Harvard[a]	1895	1887	Psychology	42
Ellor Carlisle	?	none	—	none	—	none	—	1898	Pedagogy	5
Mary Sophia Case	1854	U. of Michigan	1884	Wellesley	1926	none	—	1884	Philosophy	40
Eva Chandler	1855	U. of Michigan	1878	none	—	none	—	1879	Mathematics	41
Angie Chapin	1855	U. of Michigan	1875	U. of Michigan	1895	none	—	1879	Greek	40
Katharine Coman	1857	U. of Michigan	1880	none	—	none	—	1880	History, Economics	33

Table 5 (continued)

Name	Year of Birth	Bachelor's	Year Earned	M.A.	Year Earned	Year Ph.D.	Year of Earned	Principal Appt.	Dept.	Yrs. on Faculty
Grace Cooley	1863	Wellesley	1885*	Brown	1895	none	—	1883	Botany	21
Clara Eaton Cummings	1855	Wellesley	1880*	none	—	none	—	1879	Botany	27
Grace Davis	1870	Wellesley	1898	Wellesley	1905	none	—	1899	Physics	37
Katharine May Edwards	1862	Cornell	1888	none	—	Cornell	1895	1889	Latin	38
Margaret Clay Ferguson	1863	Cornell	1899	none	—	Cornell	1901	1893	Botany	37
Elizabeth Fisher	1873	MIT	1896	none	—	none	—	1893	Geology	32
Caroline Rebecca Fletcher	1867	Wellesley	1889	Radcliffe	1899	none	—	1894	Latin	38
Eleanor Acheson McCulloch Gamble	1868	Wellesley	1889	none	—	Cornell	—	1898	Philosophy	35
Susan Maria Hallowell	1835	none	—	none	—	none	—	1875	Botany	27
Sophie Chantal Hart	1868	Radcliffe	1892	U. of Michigan	1898	none	—	1893	English	45
Adeline Belle Hawes	1857	Oberlin	1883	Oberlin	1897	none	—	1888	Latin	33
Ellen Amanda Hayes	1851	Oberlin	1878	none	—	none	—	1879	Mathematics	37
Marian Hubbard	1868	U. of Chicago	1894	none	—	none	—	1894	Zoology	43
Margaret Hastings Jackson	1861	none	—	none	—	none	—	1890	Italian	40
Sophie Jewett	1861	none	—	none	—	none	—	1889	English	20
Elizabeth Kimball Kendall	1855	none	—	Radcliffe	1899	none[b]	—	1879	History	41

Table 5 (continued)

Name	Year of Birth	Bachelor's	Year Earned	M.A.	Year Earned	Ph.D.	Year Earned	Year of Appt.	Principal Dept.	Yrs. on Faculty
Eliza Hall Kendrick	1863	Wellesley	1885	Boston U.	1893	Boston	1895	1900	Biblical History	32
Adelaide Imogene Locke	1869	Mount Holyoke	1896[c]	none	—	none	—	1896	Biblical History	28
Laura Emma Lockwood	1863	U. of Kansas	1891	U. of Kansas	1894	Yale	1898	1899	English	31
Anna Jane McKeag	1864	Wilson	1898	none	—	U. of Penn.	1900	1902	Pedagogy	27[d]
Helen Abbot Merrill	1864	Wellesley	1886	none	—	Yale	1903	1893	Mathematics	39
Edna Virginia Moffett	1870	Vassar	1897	Cornell	1901	Cornell	1907	1902	History	36
Annie Sybil Montague	1854	Wellesley	1879	Wellesley	1882	none	—	1882	Greek	32
Margarethe Müller	1862	U. of Göttingen	1897*	none	—	none	—	1889	German	34
Julia Orvis	1872	Vassar	1895	none	—	Cornell	1907	1881	History	42
Ellen Fitz Pendleton	1864	Wellesley	1886	Wellesley	1891	none	—	1888	Mathematics	48
Frances Perry	1870	Butler	1891	Butler	1893	none	—	1900	English	9
Ethel Dench Puffer	1872	Smith	1891	none	—	Radcliffe	1902	1901	Philosophy	7
Charlotte Fitch Roberts	1859	Wellesley	1880	none	—	Yale	1894	1901	Chemistry	36
Vida Dutton Scudder	1861	Smith	1884	Smith	1889	none	—	1888	English	40
Martha Hale Shackford	1875	Wellesley	1896	none	—	Yale	1901	1901	English	42

Table 5 (continued)

Name	Year of Birth	Bachelor's	Year Earned	M.A.	Year Earned	Ph.D.	Year Earned	Year of Appt.	Principal Dept.	Yrs. on Faculty
Margaret Pollock Sherwood	1864	Vassar	1886	none	—	Yale	1898	1889	English	42
Caroline Rebecca Thompson	1869	U. of Penn.	1898	none	—	U. of Penn.	1901	1901	Zoology	20
Roxanna Vivian	1872	Wellesley	1894	none	—	U. of Penn.	1901	1901	Mathematics	26
Alice Vincent Waite	1864	Smith	1886	Smith	1894	none	—	1896	English	36
Alice Walton	1865	Smith	1887	none	—	Cornell	1892	1896	Greek, Archaeology	37
Sarah Frances Whiting	1865	Ingram	1865	none	—	none	—	1876	Physics	40
Mary Alice Willcox	1856	Salem Normal	1875	none	—	U. of Zurich	1893	1883	Zoology	27
Natalie Wipplinger	1871	Bern U.	1896	none	—	U. of Freiberg	1900	1904	German	36

aAfter "unofficial study," Calkins passed all requirements for a Ph.D. at Harvard but was denied the degree.
bKendall received a law degree from Boston University Law School in 1892.
cLocke received a Bachelor of Sacred Theology from the Hartford Theological Seminary in 1892.
dThis number reflects the fact that McKeag left Wellesley for three years to be president of Wilson College and then returned.
*Attended but did not graduate.

Mount Holyoke. Following normal school in Framingham, Massachusetts, Mary Alice taught science at secondary schools in Boston. She was recruited by Lucretia Crocker to attend the Agassiz Anderson School of Natural History, on Penikese Island, off the coast of Massachusetts, and was sponsored by Henry Durant and Alexander Agassiz for advanced training in England; instead she began teaching at Wellesley without an official B.A.[4]

Several features mark the undergraduate experiences of the forty-eight women who earned formal B.A.'s during this time and who form the second generation of Wellesley faculty. Twenty-three (43 percent) held bachelor degrees from coeducational institutions, and twenty-five (47 percent) graduated from the eastern single-sex colleges known as the Seven Sisters. Fourteen Wellesley graduates made up 26 percent of the faculty, quite a few of whom had been classmates. Although grades were traditionally not assigned in the era in which these women studied, almost all of the Wellesley graduates were known as brilliant students and were later elected to Phi Beta Kappa.[5]

Whatever type of college they attended, undergraduates in the 1880s and 1890s were exposed to a curriculum in flux. This group studied both the classics and the social sciences, which were just gaining prominence in American colleges. The transcripts of the Wellesley alumnae who became faculty show that nearly all took either Greek or Latin (and sometimes both), biblical study, mathematics, science, history, and philosophy. A philosophical idealism, set forth in courses in moral philosophy and ethics, formed the foundation of their educations. Several women adopted the moral and social idealism of professors affected by the Social Gospel movement. Emily Balch was influenced by Franklin H. Giddings at Bryn Mawr; Vida Scudder by Stuart Phelps and John Bates Clark at Smith; and Mary Calkins by Charles Garman, whose philosophy courses stressed the doctrine of service. Some women who did graduate work at Oxford became caught up in the neoromantic revival led by William Morris and John Ruskin. Those who did graduate work with William James, Josiah Royce, and Hugo Münsterberg at Harvard during its golden age of philosophy absorbed the ethical ideals of the department. They were especially influenced by Royce's belief in an ethical community. In short, idealism and social reform ethos infused the educations of many members of the Wellesley faculty.[6]

In addition to the shared intellectual milieu of their undergraduate days, the Wellesley faculty also attended the handful of graduate training programs available to women. Six women went to Yale for their masters and doctorates: Annie Sybil Montague, Helen Merrill, Margaret Sherwood, Martha Hale Shackford, Laura Lockwood, and Charlotte Fitch Roberts. Sherwood, Shackford, and Lockwood, who took degrees in English, all studied with Professor Albert Stanburrough Cook. Graduate records reveal that most did excellent work. In 1898 Martha Hale Shackford received the first award offered by Professor Cook for the best unpublished verse, the Yale University Prize for Poems. Helen Merrill recalled spending a happy and productive year studying mathematics at Yale—her "Almus Pater . . . (Wellesley being my Alma Mater)." Laura Lockwood's thesis on Milton, however, elicited a negative response from a member of her doctoral committee, who noted that "intellectually such work is not much higher than index-making—Anyone could do it, and when done it is of no value." He did not reject the thesis, however, because it showed "much industry, though industry sadly misapplied."[7]

Five Wellesley scholars received their graduate training at Cornell: Katharine May Edwards, Margaret Ferguson, Eleanor Gamble, Julia Orvis, and Alice Walton. Orvis, recommended by the president of Vassar, James Taylor, was granted a Ph.D. in history. Ferguson majored in botany, with a first minor in physiology and second minor in mycology. Her mentor wrote that she had "completed a larger amount of research work, and of a higher character, than any other candidate under my direction in the past."[8]

Although these talented women were accorded Ph.D.'s, those doing graduate study at Harvard were barred from official recognition. The Harvard case shows how patriarchal graduate programs could be. Eight full professors deemed Ethel Puffer "unusually well qualified" for a Harvard Ph.D. But the corporation refused to grant it. She later took a Radcliffe doctorate and was appointed as an assistant on the Harvard faculty, but her Smith alumnae record noted that "her name is not printed in the [Harvard] catalogue for fear that it would create a dangerous precedent."[9]

Mary Calkins was Josiah Royce's most brilliant pupil. (After hearing Calkins, William James chided the egotistical George Santayana—who believed his own doctoral defense to be a hallmark—"go hang yourself, Santayana.") Nonetheless, the Harvard corporation refused to set a precedent by granting her a Ph.D., even though the Department of Psychology unanimously petitioned that it be conferred. Calkins exemplifies another pattern common to the Wellesley faculty women. By treating her as an exception to the rule against admitting women, Harvard diminished the precedent set by her acceptance. Still Calkins felt privileged. She reported that as other members of her graduate seminar with William James dropped the course, "James and I were quite literally at either side of his fireplace." She gained much from these tête-à-tête conversations and others with Professor Hugo Münsterberg. She expressed her "gratitude for the friendly, comradely and refreshingly matter of fact welcome which she received from the men working in the Harvard laboratory as assistants and students, by whom the unprecedented incursion of a woman might have well been resented." Such friendly tolerance in graduate school contrasted with the discrimination she experienced a few years later in 1905, when the Harvard Faculty Club barred her from a luncheon meeting of the executive committee of the American Psychological Association, even though she was president of the society![10]

It was apparent that these graduate women would be filling chairs within the newly founded women's colleges and would not be a threat to the positions of men in the men's colleges or universities. The Yale President's Report of 1891 specifically stated that Yale granted women the privilege of obtaining the Ph.D. "not [as] a rival or opponent of the college for women, but an ally and helper to them." In 1892, in opening its graduate school to a few exceptional women, the University of Pennsylvania similarly explained that "this step was safe and judicious." Both schools, however, refused to accept women as undergraduates.[11]

A kind of halo effect surrounded the Wellesley women scholars. Physicist Sarah Frances Whiting had what she considered exceptional opportunities to meet male scientists and to attend epoch-making lectures in the scientific community. Male sponsors at the University of Pennsylvania, MIT, and Yale arranged for her to attend classes. Emily Greene Balch, in economics, received similar sponsorship from Professor Franklin H. Giddings of Bryn Mawr, who recommended her for the Bryn Mawr European Fellowship. Women sponsors were also important. Julia Swift Orvis was a disciple of Lucy Salmon of Vassar, who arranged her graduate work at Cornell.[12]

Underlying this widespread sponsorship was an informal ideology of the "select few" that operated in educational circles. Male educators believed that a few women geniuses could achieve eminence. Even though they nearly always associated productive scholarship with men and considered its price too high for most women, educators often allowed an exceptional handful of women to become scholars. William De Witt Hyde, president of

Bowdoin College, had this view: "No one disputes the rights of women to pursue this exacting ideal of productive scholarship"; such women, he added, would "supply our few women's colleges with professors who are productive scholars. This gift, rare in men, however, is far more rare in women."[13]

At Harvard Hugo Münsterberg opined that there were "several American women whose scientific work is admirable, to be classed with the best professional achievements of the country, but they are still rare exceptions." The great mass of women, he felt, never progressed in their science studies beyond passive learning to creative production. Women as well as men embraced the idea of a select few. M. Carey Thomas, president of Bryn Mawr, also subscribed to this ideology and argued that a college should "foster imaginative and constructive genius." Noting that such ability is rare, she looked to higher education for its cultivation: "If the graduate schools of women's colleges could develop one single woman of Galton's 'X' type— say a Madame Curie or a Madame Kovalewsky . . . they would have done more for human advancement than if they had turned out thousands of ordinary college graduates." Professor Abby Leach of Vassar agreed: "The truth is . . . that only a few will ever make, can ever make, a brilliant success of study." Such beliefs enhanced the status of the pioneering women scholars, making them appear anomalous and very special.[14]

Once they were sponsored and accepted, several of the women in this study seemed to confirm the theory of the select few. In 1894, Charlotte Fitch Roberts and a classmate shared the honor of being the first women to be granted doctorates from Yale in chemistry. Elizabeth Fisher graduated from MIT in 1896, one of two women in a class of 194 men. She became the first woman geologist sent into the field by an oil company to locate oil wells. Mary Whiton Calkins was the first woman elected to the presidencies of the American Philosophical Association and the American Psychological Association. Margaret Ferguson was the first woman to become president of the Botanical Society of America. These women, it is clear, took advantage of their uniqueness to become notable.[15]

Many Wellesley faculty saw themselves as pioneers rather than as professionals, identifying with the image of a lonely trailblazer. In "Woman as Scholar" Katharine Lee Bates wrote that the life of thought must "ever be in a large degree the life of solitude." Vida Scudder wrote that she "liked to feel herself a trail-maker, . . . hacking alone" and that she felt close only to the "spiritual leaders of all time, who have always been lonely." Similarly, Ellen

Hayes proclaimed herself "an explorer [who] goes ahead to clear the track for less daring feet." This sense of themselves as lonely may have precipitated their embrace of community.[16]

The Strains of Selection

Put upon a pedestal reserved for a select few female geniuses, yet defined as lacking normal female virtues, these intellectual women could not help but feel conflicts. It was not just the definition of a woman scholar that incited dilemmas, conflict, and confusion. Sometimes the programs entered—the unofficial courses arranged informally through special connections—reminded these women that by virtue of their sex they were imposing upon the male intellectual world. Consequently, many women felt nervous about their attendance and sought to minimize their intrusion. Vida Scudder, praising the quality of education American women graduates received at Oxford, termed herself "a queer apparition in Oxford"; her tutor, York Powell, demanded that her mother act as chaperone during their hourly sessions. In classes, Scudder noted that "the minute handful of us women [made] ourselves as inconspicuous as we could in our own particular corner."[17]

After a series of unofficial visits to European laboratories in the 1880s and 1890s, Sarah Frances Whiting recalled that having visitor privileges often meant that "I effaced myself as much as possible" in order to watch experiments. Whiting elaborated upon the tensions that her special status induced. Wherever she went she had a "nerve-wracking experience because she was doing unconventional things, in places where women were not expected." One scientist who admitted her to his lectures later quizzed her: "What would become of the buttons and the breakfasts if all the ladies should know so much about spectroscopes?" In Holland, another famous thinker boldly asked Whiting: "You have a head, where did you get it?" When she explained that she was the head of a physics department at a women's college, he "finally bowed us out of the doors, saying he had never met such ladies; we seemed to him like angels from another sphere." In Berlin, when, in the presence of Whiting, the wife of one of the professors who had granted Whiting special laboratory privileges complained to her husband that "you will get yourself into trouble with the ministry by such irregularities," more tensions erupted. One suspects that not only the ministry took a jaundiced view of such arrangements.

In 1896, "after years of peeking in cracks and opening back doors," a relieved Sarah Frances Whiting walked up to the registrar's desk at the University of Edinburgh and matriculated as a regular student. The response she got from a famous professor of physics was telling: "Two years ago I should have said no, now I have nothing to say." Obviously these brilliant women received mixed messages: on the basis of their brains and social networks they were made to feel special and select; they were excused from the regulations that barred women from major universities. Yet these scholars could not help but feel deviant.[18]

Along with exemption came onerous responsibility. These women had to be on guard lest they commit some fatal error that would tarnish the belief in women's intellect and abolish the possibility of the experience for future selected women. Recognizing her obligation, Emily Greene Balch tried to settle the recurrent questions concerning propriety, etiquette, and behavior in favor of "freedom and doing the pleasant and profitable thing. . . . I should be awfully sorry to do anything to make women *personae ingratae* in the University now [that] they are just being let in."[19]

The advanced liberal beliefs of the few professors who admitted these women to seminars did not eradicate the hostility to women that permeated the general academic climate. Katharine Lee Bates wrote her mother from Oxford that one of the lecturers, Dr. Wright, "hates American students, especially women, and says they have no ability, anyway, only a little shallow enthusiasm." Reminiscing about her graduate student days in Berlin, Emily Greene Balch complimented two of her professors, Adolf Wagner and Gustav Schmoller, on their generous outlook on women's intellect but noted that "Professor Trietschke told an acquaintance that a woman should cross the threshold of his classroom only over his dead body."[20]

Being admitted to unofficial study did not always mean that the intellectual path was smooth. On the contrary, these female scholars often found their sponsors rather neutral and untutored in supervising women. It is a credit to the intelligence, dedication, and strength of will of this group of women that they were able to take advantage of piecemeal educational opportunities and make them into legitimate graduate programs. Doing this sometimes became an endurance test. In a letter from Ethel Puffer to her mother, written in Berlin in 1896, one gets a glimpse of the stamina and perseverance required. On the advice of one sympathetic professor she sought admission to another's seminar on aesthetic theory: "I gave up two hours yesterday afternoon to hunting for him, got the address wrong, got lost, and finally discovered his rooms after dark at the top of a house—

'He—the Herr Doctor—was out!' So I had to go around again this morning." Evidently the admission was worth the price; this particular professor's lectures were brilliant. But being the only woman in the jammed room made her a little uncomfortable, "so I have persuaded Carita to come too."[21]

In addition to putting up with inadequate housing, she never seems to have found a professor who would take her under his wing. Although warned that Hugo Münsterberg, a famous psychologist located in Freiburg, was not taking on new students, she pursued him nonetheless. "Sunday morning is certainly a good time," she wrote her mother. "We found both the Frau and Herr Professor at home." Through intellect and wit, Puffer brought Münsterberg around "from a polite hospitality" to an offer to direct her work in his private laboratory, an offer that put her among his three or four disciples.[22]

Ethel Puffer next informed her mother that Münsterberg was directing her experiments on symmetry, a topic in aesthetic theory. She was required to spend the morning in his house under his direction and explicitly addressed the not-so-subtle sexual dynamics that underlay these special male professor–female student relationships. Puffer quieted her mother's fears with: "Don't be alarmed. Mrs. Münsterberg paints at the other end of the room and inquires when she doesn't understand our meaning." Evidently there was reason for alarm, for another woman student, "a German divorcee," had arrived on the scene. "I see a Münsterberg flirtation in the air—and Mrs. M. strongly objects to her."[23]

Ethel Puffer maintained a rigorous schedule, attending all of Münsterberg's lectures. She was often the only woman in the room, so "of course I came in for a good deal of staring— but I am accustomed to that." She even enrolled in an extra course. As usual, she dazzled her male mentors with her stamina and knowledge. Her ambitiousness is made amusingly clear in a letter to her mother, written while she was applying for the European fellowship given by the Association of Collegiate Alumnae: "Until Friday last, I have been sitting up all hours of the night, and am pretty worn out. I sat one day five hours in a butter and cheese store (German cheese!) dictating my seminar paper in German to a type-writer—the only one in Freiburg apparently—because I thought the German would impress them, but knew they wouldn't read it in MS—I sent besides a full abstract of my Book!" Typically Puffer agonized over being favored, for she feared disappointing those who supported her. Yet she anticipated being ashamed if she didn't get the fellowship. Puffer won the award, however, fulfilling her own and others' expectations.[24]

When she decided in 1890 to do graduate work at the Sorbonne, Emily Greene Balch confronted many of the same difficulties articulated by Puffer. In order to get what she wanted out of the program she had to take "my life in my hands." Admittedly her major professor, Emile Levasseur, was polite; he smoothed Balch's path by handing her cards of entree into the lectures of colleagues, rehearsing for her the cautions and doubts about young women gaining admittance. Beyond this, he was unable to give her any real direction. Desperate, she wrote her father that M. Levasseur was quite astute and very eminent but offered little advice or criticism. "He expects me to bring the initiative and I expect him to perhaps." Balch proposed that she do a statistical study. The most her mentor would offer was to direct Emily to take down the names of fifteen tomes, give her two books, and dismiss her with a parting word—"Courage." Understandably Balch felt confused, helpless, and worthless and was unable to evaluate whether she was wasting her time or not: "If I knew where I were steering for it would be a good deal easier to steer. I think there never was more of an idiot than I am in certain respects." She nevertheless managed to devise a study plan without help from her professor; later, her statistical study entitled *Public Assistance of the Poor in France* was published.[25]

Intellectually formidable and inquisitive women had difficulty asserting claims in the academic world. Several in this group conceived of themselves as drifting rather than steering, perhaps because it was easier for women to picture themselves floating on an uncontrollable current than to take responsibility for their actions. This inner feeling of drift was often accompanied by an actual hiatus or period of moratorium in their lives, during which they tried to find intellectually satisfying careers.

Drift and Discovery

In spite of sponsorship by families, rare educational opportunities, and special attention by male and female sponsors, many of these bright women had no specific vocation in mind throughout their years of intellectual preparation. The women's colleges had just opened, and the role of academic woman had been neither formulated nor formalized. As a result, several women experienced painful periods of drift and self-doubt at the end of their postgraduate study. They did not escape what some historians have identified as a postgraduate identity crisis called the "After college, what?" syndrome. Conflicts and failed attempts at making use of their educations were common to these future Wellesley faculty women.[26]

Vida Scudder recorded the tortuous path by which she finally arrived as an English instructor at Wellesley College. In 1885, upon graduation from Smith, she had a breakdown and was confined to bed. Summoning her energies, she left for England with a classmate and her mother to study at Oxford with John Ruskin and William Morris. Returning home, she recognized that "the hour had struck" for her to define a vocation. A "clamorous disappointment" accompanied her attempts at writing. She took stock: she had failed as an artist and had attempted writing to no avail. Claiming that marriage was "not for her," she concluded: "I was still a Lady in Waiting: waiting, not for my destined mate, but for my destined Cause." Meanwhile, she was "restless during those two years at home,—and more unhappy, I think, than ever before or since."[27]

Scudder was rescued by George Herbert Palmer, a friend of her mother's, who suggested that she apply for a position in English literature at Wellesley, where his fiancée, Alice Freeman, was president. The sudden call to a profession helped, momentarily at least, to resolve Scudder's identity crisis. The position was all the more attractive because teaching at Wellesley allowed Scudder to live in Boston and "neither uproot my mother nor desert her." Once at Wellesley, she experienced another crisis of doubt over her preparation to teach English literature, followed by "The Terrible Choice" between a life dedicated to academe versus one submerged in social reform.[28]

Although the particulars of these crises varied from woman to woman, other faculty struggled with definitions of career and self. Some found a solid mooring in academe; others were always restless. Many suffered spells of despair over their lack of preparation. The situation was additionally complex in that a sense of worthlessness often coexisted with feelings of ambition, egotism, and selection. Those from upper-middle-class backgrounds seemed fortunate in that they could afford to test the waters. In fact, this only prolonged their crisis.

Emily Balch is a good example of this bedeviled brew. As an undergraduate at Bryn Mawr, she began to feel that studying literature was "pure self-indulgence"; it would not lead to a career since "I had just enough sense . . . to know that I was not fitted to be either an original writer nor a critic." She next took up economics. Winning the first Bryn Mawr European Fellowship, she left to pursue the intellectual life. Her stint at the Sorbonne was followed by a stay at Hull House, a course at the University of Chicago, one at Radcliffe, and entry into Felix Adler's Ethical Summer School in Plymouth, Massachusetts, where she met Jane Addams and Katharine Coman. In 1893, contemplating the term at Hull House, Balch wrote her faithful intellectual seer, her father: "What should you think of my spending a month in Chicago at Hull House? I shall enjoy it immensely and do feel it might not pay for me to do it. I am a bottomless pit in which I sink teaching experience and example. Shall I give out anything?"[29]

Balch's father steadfastly advocated her continued education, which led to another year of study, this time in Berlin. Before leaving Berlin, she recorded in her diary that five years after graduation from Bryn Mawr "aspirations and failure mark the record." She felt she had little to show for several years of study, research, and work. Finally she composed a plan to teach the social sciences, because "all the questions of unfairly large consumption of the world wealth, of dependence and of compromise still puzzle me." This was written two years before she arrived at Wellesley College. Later, she recorded how fortuitous it was that on the boat home she became reacquainted with Katharine Coman, who asked her to assist her in grading economics exams at Wellesley. Happy for the rare opportunity, but plagued by her "scrappy preparation," Balch accepted the offer, which allowed her to live at home, "as so much desired by my father."[30]

The path that Mary Calkins took to the psychology department was similarly dependent upon luck and circumstance. After graduating from Smith in 1885 she spent one year at home tutoring her siblings and compensating her family for the loss of her sister Maud. In 1886, when the family took the requisite European journey, she fortunately met Abby Leach, a professor of Greek at Vassar, who invited Calkins to accompany her on a trip to Greece. Calkins took advantage of the offer, disengaged herself from her family, and began to study modern Greek. After sixteen months in Europe, she returned home, prepared to teach Greek to private pupils if she could not secure a college position. Her father, however, had forestalled her being trapped in secondary school teaching by arranging an appointment as an instructor of Greek at Wellesley. She had been teaching for three years when another stroke of luck occurred. In the course of borrowing several Greek books from Professor Mary Case, Calkins lingered to admire some of Case's philosophy texts. Impressed with Calkins and cognizant that new work in psychology and philosophy was required, Case asked Calkins whether she would consider an appointment in the philosophy department. Calkins "thought the idea preposterous and could hardly be brought to take it seriously."[31] Nonetheless, Case persuaded Calkins not to dismiss the offer entirely. Simultaneously, Case inquired of President Shafer whether, with appropriate preparation, Calkins might obtain the new position. Shafer agreed. It was up to Calkins to decide: "I know already that I should like to do this, but I do not know whether I ought." Several former Smith College advisers whom she consulted for advice responded positively. Charles Garman predicted that she would be very successful. Another, Mary Augusta Jordan, counseled that usually it "is well not to be too bold," but "I insist for the time being—be bold!" Propelled by such enthusiasm and high expectation, Calkins commenced graduate studies at Harvard and Clark universities, which culminated in her highly successful career in psychology and philosophy.[32]

Although Mary Calkins escaped years in that graveyard for women of high ambition—secondary school teaching—many of her colleagues did not. Fully 49 percent of the Wellesley faculty had taught in secondary school before continuing graduate training or arriving at Wellesley. Katharine Lee Bates's odyssey is indicative of one such perilous journey. After graduation, the "genius" of the class of 1880 busied herself teaching girls at Dana Hall preparatory school. Finding this work taxing and not as creative as she had hoped, Bates contemplated leaving but found Dana Hall's proprietors, the Eastman sisters, reluctant to let her go. "My lamp is low," she lamented to a friend. Yet when an offer of an instructorship in either Latin or English came from her alma mater, she hesitated before taking it. She felt inadequately prepared, but more than that she realized that it meant more teaching and probably the end of her hope to write poetry. Because opportunities to write full time seemed nonexistent, however, she took the offer. Within three years, she became restless and went on a paid sabbatical to England, mainly to escape her overtaxing responsibilities but also to rethink her decision. "I'm afraid going back means a long goodbye to any original writing," she wrote her mother despondently. Wellesley was "*such* a busy, feverish place," and although she loved it, she also dreaded it. She returned, partially because she knew that President Shafer thought it "dishonorable in a teacher not to return, if she could, after a year of leave." Moreover, she had already formulated her identity on the role of professor; also, too many "love anchors" held her at Wellesley. There was, first, her love for her alma mater and, conversely, the praise and acclaim that Wellesley gave her as its most prestigious daughter. She was bound no less by the love that she had developed for Katharine Coman. And so she returned. How she arrived at this decision is instructive, for it gives another glimpse of how a woman torn by doubt explained the process of decision: "After all I suppose I shall be *drifted* back to Wellesley in the end." She remained, in her words, "a reluctant captive."[33]

Those who had been trapped in secondary school teaching viewed their Wellesley positions in a brighter light. Ellen Burrell, also in the class of 1880, initially took her father's advice to be a "big fish in a little pond" and taught at Rockford Seminary. Feeling waylaid and lamenting the waste of five years, she decided it was better to be a "big fish in a big pond" and hastened to return to her alma mater to teach mathematics.[34]

Carla Wenckebach, who grew up in Germany, experienced a strikingly similar route to Wellesley. Originally she had wanted to study music, but this was a difficult aspiration for a German woman. She turned instead to studying the German language and joined a teaching staff on a pittance of a salary. To a friend who wanted also to be a professional musician, but whose family did not want her to play in public, Wenckebach bitterly asked: "What is the use of all study if it has to be carried on merely for the sake of one's self-development?" Consoling her friend, she explained that "ours is an unfortunate era of transition," one in which women desired intellectual and economic equality with men. If they had lived but two centuries later, "I just *might* perhaps be a regularly appointed professor at some great and glorious university." Wenckebach pursued normal school training but worked so hard that she suffered a breakdown. Forced to return to her family's home, she recuperated by reading and writing essays about women's higher education. Recognizing that her hopes for an intellectual life might never be realized in Germany, she seized an offer to be a governess to a family in New York.[35]

Like many of her future Wellesley colleagues, Wenckebach was rescued. Through social connections her name was given to President Freeman and to Professor Elizabeth Denio of the German department. After viewing her teaching, they offered her a position. Wenckebach was ecstatic and wrote home that she had made a "superb catch,—not a widower, nor a bachelor, but something infinitely superior!" Feeling that a "priceless gift [had] fallen" into her hands, she exhibited the immense gratefulness characteristic of many of her colleagues, thanking "my Creator, who has rescued me out of my Cinderella existence and has brought me into this Elysium."[36]

The Search for Identity

Wenckebach's reference to Cinderella is a dynamic metaphor for female identity in that it reveals a sense of these intellectual women passively awaiting a stroke of fate. As children and young women they were encouraged to think of themselves as members of a gifted elite who were entitled, indeed expected, to accomplish epoch-making deeds. Consequently, several of the women harbored visions of themselves as heroines. Yet they had also absorbed some of the popular cultural ideals of what female behavior should be. This led to episodes of confusion over their hopes and dreams or of guilt over their enormous drive.

The future Wellesley scholars felt keenly the emotional pull between domestic and social relationships and their intellectual life. Some tried to reconcile the two by living with their families while teaching. Many former self-proclaimed tomboys and bad girls wound up walking a fine line between deviant and proper female behavior as young women. In reviewing the period from their undergraduate years to their early years of teaching at Wellesley, one is tempted to conclude that they had lived out the Cinderella myth: serendipitously they were rescued from possible intellectual sterility. In this case Wellesley College was the life-giving prince, and their contract the kiss that sealed the covenant—it stood for a vow of renunciation.

One should not minimize what it meant for such women to enter an academic role. On the contrary, many faced inner struggles with cultural definitions of femininity. As Carla Wenckebach informed a friend, "we poor daughters of Eve" have to "box the ears of many prejudices sanctified by tradition, and shall, in the eyes of many . . . become . . . a bluestocking." Flouting tradition to become an intellectual, Wenckebach claimed to be immune to criticism. But she added: "You may rest assured that in my manners I shall observe simplicity and decorum, although I feel that with my pen I should like to break down a Chinese wall." Such a mixed stance sometimes produced an odd combination of genteel woman and social radical.[37]

Many of the Wellesley women wrestled with the problem of appropriate behavior. As a result, intellectual vigor and skepticism were sometimes accompanied by imprisoning notions of respectable womanly behavior. At twenty-seven, just as she was beginning her tenure at Wellesley, Emily Greene Balch listed among her goals: "To be self-respecting, to control my temper and be actively, spontaneously pleasant and cheerful; to be honest; to be discreet." Evidently she did not realize that these goals were in direct conflict with other ones recorded in her diary, among them, "not to drift into a fixed way of life but think and conclude bravely."[38]

Similarly Katharine Lee Bates struggled to reconcile her search for independence and originality with stereotypical female behavior: "Where am I discontented with myself? I must give more heed to outer appearance, dress better, walk better. I must keep a more even mood of courtesy. In the home and in the village I must be careful of the small pleasantnesses of daily life. I must study more lovingly my mother's comfort. I must be an inspiration and not a clog to Katharine [Coman]. I must respect individuality and most of all my own. As regards the College, I must study reserve. . . . I must look to my own growth, as the duty of duties. I must not let myself be a drudge for conscience's sake. *Life. Love. Aspiration.*"[39]

The origins of Bates's dilemma were of course social, and its resolution lay in social change. But still she interpreted her conflicts and restlessness as a personal problem and puzzled over her identity. In a letter to a friend she lamented, "I have been trying all my life to find out which I is I, and I don't know yet." Whether struggling with her agnosticism, her conflicts between being a poet or teacher, or her attempt to be both a good daughter and sister while living out the prophecy of class genius, Bates criticized herself for the most part, not society. Although she tried to curb her restlessness and rebellion, she was never fully able to "*melt* my stubborn members, physical and mental, into one truth." Remorsefully, she commented upon her nonconformity: "I get so weary of these other shifting selves—more angry with them than my severest judge can be."[40]

The reference to the physical self is important. These women's complaints of living life secondhand has most often been interpreted as their imprisonment within a middle-class existence and as a sign of intellectual alienation, but they also might be referring to the constraints on their sexual identity.[41] They lived in the late Victorian era, when sexuality was rarely addressed openly. Many commented instead on their social identity. It is astounding how few women approached this question of the identity of the woman scholar from a personal point of view. Rather they alluded to it in fiction, prose, or essays. Mary Calkins's writings reveal what must have been a painful process of self-diagnosis. In an unpublished essay on the problems confronting the woman scholar, she began by using the word *I*, then about halfway through the piece substituted the word *one*.[42]

A striking picture emerges, even from these oblique references. Margaret Sherwood noted that the undergraduate woman is too busy to be "seriously troubled about the uses of her existence," but after college, forced by pressure from the outside world, she self-consciously stops to wonder if she is a "little queer." Such feelings of social deviance might have clothed or included sexual impulses that were stirring. Whatever the sources, it is clear that feeling destined and special was not an unalloyed blessing. Emily Greene Balch recalled that in going to college she felt like "a marked character in the neighborhood." After college she realized that people in her town were "afraid to talk to me, I was so learned." She contrasted this alienation with the community's acceptance of a college man.[43]

In an essay entitled "The Effect on Character of a College Education," Vida Scudder noted that the bright woman was "set . . . on a pedestal of solitary intellectual eminence." She finds herself "regarded as an abnormal intellectual prodigy, a sort of logic machine to be respected. For some years after her graduation a loneliness hard for her feminine nature to bear is the almost inevitable price she pays for the delight of her college career." Ethel Puffer put it more bluntly: at times, she declared, the bright woman feels like an "intellectual Frankenstein."[44]

Renunciation: The Choice between Marriage and Career

To fulfill the role of woman scholar, Wellesley's academic women spurned marriage. For this generation, marrying would have meant abandoning a career. Renunciation became a catchword for the life of the woman scholar. Katharine Lee Bates wrote in "Woman as Scholar": "We may plead still unconquered disadvantages of domestic and social environment; but we must strengthen the scholarly resolve and purify the scholarly ideals." To accomplish this Bates offered a personal solution. She called for women to "renounce the call of love or duty . . . and hardest of all, the sympathy . . . of the beloved."[45]

Mary Calkins also took up this question of the conflicts between scholarship and social life. She explained that there was "no magic formula" that could be universally applied. For Calkins, every scholar had to come to terms with the "often conflicting claims of scholarship and life in its social relations." Although seldom easy, this adjustment was especially difficult for women. To Calkins, the social role of women as daughters and mothers was extremely important. She felt that even the unmarried woman "by virtue of belonging to the mother-half of the race, and by virtue of being or having been a potential mother should owe a peculiarly close obligation to her house." Calkins acknowledged that unmarried men also had social obligations to their families, but their concerns were less vital than a woman's duty to perpetuate and nurture the race. Whether married or unmarried, however, women scholars had "crucial obligations" to family.

Calkins questioned the justice and expediency of the laws of academe that made choosing between the two inevitable and then excluded those who chose to marry, calling this situation "sheer stupidity." Calkins admitted that "how to be a scholar, though married, is, to tell the truth, one of the most pressing specific problems of the scholarship of women." There was of course a right answer if a woman met the right man: "One should pity and condemn the woman if there could be such a woman who turned aside from marriage with a good man whose love she returned in order to pursue any end of the scholar." Women should not sacrifice love, marriage, motherhood, home, or children to the demands of scholarship; but they could easily sacrifice "cleaning the house superbly, presiding over a salon, specializing in bridge or attending the opera." Calkins decided that there was time in both the single and married woman's life for scholarship *if* she abandoned domesticity. She argued: "You have a right to spurn delights and live laborious days and save and hoard the time that is your own." Because she believed that the dilemmas confronting a woman scholar were to be resolved on an individual basis, Calkins did not offer institutional nor societal answers. She envisioned that a class of scholars would be formulated from the "as yet unprofessional women of America, married and unmarried."[46]

Emily Greene Balch also addressed the outlook for the woman scholar. She noted that the professional woman who remained single "cut the Gordian knot between the incompatibility of work and marriage." She added: "This is simple, certainly, but quite abnormal." Admitting that on an individual level it might lead to a happy solution, on a societal level it was undesirable to develop a class of celibate professional women. Balch felt that the problem of unmarried women workers and unemployed wives should be addressed by changes in the workplace and in marriage ideals that would allow for universal marriage and universal employment.[47]

Not surprisingly, the faculty member who pursued this problem most diligently was Ethel Puffer, who in 1908 married Benjamin Howes and left

Wellesley. We do not know whether she was asked to leave Wellesley upon her engagement or whether she was seeking a job closer to Howes's business dealings. But a letter written to her by L. C. Seelye, president of Smith College, informs us of how unemployable she was considered. He warned her that the rumor of her engagement had probably tainted her application to Barnard and "may have also affected the recommendation which I myself sent" and that a candidate had already been selected to present to the trustees of Columbia at their next commencement. Puffer wed Howes and learned firsthand the fate of the woman scholar who married. She obtained no professorship, and her married life allowed little time for scholarship. One letter to her mother described her frenzied efforts to finish an article, while her husband took over a few domestic chores. Puffer Howes wrote articles for the *Journal of the Association of Collegiate Alumnae*, but by the 1920s she had all but disappeared from the academic scene.[48]

She then began to write more popular pieces, launching her ideas about the problems of the professional woman in an article entitled "The Revolt of Mother," published in *Woman's Home Companion*. In 1922, in a semiautobiographical piece, she voiced her despair over her status and her marginality, noting that "it would be easier for a lapsed psychologist . . . to begin again at the beginning, than to try to make use, after fifteen years interruption of her outmoded wares." From the 1920s through the 1940s, Ethel Puffer Howes devoted herself to finding solutions to the "persistent vicious alternatives" between marriage or career for the professional woman. She sought to make "the unconscious conflict conscious." One senses that the young Puffer Howes did not fully appreciate the impact that marriage would have on her career. In looking back upon her graduate days in the 1890s, she reflected that scholarship was respected and enjoyed. At that time neither she nor her peers questioned the choice of the scholarly life for women. "The phrase, marriage versus careers, had not been invented, to bedevil both thought and action."[49]

Conforming to the dictates of society, the first generation of scholarly women entered the academic world as nuns entered a convent—with the explicit assumption of renouncing marriage. But for a few women of the period, and for many more in the 1920s, the resignation to remaining single became in the words of M. Carey Thomas, "a cruel handicap."[50]

In the late 1920s, Ethel Puffer Howes created the Institute for the Coordination of Women's Interests at Smith College. Through this institute she did research on the social and intellectual barriers impeding the professional woman from combining marriage and career. Believing that this issue dominated the twentieth-century women's movement, she eventually eschewed calls for renunciation, advocating instead an ideal of reconciliation between marriage and career.[51]

The fifty-two other women on the Wellesley faculty remained single, living in a community composed of female couples; such relationships were known as "Wellesley marriages." Biographies and autobiographies give us some clue as to how these women handled the issue of marriage on a personal and individual level. Vida Scudder claims that quite early in her adulthood she "serenely suspected without regrets" that marriage was not for her. In a semiautobiographical novel she recounts a crush she had on a male academic. Believing that marriage will confine her to secondary status in the relationship, she quashes her emotions. Years later she meets the man and his depressed wife and is consoled by the accuracy of her prediction. In fact, Scudder preferred her female friends; they were her closest intimates and helpmates who encouraged her to pursue her career.[52]

Emily Balch received a proposal from a miner who lived in a camp she was studying for her book on immigration. She told her biographer that she dismissed the man by telling him quietly what profession she was in and how little money she made! In her early twenties, Katharine Lee Bates encountered several English tutors at Oxford who admired her. She wrote her mother: "I sternly nip these frivolities in the bud." Later Bates rejected another marriage offer, preferring the companionship and love of Katharine Coman. Interestingly, several women were spared the cruel choice. Margaret Sherwood's lover drowned; later she lived with her disciple, Martha Hale Shackford. The librarian on whom Mary Alice Willcox had a crush also died. Many had resigned themselves to believing that the ideal marriage was a rare phenomenon and that the professional woman could not entertain a relationship that would impede her career.[53]

Thus for the first generation of academic women, what Puffer termed a "philosophical antinomy"—the contradiction between being a woman and a scholar—was resolved by living in a separate world of women. Having renounced marriage, Wellesley scholars combined career and personal life through intimate female friendships. Although not every Wellesley scholar shared her life with another woman, each found affirmation within the Wellesley world. The Wellesley professors affirmed their intellectual gifts and ended their psychological and social loneliness by revering other brilliant women and devoting themselves to women's higher education. For this generation of academic women, renunciation of marriage brought with it rewards.

6

Even Blue Stockings Have to Be Darned
Wages and Working Conditions
of the Women Scholars

*The central puzzle set before a Wellesley teacher for solution . . .
is a purely mathematical puzzle. How shall we divide one into
three and make each third equal to the whole? How shall the same
individual devote herself effectively to the three vocations of
woman, teacher, and scholar? For it is still a profession in itself to
be a woman. We may read Hebrew, or Sanskrit, but we are not
exempt from making calls, entertaining, chaperoning; we may
calculate eclipses, but we are not set free from the tyranny of the
needle. Even blue stockings have to be darned.*

—Katharine Lee Bates

The wry and engaging Katharine Lee Bates articulated for her audience what was to become a repeated refrain: she addressed the
conflicts between woman's social duties and the professional duties
of teaching and scholarship that confronted women scholars who
remained single. Bates noted: "We have not better halves to keep
our gloves mended for us and our bonnets in repair. We have not
homes in which to find with every sunset refreshment and repose.
We live in our workshop. We eat with our apprentices off the
bench. We sleep on the shavings." By the 1930s, another English
scholar, Margorie Hope Nicholson, at Columbia University,
asked: "How is it possible to be at once a scholar—and a lady?"
Her list of conflicts included the choice of whether or not to marry.

Notwithstanding this new quandary, her view of the dilemmas besetting the woman scholar strikingly mirrors Bates's. According to Nicholson, the woman scholar who showed no concern for attractive clothing or a fine home was not viewed in as positive a light as was her male peer. The male academic would be designated a recluse or perhaps a "campus character"; his aloofness might even make him attractive. Such was not the case for a woman: "In spite of all the feminists have yet accomplished, *the undarned hose remains the symbol of inequality! Worn by a man, it moves to pity and aid; worn by a woman, it moves even her peers to scorn.*"[1]

Although they were sensitive to cultural distinctions in the male and female professoriat, neither Bates nor Nicholson directly addressed the question of inequities in salary. Nonetheless, implicit in their discussion of how women professors economized by mending their own bonnets and darning their own stockings is the reality of their modest salaries.

Although Wellesley, with its all-female faculty, was singled out by the feminist M. Carey Thomas, president of Bryn Mawr, as "set on a hill in women's colleges," the women employed there were subject to the general ideological and economic restraints that governed the first generation of academic women.[2] Almost as soon as the first women scholars obtained graduate degrees and sought employment, the debate over the privileges and plight of female professors began to appear in journals and newspapers.

An examination of these issues is important not only for what it reveals about the quality of their lives but for the light it sheds on other aspects of their subculture. The institutional loyalty these women displayed, for example, can be explained in part by the lack of opportunity in higher education. "Where should I look for a position even approaching that which I should leave?" asked Mary Alice Willcox, who felt the tensions of Julia Irvine's presidency. In addition, the Wellesley professoriat was dependent upon the college for the hiring of family members and their housing. Wellesley was an employer that became their family. Faculty wills reveal that these women left bequests to the college they looked upon as their home and to colleagues they considered their kin.[3]

Henry Durant's commitment to hire only women professors, heralded by some and denounced by many, was of course the crucial first step in the creation of careers for women scholars. He openly expressed this commitment in 1874 in a letter to a prospective male applicant: "As all the Professors and teachers are to be ladies it will not be possible for the Trustees to consider your application." He added: "We have not engaged the Professor of Physiology and it may be that you know of some learned lady whom you could suggest as fitted for the position."[4]

Men were sometimes hired over women at the women's colleges and were almost always chosen over women in the coeducational institutions. In an article written in 1919, a woman applicant reported that after initially being courted by a department head in an eastern university, she was rejected: "We prefer to appoint a man. At one move of the kaleidoscope there seemed to be no men; and at the next change, a plenty. It was on one of the off days (for men) that I wrote you." This preference for hiring men was confirmed by several national studies. In a study of the compensation of college graduates done in 1896, one academic woman wrote despondently of having tried for two years "with all the vigor that I possess to get a position in the Philosophical Department of a coeducational College or University." The results were discouraging: "Either directly or indirectly, about one dozen institutions have been canvassed and the answers received have been disheartening. No encouragement from any; excuses of various kinds, or no answers at all."[5]

Women college professors were clearly at a serious disadvantage. In her 1898 article "The Problem of Occupation for College Women," psychologist Kate Holladay Claghorn asserted that women were rarely hired in the coeducational universities; they thus crowded one another for the few slots available in those women's colleges that promoted the careers of women scholars. Even within the women's college, however, women competed with men. Of four eastern women's colleges, she found that only one, Wellesley, offered women a free field. Only there were women at an advantage in the professorial ranks.[6]

In 1902 William Rainey Harper, president of the University of Chicago, concurred with this assessment. Harper reported that at the women's colleges "second-rate and third-rate men are preferred to women of first-rate ability." After surveying coeducational institutions in the East and the West, he noted that the hiring of women had slowed: "Is this progress? Or is it rather a concession to prejudices which, instead of growing weaker, are growing stronger?"[7]

In 1904, in a forthright and biting critique of this inequitable academic labor market, psychologist Christine Ladd-Franklin echoed the finding that gifted men with doctoral degrees were launched into the first stages of a career that would end in a full professorship. For bright women the situation was completely different, their doctorates being "but an empty honor."

She lamented: "Our clever girls—they go to Germany and get the parchments, beautifully signed and sealed, that proclaim them to be doctors of philosophy, but no further consequences follow." Women doctorates, Ladd-Franklin added, "have nothing but the empty satisfaction of exhibiting their 'tickets'; the pleasurable work and the adequate emoluments that ought to follow are not forthcoming."[8]

Because academic women faced systematic discrimination, the reverse policy of hiring only women was extraordinary. The Wellesley faculty felt privileged at having been hired as full professors, assistant professors, or instructors, with the full chance of being promoted. The psychological and professional uplift that this policy created should not be underestimated. It was visible, for example, in the attitude of Carla Wenckebach. Although the teaching position she accepted was not especially lucrative, the salary was not as significant as the chance to "plow a new field of work!" To her the honor attached to college teaching was "worth more . . . than thousands of dollars." She was not unique in this interpretation; Emily Greene Balch once admitted that "if necessary I would pay for the privilege of teaching Economics."[9]

The psychological and professional benefits of such positions buoyed the majority of Wellesley's faculty but often distanced them from the down-trodden feelings expressed in print by women professors. In general, for the first generation of academic women, college teaching was considered a calling, something almost sacred. It was just this noneconomic, spiritual reward that economist Susan Kingsbury alluded to in 1910, when she attributed the low incomes reported by women college teachers not to professional pride or a "lack of economic sense" but to a larger social, educational, and economic situation. Kingsbury concluded that college women made every effort to increase their economic standard but did not receive commensurate returns. For college teachers, their investment in their higher educations was not paying off. Still, she noted, academic women clung to this path, permitting "love of, or a devotion to, the present work, or personal preferences, to interfere."[10]

At Wellesley College low wages were the norm. The college was poor from the time of Henry Durant's death well into the late 1890s. During the Irvine era, many requests for higher salaries were rejected, and work loads were increased.[11] In terms of hiring, rank and title, and departmental autonomy, however, the Wellesley women scholars had unique opportunities. Unlike Vassar, Wellesley did not discriminate between salaries for women professors and the few men professors on the staff. At Vassar, Maria Mitchell and Alida Avery had a running argument with the administration over the extreme gender-based inequities in salary. At Smith, women were simply not given the rank of professor. Astronomer Mary Emma Byrd, who headed the observatory, held no academic rank at all. She felt compelled to instruct Professor Edward Pickering, an astronomer at Harvard, not to address her as professor. "It is, I understand, contrary to the traditions of this institution to give any woman the title and pay of Professor." Byrd, not without some rancor, informed Pickering that she was "just a teacher." By contrast, Sarah Frances Whiting was a full professor at Wellesley, as well as head of the observatory.[12]

In many women's colleges men were chosen as departmental heads over well-qualified women. Vassar's Elizabeth Hazelton Haight found it galling that a woman who held large fellowships, was well published, taught successfully, and had been acting head of the department could not expect the promotion or salary granted a man of similar attainments. She concluded that discrimination clearly existed.[13]

At Wellesley all the senior professors and heads of departments were women. Some care was taken to allow women with only B.A.'s to study for higher degrees rather than to replace them with men. Even during the purges instituted by President Irvine, some members of the Wellesley faculty were encouraged to upgrade their credentials, and teaching slots were held open for them pending their return. As we have noted, this period of uncertainty ended with the appointment of Caroline Hazard (1899–1910) to the presidency. After that, senior women professors were more or less tacitly tenured and protected in their employment. The one major exception concerned their political or reform activities—and given the faculty's bent, that was no small limitation.

In the larger job market, however, academic women were constantly confronted with unjust employment discrimination. The plight of the female professor became a standard lament in academic journals. According to Kate Holladay Claghorn, to embark upon a chosen career with no assurance of advancement meant that the woman scholar faced severe instability and anxiety and was left to drift without "a stable center." A woman scholar could hardly build a career when confronted with such uncertainty regarding promotion or recognition. This, in turn, produced inferior scholarship. Male scholars and administrators used just this kind of low achievement pattern to argue against the creation of more fellowships or job opportunities for women.[14]

Salaries

In the early years of the college, there was no generalized salary scale. Trustee papers reveal that decisions on salaries were made by the executive committee on an individual basis. In 1879 senior professors were generally paid $1,500. Instructors received between $300 and $800. Room and board, approximated at $200, was a bonus.[15]

By 1900, faculty salaries were put on a fixed scale, to be determined during February of each academic year. Full professors received $1,500, with a raise of $100 per year until they reached $2,000. First-year associate professors were paid $1,200 and were given $100 increments through their fourth year, eventually reaching $1,500. If one lived outside the college, the salary was increased by $300. Instructors' salaries were still to be calculated on an individual basis, determined by credentials and experience. According to one report published by the Association of Collegiate Alumnae (ACA) in 1907, the highest salary paid to women college teachers was $1,500, and the lowest about $300. Thus, Wellesley faculty were paid within the normal range of salaries for women faculty.[16]

In 1911 Susan Kingsbury, writing for the Committee on Academic Appointments of the ACA, reported that the mean salary for women with full professorships was $2,400, with a range of $1,700 to $3,100; for assistant professors the mean was $1,540; for instructors, $1,153. In addition, a promotion to full professor was a slow process. It is no wonder that one academic woman decried that women professors quickly found themselves "face to face with a dead wall, often made sightly by a veil of academic ivy . . . but no less hard to scale . . . and rarely worth the scaling, indeed, because there is nothing for her on the other side." The salaries offered to even the highest-ranking women were of a level that "no man of corresponding scholarship and pedagogic experience would consent to accept."[17]

The issue of remuneration was more important to some than to others. For someone like Vida Dutton Scudder, the product of an upper-middle-class background, salary was never a deciding issue. She claims to have been over forty years old before she made out a check! Earned income was important to her because it was more "respectable" than living off of inherited wealth. Margaret Sherwood was able to exist on a part-time salary for half of her career. For other Wellesley faculty, however, the small salaries were a major issue. In order to buy her own home, Katharine Lee Bates needed to borrow money from her brother, as well as work on articles and special marketable editions of the classics. In her "Autobiography in Brief," she sadly notes that "the writings of this busy life, which, falling in the day of small college salaries, was usually hard pressed for money, are in the main an extension of classroom interests or an outgrowth of holiday experiences." The toll of this need for extra income on her career is clear. Self-consciously she explained: "Though writing a lyric or a ballad now and then, the pressure of constant teaching and prose writing deferred from year to year and from decade to decade any sustained attention to poetry."[18]

In addition to a full departmental workload, Carla Wenckebach taught pedagogy as a "labor of love." Initially she had requested extra salary, but the trustees declined, stating: "It would create a very troublesome precedent to make any difference in the price paid to Professors."[19]

Although it was hard for Wenckebach to save money on her meager salary, she managed to give relatively large sums to her parents and siblings, paying for such extras as clothes, music lessons, and a yearly health cure in the mountains. She forced herself to economize on trips and books for the sake of her family and took out an insurance policy to shield them from economic problems. Although Wenckebach had to scrimp, she accepted her condition. Margarethe Müller, a colleague and her biographer, states that Wenckebach dreamed of traveling around the world but was never able to do so on her salary. Thus she compromised and became a devotee of the various World's Fairs that were presented in the United States.[20]

Wenckebach's economic obligations raise an important issue in evaluating the salaries of women professors. In 1907 an ACA study of faculty budgets showed that an outlay of about $800 could sustain a very modest lifestyle. (See table 6.) A single woman could therefore be fairly comfortable on $1,535. However, contrary to widespread assumptions that single academic women supported only themselves, and hence should not be paid as much as men, nearly one-third of single women had dependents, usually mothers, sisters, or brothers. The study concluded that "the economies to which [the woman professor] is forced are not only pathetic . . . but are belittling to the college which creates such conditions."[21]

The wills left by Wellesley faculty indicate the financial responsibilities of some faculty women toward dependents. Professor Katharine Edwards's estate paid for the funeral of her brother, who "was entirely dependent on her." The will of Professor Helen Merrill assigned monthly stipends to her brother. The estate of Eliza H. Kendrick shows that a cousin made her home

Table 6

Annual Budget for a Woman College Instructor, 1907

Living (room, board, laundry), during college year of 32 weeks	$200 to $256
Clothing	$99 to $184
Railroad fare and short vacations	$60 to $100
Long vacations	$158 to $194
Incidentals	$130 (total)
Doctor and dentist	$25
Christmas presents, etc.	$20
Entertaining	$32
Stationery and stamps	$18
Pictures, etc.	$10
Books and magazines	$10
Clubs	$5
Theater	$5
Church	$5
Total	$647 to $864

Source: Amy E. Tanner, "The Salaries of Women Teachers in Institutions of Collegiate Rank," *JACA*, 3d ser., no. 15 (Nov. 1907): 24.

with her. When Kendrick died and deeded her home to the college, her cousin wrote to ask if she might stay on.[22]

It is true that the women faculty could be sustained emotionally, as well as physically and professionally, by the same family members who depended upon them economically. Cornelia Bates looked after her daughter Katharine, sewed for her, and nursed her in illness; Katharine's sister, Jennie Bates, typed Katharine's papers. Nonetheless, Katharine felt responsible for her family; her biographer states that "for her family's sake she entertained village and college friends, learned to play whist, and took her mother for drives in the woods about Wellesley." The cost in time was "countless midnight sessions at her desk."[23]

The few financially independent members of the Wellesley faculty escaped the economic plight that plagued their colleagues. At her death in 1964 Martha Hale Shackford bestowed upon Wellesley College a bequest of $50,000. Sarah Frances Whiting left the bulk of her $32,000 estate to her sister, Elizabeth Whiting, whom she was supporting and with whom she shared a home at Wellesley.[24]

The wills of other Wellesley faculty, however, reveal that many had few financial resources at the end of their lives. Women who had no living relatives deeded what little they had to the college. Margaret H. Jackson left $2,034.96, the sum of her matured Carnegie retirement account, and lamented that the sum was "so trifling."[25]

Severe economic hardship beset some of these professors. Margarethe Müller, professor of German, is an extraordinary case. Having returned to her native Germany after World War I, she faced the terrible inflation of the 1920s and then the Great Depression of the 1930s. Even though the college cashier regularly sent her Carnegie pension allotment in ten-dollar bills, she was finally reduced to selling potatoes. Although most Wellesley professors eluded a similar fate, many did so solely by a lifetime of thrift.[26]

Frank Stricker has compared the salaries of male faculty during the period and assessed whether academics were truly middle class. Based on 1908 figures, he finds a wide variance in salaries: full professors at some universities were paid several thousand dollars; at others, no more than a few hundred dollars. Only those at the wealthiest institutions (the Ivy League and major state institutions) earned over $2,000. (See table 7.) This would place them in the top 5 percent of American family incomes. Stricker calculated that in 1900 the "edge of the middle class" was approximately $1,200. Hence, those who received less than $1,300 "straddled the border between better paid workers and the middle class."[27]

Stricker notes that married male academics issued a litany of complaints about their status and salary. Salaries were seen as declining, while prices and economic and cultural demands on income increased. In the first two decades of the twentieth century, professors felt that they lagged behind in an increasingly affluent, consumer-oriented society. He quotes one associate professor who thought that a minimum decent compensation was $3,200. Women associate professors could not hope to ever earn that much. Indeed, full professors failed to reach that salary.[28]

These academic salaries must be put into the context of a rising inflation, which began in the late 1890s. By some calculations inflation between 1890 and 1914 ran between 20 to 40 percent. From 1914 to 1920, Stricker calculates that average real salaries dropped by about 30 percent. Wellesley salaries failed to keep pace with the inflationary spiral. Furthermore, long-time full professors like Ellen Hayes and Katharine Lee Bates were making only $2,000 in 1908 after twenty years of service. This was at least $500 under the mean as calculated in a Carnegie study and at the low end of the

Table 7

Average Annual Salaries or Earnings of Male Academics
and Other Professionals, 1908

Full professor[a]	$1,652–2,500
Associate professor[b]	$1,646–1,900
Assistant professor	$1,451–1,600
Instructor	$800–1,000
Physician	$750–1,500
Minister	$833–1,578
Public school teacher	$455
Railroad executive	$3,194

Sources: Adapted from Frank Stricker, "American Professors in the Progressive Era: Income Aspirations and Professionalism," *Journal of Interdisciplinary History* 19, no. 2 (Autumn 1988): 237–38. Stricker acknowledges the necessity to mix medians and means because of limited data. Nonetheless, these data give an overview of how academics fared in relation to other significant occupations. Figures on academics calculated from a 1908 Carnegie Foundation Report of 471 institutions responding to a survey of faculty salaries and ranked according to response.

Note: In 1908 the estimated poverty line for a working family in New York City was $800.

[a]The figures for full professors are the range of means of 54 small colleges (spending $10,000–$45,000) and 102 top colleges (spending more than $45,000 annually on salaries; includes large state universities). Not represented here are full professors at 99 poor institutions where faculty earned between $200 and $799; neither are the few full professors who earned $8,000.

[b]The figures for associate and assistant professors are the range of means and medians of the 102 top institutions.

range of salaries for this rank. Associate professors such as Sophie Hart and Sophie Jewett would be in the $1,500 range; instructors like Emily Balch earned $1,250, and Eleanor Gamble $1,200.[29]

Some of Wellesley's senior women faculty bought homes during this same period, when urban home prices rose by 40 percent. To accomplish this they would seem to have been doing fairly well. Several did have independent incomes, but many homes were bought jointly. Without independent wealth, women had to take on outside writing jobs or administrative duties. Moreover, to earn their salary even full professors were encumbered with heavy teaching schedules.

Unlike the male academics studied by Stricker, Wellesley's women professors rarely complained about wages even when requests for increases were denied, as reflected in the minutes of the trustees' meetings. The faculty were grateful to be employed, and to get angry over salary scales would have breached decorum. On the monthly payroll ledger, Katharine Lee Bates signed "Many Thanks" next to her name. Wellesley did make an attempt to accommodate faculty leaves (without pay) used to pursue higher degrees. It offered jobs and provided housing for sisters who might otherwise have been unemployed.[30]

In April 1916 the Board of Trustees appended its minutes on salary with a comparative study of salaries at Bryn Mawr, Smith, and Vassar. The Board calculated that Wellesley's full professors earned a salary of $2,041, only 65 percent that of Vassar's full professors, 68 percent of Bryn Mawr's, and 72 percent of Smith's. (Full professors at these colleges were usually men.) Differentials existed at the associate level as well. Instructors' salaries at Wellesley compared more favorably.[31]

A plethora of complaints emanated from male college professors who felt they were falling beneath the standard of their class and feared proletarianization. To these complaints, women academics added the limited job market and the laws of competition that allowed men to win out and women to underbid each other in wages. One anonymous woman professor observed: "There are generally openings for the five hundred dollar woman teacher and the five thousand dollar man."[32]

This professor, who taught at a coeducational college, raised another concern: the image of the woman scholar as a freak. Her male colleagues seemed shocked that she could be interested in both scholarship and fashions. Moreover, she was plagued by what she termed the "matrimonial problem." Many of the men she met were jealous of her commitment to her professional life, as well as reluctant to believe she could combine career and marriage. So she stayed single. Although she enjoyed this status and had many male friends, she was still considered an anomaly. Moreover, friendships with noncareer women, often the wives of colleagues, were a problem. At Wellesley, without this set of issues, sisterhood was made easier.[33]

Carrie Harper of Mount Holyoke claimed that the life of a male academic appeared glamorous because of the high salary, travel opportunities, and professional conferences. Moreover, she worried that women faculty were unsuccessful as role models because "we are not married." Writing in 1913, Harper argued that better salaries would allow women faculty a better standard of living and make them attractive as professionals. Not much had changed by 1929. In "Women as College Teachers," Marion Hawthorne reported that the rank and file of women teachers at universities "developed a defensive attitude bordering on martyrdom, and complained, waxed bitter, and voiced resentment toward the conditions of which they were victims." Wellesley's women scholars were spared some of this defeating and destructive malaise. Still the benefits of a separate female academic community did not extend to the economic sphere.[34]

Sabbaticals and Summer Retreats

Another gauge of the Wellesley faculty's financial benefits is the unusual sabbatical program and pension plan provided them by the trustees under a bequest from Eben Horsford. Recognizing the faculty's need for rest, recuperation, and renewal, Horsford funded a sabbatical modeled on the Harvard College leave policy for one year at half-salary. Harvard allowed faculty either to stay at home and rest or to travel. Horsford, however, did not believe that staying at home was advantageous to the professor or to the institution. Thus his grant stipulated that faculty travel and reside abroad to keep up with research in their fields during their sabbatical year, for which they were eligible after seven years. He limited this grant for use by departmental heads.

The same bequest increased the salary of those serving over twenty-one years and provided a pension after twenty-six years of service. Horsford, who, like Durant, wished to sponsor women's careers, specified that the "offices contemplated in the grants and pensions must be held by ladies." The trustees ratified that request.[35]

Horsford acted much like a rich uncle to the Wellesley women faculty. He bequeathed a faculty parlor, which opened in September 1888. Against a backdrop of flowers and ebony bookcases that contained special collections, also a gift from Horsford, the faculty met for social gatherings, Academic Council meetings, and committee meetings. Additionally, he provided a room for faculty who lived off campus to rest in during their busy day. Horsford's generosity included a cottage on Shelter Island, New York, for the faculty's use during the summer. Many faculty "retreaters" availed themselves of the privilege of a visit to Harlow Cottage, later renamed Wellesley Cottage. Rowing, sailing, carriage riding, horseback riding, walking, and sunbathing were among the activities available.[36]

Residential Life

For many years College Hall was the primary residential unit for faculty and staff. Even after separate halls and cottages were built, it remained the center of community life, until it burned in 1917. Carla Wenckebach was impressed and intoxicated by the grandeur of College Hall, with its magnificent palms, valuable paintings, and fine engravings. "Everything," she exclaimed, "down to the bathrooms, is princely." Besides the beauty of the place, Wenckebach was wooed by the "personal freedom and independence which the new life promised, the large amount of leisure for private work, 'the splendid equipment', of laboratories and library, the association with large, well trained minds, and last, not least, the rare opportunities for learning, studying, growing." Margarethe Müller, who was also a resident of College Hall, gives us a rare and less lofty evaluation of faculty quarters: "The professors had to do all of their studying, sleeping, and a large part of their administrative work in one and the same room." Müller likened Wenckebach's room to "Bohemian quarters" piled high with books and manuscripts.[37]

These faculty women were grateful both for the beauty of College Hall and the opportunity to live in a communal residence where food service, domestic chores, and laundry service were provided. The lodging pattern also provided a chance for women to get to know one another personally. Vida Dutton Scudder, who lived with her mother in Boston, but who spent one night a week at College Hall, recalled the fun she had with Katharine Lee Bates: "We talked incessantly, especially at night, pacing to and fro by Longfellow Pond." Scudder noted that sometimes curfew overtook them, requiring shamefaced summoning of the night watchman. Once Katharine boosted Vida in through one of the unfastened Gothic library windows.[38]

One responsibility facing all faculty women was to eat at and supervise Tables, a duty considered a vestige of the seminary. Dining and supervising Tables, however, was a complex social experience, because at Wellesley as at the other women's colleges, sharing food showed friendship. A letter written in 1881 from a student to her family illustrates this: "Those two good pears were forbidden fruit, but they were too good not to be eaten, so I took them to good Miss Lord at supper and she divided them among our table companions, so I had an eighth. That is the only way in which we can have anything sent to us, and even that is frowned upon."[39]

Few Wellesley faculty objected to Tables. In fact, for many it was an opportunity to participate with students in lively repartee. There are many stories of students relating funny events and even playing tricks at Tables. Dining together and sharing the day's events or ideas was a rich experience at the very heart of this women's culture.

Prior to 1900, the first year that faculty were officially allowed dwellings off campus, few women had been granted permission to live away from the college. With Caroline Hazard's presidency a new climate began. Hazard encouraged women to move off campus and to buy or build homes. Out of her own funds she built the president's house, Oakwood.[40]

After 1900, three residency options existed for faculty. Until College Hall burned down, faculty would live and eat there, with room and board provided as a benefit. One lived either alone or next door to an unemployed sister. Other faculty, among them Vida Scudder, Mary Calkins, Emily Balch, and Eleanor Gamble, lived at home, commuted to the college, and sometimes stayed overnight. Finally, some faculty lived in private homes in the village surrounding the college.[41]

For faculty and students who remained in college quarters there could be fun and mutuality. Mary Case, paralyzed by polio, spent her entire tenure at College Hall, until it was destroyed in 1914. Case depended on students to transport her around the corridors and to wheel her out to the southern porch of the building, which overlooked the lake. Lucy Wilson recalled that Case "very much enjoyed having different ones of the students stop by and talk to her; and we all did it. Nobody felt the least bit put upon. Nobody felt anything but that it was an honor to take her out there." Such interaction made Case an important person in the lives of the students.[42] Professor Helen Merrill lived in various college dormitories for thirty-nine years. She did so in part because she liked the freedom from domestic responsibility but chiefly because it allowed pleasurable companionship. Her pleasant suite in Claflin became a center for mathematics students, who eventually formed the Mathematics Club.[43]

The residential policy of congregating single women faculty and students came under attack by Emily Wheeler in 1889. She argued that this policy was reminiscent of seminary days, when strict discipline was enforced by women professors. For her, "the life inside such walls was abnormal, unwholesome"; Wheeler proposed housing students and faculty off campus and hiring either more men or "teachers who know the world of men as well as the world of books." In her innovative book *Alma Mater*, Helen Horowitz argues that the inclination of faculty women to move off campus, and to live separately from women students, signaled professionalization and the increasing distance between professors and students. At Wellesley, however, this was not the case. Personal finances most often governed this decision, forcing some to wait a long time before moving off campus.[44]

Some of this financial constraint and life-style was due to the fact that single women numerically dominated the faculty. Yet women were allowed to marry and stay at Wellesley. Wellesley employed a few academic couples, but none of these married women, or pairs, was in the prestigious departments.[45]

Professional Duties

By 1900 professors normally taught three 3-hour courses per term, although several professors were responsible for four and even five full courses. In addition, some full professors directed the work of their departments and held departmental meetings. The normal load for an associate professor was four 3-hour courses or three unrelated courses with different preparations. Instructors' hours were fixed individually depending on the amount of work and years of college service.[46]

Whereas during the Freeman and Shafer administrations, professors needed to demonstrate only piety, innovation in curriculum, and good teaching, during the Irvine era, and thereafter, research and original scholarship became requirements. So did the acquisition of a doctorate. The circumstances impeding the production of scholarship became a subject of debate among women college professors. Katharine Lee Bates reminded her peers that the feminine conscience was the greatest constraint: "Feminine ministrations of sympathy" constantly eroded the time for fruitful study; faculty laid down their books to comfort homesick freshmen or dropped their pens to counsel a sophomore. Instead, she proposed that faculty subordinate students to scholarship. Bates also suggested that Wellesley follow the English model of endowing separate chairs for teaching and research.[47]

To increase female productivity in the academy, Christine Ladd-Franklin in 1904 proposed endowed professorships for women "by hothouse methods." She called upon the ACA to found a few distinguished professorships for productive scholars and thereby reduce the prejudice against women professors. She also asked for the establishment of "peripatetic professorships," endowed chairs that would rotate at major universities in order that brilliant young women have access to good libraries and time to concentrate on scholarship. By supporting select young women at the beginning stages of their careers, Ladd-Franklin hoped to prevent them from "sinking into plain school teachers, and losing in the treadmill of ceaseless duties, all their fresh interest in their work."[48]

Although few women professors held positions favorable for original scholarship, most critics faulted women themselves rather than the academy. Louise Pound, president of the Modern Language Association, pointed to an "internal barrier" to productive scholarship, the lack of self-confidence. She claimed that women distrusted their own abilities and, unlike men students, underestimated their talents. Vassar's Elizabeth Hazelton Haight noted that a woman scholar "has no husband to read her proof, make her index, or verify her references, whom she may gracefully thank in the preface; nor for daily work has she a consort who will relieve her of much of the drudgery of correcting papers. And she has no homemaker."[49]

Helen Sard Hughes, a professor of English at Wellesley, agreed that women scholars, though often bogged down in grading freshman themes, felt fortunate to have any position at all. This engendered timidity: "Made cautious—and women are not apt to gamble in any case—by the scarcity of positions open to women, and by the inferiority of most of these, she prudently devotes herself to doing with all her might the infinite number of pedagogical and social trifles which her hand finds to do." The end result was a loss in time and energy; research goals were soon dropped.

In the hope of breaking the cycle, Hughes warned young women starting academic careers of the rigors ahead: the woman scholar must recognize that "she will have to fight and fight alone, with 'foes without and foes within.'" Her only stimulation would be her love of work; she would often lack congeniality and encouragement; most of all, "she will lack the extrinsic incentives of a realizable professional ambition." In this Darwinian struggle for survival, Helen Sard Hughes concluded that "only [a few women] will fight with success the lethargy induced by their positions." Rather than criticize the norms of scholarship as disregarding the reality of women's lives, these women professors demanded that women meet the exacting standards of productivity. Self-sufficiency was exalted.[50]

Career Conflicts and Limitations

All of the pressures confronting the woman scholar—the heavy teaching schedules, physical and emotional exhaustion, and creative sacrifice—are evident in the careers of the Wellesley faculty. Faculty biographies, often written by colleagues, document the sacrifices that teaching entailed. Sophie Jewett, whose creative outflow was checked by her academic responsibilities, laughingly referred to Amy Lowell's complaint of the distractions that teaching brings to the poet, "as if a brooding hen should have to mind the door bell."[51]

The pressure of constant teaching kept Katharine Lee Bates from devoting herself to writing poetry. Not until 1911, twenty-six years after she started teaching, did Bates collect her verse in a volume, entitled *America the Beautiful*. In addition to teaching, Bates chaired the English department, a burden she dropped only in 1920.[52]

Vida Scudder looked forward to the day when college professors would receive more time and opportunity to do their own creative work. In 1919, when Katharine Lee Bates gave up chairing English and made plans to retire, Scudder confided that she too yearned for retirement. After thirty-two years, teaching inspired only "distaste and revulsion," because so many other interests claimed her in what she hoped would be her most productive years. She rejoiced for Bates, who could now listen to her own music, which had "been a bit smothered at times" by the "drone of student recitations!"[53]

Teaching and committee work relegated original research to "odd moments." Moreover, teachers sometimes succumbed to pressure by the trustees to create courses against their better judgment. Emily Balch hated this "wasteful effort and hack-work" but consoled herself about the extra work involved by claiming that she would be "glad to do much of the new reading."[54]

Scrupulous attention to detail hindered the productivity of other faculty women. Bates was overzealous in this regard. So was botanist Clara Eaton Cummings, whose work on lichens was "very conservative." She never rushed to announce new species, although other botanists readily found new species in their smaller collections. Furthermore, by examining and classifying hundreds of specimens, she provided the material from which others wrote several books. A co-worker commented that male botanists issued these books, but "it is well known that [they] . . . are after all very largely the work of Miss Cummings." Cummings never publicly confronted these scientists, but privately she wrote that much of her work appeared in the books of others.[55]

Success presented as many obstacles as failure, however. When called upon for a resume, Margaret Ferguson, head of the botany department and the first woman president of the Botanical Society of America, was reluctant to report her honors but agreed to list them for the college and not for herself. When a wealthy friend, Susan Minns, left Ferguson money to carry on research, Ferguson was flustered. She denied any knowledge of her friend's intentions, lest she appear to have solicited the gift.[56]

When the Wellesley publicity bureau requested a list of publications, Margaret Sherwood complied but sent a follow-up disclaimer explaining that she had accomplished so much only because she was on a half-time schedule by special arrangement with the college. Sherwood obviously felt guilty about her achievements, adding that some of her colleagues had at times "misunderstood," which is to say envied, her privileged situation. In response to a similar request for a career summary, Mary Alice Willcox responded that she wished her name to be omitted altogether from the list of Wellesley faculty and their works. "My list would be very short even if I could remember everything." In spite of being a leading zoologist, Willcox felt her work had "many imperfections and inadequacies" and that her main contribution lay in establishing the foundations for the later success of Wellesley's zoology department.[57]

The founding mother of the English department, Louise Manning Hodgkins, similarly shied away from publicity. She was distressed, for example, that her biography appeared in about a dozen books, including *Who's Who,* without her consent. A request from the Bibliothèque Nationale for biographical information to be included in a volume on one hundred notable American women evoked this tart comment: "I sent it but must confess I did not approve their judgment."[58]

In later life, Emily Balch reflected: "We *ought* to be ambitious, expecting and meaning to do the best thing we can, expecting much of ourselves, making much of ourselves, keeping ourselves up to a high standard. There is always room at the top!" Yet too much ambition was a crime. "If you have too little salt your soup is tasteless and worthless. If you have too much it is uneatable. That is the way with ambition." Still Balch said of her extraordinary life, "I am not a princess but the plainest of New England spinsters and ex-teachers but for one brief, accidental episode in my life I consorted with men in the seats of power."[59]

The price of achievement could also mean overshadowing sisters who had been playmates and soul mates as well as distancing oneself psychologically and often geographically from family members. Several women chose to renounce success rather than family. Mary Alice Willcox cut short her zoology career, retiring in 1910 at the age of fifty-four, ostensibly because of ill health, although she lived another forty-three years. Willcox's autobiographical reminiscences suggest other, truer causes for terminating her career. She was torn with guilt because of her preeminence over a sickly sister who never succeeded professionally. After her retirement, Willcox devoted herself to her sister, traveling and living with her.[60]

Mary Calkins provides another example of this self-imposed ceiling on achievement. Calkins was offered a joint appointment in the philosophy departments of Columbia and Barnard, where she would have taught graduate students as well as undergraduates. In a letter to her mentor, Hugo Münsterberg, she wrote: "I was unwilling to leave my home, both because I find in it my deepest happiness and because I feel that I add to the happiness of my mother's and father's lives."[61]

Discrimination cannot be slighted as a limiting factor in these women's careers. Calkins, for example, was never awarded the Ph.D. due her. In her case it did not hamper her intellectual growth or her career, but she was an exception. Mary Alice Willcox might have been employed at the Museum of Comparative Zoology at Harvard, except that Alexander Agassiz informed her that there were "three windows and a man for each window." He nonetheless sponsored her to establish the zoology department at Wellesley. Once at Wellesley, however, friction with the botany department isolated her within the community. In her professional career she never fulfilled the promise of her earlier graduate training.[62]

Margaret Rossiter has analyzed the ceiling on women's energies and output that existed in the women's colleges. Recognizing that they could not and would not go further, many academic women settled into lives and careers that were only moderately productive. She concludes that they knew they had reached the pinnacle of their profession and that even with outstanding research accomplishments, they would not be summoned to a major university. Just as the first generation of women scholars predicted, Rossiter finds that "pervasive discrimination and institutional poverty . . . diminished the energies and motivation of even these most favored women of their time and made them less productive than they might have been."[63]

But discrimination and despair are only part of the Wellesley story. Often a missionarylike devotion to social reform precluded a full-time commitment to scholarship. Indeed, several of the most academically distinguished faculty were social radicals who led or participated in the major Progressive reform movements in addition to teaching and writing. Seen from this perspective, many faculty were able to juggle two or three vocations remarkably well.[64]

What most limited, yet ironically most liberated, the Wellesley faculty was their attachment to their community. To succeed outside of Wellesley would have meant forsaking a genteel style of life that included travel, gracious houses, and the cultivation of deep and abiding friendships. For all of the Wellesley faculty, continuity and stability within community took precedence over career. Vida Scudder captured this spirit, noting that "more and more, members of the college faculty were establishing homes in the town . . . and we enjoyed . . . interchange of ideas, friends, household problems and seedlings. It was a good life." Ultimately the community that the faculty created overcame or vitiated the claims and conflicts of careers.[65]

7

The Bonds of Wellesley
Academic Work Culture

*I think I gave you the impression that I wanted to tell you more
about College Hall and its history. No one can reconstruct that. Its
picture lives only in the hearts of those who lived there. I write all
this that you may know my love for Wellesley is not a thing of
landscape and building but of the soul of it. With my sincerest
good wishes . . . I am yours in the bonds of Wellesley.*

—Ellen Burrell, letter to President Horton, 1938

The first fifty-three senior and associate professors at Wellesley
were the intellectual architects of its academic community. They
designed the courses, wrote the texts, made the rules, and controlled the appointment of faculty, creating departmental dynasties.
In addition, the president's appointment of department heads on a
permanent basis further strengthened the power of their position.
A system of rotating heads chosen by members of Council was not
adopted until 1917.[1]

Alice Freeman first organized the departmental structure in the
1880s. During the Hazard era (1899–1910), Dean Ellen Pendleton
and the departmental heads consolidated their control of the college. The president and the trustees had ultimate authority on such
matters as promotions, faculty hirings, and departmental budgets,
but often they merely ratified pro forma the recommendations of
the faculty. Even as late as 1934, Marian Hubbard, head of the
zoology department, expected the instructors of freshman courses

to adhere to the topics she had meticulously set forth in a manual and to conform to her time schedules. One instructor recalled: "I . . . don't remember any meetings. The department just ran." Yet within the classroom there was complete academic freedom.[2]

Given this independence, few associate professors or instructors objected to the way their heads administered the departments. Most were like Vida Scudder, who acquiesced gladly to Katharine Lee Bates's benevolent despotism in the English department. Scudder knew that administrative affairs could be time-consuming; intent on pursuing her social reform activities, she willingly eschewed departmental matters. Helen Merrill, an instructor of mathematics under Ellen Hayes, who chose texts and made out examinations but rarely visited classes and never held departmental meetings, "enjoyed being left alone in all that really mattered." Some junior faculty went beyond acquiescence to frank admiration. Margarethe Müller nearly worshipped Fräulein Wenckebach, her mentor in the German department, asserting that "there ought to be one, and only one, responsible person to keep her finger on the pulse of things."[3]

Autocratic departmental leadership was tolerated—or extolled—for several reasons. One was personality. Helen Merrill later smarted under Ellen Burrell's directorship in the mathematics department, finding her less easygoing than Hayes. Another was self-interest. Alice Van Vechten Brown's domineering style of running the art department bothered Agnes Abbot, yet Abbot resigned herself to Brown's leadership because Brown helped her career.[4] A third, paradoxical reason for departmental dynasties was that a pioneering sense of equality pervaded entire departments, undercutting the distance between heads of departments and other departmental members. Most of the prima donnas in this group respected one another's gifts.

In some departments, such as English, informal friendships muted the distinctions between head and underlings, with the result that departmental and personal affairs became inextricably interwoven. Martha Hale Shackford remembered that Katharine Lee Bates was the "soul of hospitality and made English Department meetings little oases beside her open fire at her house." At these gatherings, Shackford recalled, "a seemingly casual but really effective consideration was given to academic problems."[5] Finally, authoritarian departmental administration was subtly subverted by the presence of so many idiosyncratic individuals—mavericks who could not or would not be controlled. Katharine Lee Bates offered a view of her department from her perspective as head:

Please forgive me for so late an acknowledgment of your most delightful missive. I waited until we should have had a Department meeting, and you know how hard it is to herd that vigorous Department. Whenever I tried to get them together, Miss Scudder would be writing an article for a Socialist magazine or addressing a foreign concourse in her most picturesque Italian, and Miss Sherwood would be in the throes of imagination . . . and Miss Shackford would be reading the proofs of her new rhetoric, and Miss Jewett half way through the translation of some weird old ballad in a lost language of which she had never heard until the day before,—and so on and so on. It is a grand thing to have a gifted Department, but it is very difficult to get a Department meeting.[6]

No other description better—or more amusingly—conveys the actual departmental dynamics.

Matriarchal Mentors

An informal mentor-disciple system cemented the already-strong bonds of Wellesley. Women well established within their departments commonly guided inexperienced young instructors into the profession, helping them develop teaching skills and self-confidence. The all-female milieu gave a particular flavor to this recruitment and socialization process. Older women nurtured, protected, and promoted younger women almost as if they were daughters, not disciples. Katharine Balderston remembered that Martha Hale Shackford took a "very maternal kind of attitude toward her." Lucy Wilson spoke of Eleanor Gamble as "foster mother." On the practical level, senior academic women were able to train successors to carry on their work. In addition, the cultivation of "devotees and disciples" had important social and psychological significance for these women, all of whom were unmarried. To Vida Scudder, the role of mentor was a form of "spiritual maternity."[7]

The English department offers a good example of the mentoring that underlay the community. In 1885, Louise Manning Hodgkins, the head, succeeded in persuading a young Katharine Lee Bates to give up her secondary school post at Dana Hall to become an instructor at her alma mater. Among the reasons for Bates's initial reluctance were her misgivings about the "peculiar strain attaching to that life."[8] Hodgkins assuaged her anxiety, honoring Bates's requests for small freshman classes in subjects she knew well. Hodgkins and Bates developed a close relationship characterized by girlish frivolity, emotional dependence, and little separation between the private and professional. Bates soon lost some of her shyness and became something of a coquette. In 1886, during her second year at Wellesley, when illness prevented her from teaching, she wrote to Hodgkins: "Dear Crocodile: If you have (chocodile) [sic] tears, prepare to shed them now. . . . Literature V must slip one day more. . . . The pansies send their love. They say they miss you and are a little downcast in their pretty faces, but they've done me so much good they're glad they came. Still, most gentle crocodile,/In the path of life I lag on/Thine for many a weary mile, The Dragon."9

From 1885 until 1896, Bates suffered intermittently from what she called the blues—headaches, depression, and melancholia—apparently brought on by insecurity and inner conflict. She wrote often to Hodgkins, expressing her feelings of inadequacy and chastising herself for being an uninspiring teacher. Signing her letters with such phrases as "Your-Neer-Do-Well" or "Your-No-Count-Professor," Bates constantly sought advice and reinforcement. Hodgkins gave her the guidance and support she needed. Bates, in turn, concerned herself with Hodgkins's health, worrying that her mentor was overworking and often suggesting that Hodgkins rest. Such reciprocal concern was common in the Wellesley mentor-disciple relationships.10

Hodgkins remained a mother figure throughout Bates's life, as indeed she did for many members of the English department. In 1916, years after Hodgkins had retired, the entire department fervently set aside a day in honor of "Professor Louise Manning Hodgkins, our beloved and honored Pioneer." As Bates faced death in 1929, she dictated a letter to Hodgkins in which she praised her mentor's pluck and looked forward to having some "very good times together, by and bye."11

Vida Scudder, even before her arrival at the college, looked to Hodgkins for advice and emotional support. She eagerly awaited a "fat envelope" from her containing all the information she needed to plan her course. Just before Scudder was to start teaching at Wellesley, she appealed to Hodgkins: "What shall I do when I appear at Wellesley on Tuesday? You know I never taught before. . . . I have a sense of being very young. Where shall I find you?"12

Like Bates, Scudder soon teased Hodgkins. One note read: "Dear Head: I'm using your paper. Now are you unhappy? I can't come to the department meeting this afternoon. Now aren't you unhappier. And I don't want ever to come to Department meeting at 3:10 again. Now I don't wonder what your frame of mind will be."[13] Still, Scudder was not free from a haunting sense of incompetence, of being ill suited to teaching. In addition she struggled with the conflict of whether to teach or to live in a social settlement and devote herself to reform. A problem-ridden class caused Scudder to doubt herself again, and she admitted feeling frightened to Hodgkins. Finally, however, her common sense returned. In closing a letter to Hodgkins, Scudder described her insecurities: "Goodnight. You'll tell me if you're tired of me? Then I'll retire and write my magnum opus. Lovingly yours, Vida."[14]

Hodgkins and Scudder frequently exchanged loving thoughts and gifts, as was customary in such relationships. Scudder accompanied a gift sent to Hodgkins with this message: "Will the dear Professor wear this silvery, shimmery, moonshining little pin when she feels in the mood for day dreams?"[15] Their relationship—and this practice—endured. When Scudder was about to retire in 1928 she responded to a note from Hodgkins: "How good it is of you to write me! The long years vanish like shadows, and my mind goes back to those days of the last century when you were so heavenly good to a very scared, very prim, very inwardly tremulous young instructor,—who was finding under your friendly encouragement that she had really discovered the love of her life, in the classroom! They were good days, and teaching, ever since has not lost its fine excitement."[16]

Hodgkins was also a mentor to Sophie Jewett, who joined the Wellesley faculty in 1889. Their correspondence shows that Hodgkins's relationship with Jewett paralleled her friendships with Bates and Scudder. Later Bates became a mentor to Jewett. Jewett wrote: "My dear Confessor—who gives me joy for weariness and absolution without penance." Jewett admired Bates and tried to appropriate her "sweet sunshine."[17] Like Bates, Scudder and Jewett were to have disciples of their own. Jeannette Marks, class of 1900, was a protégée of both Bates and Scudder. Bates supplied her former pupil with ideas for course outlines and constructively criticized her syllabi. She also gave Marks psychological support and career advice, once counseling her to get her Ph.D. at Yale or Columbia (something Bates had not done): "Europe and books—many things can come later, but you want—I speak very earnestly—to complete your formal academic studies under thirty, if possible." When Marks joined the Mount Holyoke faculty, Scudder felt anxious but proud. Reading a syllabus prepared by Marks, she experienced "happy, sweet, impersonal pride in the hard work and excellent achievement of one of the girls I love."[18]

Prima Donnas and Protégées

Mentor-disciple relationships developed in all departments at Wellesley, though they did not always follow the model of the English department. The role of protégée could differ considerably. Some fulfilled their mentor's dreams by becoming true scholars; others were more like good drones, bearing a heavy teaching load while their mentors pursued their research projects; and still others played an integral part in building Wellesley's departments.

In chemistry, Charlotte Almira Bragg fostered the research career of Helen French, who appreciated Bragg's unselfishness and support. Bragg kept in the background while pushing her younger colleagues to the fore and deliberately passed along to them opportunities for research and study that were rightly hers. She encouraged the fainthearted and praised those who succeeded through her self-effacement. Helen French thrived under such benevolent tutelage. Thus launched, she went on to enjoy a distinguished and productive career in chemistry at Wellesley.[19]

Mary Case helped launch the careers of two Wellesley psychologists, Mary Calkins and Eleanor Gamble. Case so inspired Gamble, class of 1889, that at her first teaching job Gamble wrote of "playing Wellesley and emulating Miss Case." Gamble joined the Wellesley faculty as an instructor in psychology in 1898, the same year that Calkins became a full professor. Together they built the psychology department, while Case retained her senior position in philosophy.[20]

Calkins soon gladly left operation of the psychology laboratory to Gamble, whom she considered a superior experimentalist, while she devoted her time to philosophy. Gamble served under Calkins, whom she called her "Chief," during her entire Wellesley tenure, which lasted until 1930. Although they produced several joint papers and got along well day-to-day, Calkins clearly was the preeminent scholar. Gamble labored contentedly in Calkins's shadow.[21]

A succession of protégées built the botany department. Susan Hallowell, who held the chair in botany from 1875 to 1902, convinced Margaret Ferguson, class of 1891, to major in botany, invited her to become an instructor in 1893, and selected her as the next head of the department in 1904.

Ferguson was absolutely loyal to Hallowell and praised her fulsomely. She defended Hallowell's lack of productivity, explaining that publications had not been necessary for the first academic women. Hallowell's influence, she asserted, would outlast that of "cold bibliographies." Wishing to leave some lasting monument to her mentor, Ferguson once asked President Hazard to endow a "Hallowell Hall of Botany"; years later Ferguson wrote that "what pleased her most about her work at Wellesley" was that she had secured money for a library as a memorial to Miss Hallowell. When Hallowell died, Ferguson made the long journey to Bangor, Maine, for the funeral.[22]

As the new head of botany, Ferguson perpetuated the tradition of department building, emphasizing laboratory work and the importance of chemistry and physics for botanical students. She also established what are now the Ferguson greenhouses at Wellesley. A productive scholar, she published twenty-seven papers and was elected president of the Botanical Society of America. Margaret Ferguson, like Susan Hallowell, cultivated her disciples. She shared her research projects—and her home—with her niece, Alice Ottley, a zoologist. Together they made several expeditions to the West Coast and to Australia to collect specimens.[23] Ferguson trained another young woman, Mary Bliss, primarily as a teacher. Throughout her career, Bliss sought "not simply to please" Ferguson but to be worthy of her confidence and approval; Bliss was therefore elated with her promotion to assistant professor in 1916. She told Ferguson that "what I am as a scholar and a teacher is largely the result of your example and influence."[24]

As in other relationships at Wellesley, Bliss was solicitous of her mentor's health, grieving when Ferguson was not well and assuring her that she would fully bear the burden of the department until she recuperated. In Ferguson's absences from the department, Bliss faithfully followed her mentor's prescriptions. Whenever Ferguson went on leave, Bliss reassured her: "We shall not do anything radical in your absence." Like the sisters who served as hostesses and administrators, devoted but deferential protégées were invaluable to the woman scholar.[25]

Warring Giants

The mentor-protégée system at Wellesley made generational rivalry between younger women and senior professors rare, as did the pervasive attitude of yielding to one's seniors. But such conflict did occur occasionally. In zoology, Mary Alice Willcox clashed with Caroline Burling Thompson, a Ph.D.

from the University of Pennsylvania. Neither protégée nor disciple, Thompson joined Wellesley with a "natural feeling of superiority" because she came from a large coeducational university. Thompson found the zoology library compiled by Willcox "woefully lacking" and wrote her male professor at Pennsylvania for a list of the latest reference books. Willcox took malicious pleasure in showing the "cocky young instructor" her personal library, which contained the recommended books and many more besides.[26]

A similar case involved professors Sophie Hart and Laura Lockwood of English composition. Lockwood had a Ph.D. from Kansas and did not like being subservient to Miss Hart, who, she felt, "tried to get people to work for her as much as possible." Lockwood organized the Scribbler's Club, a devoted following of student and faculty writers who gathered round her each week. Hart was more than a little jealous. Lockwood, unperturbed, sniffed, "Miss Hart is someone who always wanted power and she's got it."[27]

More common than generational rivalries were competitions between peers. These sometimes existed within departments but more often cropped up between powerful women in different departments. Wellesley had several "warring giants" well known for their long-standing feuds. In addition, departmental dynasties sometimes spawned conflicts between entire departments.[28]

One such rivalry, between the botany and zoology departments, had deep roots. Henry Durant, who had always favored botany, bought Susan Hallowell the latest equipment and accorded her high status within the community. He was less enamored of zoology and in 1881 dismissed Emily Nunn, the first professor of zoology; that same year he recruited Mary Alice Willcox. Because Willcox wanted her department to encompass the study of plant life, she renamed it biology, though she recognized that this was "trenching" on Susan Hallowell's preserves. When Hallowell refused Willcox's invitation for a meeting, "a hostility was born." Hallowell spread her jealousy and distrust of Willcox throughout the botany department, and for years department members hardly spoke to one another. Although Willcox yielded to renaming her department zoology in 1900, a zoology instructor hired nearly three decades later was still advised not to be friendly with instructors in botany.[29]

For a short time the mathematics department contained two strong personalities of starkly different temperaments. Ellen Hayes was a flamboyant radical, Ellen Burrell a staid conservative. They clashed bitterly over both curricular and pedagogical issues. Hayes dismissed the suggestion that Burrell's work in geometry was beautiful by saying, "Beautiful perhaps but it doesn't lead anywhere." She used her power as departmental head to delay offering Burrell's geometry course. Burrell, although initially loath to challenge Hayes, eventually became "utterly fearless"—refusing, for example, to use Hayes's textbooks in algebra and trigonometry. Dissension between the two became so intense that in 1897 President Irvine created a special department of applied mathematics for Hayes and named Burrell head of pure mathematics. Helen Merrill, an instructor in math at that time, observed archly that "relations between the heads of the two departments were not cordial." She termed their relationship an "armed truce, breaking out at times into open hostility." When this happened, their battlefield was as likely as not to be Academic Council.[30]

For the Wellesley community, Academic Council was their Colosseum — a sparring ring for intellectuals. There one exercised one's verbal powers and played academic politics. There high-powered women engaged in a "continuous war of wits."[31] The intellectual jousting of the senior professors both dazzled and dismayed the assistant professors, who never entered the lists themselves. Their elders, especially the aggressive or verbally adept ones, relished the fray. Women like Martha Hale Shackford, Sophie Hart, Vida Scudder, and Julia Orvis dominated Council. Shackford was particularly impressive at making "well-worded and firmly expressed statements. When she rose to speak in Council you knew something was coming, you really did." There were some "wonderful confrontations" between the warring giants—whether Hart and Avery or Hayes and Burrell. Then Julia Orvis would produce "some very clever, very caustic remark that deflated everybody and everybody laughed and the tension eased." Academic Council vented potentially destructive energy harmlessly, converting it into an annealing force that bound the community ever more cohesively.[32]

A Hotbed of Radicals

"The Wellesley faculty is a public-spirited body," wrote Florence Converse, an early chronicler of Wellesley; "its contribution to the general life is not only abstract and literary; many of its members are identified with modern [social] movements."[33] Indeed, the social impulse had imbued Wellesley from its founding, and by the 1880s and 1890s new social notes were being sounded. The faculty vociferously espoused such causes as the rights of women and Indians and such cures as social settlements and consumer leagues.

Wellesley in the Progressive Era was a hothouse for reformers. Many faculty members split their time between teaching and social reform. Katharine Coman founded a club for working girls in Boston and served on the executive committee of the Massachusetts Consumer League. Vida Scudder once proudly proclaimed that she belonged—and paid dues to—fifty-nine reform organizations! In 1912 Ellen Hayes was the Socialist Party's candidate for secretary of state of Massachusetts.[34] An overwhelming consensus decreed that faculty women be social activists. Although they sometimes held opposing political views, a shared commitment to activism and the bonds of friendship contained any conflicts. Indeed, friendship was one of the mechanisms that precipitated social activism. Thus in 1887, Katharine Lee Bates introduced Vida Scudder to Katharine Coman, who shared Scudder's interest in working with the urban poor. Coman and Scudder jointly formed Denison House, a social settlement in Boston. Florence Converse, who lived with Scudder, soon joined them. All four women helped to recruit Emily Balch, who became a head worker at the Denison House Settlement. In all, fifteen members of the Wellesley faculty community were sponsors of the College Settlements Association.[35]

The Wellesley College faculty were particularly supportive of women's education. Several members of the Durant-Howard faculty were among the founders of the Association of Collegiate Alumnae, which is now the American Association of University Women. The faculty also demonstrated concern for the education of women overseas and for working-class women in America. In 1929 Ellen Hayes founded the Vineyard Shore School in West Park, New York, a summer school for working-class women modeled after the Bryn Mawr Summer School for Women Workers. Her colleagues at Wellesley donated scientific equipment to support this endeavor.[36]

Tainted Money

Several causes within the college community itself stirred the more radical teachers. In 1899, the Rockefeller-owned Standard Oil Corporation offered the college a grant of one million dollars for the purpose of modernizing the physical plant. Certain faculty believed the college should not accept the grant. Vida Scudder, who saw acceptance of the money as a "serious moral offence," led the protest. In her words: "I caught the distaste for 'tainted money' infectious among radicals at that time, and joined, if I did not instigate, a vehement protest made by sundry members of the Wellesley faculty against accepting money from the profits of Standard Oil."[37]

Scudder alerted the Board of Trustees that "many consciences beside my own are honestly troubled in this matter." Some faculty members threatened to resign if the money was accepted. Margaret Sherwood, in Italy at the time, wrote to Scudder expressing her solidarity. In the end a "small knot of faculty" that included Scudder, Coman, Balch, and Alice Brown addressed individual appeals to the trustees. This opposition notwithstanding, the trustees placed the financial well-being of the college above moral principle and voted to accept the money. Scudder felt in retrospect that "our little movement of revolt and inquiry" disconcerted the trustees, and she thereby took some solace in its defeat: "We radicals were at least glad that the money didn't go into salaries." A few considered resigning; but all stayed on, because, as Scudder explained, "short of fleeing into a hermitage, we could not escape the taint of communal guilt."[38] Margaret Sherwood's response was more immediate. She fictionalized and publicized the issue in a novel, *Henry Worthington, Idealist*.[39]

The tainted-money incident tested the bonds of friendship, as did any issue over which reasonable women could disagree. Such trials usually served to temper, not sever, those ties. Mary Alice Willcox believed that Scudder's position was uninformed and her tactics unwise. Nonetheless, she defended Scudder's right to voice her dissent. The controversy, Willcox discovered, had a "heart of sweetness in it all in the deep realization of how little after all such things matter to the essence of friendship." Their disagreement strained their friendship, but for Willcox it ultimately "strengthened rather than weakened the bond" between them.[40]

Vida Scudder again tested the "habitual liberality of Wellesley toward its most troublesome teachers" in 1912, when she and Ellen Hayes gave speeches supporting the strike at the mills in Lawrence, Massachusetts, which had been organized by the International Workers of the World, a group popularly believed to be dangerously militant. Hayes, even more radical than Scudder, laced her speech with calls for women's suffrage and socialism. There ensued, in Scudder's words, a "tempest in our little academic teapot." *The Boston Transcript* demanded that Scudder and Hayes resign. Many letters, mostly denouncing the professors, deluged the Wellesley trustees.[41] Wellesley did not ask for their resignations, but the recurring question of where commitment to social activism should yield to institutional loyalty once again strained friendships on campus. Katharine Lee Bates, Scudder's mentor, close friend, and department head, believed that actions which engendered vehement criticism of the college were tantamount to treason. During the uproar over the Lawrence strike, Bates asked Scudder to resign but quickly rescinded the request: "I felt with penitence, after our scraps of talk . . . that I had rather stubbornly pressed my point of criticism instead of assuring you of my fundamental support, and my essential fellowship, in the ideals toward which I hope the socialist movement is working." Bates told Scudder that she would "defend anywhere and to anybody your right to express under proper circumstances your social creed." For Bates, however, the circumstances at Lawrence had been improper. Worried that propaganda might intrude into the Wellesley classroom, she would not permit Scudder to teach her course on Social Ideals in English Literature that year. Many years later, Bates did not recommend Scudder to succeed her as head of the English department.[42]

In spite of the pain and punishment of commitment, Wellesley women continued to advocate reform. Vida Scudder spoke for many when she reflected: "How dull it would be . . . to live in an acquiescent milieu." Yet she also acknowledged that "freedom is little more than a mirage, as soon as one is committed to group activity of any type." She struggled with an "enduring strain" and a "tormenting uncertainty as to what loyalty involved." But even for the most radical Wellesley professors, institutional loyalty prevailed over radicalism. No professor or group of professors ever resigned. Even when clashes developed between radical causes and commitment to college and community, the faculty almost invariably subjugated their individual concerns and convictions to the greater good of promoting women's higher education and sustaining their group life.[43]

8

A Colony of Friends

I wish poets and novelists would celebrate more often the
friendships of women. . . . The women's colleges have helped to
develop such friendships, which albeit beset by perils, like all
worthwhile relationships, can and do supply a great need. The
devoted loyalty they engender, their persistence from youth to age
. . . are moving to watch. Endless in variety, they wait their chronicler.
—Vida Dutton Scudder, *On Journey*

The Wellesley faculty, beyond being professional associates, were remarkably good friends. They formed a community based on respect for learning, love of nature, devotion to social activism, a fondness for wit and humor, frequent emotional exchanges, and loyalty to Wellesley and to one another. Members of the community recruited friends, disciples, and relations into the fold. Mary Calkins, for example, succeeded in having her childhood chum Sophie Jewett appointed to the English department. Ellen Hayes sponsored Katharine Coman, whom she had tutored. The number of sisters simultaneously on the faculty is notable: Mary Alice and Nellie Willcox, Sarah and Elizabeth Whiting, Alice and Louise Waite, and Katharine and Harriet Coman. Carla Wenckebach had two sisters, Helene and Louise, working with her. Additionally, thirteen Wellesley alumnae comprised 30 percent of the senior faculty by 1910. Given their shared backgrounds and tastes, shared visions of life and work, and, often, shared family bonds, it is hardly surprising that the Wellesley faculty produced an extraordinary community.[1]

In contrast to today, when occupational and private selves rarely meet, the academic women of Wellesley melded public and private spheres, camaraderie and intellectual stimulation. Individual associations overlapped; one's friends were also friends and colleagues to one another. In this milieu no one was isolated, no one forgotten.

Most of the faculty were young when they began teaching at Wellesley. In 1890, for example, members of the English department ranged in age from twenty-six to thirty-one. Their youthfulness made them so "brimful of life" that freshmen confused them with brilliant seniors. When someone entered the colony they had created, there was joyful exhilaration. The mean tenure of the group was thirty-two years; fifteen women spent more than forty years at Wellesley.[2]

The communal life at Wellesley touched all areas and levels of behavior.[3] Women worked, lived, and traveled together. Vacations sometimes provided the opportunity to teach others about one's field. In 1901, Alice Brown, a scholar of Christian art, joined Vida Scudder, Scudder's mother, and Florence Converse in Europe "for a few happy weeks of companionship and instruction." At other times, conviviality was the catchword. On one European journey Ellen Pendleton was the life of the party, entertaining Edna Moffett, Charlotte Roberts, and other Wellesley travelers with charades and limericks.[4]

Faculty homes became academic and social centers. Although these women saw one another frequently during the day—between teaching assignments and at teatime in the faculty parlor—in the evening they often came together again at a faculty member's house. Geraldine Gordon, a young instructor, recounted her reactions to the nightly roundtables at the home of Katharine Lee Bates, where she lived for a year: "Miss Jewett lived [with us]. Miss Balch lived down the street on Weston Road and had her dinner with us every night. And if you ever sat at a table night after night after night with Miss Jewett, a poet, Miss Bates who was a poet and a joker . . . and Miss Balch . . . well . . . that was a wonderful year."[5]

The history of the Wellesley faculty community is deeply intertwined with a nostalgia for rural nature. For these women, the physical beauty of Wellesley College, with its three hundred acres of fields, woods, and lake, was an idyllic source of pleasure, inspiration, and solace. Wellesley's environment was so important that a plan to crowd buildings around College Hall provoked strong objections from the faculty. Vida Scudder argued that such action would "rob us of spot after spot of quiet natural beauty. . . .

That stretch of verdure unbroken is one of the most refreshing of our College possessions." Ellen Burrell argued that the "atmosphere of being . . . in the heart of nature" should not be sacrificed, for it was "a part of those higher values for which the college exists." In an essay entitled "Old Trails," Margaret Sherwood articulated the feeling of many faculty women that Wellesley's scenery was not only a welcome antidote to work but a tonic to the spirit and a stimulus to creativity.[6] In general Wellesley faculty women passionately loved the outdoors. They were never so happy as when they were mountain climbing, hiking, or bicycling. Sometimes such passion led to humorous extremes, as when Sophie Jewett explained that she "took a type-writer up into a green tree," having had a loft, complete with tables, chairs, and a hammock, built into the huge maple![7] Conscious of living in a beautiful environment, these women reveled in their secular retreat. So strong was the belief in nature as therapy that some of the faculty built summer compounds in even more rustic Maine, Massachusetts, and New Hampshire.[8]

Many faculty members who built homes near campus planted gardens that enhanced the surrounding splendor. These gardens provided distractions from the demands of work and opportunities to create and nurture. "My garden," wrote Margaret Sherwood, "has a thousand feminine wiles for keeping my mind upon itself; distracting ways of demanding attention, . . . jealous lest it be forgotten for a moment. . . . One finds an absolute content in coming alive with one's garden." Numerous photographs of faculty women in their gardens attest to the popularity of this activity.[9]

Just as Wellesley fit the vision of an ideal place in which to work and establish roots, so too it seemed a good place to die. Again Margaret Sherwood spoke for the group when she said: "I know the way I shall take, when the last moment comes. . . . Bare hill and hollow . . . a glimpse of the lake and beyond. . . . It would seem but an easy step from this world to a fairer—if indeed any could be more fair, which I doubt."[10]

In health, in sickness, and at the hour of death, Wellesley academic women were rarely alone. They mourned those who died and consoled themselves that their departed friends had "joined our advance guard on the other side."[11] Indeed, death did not banish women from this community. Sophie Jewett's death in 1909 evoked a strong response from all. The President's Report for the year 1909–10 chronicled an outpouring of tributes to Jewett, including a window in the chapel and a small library of choice books. Such gestures were intended to keep "her name and her work closely associated with the future life of the College, as it has been in the past."[12] Margaret Sherwood, one of Jewett's closest friends and colleagues, captured the community sentiment: "Wellesley is indeed a changed and lonely place without Miss Jewett, and yet I should not say 'without,' for everything brings a constant reminder of how deeply she is a part, for all time, of all that is most lovely in the life of this place." After Jewett's death, the community informally adopted as its symbol the pilgrim, which she had used as the title and subject of one of her poems. Vida Scudder intoned, "We are pilgrims of truth together, here at Wellesley."[13]

The Wellesley fellowship nurtured kin as well as colleagues. Indeed, a distinctive feature of the Wellesley academic community was the size of its mother-daughter colony. Katharine Lee Bates and her mother shared a home with Katharine Coman and her mother; Vida Scudder lived with her mother, Florence Converse, and Mrs. Converse; Elizabeth Kendall, Adelaide Locke, Laura Lockwood, and Margaret Jackson all lived with their mothers. Much socializing occurred between the two generations. When Mrs. Coman came to live in Wellesley, Coman and Bates gave their mothers a coming-out party. Upon Coman's retirement, Mary Calkins proclaimed her delight that Coman had been close to her mother. When a faculty mother died, the condolences of friends in the community were heartfelt expressions of sorrow, not mere formalities.[14]

The faculty women of Wellesley also served as models for one another. The "absolute fearlessness" of Elizabeth Kendall, an intrepid wanderer who traveled alone through much of Asia and the Middle East, made her a source of strength for many of her Wellesley friends. Margaret Sherwood in particular drew inspiration from Kendall's "staunch courage."[15] In return for being a model of independence and daring, Kendall earned the admiration of her colleagues. Bates, Scudder, Coman, and Balch kept vigilant track of their friend; each time Kendall left on a trip a slew of letters followed her. Besides expressing concern about Kendall's welfare, these letters kept her abreast of events within the college community. Katharine Lee Bates addressed Kendall in China: "Dear Adventurer: My, but we are glad to know that you are alive and well! . . . Miss Eastman . . . called me . . . to say in the most distressed and plaintive voice: O Katharine, you don't think Miss Kendall is dead, do you? . . . I told her we all expected to see you . . . bob over the edge of the horizon . . . almost any time. I have written you several times. . . . I wrote you a few weeks ago of the very sudden and gentle death of Miss Roberts. . . . Miss Moffett is very brave. . . . The best of luck to you

wherever you go, and the best of welcomes whenever you come."[16] Notes
and greetings continued to accompany Kendall on her travels even after she
moved to England at the age of ninety-six.

Wellesley Marriages

In the process of sharing professional and social lives, the academic women
of Wellesley forged deep emotional bonds. Single faculty members expected
and derived all the satisfactions of a family from their female friendships.
Frivolity, intimacy, and emotional interdependency often developed, both
between peers and between senior and junior professors. Lifelong relationships of deep significance were commonplace at Wellesley, fostering verbal
and physical expressions of love. Emily Greene Balch wrote a valentine to
Elizabeth Kendall; Katharine Lee Bates considered Katharine Coman her
partner and "Joy-of-Life." Students gossiped that Miss Shackford stole Miss
Sherwood from Miss Jewett.[17]

Historians are currently debating how to treat such relationships. We
know that mid-nineteenth-century women inhabited a separate homosocial
world of love and ritual in which female friendships were the norm.[18] But
the private lives of late-Victorian or Progressive Era (1870–1900) women
were changing. Historians view the turn of the century as a transitional
period in the history of sexuality. Debate rages over the nature and extent of
the changes, as well as over how to interpret them. Blanche Cook believes
that the term *lesbian* should encompass "women who love women, who
choose women to nurture and support and to create a living environment in
which to work creatively and independently."[19]

Lillian Faderman, in contrast, maintains that "lesbian identity is peculiar
to the 20th century" and offers an evolutionary framework from which to
understand the transformation of women's relationships. The romantic
friendships common between women in the late nineteenth century
(known as Boston marriages) evolved into the accepted notion of educated
spinsters renouncing marriage in favor of intimacy and support from other
women. These women were not referred to as lesbians, however, because
the term was not yet in currency. By the early twentieth century, because of
the impact of Freud and the sexologists, these romantic relationships were
deemed morbid, and the lesbian label—defined as abnormal sexuality—
was applied. Faderman sees the conscious construction of a lesbian sexual
identity as possible only *after* the new category was created. By the 1930s a

lesbian subculture was beginning to emerge out of this new sexual recognition. Women who chose to identify themselves as lesbians therefore differed from previous generations of women, not because the "quality of their love for other women was necessarily different" but because "their awareness (especially of genital sexual potential between women)" and society's awareness of their "decadence" were different.[20]

Other scholars put less weight on the role of the medical profession in defining the term *lesbianism* but agree that consciousness of sexual activity and participation in a lesbian culture is critical. Leila Rupp, who studied couples in the women's rights movement in the 1940s and 1950s, found that none of these women identified themselves as lesbians. She concludes that even with the "'discovery of lesbianism'" romantic friendships continued to exist. Rupp's framework is useful: "We need to distinguish between women who identify as lesbians and/or who are part of a lesbian culture . . . and a broader category of women-committed women who would not identify as lesbians but whose primary commitment in emotional and practical terms was to other women."[21]

The women who formed companionate relationships at Wellesley in the late-nineteenth and early-twentieth centuries did not consider themselves lesbians, as the term is used today. They spoke of themselves as "spinsters," celibate women, or women involved in romantic friendships; some used the term "Wellesley marriages."[22] The twentieth-century historian cannot determine conclusively what transpired in private in the homes of these women, but the possibility exists that some of these relationships included physical intimacy, given our knowledge of the wide spectrum of female sexuality. I believe it is best to consider Wellesley as a community of women-committed women, because this approach acknowledges the elements of love, physical affection, and openly sexual behavior in some Wellesley marriages and reserves the term *lesbian* for women who have consciously claimed that identity.[23]

Describing a few of these relationships evokes their essence. Vida Scudder and Florence Converse met as teacher and student at Wellesley and became lifelong companions. Scudder wrote that although she had been close to perhaps thirty or forty students out of the three thousand she had taught, Converse had "entered the inmost region" of her heart.[24] Scudder and Converse worked as shopgirls for a time in order to acquaint themselves with industrial conditions and volunteered jointly in the Denison House Settlement. Scudder encouraged Converse to be a novelist. In 1899, at the publication of one Converse novel, Scudder boasted: "We hold high jubilee." In 1907, she lauded Converse's *Long Will* because it was on the verge of "real recognition."[25] Several times they were traveling companions in Europe. They shared a summer cottage in Shelbourne, New Hampshire, to which they invited their friends. Contemplating retirement from Wellesley, Scudder anticipated a new life of thinking and writing. Converse helped Scudder prepare *On Journey,* Scudder's autobiography; the dedication to Converse read: "Comrade and Companion." An aged Scudder wrote that despite being increasingly feeble she was content "to stay in my prison of Time and Space on Florence's account." When Scudder died, she left their home, which Scudder owned, and the bulk of her money to Converse.[26]

Katharine Lee Bates fell in love with Katharine Coman in the 1890s. She recorded in her diary: "Katharine lunches me and dines me, approves me and puts me to sleep." Writing from England during their first separation, Bates reminisced about a journey to Princeton when "there were two hands in one pocket." Anxious about even this brief separation, Bates wrote Coman: "You are always in my heart and in my longings."[27] She and Katharine Coman lived together for nearly a decade in a house they called "The Scarab." They also traveled together and collaborated on a book. In letters to mutual friends they fondly detailed their numerous walks and conversations and praised each other's accomplishments. When Coman became terminally ill, Bates nursed her for almost a year. Bates's ministrations prompted this last note from Coman: "I have no fear Dear Heart, for Life and Death are one and God is all in all. My only real concern to remain in this body is to spare you pain and grief and loneliness. But I should come to you as my mother comes to me, in my best moments, when my heart is open to her."[28] Coman left all her personal possessions to Bates. After Coman's death Bates moved into her room, known as "Bohemia," and did all her writing there, including *Yellow Clover,* a volume of poetry dedicated to the memory of her lifelong intimate.[29] Publication of these poems inspired the entire friendship network to send Bates notes of deep appreciation for having captured a "woman's love for a woman"; Jane Addams praised her for chronicling the "new type of friendship between women."[30] Bates never totally recovered from Coman's death. She wrote to a friend: "So much of me died with Katharine Coman that I'm sometimes not sure whether I'm alive or not. . . . We were merry together." When Bates died, she willed money for a Katharine Coman memorial at Wellesley.[31]

Bates's intimacy with Coman did not prevent her from having other deep relationships. The most notable of these was with President Caroline Hazard, who herself formed close friendships with several faculty women. Before coming to Wellesley, Hazard's life had been marked by the kind of drift that plagued many of the faculty women early in their careers. Her essay entitled "At Eight and Twenty" describes the plight of the unmarried woman who nearing thirty "finds her brothers going off to be lawyers and doctors and her own social and intellectual usefulness limited."[32]

Hazard went to Wellesley without academic experience. Insecure about carrying out her professional duties, she found the emotional support she needed in Bates. The evolution of their friendship can be traced by the frequency, tone, and substance of their letters, but a glance at the salutation serves almost as well. Early in their relationship they headed their letters "My Dear Miss Bates" and "My Dear President." The exchanges of these women, both in their forties when they met, soon acquired a girlish exhilaration, as if the two were infatuated. Headings such as "Beloved," "Dear Heart," and "Gentleheart" became common. Hazard once jokingly addressed a card to "Professor Bates" and then wrote, "Here is the formal word dear friend, and now the informal loving addition."[33]

The Hazard-Bates correspondence is particularly rich and revealing. A letter from Hazard written in July 1905 shows the romantic yet unpossessive quality of such relationships: "I have been thinking of the mercies of the year. And among them all the chiefest is that you have let me in a little into your heart—that you have let me count you as my friend. . . . Of course, I always liked you, who could help that? But that you let me love you is a gift to be gratified for. Good night dear friend—give my love to Miss Coman and keep your own special share."[34] In December of that year Bates wrote to President Hazard in a similar vein: "I have been dreaming . . . of your presence, your dear look and voice and touch enfolding me. I must own straight up and confess that I've opened the package! . . . If love could be made into bundles, I would fill your stocking with love, or if it could be made into candles, your Christmas tree should shine with them. It can't even be made into kisses, across this distance, but I think you must feel it flowing out to you and rejoicing over you, you, my sweetest of Christmas gifts."[35] Hazard wanted to mother Bates and expressed her need to nurture: "I wish I could take care of you. I can take care of people." She depended upon Bates for reciprocal support. In 1906, after leading a college chapel service, Hazard wrote to Bates: "Dear, it's 2 o'clock. Everybody's gone and I long to put my head on your shoulder to feel your arms of love. So I'll just tell you—it all went well. The chapel service fitted together as planned. People here said such nice things. I could cry, if I let myself. So, I'll just send this note of love to you. It is exhausting to bare a bit of one's soul. How I count on your love."[36]

Bates depended on Hazard as well. Weighted down by "two horrid messes in my own beloved department," Bates wrote, "when . . . we are together on that confidential sofa again, I'll tell you all about them." When Hazard announced her retirement in 1910, Bates confided: "I have been going through my letter-chest as well as my diaries, and everywhere I come on signs and tokens of yourself, letters and notes and photographs, with entries of the beautiful drives, and talks, and travels that we have taken together. You are always deep in my heart."[37]

When Katharine Coman was dying, Hazard kept up a daily correspondence from California, where she lived at the time, sympathizing and consoling: "My, my dear. Why do we all have to suffer so for each other? And yet if we didn't, we couldn't love—one is the measure of the other. Words are useless dear— but you know how I suffer with you and for her."[38] Bates acknowledged her appreciation of this support after Coman died in 1915: "In two great griefs of my life, the loss of my mother, and the loss of Sophie Jewett, you were my daily comforter, and I often long for you. . . . I am living with Katharine's spirit. I put on her breast a little olive-wood cross we brought, you and I, from Bethlehem."[39] When in 1926 Bates became very ill, she wrote her "Dearest Sister Caroline": "My thoughts turn constantly to you in the deepest love and longing." In 1929, with great appreciation for the automobile—named Abraham—that Hazard had given her, Bates acknowledged that "your kindness . . . has so surrounded my life with ease and beauty and freedom from anxiety that I cannot be grateful enough." Bates was sustained by Hazard: "Every word from you is nectar. I am living in your splendid energies and achievements."[40] The Bates-Hazard relationship contains in microcosm many of the features of the female friendships of Wellesley: emotional interdependency; a fusion of private and public roles; and mutual support and continuity from youth to old age.

Wellesley faculty women built a world around the sharing of ideas, emotions, and values. Their community offered them the matrix for self-identity and allowed the individual myriad opportunities to confirm and reconfirm the worth and purpose of life. Until the end of their lives these extraordinary women remained loyal and committed to one another. The constant stream of life that flowed among them permitted them to reflect that they had been truly "blessed with friendships."[41]

Part III

Trailblazers in Women's Higher Education

1880–1900

9

Symmetrical Womanhood and the Claims of Community
Educational Ideals of the Faculty

*You cannot find any longer, except in obscure corners, the old
ideal of womanhood—the gentle, docile creature, absorbed in the
cares of the household.*

*A symmetrical womanhood . . . must always be the object in the
education of our girls.*

—Vida Dutton Scudder,

"The Effect on Character of a College Education," 1887

In 1887, the *Christian Union* carried a series of articles by the young
literature professor Vida Scudder, entitled "The Effect on Character
of a College Education" (written in two parts) and "The Educated
Woman as a Social Factor." In them Scudder noted that women's
access to higher education was the most significant reform of the
century. Indeed, "to inveigh against the higher education is now as
foolish as to plead for it." Scudder boldly pronounced any criticism
to be irrelevant; "a mournful protest no longer excites our indignation; we dismiss it with a quiet smile." Nonetheless, she added,
educators should not treat the subject complacently: "The problem has shifted its ground. . . . The premises are won; but what
will be the conclusion?"[1]

In these articles, Vida Scudder set the intellectual framework
for an educational debate that would occupy her colleagues at

Wellesley from the late 1880s until 1915. This discussion centered on how higher education would affect the middle-class woman's character and alter her life and, in turn, how this new woman would develop a socially responsible civic role and a career.

A number of cultural elements merged to produce a new conversation about middle-class women's social destiny. One of the most important was the improved status of single women and the concomitant critique of the institution of marriage. Lee Chambers-Schiller traces the "cult of single blessedness" to the period 1780–1840. The Revolutionary War had produced an articulate defense of independence and autonomy. Although marriage was still the norm for the majority of American women, those who did not marry came to be accepted and sometimes even revered. Prescriptive literature claimed that "a single lady, though advanced in life, is much more happy than an ill-matched wife."[2]

Although the trend toward American middle-class women remaining single started with the antebellum generation, the highest percentage of women who never married occurred among those born between 1860 and 1890. (See table 8.) By the 1870s, a demographic and economic transition had created a superfluous number of single women in New England. In the antebellum generation, a single daughter had been unable to make a vocational commitment because of family needs. But by the 1880s and 1890s, more single women were gaining higher education and moving into the public sphere. The first generation of faculty women at Wellesley took the "cult of single blessedness" another step forward. They chose to stay single and to commit themselves to causes and careers. Furthermore, they advocated a similar devotion to public life for their students if a feasible marriage offer did not present itself.[3]

In their life choices, the faculty clearly emblematize what social thinkers of the 1870s and 1880s termed a transitional era in women's roles. Feminists such as Susan B. Anthony spoke of an "epoch of single women"—the result of the noted demographic imbalance and a rejection of conventional marriage. "The women who will *not be ruled* must live without marriage," Anthony proclaimed. In an 1880 article entitled "The Transitional American Woman," a far less radical social observer, Kate Gannett Wells, made a similar observation: "The simple fact is that women have found that they can have occupation, respectability, and even dignity disconnected from the home." While at graduate school in Europe, M. Carey Thomas pondered her life choices, noting that women needed wider interests whether they mar-

Table 8

Percentage of American Women Who Never Married, 1835–1930

Year of Census	Birth Cohort	Age at Enumeration	% Who Never Married
1910	1835–39	70–74	7.3
	1840–44	65–69	7.1
	1845–49	60–64	8.0
	1850–54	55–59	7.7
	1855–59	50–54	8.9
	1860–64	45–49	10.0
1940	1865–69	70–74	11.1
	1870–74	65–69	10.9
	1875–79	60–64	10.4
	1880–84	55–59	8.7
	1885–89	50–54	8.8
	1890–94	45–49	8.6
1950	1895–99	50–54	7.7
	1900–04	45–49	8.0
1960	1905–09	50–54	7.6
	1910–14	45–49	6.5
1965	1915–19	45–49	4.8
1969	1921–25	45–49	4.5
	1926–30	40–44	5.0

Source: Adapted from Daniel Scott Smith, "Family Limitation, Sexual Control, and Domestic Feminism in Victorian America," in Clio's Consciousness Raised: New Perspectives on the History of Women, ed. Mary S. Hartman and Lois Banner (New York: Harper, 1974), 121, table 1.

ried or not. A life devoid of such interests "is a blank." Highly critical of middle-class marriage, she wrote to a potential suitor: "In a transition state I think it would be quite often a *duty* and a pleasure not to marry until the supply of parties of either sex equalled the raised demand."[4]

The Wellesley College faculty believed a time of transition in American culture required a new set of cultural ideals for middle-class women. As educators, the faculty set out to define and transmit these ideals, terming this new ideology "symmetrical womanhood." The new social type would be a healthy woman who moved through her adolescence and into middle age without physical or psychological ailments; marriage would not necessarily be her supreme goal. Even though marriage was not completely scorned, symmetrical womanhood often meant that women would reject their previously ordained domestic roles and step out of the privatized sphere of the family and onto the public stage of community activism and careers. The symmetrical woman's life course would not be identical to a man's, but neither would it replicate that of previous generations of American women.

To help women break away from absorption in the family claim, the Wellesley faculty emphasized what Emily Balch called the claims of community. The responsibilities of citizenship and community activism were therefore elevated above a woman's role as either daughter or wife.[5]

Additionally, the faculty concerned themselves with the collegian's occupational or professional role. Launching an attack on amateurism, they encouraged their students to join men in the culture of professionalism. They insisted that educated women become knowledgeable in the new social sciences in order to contribute their social expertise to society, often as social workers, doctors, academics, or teachers.[6]

The Wellesley faculty were not the first women intellectuals to use the concept of symmetry as a model of stable and wholesome womanhood. Such discussions arise in feminist literature as early as the 1860s and 1870s, particularly in relationship to women's health. The term is also found in Julia Ward Howe's *Sex and Education* (1874), a book of essays that disputed Dr. Clarke's claims that a woman's biology limited her intellectual capacities. The Wellesley faculty, however, were the first to fully articulate the norms of symmetrical womanhood within an institutionalized setting of higher education and to inculcate those ideals in a generation of young women students. Moreover, their model of womanhood was infused with profoundly mixed and even critical views of the family. They believed that character was best shaped and best served in community. They represent the first generation of women educators to expose the limitations of the privatized family, which absorbed woman's energies and prevented her from reaching a consciousness of self that would allow her to participate in public life. In this educational philosophy they are connected to the new aims of the Progressive Era.[7]

Because the ideology of symmetrical womanhood espoused women's entry into public life, it contravened the conventional middle-class rhetoric governing women's roles and advocated a rebellion against true womanhood. It repudiated as well the concept of the "female animal," the biologically based viewpoint that women are prisoners of their reproductive capacities and that higher education would cause physiological damage. It even challenged republican motherhood, a conservative ideology that favored educating women as a means of enabling them to raise virtuous sons. In short, symmetrical womanhood overturned all the social norms about the purposes and effects of women's higher education. For the Wellesley faculty, higher education was not the cause of women's problems but a powerful remedy.[8]

George Peterson argues that the concept of the "whole man" or the "symmetrical man" connects the nineteenth-century New England college with the creation of the Progressive Era male reformer. The language of symmetrical womanhood demonstrates how the women's colleges also incubated social reformers. Sophie Hart envisioned the women's colleges as "great clearing houses for the new thought, the new activity in social welfare."[9]

At Wellesley, socialization aimed to break the old bondage to family and to create a female cultural elite that could contribute to public life and also assume control in emerging areas of the professions. Vida Scudder believed that this new generation of women would spearhead major social change: "Into this world:—a world of paradox, weary with age, yet eager with the excitement of youth; ardent with hope, yet sick with half despair; rife with bewilderment and contradictory theories, yet bent, as no other age has ever been, on the analysis of social evil and the righting of social wrong—into this world we are born—we, the first generation of college women. In a sense, we represent a new factor in the social order. . . . We embody a type, in some respects, hitherto unknown. . . . Our lives are in our hands. In a sense, the lives of the two or three generations of college women who are to follow us, are in our hands also." Scudder explained that the professional class was "a mediator between the idle rich and the great mass sunk in mechanical labor." As professionals, college-educated women would be free from poverty yet disdainful of luxury. From that special vantage point they could devote themselves to the study and alleviation of social ills.[10]

In the post–Civil War era, higher education allowed middle-class women to lay claim to careers and to a public role in history. To Scudder and her Wellesley colleagues, the 1890s presented women with an opportune sociohistorical moment. The combination of highly educated single women coming of age in a world bursting with economic and social problems produced, in Scudder's view, a "beautiful concurrence which we are pleased to call Destiny." The millennial tone of women's higher education is apparent in her declaration that just when the "disintegration of older cultures [has] precipitated society into a chaos before which men are helpless . . . this throng of educated women has been released into the larger life." Educated women were to bring a new ethical awareness to civilization, and the faculty had the privilege of creating that climate.[11]

In their educational philosophy, the Wellesley faculty illuminate the ideology of activism and the impulse to create a new social character, one based not on evangelical piety but on the social bonds of society. They epitomize what John Higham calls a reorientation of American culture, in which "the acid of defeat and the elixir of liberation mingled in the intellectual ferment of the decade."[12] This new vocabulary of the social self forged in society connects them with such intellectuals as Josiah Royce, Mary Follett, John Dewey, and Jane Addams, who saw education as a vehicle for creating a new organic culture.[13] Hence, the faculty's concern about a woman's social character is not simply a reiteration of traditional ideals about woman's religious, moral, or domestic role. The rhetoric these women used also differs substantially from the ideology of the women's club movement that transformed the concept of true womanhood into a palatable model.[14] Rather, the new faculty ideals emphasized "action, direct and deliberate . . . replacing previous interpretations of liberal education as passive."[15]

Creating Symmetrical Womanhood

The Wellesley faculty challenged expectations about the lives of middle-class women, starting with cultural definitions of the female self that emphasized physical beauty. In 1879, as a senior at Wellesley College, Katharine Lee Bates wrote an essay entitled "The American Heroine," in which she registered her dismay over the "blank in our existence—the lack of an American heroine." While reading William Dean Howell's "The Lady of the Aroostook," she had noted that the author was consumed with the female protagonist's physical attributes, especially her slim figure and her attention to beauty and attire. Bates rejected Howell's heroine, who had no mind of her own and read only what the hero suggested to her. To Katharine Lee Bates, this "maiden, does not possess outside of her beauty of face and voice, one characteristic of the heroine," for, Bates pointed out, "the predominant stamp of heroism must be activity . . . and this girl is as passive as a wooden angel or a wax rose." Bates concluded that the American reading public awaited a heroine who would display daring, intelligence, and force.[16]

This emphasis on women's physical beauty also repelled Vida Scudder.

In an essay entitled "Womanhood in Modern Poetry," Scudder reviewed poets from the sixteenth to nineteenth centuries and complained: "Sometimes it almost seems as if beauty used to be considered, not alone the supreme crown, but the only essential to normal womanhood." Male poets were either enrapt by a woman's form, hair, and lips or absorbed in defining the emotion of the lover in the presence of this beauty.[17]

Ethel Puffer argued that woman's social value is "after all too often measured in terms not of appreciation but of admiration. The outwardly beautiful, rather than . . . accomplishments, is required of her." Such social training, Puffer claimed, is aimed at the "career of marriage." Judged by such an artificial standard a woman forgets sometimes that she must live out her life as a moral being. The empowerment of beauty, Puffer wisely insisted, is not power at all, because it is only accidental to the real self.[18]

For these women, the old Victorian ideal of womanhood — the docile figure absorbed in household cares — was defunct. The new times confronted middle-class women with a new set of economic and social conditions, including the use of leisure. Citing her own experience, Vida Scudder said that the contemporary young woman was restless: "Nothing can satisfy her long. A protracted book wearies her. . . . She dashes from charities to fancy-work, from church to ball-room." As a result, Scudder argued, discontent had reached epidemic proportions among this class of women. A young woman who lacked training was narrow; her intellect danced obediently to the tune of her emotions. In everyday affairs her life was therefore without balance, control, or method. This lack of direction, Scudder insisted, led women to become high-strung creatures and left them with a "morbid conscientiousness" of emptiness. Ultimately, women confronted an adulthood, and in particular middle age, devoid of purpose. Scudder lamented: "Do we not all know her, the pathetic woman of thirty-five, struggling in vain to occupy herself, unfitted for anything in particular." Not all women could or should marry, she declared, and marriage should not be considered "a panacea for discontent."[19]

In 1897, former president Alice Freeman Palmer echoed this sentiment: "The old fairy story which charmed us in childhood ended with—'And they were married and lived happy ever after.'" Mistakes and problems were never acknowledged, as if "life would be one long day of unclouded bliss." Arguing that perfect companionship in marriage was rare, Palmer exhorted that if a "marriage of comradeship" eluded a woman she must confront the question "What shall I do with my life?"[20]

The solution lay in higher education. For Vida Scudder a college course would allow a woman to develop some unity in her life—to move through middle age with purpose. It would bring a balance to female adolescence; it would be an antidote to the dissipation of energy characteristic of middle-class women and to the emptiness caused by the lack of a valid and authentic social role. Higher education that culminated in productivity—a career—would bring a woman's life stability instead of futility.[21]

The faculty was convinced that a college education would shape a new womanhood. Ethel Puffer drew a distinction between the aesthetic ideal of outward appearance and charm that governed the ordinary woman and the ethical ideal that she hoped would be the norm for college women. The aesthetic ideal was passive; the ethical "represents force, action, change." Puffer believed that as the college woman advanced toward middle age, she would represent "a noble and a stronger type of womanhood than any other."[22]

On an individual level, higher education empowered women, offering them, in Vida Scudder's words, not only a change of "social opportunity but of psychological make-up." On a social level, it had the potential of shaping a generation of highly trained women, whose energies would significantly alter the political and social fabric of the nation. Higher education would allow women to break the confines of personal and immediate interests, link women's lives with work and the public realm, and "enlarge consciousness till we recognize ourselves as parts, responsible parts of . . . national life." Katharine Lee Bates reminded women that education would allow them to appropriate learning; the final outcome of study was power.[23]

Vida Scudder also pointed out that society had lost the intellectual contributions of previous generations of women. "Few things . . . are more depressing to a thoughtful mind than the tremendous amount of misdirected and non-utilized power latent in the feminine half of humanity." Scudder lamented: "Often with a mistaken sense of sacrifice women subordinated themselves until this was their second nature." Rhetorically she asked: "How many women of rare capacity have fairly blotted themselves out from a mistaken sense of duty!" Scudder painted a sorry picture of women's history in her characterization of a woman's suffrage bazaar. Banners inscribed with "'Our powers demand our rights' and the like" draped the room. She mocked woman's "vaunted powers: crocheted mats, tidies of all descriptions, hand-painted screens, fans, dinner-cards, kickshaws, and sachet-bags by the score—all the usual dreary, futile, and petty array presented by women's work when the masculine element is ruled out."

Although one might be amused by a grandmother who whiled away her leisure, it was sad to see women devoting their lives to decorating china. She recalled an exhibition of women's quilts: "Think of it! Think of the years of labor involved and the tons of patience! . . . Here is a world of suffering needing to be healed, of ignorance longing to be enlightened; and here are women . . . devoting their energies to the embroidery of doilies or the analysis of their own emotions, while they mourn over the narrowness of their lives."[24]

Scudder did not deny that younger women should and did honor the work done by the exceptional women of the prior generation, but she noted that as a rule, men's criticism of this work is true: "Feminine work is vitiated by an excess of those very qualities wherein ought to consist its power—by an intensity which ignores proportion, and a sentimentality which ignores law." Unlike contemporary feminists who celebrate women's quilt making as a potent symbol of women's culture, Scudder rejected such amateur endeavors. Instead she envisioned educated women entering public life in a professional manner. The larger problems of the day, such as housing, public morality, and the wages of working women, would not be solved by charity but by complex thinking and social science methods.[25]

In analyzing women's place in society, Scudder employed a dialectical framework: women could make use of the feminine element derived from their historical seclusion from public life if they added to it the masculine element—training in abstract thinking and the comprehension of universal rules. Scudder insisted that men had developed this approach because of the need to be efficient and to execute policies. Women, by virtue of their past seclusion, had not been able to tap into this power. In the 1880s and 1890s, however, women were "called out . . . from the privacy of the hearth"; their lives linked up with a "more public struggle." In the words of Emily Greene Balch, women would no longer be "lookers on at the game."[26]

The faculty stressed that their students had come of age at a unique moment in cultural and political history. Balch explained that economists and philosophers, supported by the church and press, had for generations preached self-interest as moral and economic law. Yet, she remarked, "gradually it is dawning on men's minds that there is no department of life in which they are at liberty to act purely selfishly." Women who cultivated a cooperative spirit would therefore be in demand in the new state. Vida Scudder argued that the objective and dry doctrines of the Manchester School, which taught that the relations of man to man were subject to purely mathematical laws, were falling into disrepute. She saw the new generation of economists as emphasizing ethics, a shift that meant greater opportunities for women. Scudder was convinced that "men will always continue to judge matters largely from the standpoint of the expedient, women from the standpoint of the ethical." But Scudder reminded her audience that the "typical feminine answer: 'I cannot understand; I feel'" was inadequate. "She must say: 'I both feel and understand;' or, indeed, in some cases: 'I feel because I understand.'" Scudder believed that the feminine instinct had to be disciplined and made active, not self-centered. It should not, however, be totally eliminated.[27]

The Wellesley intellectuals did not repudiate all feminine values, nor did they simply adjust to bureaucracy and corporate organizational structures. Rather, their female version of community became the model for the state; the state then became a moral organism. Women brought a moral purpose and energy into political and professional causes.[28] Vida Scudder commented: "The chief need of American politics . . . [is] a larger introduction of the ethical element. . . . Who so fitted to emphasize these matters . . . as thoughtful women?" The methods of social science, tied to science yet infused with moral ideals, appealed to college-educated women.[29]

The College as a Workshop

Training the college woman to participate in this female vision of the Progressive society was a major goal of the Wellesley faculty. In 1890, Margaret Stratton, dean of Wellesley, stated that "the modern college does not aim to make ascetics; it seeks to make men, whole men and whole women, ready for the duties of modern life." For Sophie Hart, college was the means by which middle-class women gained access to the traditions of our collective heritage. Colleges were preparing women to become active citizens and to partake of corporate life. Training led to social and political consciousness.[30] Katharine Lee Bates found that "the college girl of the period is not only eminently executive, but she is trained to corporate action." Bates asserted that the collegian "must continually subordinate herself to her society, her class, her college." This was a desired form of discipline, because the American girl was too often an autocrat at home.[31]

One of the most important functions of colleges was not only to integrate different social classes but to diminish social class as an indicator of station in life. Wellesley intellectuals were seeking to establish new categories of authority and status in which public service, not private wealth, was the badge of social distinction. Vida Scudder stated that the college community influenced a woman's character even more than it did her mind. She argued that in coming to college, a young woman left behind the narrow social world and environment of her family. Scudder predicted that the upper-class girl's "mild, unconscious snobbishness will soon be knocked out of her" as she learned that young women of all classes could be of superior intellect or moral force. Sophie Hart supported the notion of service, stating that wealthy young women will be "sucked into this new vortex of college thought, which discloses . . . the conduct of life in accordance with the ideals of service."[32]

Character and intellect were elevated over all other personal attributes. In Katharine Lee Bates's words, "[Wellesley] honors character, she believes in brains." But far more significant than the intellectual training was, in Margaret Sherwood's view, "the companionship in work and play, standing shoulder to shoulder with . . . fellows," which would "bring into women's lives . . . a certain breadth and largeness." Scudder agreed. College would help women replace egotism with a more impersonal or universal stand-point. Working within a framework of public service the symmetrical woman would serve society but also be served in that her character and outlook would be shaped in a communal social context. Ethel Puffer spoke of the psychological transformation that would ensue: "From dwelling in an Adamless Eden of moral and intellectual effort" college women would cast off a narrow masculine or feminine identity to become "simple human beings and workers after the law."[33]

To Professor Hart the sense of belonging to a college community created a shift in mental attitude. The orientation toward public life amounted to a political and intellectual liberation. An adjustment to communal rules and standards over family loyalty corrected, in Hart's opinion, women's tendency to be overindividualistic and self-absorbed. Society needed women who could work on boards of business enterprises where collective teamwork shaped policies. In 1908, when Hart developed her philosophy, women lacked the right to vote. Yet Hart, like other members of the Wellesley faculty, called for women to attain citizenship in the civil life of the nation.[34]

Echoing this call, Emily Greene Balch observed that "obviously life is not an individual affair." She wrote: "We are not Robinson Crusoes. We have our places not only as members of families, as friends, as neighbors and workers in one or another field, but as members of the community with claims as such and duties and opportunities." For Balch, the Greeks provided a model of civic responsibility, as reflected in their devotion to public service: "[The] most that a man can do is to find his life by losing it, by merging it in a larger whole." Although historically women had been marginalized, Balch felt that they now had the opportunity to join men and become the guardians of civic life.[35]

The faculty offered a variety of strategies to put these educational ideals into practice. Emily Balch explained differences in sex roles on the basis of children's games. Boys' games were based on loyalty and subordination; the good player subordinated his individuality for the success of the game. But girls customarily did not play games requiring team play and self-subordination. From our twentieth-century vantage point, the call for self-subordination is ironic, for is this not the most damaging part of woman's common lot? Yet Balch is rejecting women's absorption within the private family. Recognizing that games often provide men with anticipatory socialization necessary to their future roles as leaders in public life, Balch wanted women to develop new games, yet she did not want women to copy men's aggressive striving for total victory. She would have women find a team sport (theatricals perhaps) that allowed them to be part of the social whole without the negative results of annihilating victory.[36]

The Wellesley faculty's educational ideology was imbued with the Progressive spirit of preparing women to live together within community. President Hazard expressed this idea in her commencement address of 1901: "We are an isolated community at Wellesley, and are thrown much upon our own resources. It is most wise and fitting that the civic spirit should be aroused, that young women should here learn what it is to be a vital part of community, what the duties of true citizenship are. Individual relations are easy to establish. . . . College is certainly the place to find fellowship on the broadest human grounds. It is the place for the development of natural leaders." In another talk, she praised women's colleges for providing women the opportunity to serve on journals, in student government, and in debating, literary, and scientific societies; such experiences equipped women as never before to become leaders in society.[37]

This view of the college as a "little commonwealth" was widespread. College developed what Progressives called executive ability. In societies and class meetings young women learned to speak concisely, to conduct business in an orderly and efficient manner. Sophie Hart pointed with pride to student government meetings, conducted according to parliamentary procedure, where young women adjudicated all sorts of problems. They held their meetings "as gravely as the President of the U.S. might hold a Cabinet meeting over a proclamation of war."[38]

On the one hand, this call for women to work in concert can be seen as an extension of nineteenth-century women's culture. Women had worked in voluntary organizations and women's clubs and had formed alliances based on shared conceptions of their gender role. The conventional bonds of womanhood had allowed women to participate in reform activities.[39] The Wellesley faculty sustained this tradition of women's bonding, but dissociated themselves from what they termed the amateur status and behavior of previous generations of women. In fact, they denigrated certain aspects of women's culture—the sentimentality, the confinement to domestic life, and the lack of access to the public realm. Higher education was now to be the glue that cemented this radical generation of middle-class women; trained in history, literature, economics, science, and government, they were to be creators of the new social order.[40]

The Wellesley faculty self-consciously attempted to create a network of educated white middle-class women who would be active participants in social causes and social change. Katharine Coman spoke of the Wellesley alumnae as "social servants" who could see things clearly and judge them without prejudice. Coman aimed to produce such women in the Department of Economics. She was successful, for the department received many calls for women trained to serve as settlement headworkers, tenement inspectors, and probation officers.[41]

Even the woman trained to be a scholar operated on these principles of social service. Katharine Lee Bates explained that the scholar "would hope to discover new heart-space . . . to humanize and spiritualize learning."[42] Along with opportunity came responsibility. Emily Balch reminded Wellesley College students of their debt: "Our education is not paid for . . . but given us—as a charity if we like to call it so—by strangers on whom we have no claim. . . . We rise on stepping-stones of the lives of those who have struggled in this tough old world before us. We must, if we can, at least maintain what they have left us."[43]

Although Wellesley took a firm stand on social responsibility, some faculty in the 1880s and 1890s were cautious on the subject of suffrage.[44] In the mid-1880s, Vida Scudder, who advocated women's participation in national politics, still disclaimed any intent to speak on behalf of the vote.

In 1906, Emily Balch, who supported suffrage, claimed in her article "Citizenship in College" that in arguing for women to feel a stronger public spirit, she was not taking any position on the question of their participation in public life. Nonetheless, she warned that without civic consciousness women would be no more than actors in a crowd.[45]

Other faculty supported suffrage as early as the 1880s. Ellen Hayes, in her column for the *Courant*, reported on suffrage conferences and progress toward the ballot. In the 1900s several faculty were active in the Wellesley Woman's Suffrage League. In 1906, Mary Calkins represented Wellesley at the College Evening of the National American Woman Suffrage Association. In 1911, in explaining the ethos of the economics department at Wellesley, Katharine Coman specifically stressed that as early as the 1880s, the program was intended to prepare women for the vote. Mary Woolley expressed the sentiment of many when she said that "it is impossible to consider the question of civic responsibility without reference to the question of suffrage." An awareness of civic problems, including a knowledge of economics, political science, and history, was "one of the first steps in preparation for the wider citizenship coming so surely to women."[46]

In 1917, Katharine Lee Bates wrote to the editor of the *Lewiston Journal* that she was glad to support suffrage: "*Why not?* Women are tax-payers, patriots, workers for every national cause,—why not citizens? Women may and do express their opinions freely on public questions, in the home and schools, from the platform and in the press,—why not through the ballot."[47]

Higher Education and the Rhetoric of Reform

The early Wellesley faculty outlined what I would call the rhetoric of reform for college-educated women. On the surface their ideals meshed with those of other educators and public servants, including Theodore Roosevelt. In *American Ideals,* Roosevelt articulated the gospel of character and community, stating that public life depended on the love of order, the ability to fight well, the devotion to family, and the capacity to serve the community. To Roosevelt, "character is far more important than intellect to the race as to the individual. We need intellect, and there is no reason why we should not have it together with character; but if we must choose between the two, we choose character without a moment's hesitation."[48]

When applied to women, the concept of symmetry, wherein character was shaped by and displayed in a commitment to public life, subverted the conventional ideals of womanhood and hence caused tremendous alarm. The whole woman of this era was not simply the mirror image or analogue of the whole man. Educators who supported the concept of the whole man were intent on keeping women in an old-fashioned sphere. Although they saw deficiencies in the behavior of middle-class women and were struck by young women's restlessness and emotionality, their remedies differed greatly from those proposed by the Wellesley faculty.

The president of Bowdoin College, William DeWitt Hyde, warned against women squandering "the wealth of physical vitality meant for twenty generations to gain some paltry academic honor." He believed that higher education would sap women of their sexual and emotional strengths—just the opposite of the conclusion reached by the Wellesley faculty.[49] In his authoritative volume *Adolescence,* G. Stanley Hall worried lest woman lapse into "mannish ways, methods and ideals, until her original divinity may become obscured." He scorned women's intellectual aims, arguing: "Who ever asked if the holy mother, whom the wise men adored, knew the astronomy of the Chaldees or had studied Egyptian or Babylonian, or even whether she knew how to read or write her own tongue. . . . The glorified madonna ideal shows us how much more whole and holy it is to be a woman than to be artist, orator, professor." Hall concurred with the conclusion reached by another educator who warned that "unless there is a change of trend we shall soon have a female sex without a female character."[50]

The ethos of symmetry and wholeness ruptured the ideology of separate spheres. In particular, the ethos that inculcated in an educated woman a commitment to community over family, to public service rather than to reproductive values, disrupted conventional sex roles. Male educators eventually attributed low marriage rates and low fertility in Anglo-Saxon college-bred women to this disruption. Roosevelt condemned this upheaval in cultural roles as "race suicide" and thus wound up criticizing well-educated women for pledging themselves to public life, demonstrating that his philosophy of life was only for educated men.

In the Progressive Era (1890–1920), society was viewed as an organic whole; no class or part of society could or should separate itself from the rest of the body politic. No class should feel itself so privileged as to lie in isolation from problems or so oppressed as to demand a full-class revolution. Rather, society existed, functioned, and flowered because of social symmetry.

There was also a rejection of the growing trend toward specialization in the academy and particularly within universities and the field of science. To distinguish the role of the liberal arts college from the university, many a college president used the metaphor of the whole man. George Peterson rightly connects the whole man and the whole woman with the social type who would fill the ranks of Progressive Era reformers.[51]

This meant that male educators in the late nineteenth century called upon the whole man to use his liberal education for action, to employ his newly acquired social science learning to remedy social evils. By 1905, however, much of this rhetoric sounded hollow. The metaphor of the whole man began to decay and became an anti-intellectual symbol that denoted an empty gentility. Principles seem to have become platitudes. One might argue that for middle-class educated men, the emphasis on social character and symmetrical manhood began to be equated with effeminate decay as professionalization became the "manly" norm.[52]

Although the term "symmetrical manhood" might have become a hollow phrase, at Wellesley symmetry was part of a robust and productive language of social change, at least from 1870 through 1915. For educated middle-class women, the discourse of symmetrical womanhood seemed to gain energy during this period. A life embodying physical and mental culture in balance, usefulness to society, and dignity in old age augured hope. The aim of all of this education, Vida Scudder stated, was "not primarily . . . to develop the intellect; it is to balance the powers." Similarly, Katharine Lee Bates predicted that higher education would produce "a harvest of women, sound of body and of mind . . . paying back in original achievement some fraction of their debt to the man-accumulated learning of the past, and recompensing society for its educational venture in their behalf by a richer and more symmetric womanhood than the world has ever known."[53]

10

Adventures in Pedagogy
Teaching Styles and Curriculum Reform

*To plan a curriculum . . . to distinguish intelligently between the
elective system and its disadvantages . . . to try out the pedagogic
methods of the men's colleges and to discover which were
antiquated and should be abolished, which were susceptible of
reform . . . to invent new methods—these were the romantic
quests to which these enamored devotees were vowed.*

—Florence Converse, *Wellesley College*

Standard historical accounts of women's colleges fail to record how
curricula were developed. Indeed, a disconcerting consensus governs the literature—namely, that the women's colleges, bent on
proving their equality with men, merely mimicked the curriculum
of men's colleges. Because this curriculum was considered "on the
brink of collapse," the women's colleges appear to have adopted
the shopworn, classical education of gentlemen for their clientele.[1]

Yet a survey of the major departments within Wellesley, and the
faculty who brought renown to them, indicates that Wellesley's
golden age is marked by significant departures in curriculum and
educational pedagogy. Fired by energy and commitment, academic
women incorporated into their classrooms the most innovative
methods in their fields and created new ideologies within their disciplines. Rather than simply rely on conventional pedagogy, which
stressed mental discipline through rote memorization of details,
the faculty combined lectures with discussions, seminars, field

trips, and laboratory work. Moreover, these professors had what contemporary educational theorists term "a pedagogical project"—a larger moral and social vision that in this case allowed for the self-empowerment of women. The contributions of the Wellesley faculty in the areas of curriculum reform, the writing of textbooks, and teaching styles helped revolutionize post–Civil War intellectual life.[2]

English

The most subscribed courses at Wellesley during 1890–1910 were in the English department. Whereas at Harvard philological analysis and linguistics made up the "steel core work" of the department, at Wellesley the concentration was on intellectual and social themes in literature, reflecting the humanistic approach that many of the faculty had learned as graduate students at Oxford. Under the inspired direction of Katharine Lee Bates, who taught at Wellesley from 1885 to 1925, English teaching avoided both excessive sentimentality and the dry, detailed scholarship emanating from Germany. At Wellesley, English literature courses involved textual analysis mixed with critical social commentary or stressed creative writing. The fact that more than half of the members of the department were poets added to its distinctive style.[3]

The most famous poet was Bates herself. Shy, chubby, and merry, with a contagious chuckle, "Kitty" Lee Bates was at her best in small seminars that she conducted in her home. Other kinds of teaching did not come easily to her, and she often felt "like a round peg that didn't fit a square hole." At the beginning of her Wellesley career, she predicted: "I think I should make a horribly bad professor—honestly I do." Nervously she analyzed her lack of qualifications for lecturing: "I can't speak well, I dread to face even a class audience, I'm sinfully bored by critical works of literature, I would like to hold my peace instead of always having to talk, and a crowd of people takes all the magnetism out of me." Bates admitted: "I don't mind the essential teaching, tho' I abominate 'lecturing,' if only I could teach under a bushel, like a nice grey toad, with time for moonlight excursions in the grass." In spite of her disclaimer, Bates made English literature come alive for many of her students. One student recalled that Bates was "larger than books and bookishness . . . so that in her hands, imaginative works, however old, were as full of new feeling as [a] New England springtime."[4]

Bates did not have any special pedagogic method but constantly created in her classes a fresh outlook just by the vivacity of her imagination and intellect. She taught a basic survey of American literature, for which she wrote *American Literature* in 1897. But she is best remembered for her Elizabethan seminar; in that class students willingly stayed four or five hours instead of the required three. There was no chance for note taking, because she showered her students with Socratic questions. At her best when roused by class discussions, she was "unmatched in repartee." With one sudden, piercing comment she could illuminate a text.[5]

Bates's professional distinction came from her poetry, the most famous of which is "America the Beautiful." She wrote in the Longfellow tradition, and her style was eclipsed in the early twentieth-century by modernists like Amy Lowell, whose work Bates knew and sponsored. Today, Bates ranks with Louise Imogen Guiney as a minor lyricist, but in her prime she was extraordinarily well received. Her poetic humanitarianism inspired college youth of her day: "The Ideal" was a clarion call to the young, summoning them to "rise and follow thy dream." Richard Cabot, who later became famous for his pioneer work in the social ethics of medicine, wrote of this poem that his friends at Harvard felt "every line in it . . . rings true."[6] In "The Remonstrance" Bates exemplified her central creed:

> For none shall walk in perfect white
> Till every soul be clean.

She demonstrated this idealism and concern for people not only in her poetry and in the classroom but within the English department. Her love of the "dear department" allowed her to genuinely cultivate an esprit de corps among its members. Unlike the English department at Harvard, the Wellesley group were good friends and social intimates. Although at times Bates demanded conformity to her ideals, for the most part she allowed members of her department enormous freedom and cultivated their friendships and careers.[7]

Such was the case even with so radical a member as Vida Dutton Scudder. In 1888, Scudder, fresh from her studies at Oxford with William Morris and John Ruskin, began teaching the modern English poets and quickly assumed responsibility for courses in Victorian literature and romanticism, offering a seminar on Browning, Wordsworth, and Shelley. By 1897 the catalog listed a new course, Social Ideals in English Literature, in which she combined her interest in literature with philosophical analysis and social criticism. Treating novels as social documents, with a section devoted to the status of women, Scudder judged this course her most original and important contribution to the department. From it, she produced a book, *Social*

Ideals in English Letters (1898). At times the course was considered so politically radical that the college administration and some faculty balked at its
being offered under the auspices of English. But Katharine Lee Bates
endorsed it. Only once, in 1912, when Scudder participated in the strike in
Lawrence, Massachusetts, did she forfeit the right to teach the course for a
year.[8]

Scudder, a squat figure who almost always dressed in black, was Wellesley's preeminent lecturer. Students remembered her as "indomitable, inspiring, never-to-be forgotten." Like many of her colleagues, she came to the
profession as a novice, insecure about her role. When she began her teaching career, each class filled her with "sheer terror." She conquered these initial fears, but until the end of her career she believed that "anyone who does
not find the process of teaching as alarming as it is exhilarating would better abandon the profession."[9]

Scudder felt the largest puzzle confronting the teacher was learning to
adapt to the varying levels of student abilities and temperaments. Her central pedagogic method was never to ask a question that could be answered
by yes or no. One favorite technique was to have the class quiz her instead
of quizzing the class. She boasted, "When I do it, it works." She always
sought to develop within her students a self-confidence in their powers of
analysis.[10]

In what she termed "liaison" courses (what we might call interdisciplinary ones), Scudder touched on such diverse subjects as religion, art, science, and history, leaving her students dazzled with the breadth of her
knowledge. Mary Gilson, a Scudder devotee, found her transitions from one
subject matter to another "breath-taking, and sometimes a bit of a strain on
a dull imagination." Scudder's proficiency with words could be haunting;
one student recalled: "Those curious fresh cadences, the varying tone for
tart asides, those unwavering solemn periods; the sound lurked in our ears
as we wrote our college papers." Whether speaking to a few girls or in front
of several hundred, she had an "electric fervor."[11]

An active social reformer, Vida Scudder awakened a feeling of social
responsibility in her students. One said: "When you touch her, sparks fly."
The young woman's father reportedly refused to send another daughter to
Wellesley to be so inflamed! After forty years Scudder's zest remained
undimmed. She seemed never to attain a "smug peace of mind or peace of
soul," yet she was careful never to indoctrinate students.[12]

Two other women, Sophie Jewett and Margaret Sherwood, were also central to the English department. Jeannette Marks, a Wellesley graduate who later became an English professor at Mount Holyoke, described studying with them as discovering "what it is to be a student and to love learning somewhat as the ancient Greeks must have loved it." Jewett, a poet, studied nineteenth-century poetry as well as the literature of the fourteenth century, especially English balladry. She produced a masterful version of a fourteenth-century elegy, "The Pearl." Bates remarked that Jewett's work was "like handmade lace whose exquisite quality no Ph.D. machine product can equal."[13] Margaret Sherwood was a reputable scholar in her own right. She began her Wellesley career working on the history of the novel and teaching the prose and poetry of the nineteenth century. Sherwood wrote several novels, many of which employ themes of social radicalism. Later, she concentrated on the English poets of the nineteenth century and developed a seminar on English romanticism. One of her students recalled that studying under her was "an experience of challenging value for life." Another, who took her seminar in the 1920s and then went on to Harvard for a master's in literature, said nothing there equaled Sherwood's class.[14]

Sherwood's disciple in the department, Martha Hale Shackford, was a Wellesley undergraduate who followed in Sherwood's footsteps and got her Ph.D. from Yale. At Wellesley she became a specialist in Renaissance literature. In later years, she taught the Shakespearean seminar that commanded such respect that she became known as the female counterpart to George Kittredge of Harvard.[15]

The handmaiden of English literature was English composition. Although some of the literature faculty also taught writing, the composition courses were mainly handled by Sophie Hart, Laura Emma Lockwood, and Frances Perry. Lockwood, a Milton scholar, had an infallible memory and loved to challenge her students to walk up the highest hill in South Natick reciting *Paradise Lost* from memory. She never forgot a line.[16]

At times Lockwood clashed with Sophie Hart, the senior member of the department and a controversial figure. Stately, with reddish blonde hair, clear blue eyes, and a long, thin neck that gave her a Botticelli-like appearance, Hart dressed in long flowing capes and resembled a medieval lady out of a French tapestry. Although some students bemoaned the fact that she never altered her lecture notes, others were awed by her "exquisite language." One recalled that Hart had the "most differentiated vocabulary we ever heard, it cast a spell on us." The husband of one of Miss Hart's former students recalled that "if she were in the business world her vocabulary would make her a $100,000 a year man." Geraldine Gordon, class of 1901, noted that Hart "knew how to put over what she wanted and how to draw students out." Hart also was a recognized social activist who inspired her students to do something with their lives.[17] Given the special nature of the Department of English Literature, it is not surprising that more Wellesley undergraduates went on to obtain Ph.D.'s in English than students from any other women's college.[18]

Classics and Modern Languages

The staple of the traditional college curriculum was Greek and Latin, and Wellesley was no exception. Greek was not required of entering students until 1881, after which time it became a prerequisite for admission to the Classical Course. Wellesley reached its high point in Greek studies in the 1890s with the appointment of Julia Irvine. But when Irvine became president in 1895 and the elective curriculum was passed, both Latin and Greek were made electives and the number of students studying the classics dropped precipitously.[19]

From 1890 through 1920 the senior professor of Greek was Angie Chapin, whose specialty was the origin and development of Greek drama. In 1906 Chapin became the first woman professor to study at the American Classical School in Athens. In 1889, Katharine May Edwards joined the department to teach Greek, classical philology, and a Homeric seminary. The teaching of Greek syntax was left to Annie Sybil Montague, who studied at the American Classical School in Athens, Radcliffe, and Yale. The appointment of Alice Walton in 1896 enriched the department because she offered a course in classical archaeology.[20]

A rivalry for students existed between the Greek and Latin departments. Katharine Edwards was so hostile toward Latin that she would not permit a Latin dictionary in the Greek office. Latin was offered by two women who reached no particular prominence—Adeline Hawes and Caroline Rebecca Fletcher, both of whom were affiliated with the American School for Classical Studies in Rome. Alice Walton, who taught both Greek and Latin, recalled that Hawes was unstinting in her devotion to the members of Latin, whom she affectionately termed "il departimento." She allowed them to engage in "new and often wild projects" and selflessly applauded even their modest achievements.[21]

Until World War I the most famous and well-attended language courses at Wellesley were offered by the German department. Chaired by Carla Wenckebach and sustained by her disciple, Margarethe Müller, the department introduced hundreds of students to the German language and literature. In 1904, Natalie Wipplinger, who held a Ph.D. from a German university, completed the faculty.[22]

The administration endorsed Wenckebach's innovative teaching methods. She emphasized class discussions in German and wrote her own textbook for the course. Upon Wenckebach's death in 1902 Mary Haskell, class of 1896, wrote that "Fraulein Wenckebach fairly sparkled with vivacity and humour. She never padded a lecture for us, nor threw away a minute nor gave us anything but her best." Haskell acknowledged that students modeled themselves on Wenckebach: "She was brimful of life, thinking life . . . inspiring life, life in achievement."[23]

History and Economics

The history department at Wellesley also revolutionized teaching methods. In 1876, Henry Durant appointed Mary Sheldon (Barnes) as professor of history. Sheldon, along with Lucy Maynard Salmon, Alice Freeman, and Katharine Coman, had studied at the University of Michigan with Charles Kendall Adams. Like her mentor, Sheldon used no textbooks but had sets of primary sources duplicated each week for students. Her seminars focused on discussions of historical problems. When in 1879 Henry Durant forced Sheldon to resign, she was succeeded by Alice Freeman, who also taught history from primary-source documents. But Freeman's rapid rise to the presidency made it impossible for her to continue teaching history, and she promoted her old friend Katharine Coman from a teacher of rhetoric to history.[24]

Tall and queenly looking, with a braided coronet of auburn hair, Katharine Coman was considered one of Wellesley's greatest and most stimulating teachers. She became interested in economic history and wrote two major works in the field: *The Industrial History of the United States,* published in 1905, which was widely used as a textbook for high schools and colleges and which went through eleven editions; and the two-volume *Economic Beginnings of the Far West,* published in 1912. She conducted primary research for this book by traveling with her mother to the West Coast, Alaska, and Hawaii.[25]

In spite of Coman's strengths as a teacher of economic history, the history department suffered a blow when Lucy Maynard Salmon of Vassar rejected Alice Freeman's offer to join the Wellesley faculty. Salmon eventually placed two of her students at Wellesley, Julia Orvis and Edna Moffett, both of whom held Ph.D.'s from Cornell. Orvis, who came to Wellesley in 1899, taught European history, especially the French Revolution and the history of modern Germany. By 1901 Orvis was teaching what was to become her specialty, European diplomatic history. In class, Orvis was an unusually vivid lecturer, speaking from only a few notes. Her mind was so lucid that it seemed as if "a searchlight . . . had been [turned] upon the principal topic in question."[26]

Edna Moffett was hired to teach medieval and Renaissance Europe. Prior to her coming to Wellesley, the department offered only one premodern European history course, a history of Rome. She thus helped to expand the European offerings. Moffett made several discoveries of medieval manuscripts, which she successfully dated. She published few articles, however, and no books. In fact, neither Orvis nor Moffett ever reached the stature of their famous mentor, Lucy Salmon.[27]

After 1900, when Katharine Coman changed to the economics department, Elizabeth Kendall became the real center of the history department. Kendall's education reflects the influence of her father's diplomatic career. During his appointments as American consul in Europe, she studied in Austria, Germany, and France. After an initial period of teaching French and German at Wellesley, she went to Oxford to study history. Returning to her history post at Wellesley in 1885, she proceeded to acquire a law degree from Boston University in 1892 and a master's degree in history from Radcliffe in 1899. In the 1890s Kendall taught English constitutional history and the political history of England and America. In 1894, she and Katharine Coman wrote *The Growth of the English Nation* for the Chautauqua Reading Circle; in 1899 they collaborated again to produce *A History of England for High Schools and Academies.*[28]

Elizabeth Kendall loved to travel. She recorded her extensive travels in China (she was the first Caucasian woman to cross Tibet) in *A Wayfarer in China* (1911). For her exploits she was elected a Fellow to the Royal Geographical Society. Her love of the international scene inspired her to create courses on the growth of the British Empire, which included segments on India, the Near East, and the Far East.[29]

Kendall was ahead of her times not only because she was internationally oriented as a historian but also because she held distinctly radical social and political views. One of her students, Molly Dewson, a nationally prominent social reformer and New Deal activist, wrote Kendall: "You were a real influence in my life, one of the milestones." Kendall's course on English constitutional history enjoyed great popularity. At the end of the first semester, students staged a Parliamentary debate, complete with wigs and robes.[30]

Political Economy and Economics

In 1883, the *Wellesley College Calendar* started listing a course in political economy taught by Katharine Coman. By 1887, Coman had built a two-part course: the first-term students read the works of John Stuart Mill, Alfred Marshall, and Francis Amasa Walker; the second term consisted of a study of social problems by means of lectures and special investigations of industrial conditions. In most colleges, political economy emerged from the moral philosophy curriculum. But at Wellesley, because of Coman's influence and interest, political economy was rooted in the historical school. Whereas at Harvard economics was studied as a scientifically closed, theoretical system, at Wellesley economics embraced social study and veered away from the peculiar concerns of economic theory.[31]

Coman's courses in political economy demanded a large amount of independent work. She used no textbooks; instead she provided outlines and references from authoritative writers. She lectured when necessary but felt students should be left to master much of the readings on their own. By 1894, Coman was offering courses in economic theory that included a study of contemporary theories of industrial relations. She also offered a course in the historical development of socialism in which students read selections from Jean-Jacques Rousseau, Charles Fourier, Robert Owen, and Karl Marx. She pioneered a course in the Statistical Study of Certain Economic Problems, encouraging students to learn how to produce statistical economic models like those offered by the U.S. Census, the Census of Massachusetts, and the U.S. Labor Bureau.[32]

Coman's interest in industrial relations was not merely academic. She applied her economic training to helping investigate and solve problems of women workers, consumers, and immigrants. She took a personal interest in her students. Gail Laughlin, Molly Dewson, and Harriet Rice are among those whose later careers testify to Coman's impact on their lives.[33] Rice, who became a doctor and was one of the first black women to graduate from a woman's college, wrote Coman in 1913: "I was a 'Wellesley girl' in the days of 'personal influence.' . . . I often think that the values of a teacher's life . . . are not measured wholly by the numbers of her special pupils or by the knowledge or renown which she or they may win along her special line of work; but also by the unseen and immeasurable effect of her daily walk and work upon the many lives she is bound to touch. . . . I confess that many a small kindness received at your hands . . . made a far more lasting impression on my young girlhood than many pages of history. . . . I would part sooner with much than with my lovely and abiding memories of you."[34]

Coman's disciple in economics was Emily Greene Balch, who had an intense, driving energy coupled with a devastating intellectual curiosity. Having studied with William Ashley at Harvard and Gustav Schmoller at the University of Berlin, Balch became interested in the historical approach to economics. Influenced by her mentors and her work with Coman, Balch lost her initial fascination with Adam Smith and abandoned abstract economic theory for the inductive method of German historicism. Thus both she and Coman taught economics from a historical and sociological viewpoint. In 1906, Balch declared herself a socialist.[35]

More than one hundred students at a time enrolled in Balch's courses in social economics. In part one of these courses she studied the "defective, dependent and delinquent classes"; in part two, the "methods of meeting normal social needs like sanitation, housing, education, recreation and leisure." In 1899, Balch inherited Coman's course in socialism and chose to emphasize the study of German scientific socialism. Another innovative course was her study of immigration, in which she explored ideas compiled in her book *Our Slavic Citizens* (1910). The book uniquely presented a firsthand account of an immigrant community and also countered much of the prejudice against the new immigrants of the time.[36]

In consumption economics, which Balch offered for the first time in 1908, she explored in detail contemporary American women's roles as "wives, administrators, industrial inventors, parasites, conspicuous spenders, wasters, and custodians of the race." The reading list included Charlotte Perkins Gilman's *Women and Economics,* as well as works by Thorstein Veblen, Ellen Swallow Richards, Edith Abbott, Dorothy Richardson, and Balch herself. None of the men's colleges in the United States offered such a course, and its duplicate probably did not exist at many other women's colleges.[37]

In all of her courses Emily Balch emphasized fieldwork. She took field trips to immigrant neighborhoods in Boston's North End, to factories, and to prisons. The college once received letters from parents protesting that she was taking their daughters to investigate brothels! Besides her involvement in Denison House Settlement, she became a cofounder and president of the Boston Women's Trade Union League (1902), supporting striking workers and speaking out against class exploitation. This activism infused her courses with a contagious enthusiasm.[38]

Nonetheless, Emily Balch had a mixed reputation as a teacher. Although many considered her brilliant, her lectures were sometimes too abstract for her students. Also, she would sometimes forget to show up for classes because she was so engrossed in a study of social conditions in Boston. Still, she taught her students to think. And when she presented statistical data, she "never lost sight of the individual involved or affected by the figures."[39]

Balch aimed to have her students examine the social order critically and to make themselves serviceable to society. She had a good sense of humor and for the most part was patient with students who were not as intellectual as she. Like Vida Scudder, Balch tried hard not to propagate her social views among students. One of her students noted that "it was impossible to decide from her classroom presentation which 'side' she considered 'correct,' or in which she believed."[40]

Philosophy and Psychology

As in many colleges, Wellesley at its founding offered seniors a year-long study of mental and moral philosophy, a topic traditionally at the heart of the classical curriculum.[41] Mary Sophia Case, who came to Wellesley in 1888, studied Hegel on her own and eventually became expert enough to teach a seminar in Hegelian philosophy. In later years she taught a variety of social ethics courses, thus making her philosophically consonant with her colleagues in literature and economics. But Case's greatest contribution to philosophy was her sponsorship of Wellesley's most stellar professor, Mary Whiton Calkins.[42]

Calkins established a psychological laboratory in the college, one of the first dozen in the United States and the first in a woman's college. It began in a one-room attic with two hundred dollars' worth of equipment. Calkins almost single-handedly taught all of the psychology offerings and directed the laboratory until 1898, when she was joined by Eleanor McCulloch Gamble. By that time, the laboratory had expanded to five attic rooms; in 1906 Calkins noted that it was housed in six rooms and had "moderately good equipment for beginners and a few good pieces for advanced investigations." A steady stream of publications flowed from this laboratory. Most of the studies appearing between 1893 and 1916 were the work of undergraduates supervised by Calkins and, later, Gamble. Fifteen masters' degrees were awarded to women who had worked in experimental psychology. During this period, Calkins herself also published numerous studies on color theory, time, space, and children's dreams. As an empiricist she demonstrated the existence of dreams and examined their manifest content rather than analyzing them, as did Freud.[43]

With the arrival of Gamble, Calkins happily left experimental work behind and began to direct her energies toward her long-standing interest in philosophy. She became recognized as the most prominent pupil of Josiah Royce, an idealist. Rejecting behaviorism and materialism, she believed that the universe is mental in nature and that ideas cannot be treated apart from the selves that conceive them. Her most important book, *The Persistent Problems of Philosophy,* appeared in 1907.[44]

During her career as teacher and administrator, Calkins produced four books and well over one hundred papers. In 1903, Calkins placed twelfth on a list of the fifty most distinguished psychologists in the United States. In spite of her rigorous research schedule, she put great emphasis on teaching. She claimed that the main virtue of the lecture system is that of economy and a "summing-up method." Like other members of the Wellesley faculty, Calkins emphasized independent reading courses and small tutorials. Yet even in large courses she devised ways of engaging students in fruitful discussion: "I think that one may lecture for a while, and notice somebody that looks interested and ask for a question, and then ask a question of one's own."[45]

Completely devoted to her teaching, Calkins kept a sign on her office that read: "Office hours daily from 7 A.M. to 10 P.M. and at other times by appointment." She commuted daily to the college from Newton, where she lived with her parents, yet never missed a lecture. Students appreciated her extraordinary commitment to them, coupled as it was with an intense dedication to research and publishing. They admired her also for combining an interest in political and social activism.[46]

Between 1901 and 1908 Ethel Puffer taught the philosophy of aesthetics. Like Calkins she had attended graduate school in psychology at Harvard, where she also studied with Münsterberg and Royce. At Wellesley, she is most remembered for her course on aesthetics. While teaching, she published *The Psychology of Beauty* (1905), which she used in her classes and which was adopted widely in American colleges. Puffer's work in the field of aesthetics theory places her as a forerunner to contemporary philosopher Susanne Langer.[47]

Education

Wellesley had been founded explicitly to upgrade the teaching profession, and it carried out this mission in developing a department of education. In 1887, President Freeman convinced Carla Wenckebach to offer a course in the fundamentals of pedagogy; by 1890, a department had been formed. The program covered both theoretical and practical components of the subject: the theoretical covered educational philosophy and the study of the child; the practicum gave particular attention to the kindergarten system and the methods of instruction in primary and secondary grades. Students who enrolled in such courses taught lessons and were criticized by their instructors and classmates. By 1895, the pedagogy department was offering courses in the history of educational theories and teaching methods. These courses were always coupled with course work in appropriate academic disciplines such as science, art, or history.[48]

In 1902 Anna Jane McKeag, who held a Ph.D. in psychology from the University of Pennsylvania, became an instructor in pedagogy; in 1909 she was made a professor of the history and principles of education. While teaching, she also studied under G. Stanley Hall and William Henry Burnham at Clark University. Three times president of the New England Society of College Teachers, she was also president of the New England Association of Colleges and Secondary Schools. In 1912, she was called to the presidency of her alma mater, Wilson College. Staying only three years at Wilson, which was rife with financial problems, McKeag returned to Wellesley and served as a full professor of education until 1932.[49]

The Sciences

Wellesley exceeded all other women's colleges in the number of distinguished women scientists it employed. In 1906, Wellesley had fourteen such scientists, while its nearest rival, Mount Holyoke, had eight. Twenty-five years later, Wellesley still led, twenty-two to fifteen, over Vassar.[50] Fourteen Wellesley professors earned listings in several editions of James Cattell's *American Men of Science*. It surpassed even the men's colleges in the East in having first-rate laboratories where students could conduct their own investigations. Although pioneering work in botany had been done at women's seminaries like Troy and Mount Holyoke, Wellesley was the first women's college in the world to have a separate chair of botany and one of only five colleges in the United States with a separate department.[51]

Susan Hallowell employed modern research methods. She emphasized laboratory work in subjects like histology and photogenesis, reversing the tradition of merely cataloguing specimens.[52] Hallowell's most famous protégée was Margaret Clay Ferguson, who studied at Wellesley from 1888 to 1891. While there she was classified as a special student (one who was allowed to study without taking a degree), but she went on to attend Cornell, where she earned a B.S. in 1899 and a Ph.D. in 1901. Returning to Wellesley in 1901, Ferguson worked on plant life histories. She was a painstaking observer and illustrator, and her study of native pine was published in 1904 by the Washington Academy of Sciences. Ferguson helped make the Wellesley botany department an undergraduate center for the study of plant science. With the support of Caroline Hazard, Ferguson planned and designed the college greenhouses and a new botany building.[53]

Hallowell trained two other women who served in the department. Grace Cooley spent three years (1881–83) as an undergraduate at Wellesley and then immediately became an instructor in botany. She stayed at Wellesley until 1904, rising to the rank of associate professor. Clara Eaton Cummings was better known. Born in 1855, Cummings was more a peer of Hallowell than a disciple. She attended Wellesley from 1876 to 1879, becoming curator of the botanical museum in 1878 and then an instructor in botany. In 1904 she was made professor of cryptogamic botany, a post she held until her death in 1906. She was internationally recognized for her contributions to lichenology. Both of these women were overshadowed, however, by the research-oriented Ferguson.[54]

An emphasis on observation and experimentation prevailed in the zoology department. In 1878 Henry Durant had appointed Emily Nunn to the chair in zoology, but Nunn was either too eccentric, too independent, or too agnostic for Durant, who terminated her contract in 1881. Looking for a replacement, he found Mary Alice Willcox. Durant sponsored Willcox's training in Cambridge, England, but did not live to appoint her officially to the Wellesley faculty. In 1883, Willcox joined the faculty under President

Freeman and began to build what became one of the foremost departments in the country. Willcox was to become an outstanding malacologist with impeccable credentials.[55]

She tailored her courses to students preparing for medical school. In the 1890s, several zoology courses were listed as meeting the biology requirements of the Johns Hopkins Medical School. After visiting two eastern medical colleges for women, Willcox concluded that dissection opportunities were extremely limited. She returned to Wellesley "hot with indignation," determined that her students begin medical school with some firsthand knowledge of mammalian physiology. She therefore initiated a course on the cat, bred rabbits to demonstrate placental circulation, and got permission to go with her classes to the Harvard Medical Museum to study the differences between humans and other mammals. Her one-year course in laboratory physiology included four hours of lab work weekly. At Harvard, the comparable course had only one hour of lab work.[56]

The department's most prominent researcher, Caroline Rebecca Burling Thompson, was a leading authority on termites. Her laboratories at Wellesley were run with "contagious enthusiasm." Mary Collett, class of 1910, recalled that Thompson introduced her students to scientific problems that they might someday hope to solve and helped them gain self-confidence and independence. Never harsh or patronizing, Thompson offered her students good-humored criticism. With Thompson's death in 1921 the department suffered a setback.[57]

A similar meteoric rise followed by a decline characterized the Department of Chemistry. Henry Durant's interest in chemistry is evident in the early curriculum. In 1876–77 students could elect chemistry in their junior and senior years. By 1879, there were still two years of chemistry offered for juniors and seniors within the General College Course: qualitative analysis and chemical theories. Students participated with professors in chemical experiments and were instructed in the use of the spectroscope and compound microscope. Because it was expected that many of the students would eventually teach chemistry, they were required to conduct both lectures and experiments.[58]

The first professor of chemistry was Maria Eaton, who held the post from 1876 to 1886 and about whom very little is known. In 1881, Charlotte Fitch Roberts, a Wellesley graduate, joined the department as an instructor. In 1886 she was promoted to associate professor, a rank she held when she went to Yale for a Ph.D., becoming the first woman in the

United States to obtain the degree. Graduating in 1894, she attained a full professorship and taught general chemistry, organic chemistry, and her specialty, stereochemistry.[59]

The other professor of chemistry was Charlotte Almira Bragg, whose course in general and theoretical chemistry was so intellectually rigorous that her students were credited for it in lieu of a corresponding graduate course in the Women's Medical College of New York Infirmary. Bragg was a devoted teacher and administrator who taught thirty-nine years without interruption. Helen French, a Bragg disciple, calculated that Bragg had taught chemistry to fifteen hundred freshmen. Bragg's classroom was considered "a joyous homeland for those who worked hard, but a bit forbidding to any stray loafers."[60]

Bragg contributed more as a teacher and mentor than she did as a researcher. She recognized her deficiencies and took pride in announcing that other members of the department were working on research projects at MIT and Harvard. Nonetheless, the Wellesley chemistry department, which had been extraordinarily well endowed at the start, soon fell behind. From the 1890s until 1925, reports of the chair enumerated the limitations of the department, focusing on the need for a new building. As a result, Wellesley never reached the distinction of the Mount Holyoke chemistry department, lacking Holyoke's *esprit de corps* and producing fewer Ph.D.'s. As in the case of the zoology department, however, the chemistry department took pride in fostering the careers of many women doctors.[61]

Marion Talbot came to Wellesley in 1890 to introduce a course in domestic science. Although it was rigorous—knowledge of chemistry and physics was a prerequisite—the course met with little faculty enthusiasm. In 1891, Talbot left Wellesley for the University of Chicago, where she taught the course under the auspices of the Department of Sociology. After Talbot's departure, the course was listed as "not offered" and then dropped.[62]

Wellesley was quite advanced in the field of physics. In 1876, Sarah Frances Whiting set up an experimental physics laboratory in College Hall—the second such laboratory in the country and the first for women. Three male benefactors aided her endeavor: Henry Durant, Edward Pickering, and Eben Horsford. Durant insisted on having experimental laboratory facilities at Wellesley, even though they required costly apparatus and in many instances had to be made to order. With introductions from Durant,

Whiting attended physics lectures at MIT given by Edward Pickering, who took an interest in Whiting's career and advised her on how to equip the laboratory. As a result, physics soon became one of Wellesley's outstanding offerings.[63]

Whiting attempted to open the research laboratories of America's major industries to women with physics training, but her efforts met with little success. Although a few female physics graduates were hired as researchers in industrial chemistry and bacteriology, most were forced to teach. Reluctantly, Whiting responded by developing courses in how to teach physics and astronomy in secondary schools. Before physics became an elective in 1895, over twenty-five hundred women took the course.[64] In 1879, having been invited by Pickering to view the new applications of physics to astronomy at the Harvard Observatory, Whiting introduced a course in astronomy, using only a celestial globe and a four-inch portable telescope as teaching aids. In 1900 her friend Mrs. John C. Whitin, a Wellesley trustee, advanced the study of physics at Wellesley by endowing the college with an observatory that housed a twelve-inch refracting telescope with spectroscope and photometer attachment. The new facilities enabled Whiting and her students to contribute to the new work on stellar spectra. Although Wellesley's astronomy department was overshadowed by Maria Mitchell's world-famous department at Vassar, it produced a sizable number of teachers and a few notable scholars, such as Annie Jump Cannon.[65]

Ellen Hayes, a professor of applied mathematics who also did graduate work at the University of Virginia in astronomy, taught several courses in the astronomy department, including mathematical astronomy, theoretical mechanics, theoretical astronomy, and the theory of orbits. In 1888, while at Virginia, Hayes had defined the orbit of a minor planet, for which she was included in Cattell's *American Men of Science*. Although Hayes had only a handful of students in her rigorous courses, one of these testified to Hayes's extraordinary "mental integrity."[66]

Mathematics

Members of the pure mathematics department never really achieved prominence outside the college. Although two professors, Helen Shafer and Ellen Fitz Pendleton, ascended to the presidency of Wellesley, the mathematics faculty were noted mainly for their good teaching. Helen Shafer trained three disciples—Ellen Burrell, Helen Merrill, and Ellen Fitz Pendleton—who were all good friends. Burrell, who became head of the department after Hayes was forced out, completely dominated it, requiring members to adhere to her ideals. She rejected the use of outside texts, favoring instead materials produced from within the department. Before leaving Wellesley she cautioned the incoming chair, Helen Merrill, to relegate all published texts written by men to a reading shelf: "Let the students regard your own lectures as the backbone and ribs of the course." As a result of this emphasis, the department produced a number of textbooks.[67]

Toward a Women-Centered Curriculum

The Wellesley faculty reinvigorated a declining liberal culture curriculum in the late nineteenth century. Far from mindlessly imitating the men's colleges, the faculty forged a creative link between the humanities, social science, and social reform. In addition to introducing students to the latest research and teaching methods, they addressed the important issue of women in the professions.

Some historians of higher education have condemned pioneering academic women for adhering to traditional ideals about the nature of women; others have accused them of disregarding women's special place in society and have assumed they lacked a feminist consciousness. One will never find a statement of women's studies courses in any Wellesley catalog written during the Progressive Era, but it is not true that the faculty merely mimicked the men's curriculum and remained oblivious to questions concerning women's roles, status, and power. Indeed, their concern for women's educational and professional status caused them to create courses in which women were the subjects of study—for example, in literature and economics. A sizable number of Wellesley's courses required that students read women authors. The faculty also focused on women in their own writings, namely, their novels, plays, poems, and literary criticism. Thus the informal curriculum at Wellesley was also feminist.[68]

Interestingly, just as the women's studies programs of the present are beset with tensions, there were frictions in the 1900s. Although Wellesley faculty tailored their courses to suit women students, they rejected a specifically sex-differentiated curriculum. At the time, antifeminists demanded a special education based on their vision of educated women's future domestic roles. The Wellesley faculty's high career expectations for their students meant that they rejected what M. Carey Thomas termed a "geisha" education, because they believed women were men's intellectual equals.[69]

Mary Calkins refused to stereotype either men or women. She rejected any discussion of a distinctive course of study for women, commenting that favoring such a curriculum is very much like advocating a specific diet. "Is it not, in a word, as futile to differentiate feminine from masculine studies as to distinguish between women's and men's foods?" Calkins published a number of experiments aimed at refuting ideas about sex differences in the mind, using women students as her subjects. In one early study she compared the "mathematical consciousness" of students from Harvard and Wellesley and discovered no difference between them. When in 1891 Joseph Jastrow, a psychologist at the University of Wisconsin, reported that a study of male and female college students revealed the existence of innate feminine and masculine traits, Calkins attempted to replicate the study but found no evidence for Jastrow's findings. Debating him in print, she argued that so-called innate sex differences resulted from differential sex-role training and expectations that begin in the earliest months of infancy and continue through life.[70]

Perhaps the most strident feminist was Ellen Hayes, who constantly cautioned against speaking in terms of innate sex differences. In 1910, Hayes published a retort to James Cattell's conclusion that since few women were found eligible for inclusion in his *American Men of Science* there were signs of an "innate sexual disqualification." Hayes argued that the only distinct differences involved the ways boys and girls were socialized: "Who concerns themselves with taking a girl to the blacksmith shop, the powerhouse, and the stone-quarry?" Rather, girls were given dolls to play with and were treated as ornaments. Unable to recognize the insidiousness of this sexism, scientists and educators continued to advance "theories about feminine predilections." Hayes questioned how many brilliant men would be strongly inclined to devote themselves to science if confronted with dire statistics, as were women, as to how few would achieve high-ranking academic posts.[71]

The Wellesley faculty took pride in preparing women for careers. For faculty women like Vida Scudder, teaching was like an "initiation rite." She proclaimed: "What a joy to lead the neophyte to the altar of her consecration, with her tiny flame alit!"[72]

At Wellesley, "Non Ministrari sed Ministrare" (Not to Be Served but To Serve) was more than an ideal affixed to a college seal. Ruth Sapin Hurwitz, class of 1910, defined her "Coming of Age at Wellesley" as an intellectual growth that resulted from working with teachers who turned out students "consciously faithful to the ideals of the founder."[73]

11

Daughters of My Spirit
Faculty-Student Interactions

*My own darling Mary: But now I am ready—I hope—for home
and the last lap of teaching—only 2 years more of it! And how
I've loved it, and how badly I've done it! But it brought me you,
and many other daughters of my spirit. . . . Most lovingly, Mother
Vida*

—Vida D. Scudder to Mary Gibson

But as life architects we must have our models.
—Tree Day Oration, Class of 1888

During the early years of the college, the faculty promoted visionary educational principles, teaching practices, and curriculum
reform, all of which advanced the lives of their students. The influence of the faculty, however, extended far beyond the classroom.
Students also felt a combination of awe, admiration, and attachment toward these women whose ideals and patterns of living they
wished to emulate.

This closeness was often strengthened by the fact that the first
faculty were hardly much older than the first group of students.
Katharine Lee Bates, in paying tribute to Eva Chandler and Elizabeth Kendall, her former Wellesley teachers who later became her
colleagues, hinged her tribute on "three catch-words: Seventies
[1870s], Subjects, Symbols." She noted: "We were juniors . . . when
the girl from the western university slipped into the faculty; seniors

when the girl from England . . . made her shy appearance. . . . So our relation to them was nearer that of playmates than of pupils." In 1898 Betsy Manwaring, a freshman, wrote home to her parents: "My Latin teacher is Miss Fletcher. The girls just about worship her. She is just like a girl herself; very jolly and kind. I couldn't stand in awe of her if I tried."[1]

This camaraderie is seen, for example, in the *Annals,* an annual student newsletter. In 1884 it reported with glee: "And Miss Coman is Prof. Coman. Great was the joy and pride of her History Classes at the news; and under her window the entire Junior Class, including the latest honorary member, rendered their choicest selections in music and flowers, until the selections gave out and Stone Hall's doors opened to the minstrels. Dr. McKenzie's suggestion that she should not be called Professor of *History* since in this case it was " '*Herstory,*' " was received with applause."[2]

This celebration of the promotion of a woman professor also conveys the particular self-consciousness about women's status that characterizes the early generations of Wellesley students. The classes in the 1880s and 1890s were keenly aware of the history of women's exclusion from higher education and knew that they were privileged to attend college. In their poems, plays, and prose essays they expressed feminist sentiments and referred to famous women in history. Annie D. Rhea captures this in her poem "Woman," when she states that in the past

> women untaught could never be
> What they might be now if they will
> Believe in themselves and work until
> They learn what their brothers learn,
> and full equality earn.[3]

The students in the closing decades of the nineteenth century clearly showed a sensitivity to women's powers and the need for models. Inspired and taught by such faculty as Elizabeth Kendall, Katharine Coman, and Ellen Hayes, the graduating classes of the 1880s and 1890s were immersed in women's history; they linked their lives with those of other talented women. At their Tree Day Oration, the class of 1888 spoke of their belief in the significance of women in the past and cited important women from European and American history. "To see that through the proven ability of these women we have the greater chance to prove our ability." The oration stated that it was not mere interest or gratitude that led students to see notable women as the "high water marks of their day and generation." The class felt they had to sustain women's efforts. "Their lives are over: they are far from perfect. Their work is begun: to finish it is left for other hands than theirs. Some among us there will be to take the broken, scattered strands and weave them into the perfect whole."[4] This philosophy was prescient, for the class of 1888 produced several achievers: teachers, ministers, school principals, and lawyers. The most notable was Sophonisba Breckinridge, who acquired a Ph.D. and a law degree and went on to help found the School of Social Work at the University of Chicago. At their thirtieth reunion in 1918, this same class spoke with pride of being the "burden-bearing generation" whose motto was "not for ourselves."[5]

Clubs and Causes

From the 1880s through the 1900s, faculty and students jointly initiated a number of clubs and social reform projects that brought a common purpose to their relationships. In the 1880s, there were several societies: Zeta Alpha, Phi Sigma, Shakespeare, Beethoven, and Microscopical. There were also clubs devoted to the study of Browning and Dickens. One alumna recalled that Zeta Alpha and Phi Sigma (the literary societies) took themselves very seriously and "for recreation" discussed such themes as "Transcendentalism, Evolution, Higher Education of Women, [and] Darwinism." When the entire college was invited to public forums, the level of their eloquent oratory was said to "put to shame a U.S. Senate."[6]

The Microscopical Society, which was started by Henry Durant and Sarah Frances Whiting, pursued all sorts of scientific investigations using the microscope. Each member was required to spend an hour a week doing research. The constitution noted that students who wished to join merely for pleasure and entertainment would find themselves without a place. "Better a society with but ten earnest, working numbers than five times that number of the indifferent." Beginning in 1879, the society mainly invited guests from Boston to deliver papers. In the 1880s faculty such as Grace Cooley, Ellen Hayes, Grace Davis, Mary Alice Willcox, and Clara Eaton Cummings delivered lectures on Darwin and on research possibilities open to women in England.[7]

This society was tinged by a social reform ethos. In April 1886, Boston ornithologists delivered a talk on the destruction of birds in the interest of fashion and informed the audience that it would take two or three generations before the woods and orchards would be repopulated with singing birds. Wellesley women needed to concern themselves with the consumption habits of millions of American women who were purchasing bonnets, shawls, and gowns that had been made out of bird skin. With humor, the *Courant* of April 22, 1886, reported that "several birds which came into the chapel on hats came out rolled up out of sight in handkerchiefs."[8]

Wellesley faculty were inextricably involved in the College Settlement Movement and used that experience to energize their classrooms and their students. Settlement houses, located in slums, were centers for the diagnosis of urban problems; settlement workers established programs in education, nutrition, and recreation. Vida Scudder, in particular, took an active leadership in the movement. After graduating from Smith, she had tried along with two other women to open a settlement in New York. When this failed, she brought the idea to Wellesley, where her colleagues supported the project.[9]

At the first annual meeting of the College Settlements Association (CSA) in 1890, Scudder argued that the settlement reflected educated women's "responsibility towards the social needs of the times and their faith in the method of friendship and personal communion, as the most direct mode of ministering to that need."[10] That year the membership of Wellesley faculty in the CSA outnumbered that of Smith, Vassar, and Bryn Mawr. Wellesley also led the list of financial donors, with contributions of $267.50.[11]

In 1891, Wellesley College opened a chapter of the College Settlements Association. Testifying to the impact of faculty on this decision is a student report from the previous year that stated: "We, who have listened to the glowing reports of Miss Coman and Miss Scudder, cannot but hope that we, too, may be of some use in a similar form of work in our own city."[12]

John Rousmaniere finds that a high proportion of classmates from Wellesley and Smith entered the college settlements. Rousmaniere interprets this as peer group influence and a quest for a stable home in a world filled with hostility toward well-educated women. For him, this is how women graduates, particularly at these two schools, solved their "After college, what?" identity conflict. But it may simply have been the depth of faculty commitment and their capacity to recruit disciples that made Wellesley and Smith students so active in the CSA.[13]

Wellesley was also active in the National Consumers' League, an organization committed to prevent the evils of the sweatshop. Founded in 1902, the Wellesley chapter was one of only five local leagues. Professors Coman and Calkins, members of the Massachusetts Consumers' League, were active in founding and guiding this local chapter.[14]

The Wellesley chapter regularly invited Florence Kelley, the national chair, to speak. An article entitled "The Spectator," written by a student for the *Wellesley Magazine*, detailed the working conditions of hundreds of men and women in the garment industry in Boston and urged consumers to purchase only goods with the league's label. The student advocate argued that because merchants depended on sales to Wellesley girls, the students could "make our influence a power, and force them to find it to their advantage also to place on their counters honest goods which have been made under conditions of which we need not be ashamed."[15]

In her memoir *What's Past Is Prologue,* economist and reformer Mary Gilson recalled being inspired by one of Kelley's visits to Wellesley. Gilson and a friend decided to help a worthy cause and spent a day in Boston chiding clerks in stores that sold unlabeled goods. The two women finally purchased underskirts and corset covers that bore the label. Gilson notes: "They were clumsy and coarse and ugly, but we unctuously displayed them to our unregenerate friends, conscious of having performed a noble duty in the interests of the working class."[16]

There were other political and social reform clubs on campus. In 1891, Academic Council gave official recognition to the Agora Society, which grew out of a small freshman club, The Cottage Street Political. Gail Laughlin, its leader, later distinguished herself as a lawyer and feminist. Discussions centered around political issues such as the protective tariff, free trade, and women's rights.

Agora demonstrates that students were sympathetic to the new ideals of womanhood promulgated by the faculty. The society was committed to helping students confront national problems and to keeping them in touch with international politics. Agora attempted to create a "higher ideal of womanhood, which shall lead them [students], throughout their lives, to work for their country, for their fellow-men and women."[17]

Several faculty were ongoing members of Agora. Records show that in the mock House of Commons held on February 15, 1896, the whips of the several parties were all faculty: Dr. Roberts, Miss Woolley, Miss Calkins, Miss Edwards, Miss Pendleton, and Miss Kendall.[18]

Debates, mock conventions, political rallies, and elections were the trademark of Agora. In 1901, Agora arranged a rally for William McKinley. On election day, polling booths were installed on the first floor of College Hall and "the voting was conducted with the strictest observance of the law." After McKinley's assassination, Agora again sponsored a mock convention of the Republican Party. The barn was decorated with flags, music played, and convention members wore blue badges. Chairman Elihu Root called the convention to order. Planks were offered on behalf of American labor, emigration, the Isthmus Canal, and international arbitration. Students nominated Theodore Roosevelt for president and Charles Fairbanks for vice-president. Such student simulations of national elections were common during this era.[19]

These mock elections are a companion to the faculty's emphasis on citizenship: they seem geared to preparing women for getting the vote. A decennial reunion poem written by a member of the class of 1894 self-consciously conveys this ethos:

> A class there was by Waban's shore, '94, '94,
> Its like was never seen before, never seen before;
> It took a dose of Pol. Econ.,
>   And women's rights it lectured on,
> It studied Parliamentary law, 'mentary law, 'mentary law,
> It could debate without a flaw on everything it saw.
> This class did found the Agora, Agora, Agora
> *Where a girl could vote just like her Pa, Vote just like her Pa;*
>   It mixed itself in politics.
>   Election speeches made prolix.[20]

The society argued the need for suffrage in March 1896 and again in 1900.

Agora clearly reflects the influence of Elizabeth Kendall, who held a law degree from Boston University and who taught parliamentary law. And it offered students another route to camaraderie with the faculty. In 1901, the newsletter recorded that Miss Coman had entertained Agorites: "Gathered around the blazing fire we talked of Queen Victoria and read aloud some of the beautiful things the poets had said about her noble life."[21]

The Faculty as Models

Throughout the period 1880–1910 students revered the faculty. Letters home reveal that students were awestruck by these remarkable women. One alumna spoke of the faculty as "aspiring women" who created high-achieving disciples through personal relationships. The faculty's belief in learning through friendship and informality seems to have successfully taken root.

Geraldine Gordon, class of 1900, commented in an oral interview conducted in 1975, "Students now . . . don't know the faculty as people, but we sat at their table three meals a day—and you get to know people that way."[22] In explaining the ambiance at her table, Louise Sherwood McDowell wrote her mother that much of it was due to the assigned teacher, Miss Locke, "a new member of the faculty and a *minister*. She is very jolly, however, and doesn't remind me painfully of the pulpit." McDowell noted that "she is exceeding tall, and looks quite stiff and awkward enough to be a minister." McDowell was thrilled to see her professor "climbing stone walls and crawling through holes in the fences when we were on our tramp [looking for chestnuts] yesterday."[23] Female sociability and the shared sense of intellectual life is conveyed in a letter written by Betsy Manwaring in 1898. She noted with pleasure that Miss Hubbard, the faculty member at her table, asked her what she was reading and offered to lend her some books. Manwaring accompanied Hubbard to her lovely room, whereupon Hubbard heaped her arms with works to choose from. Manwaring wrote: "I told her I loved books and she said she knew that by the way I handled them and looked at them. Finally, I chose some and she told me to come for more when those were finished, for she would be delighted to lend them."[24]

Another night at her Table, Manwaring was told by one of the teachers, Dr. Cooley, that she reminded her of another faculty woman. She was "wild to know which one, for there are faculty—and faculty!" She finally learned it was Miss Bates, "who is one of the heads of the English Department here, as well as an authoress" and felt really proud when "Miss Morgan said that I might feel complimented for she [Bates] was lovely." Soon Manwaring eagerly looked forward to the sophomore reception when the sophomores took the faculty to the dance. She was to dance with four faculty in a row; hardly intimidated, she was ecstatic, "for the Faculty here are 'super-mellow gorgeous.'"[25]

Manwaring was not alone in adulating the faculty. An alumna of 1895 phrased it this way: "Our professors were a truly grand, and even great galaxy." And in 1896, the class wrote that "the 'new woman' is best personified in: Prof. Webster; Mrs. Alice Freeman Palmer; Mrs. Irvine; Dr. Ritchie; Miss Scudder; Miss Hayes; Miss Hill; Miss Wilcox on [a bicycle] wheel." Grace Cook, class of 1899, fondly recalled the "enduring influence" of the "great women and fine teachers . . . names to conjure with."[26]

Students understood that faculty and alumnae were part of a new womanhood engaged in shaping modern cultural roles for women. On June 10,

1897, for example, Mary Gilson wrote to ask her parents if she could stay at Wellesley until commencement. "We girls thought it would be fun to stay and see all the old alumnae, Woman's Suffrage freaks, dress reformers, and old maids flock around here." In response to the idea of having more men on campus Gilson wrote: "I am perfectly content to be in this so-called Adamless Eden."[27]

It was not only the heady life of the mind that was shared, however. The faculty were reputed for their wit and, at times, their abandon. Ellen Hayes was complimented for the frivolity she displayed when she received some mathematical objects and treated them as toys. She also liked to frolic with freshmen, playing tag.[28] In 1898, Betsy Manwaring wrote her parents about Halloween: "It is too funny to see how sociable the faculty are with the students. Miss Hart, our English instructor, was meandering about in the crowd, in full ghost costume like any of us, and Fraulein Habermeyer, the dignified, was amusing herself by poking up our masks to find out who we were." Manwaring was thrilled when the faculty who resided at College Hall gave a farce for the benefit of the students. The usually serious President Irvine and Dean Stratton became performers in a bogus mandolin club.[29]

Admiration for women faculty and the closeness of this female-centered world lasted well into the 1910s. In November 1912, Mary Rosa excitedly wrote her mother that she had dined with one of the psychology professors, Miss Gamble, who resembled "a second Samuel Johnson in unkempt appearance." Rosa added: "We had lots of fun as she is not a bit terrifying, and very funny. We discussed everything from Faculty love-affairs to forensic burning."[30]

Respectable Spinsterhood

Although Wellesley students saw marriage and children as a perfectly reasonable choice in life, so, too, was remaining single and having a career. Spinsterhood was a respectable option for Wellesley faculty and, apparently, their students.

Several demographers and social historians have commented on the low marriage rates among the graduates of women's colleges between 1885 and 1905. Mary Cookingham notes that rates were high up until 1885 and then declined in the period 1885–1905, only to rise again after 1905. At Wellesley, for example, she explains this V-shaped pattern that characterized many women's colleges by the increase in economic opportunity for college

women between 1885 and 1905, arguing that college women could expect
to earn more money and to enter occupations previously closed to them.
Women displayed rational economic behavior in passing up marriage,
because during this same era men experienced a drop in income owing to
an economic depression. Cookingham concludes that "spinsterhood . . .
became a viable lifestyle, associated with financial independence, social
reform, and productive work." She gives no weight to institutional ideals,
except to note that the women's colleges implicitly acted as incubators for
women entering the new professions. She also minimizes the impact of a
special generational ethos that perhaps caused the pioneering students to
renounce marriage.[31]

Economic arguments about social class or available income from new
careers cannot fully explain the behavior of college-educated women, however. Educated women of that generation had to make a choice between
career and marriage. Students frowned upon the stereotypical nineteenth-
century marriage in which women were subjugated. At the encouragement
of their faculty, these students entered careers in social work, medicine,
library science, and journalism, and in doing so consciously acted as agents
of social change. In addition, Barbara Sicherman has noted that many students in this period were already in their twenties when they went to college. Their advanced age may have meant that they had already made a
choice of career over marriage before entering college.[32]

This respect for a variety of life choices is reflected in a poem written for
the twenty-fifth reunion of the class of 1888, entitled "Twenty-Five." The
poem refers to "a union in diversity" within the class:

> We've one who heals the ills of men
> And one who writes with gifted pen;
> One who in law has qualified.
> And one a saint now glorified.
> A missionary sister, too,
> And mothers wise, and teachers true;
> And some who with home problems strive,—
> How dear the list, at twenty-five.

In another poem, "The Call," an 1888 graduate summoned her classmates:

> Wives and mothers, with no regrets,
> Aunties and Antis and Suffragettes,

Teachers, and Spinsters who love their fate,
Cherish this purpose! Be not too late![33]

Although family and the joys of having children were praised, marriages did not escape critical attention or satire. Various poems and talks from reunions reflect a mocking attitude toward marriage and its supposed romantic bliss. The class of 1894 at its tenth reunion listened to a talk entitled "Husbands, Pro and Con."[34] A lawyer who graduated with the class of 1882 billed herself this way at her fifteenth reunion:

Have ye any cause for lawsuit?
. . . .
Any longing for divorcement?
Ye who wedded your *ideal* —
Wedded him and found him *real*?
Lawyer Matteson will counsel
For sufficient compensation,
Will assuage your wounded feelings
And adjust your luckless quarrels.[35]

The class of 1907 issued a sober message and a double entendre as they envisioned their future.

There'll be those who have left single blessings
To take on matrimonial bonds.[36]

The critique of marriage—or suspicion of it—fits in with larger cultural trends, namely, the rising divorce rate in the Progressive Era. In 1880 only one in twenty-one marriages ended in divorce; by 1916, the rate had risen to one in nine. Marriage was under fire from several corners. Among the reasons for changes in the marriage ideal and for easier divorce laws were higher education, the increasing affluence in the middle class, and the financial and social autonomy of women. Educated women understood that they had the choice of living a portion, or all, of their lives unmarried.[37]

The Wellesley faculty endorsed and epitomized this belief, even though they rarely delivered overt pronouncements on the subject. As reflected in their private lives, their personal letters, and their fiction, however, it is clear that they upheld the choice of spinsterhood. Katharine Lee Bates, a committed spinster, communicated such values in a number of ways.

Bates mocked marriage in 1889. She began a letter to her fellow editors on the college *Courant* by at first withholding information on the marriage of Miss Mary Roberts, who had taught for a time at Wellesley, explaining: "I don't wish your thoughts, as I have already had occasion to say, to run on widower-marriages too much. I want a first-love young hero, a genuine Gabriel, for you." Then she announced that "Miss Mary E. B. Roberts has gone and promised to make happy the mortal life of one Prof. Smith at Cornell. *What* he professes, besides undying devotion, I forget." Bates recounted that the two had been classmates but that he had married another woman, who soon died thereafter. He developed melancholia and saw a lifting of his spirits only after reuniting with Miss Roberts at Cornell. "Then they fell in love and owned it up and *next June* Miss Roberts says goodbye to Wellesley and becomes a [Professor in] the select university society of Cornell, Ithaca. And she seems to like it all immensely."[38]

Bates was proud of her spinster status but understood well that it was not the choice of most women. In 1901 she spoofed the situation—and sized it up realistically—in a letter to Anna Stockbridge Tuttle concerning arrangements for their class union. "It is to be a *Mothers' Meeting* this time," Bates acknowledged, "but next year it shall be a *Spinsters' Symposium,* if there are any spinsters left."[39]

In 1910, Bates defended the choice not to marry to Mary Russell Bartlett: "I am mightily amused over your metaphor for us free-flying spinsters, of 'a fringe on the garment of life.' I always thought the fringe had the best of it. I don't think I mind not being woven in. As for children, whenever we have time and money we can adopt a dozen, and without time for them—and money—think what a life they would have had! . . . I was at a Wellesley luncheon, and several of the girls told me how nice their husbands were, but that none of the other girls' husbands were at all good enough for them. So let's be fluttering fringes."[40]

Careers

There is a great deal of evidence suggesting that faculty were successful in influencing the career paths of their students and in grooming successors. A particularly large number of Wellesley graduates went on to seek Ph.D.'s at the University of Chicago and Cornell. Moreover, a significant number of alumnae returned to Wellesley to assume academic slots at their alma mater.[41]

The class sibyl of 1896 reflected this ethos and expectation, prophesying that there would be astronomers, writers, inventors, doctors, and professors among its graduates. The sibyl was also accurate in predicting that some would come back to Wellesley, for three graduates of the class of 1896, Josephine Batchelder, Annie Tuell, and Martha Hale Shackford, returned to teach in the English department.[42]

Recruitment of women into the ranks of college professors is indeed one of the features of faculty-student interactions at Wellesley from the 1880s through the 1910s. The English department replicated itself by sending several of its students on to Yale (the predominant choice of women entering graduate school in English). These disciples studied with the same Yale professors as had their Wellesley teachers. Indeed, one of the smoothest transitions for academically motivated Wellesley students was the progression from undergraduate to graduate school.

Betsy Manwaring exemplified this tradition. Doted on as an undergraduate, Manwaring formed close-knit friendships with several faculty women, particularly Sophie Hart, Marian Hubbard, Carla Wenckebach, and Margarethe Müller. Katharine Lee Bates also provided support and references endorsing her entry into magazine writing. Manwaring's undergraduate letters are filled with reports of being complimented by her faculty. Upon submitting her first English theme she noted that Hart had found it worthy enough to read aloud in class. After soliciting the opinion of the class on Manwaring's style, Hart stated that it was the best in the division. "I was quite embarrassed," confessed Manwaring. Eventually, however, she was delighted by the attention and praise, writing her parents that she had become a regular "Faculty pet."[43]

Louise Sherwood McDowell, Wellesley's future physics professor, felt privileged to be given special attention and critical insights by her faculty. She wrote to her mother that Miss Hart had returned one of her weekly compositions with the remark, "'Very carefully prepared, development steady and natural.' I feel quite 'set-up.'" Ellen Fitz Pendleton influenced McDowell greatly. In 1894 McDowell spiritedly informed her mother that "my mathematics teacher is 'perfectly lovely' even if Miss Hart does say that expression is perfectly meaningless. She (i.e. Miss P.) is very calm and dignified, almost cold but I like her the best of my teachers."[44] Several of the women who went on for Ph.D.'s spoke of the faculty as bringing out the best in them. One noted, "We were being trained as scholars. We really learned something about thinking. Integrity and mind were put together."[45]

For some Wellesley graduates the choice of career was more tenuous. Yet even when women had no specific goals after leaving college, the faculty continued to guide them and to help shape their choices. Mary Gilson, who eventually joined the economics department at the University of Chicago, left a good account of her uncertain path in her letters to family and faculty while at college. In her autobiography, *What's Past Is Prologue*, Gilson recalled: "Vocational information was unheard of in the Wellesley of my time. I vaguely knew that some women had boldly broken into medicine and law and a few other fields generally considered exclusively masculine bailiwicks. But most women who went to college taught school if they did not marry, and if a woman's nostrils sniffed for other academic trails she had little encouragement."[46]

During college, Gilson, like Manwaring, was rewarded for her intellect and her public speaking talents. Although she was a serious student, she also liked to dress fashionably and to participate in extracurricular political and social clubs. After graduating from Wellesley in 1899, she returned home, as planned, and worked in a library in Pittsburgh for lack of anything else to do. By 1910, however, she had returned to Boston to train for a sales position. Initially she liked her new job, which soon led to her teaching young women clerical, sales, and industrial principles at the Boston Trade School. "I think this experience, hard as it seems at times, is just what I needed to jolt me out of the ruts and make me use my mind better."[47]

Later, assigned to the sales floor at Filene's department store, Gilson soon found herself overwhelmed with the drudgery and exhaustion of the job. She was working in one of the noisiest and most crowded areas—the department that sold veiling for women's hats. "I got mortally sick of peering through dots and meshes all day. But it was a good way to see what those poor girls have to put up with." She confided to her mother that "I am afraid, as Vida Scudder says, there are very very few people in the world who are willing to live the life of *voluntary poverty* for the sake of others." She added that she was doing almost all her own laundry so that she could occasionally treat the poorer girls to dinner—though it seemed so little to do. She then attended a socialist meeting in Boston and sent her mother the flyer that announced the call for a meeting on "Votes for Women."[48]

By 1910, Mary Gilson had come to understand how "the high cost of living" was correlated with middle-class women's parasitism. "When I see these crazy women jumping over tables in department stores, buying things they could do without, I am *sure* of it. If they'd go home and wash their corsets instead of buying new ones it would be more to the point." Soon

Gilson was lured to Cincinnati to do time management studies for industry there. She eagerly accepted.[49]

By 1912, Gilson was teaching vocational skills to poor girls in Boston and becoming increasingly aware of how she had escaped the futility and emptiness of ordinary middle-class women's lives. Her letters to her mother reveal the degree to which she had adopted the Wellesley faculty ideals of symmetrical womanhood and the need for service. "When I think of the year I sat in that library when I ought to have been out increasing my knowledge of conditions as they really are!"[50] She contrasted her life with that of a friend:

> I have pitied Lucy from the bottom of my heart but I can do nothing. She feels so "useless," so "born-for-nothing," etc. etc. And I just told her mother last night that Lucy was too full of power and ability to be happy waiting for jobs about the house to "turn up." She must have her definite responsibilities and cares. . . . The happiest girls I know today are girls who definitely prepared for some kind of work and then went on developing and becoming more and more useful in it. . . . When girls like that marry they marry because they are in love and not because they are afraid of being old maids. The numbers of divorces may be traced . . . to the fact that up to very late years women have been deprived of the greatest blessing on earth, the right to congenial work. Read "Olive Schreiner's *Woman and Labor*." It is *wonderful!*[51]

During her early adulthood, and indeed throughout her life, Mary Gilson corresponded with and sought the advice of Sophie Hart, Margaret Sherwood, and Vida Scudder. Scudder beamed with pride over Gilson's career and showered her with praise when in 1939 Gilson won a Guggenheim fellowship. Scudder gloated: "Ha, ha, Hurrah! Florence just read out your Guggenheim from the paper,—and how we chortled! . . . And you must write M.V. [Mother Vida] all about it, and what you are going to do. She is puffed up with majesticke [*sic*] pride when she thinks of you, and that she is truly your Mother Vida."[52]

Gilson was so attached to her professors that in the 1940s, after producing two books on industrial management and teaching as an assistant professor at the University of Chicago, she considered moving back to Wellesley. Sophie Hart dissuaded her, however, because she felt that the community had by then become too politically conservative for someone like Gilson.[53]

The circuitous path that Mary Gilson took was a familiar trajectory in the lives of educated women during the Progressive Era. Many outstanding Wellesley alumnae from the period 1880–1910 exemplify this pattern, including political and social reformers Gail Laughlin, Belle Sherwin, Molly Dewson, social researcher Grace Coyle, and doctors Harriet Rice and Connie Guion. These women did indeed come to represent, as Vida Scudder termed them, new factors in the social order.[54]

At Wellesley there was a close fit between the ideals and life choices of the faculty and the occupational and marital choices of this generation of students.[55] Vida Scudder told Mary Gilson, "I am terribly proud of you. You are one of the brightest jewels in my shining Alumnae crown." Through this conscious cultivation of student protégées, the Wellesley faculty recruited a generation of followers infused with a shared sense of mission.[56]

Margarethe Müller (*left*) and Carla Wenckebach, both members of the German department during the 1890s, were a romantic pair.

Margaret Pollock Sherwood (*left*) and Martha Hale Shackford lived together in a Wellesley marriage.

TO FLORENCE CONVERSE
Comrade and Companion

Twenty-five years ago, writing from the holy mountain of La Verna, I dedicated my book, "Socialism and Character," to you in these same words. A quarter of a century is a long time; each passing year has deepened our loyalty to the ideas in that book, and the meaning to us of those words.

To Vida D. Scudder

"Lo, here is fellowschipe;
One fayth to holde,
One truth to speake,
One wrong to wreke,
One loving-cuppe to syppe,
And to dippe
In one disshe faithfullich
As lambkins of one folde.
Either for other to suffer all thing.
One song to sing
In swete accord and maken melodye.
Right so thou and I good-fellows be:
Now God prosper thee and me."

◆⟨⟩◆

Vida Dutton Scudder (*left*) and Florence Converse in the garden of their home at Wellesley. Book inscriptions in *On Journey*, by Scudder, and *Collected Poems*, by Converse, reveal their lifelong devotion to each other.

Carla Wenckebach (*second from right*) presides at her German Table in the College Hall dining room, May 17, 1889.

When domestic service was abolished in 1894, more maids were hired to clean students' rooms. The added costs forced a tuition increase, which in turn required that wealthier students be recruited.

The first biology class at Wellesley, 1883–84. In the center of the class is Professor Mary Alice Willcox, who prided herself on the number of women she encouraged to become doctors.

Professor Charlotte Bragg (1900) in her chemistry lab, where she taught for thirty-nine years. During her career, Bragg had over fifteen hundred students.

A class in physiology shows Martha Hale Shackford (*fourth from left*),
future professor of English, studying science.

Professor Elizabeth Fisher in her geology classroom in the 1910s or early 1920s.

Professor Katharine Coman (in wig) with her constitutional history class, 1887. The students are costumed for a mock House of Commons.

The Agora Society, composed of students and faculty, was famous for its debates on suffrage, labor reform, and other social and political issues of the day. Katharine Coman (*second row, second from left*), Carla Wenckebach (*second row, fourth from left*), and Mary Whiton Calkins (*first row, fourth from left*) were members.

To Katharine Lee Bates —
"literary godmother to all good — or indifferent good
young poets,"
with love from
Florence Converse

Florence Converse, class of 1893, dedicated her novel *Into the Void: A Bookshop Mystery* to
Katharine Lee Bates, "literary godmother" of young poets.

For
    Miss Bates
with love and gratitude
for all I owe her
and to others who
were, and still seem
to me, among the
great teachers
    from
    Jeannette Marks

October, 1926

Jeannette Marks, class of 1899, writer and professor of literature and drama at Mount Holyoke, inscribed her book *Genius and Disaster* to Katharine Lee Bates, one of her "great teachers."

During its golden age, the Wellesley faculty had several noteworthy students who went on to have distinguished careers: Mary Barnett Gilson (*top*), class of 1899, was a pioneer in the creation of industrial vocational guidance and personnel management for women, received a Guggenheim fellowship, and became a member of the faculty of the University of Chicago. Gail Laughlin, class of 1894, attended Cornell Law School, practiced law, and campaigned for women's suffrage.

By the turn of the century, dramatics had become a popular
extracurricular activity. In 1906 the sophomore class produced
School For Scandal.

Junior Barnswallows, the college dramatic association, staged *An
Unlucky Tip* with members of the class of 1911. Women students
commonly cross-dressed and assumed men's roles in plays.

NO MAN FOR WELLESLEY'S HEAD, DECLARES WIDOW OF THE COLLEGE FOUNDER

Pauline Durant adamantly rejected the idea of recruiting a man as president of Wellesley (clipping from the *Boston Post*, July 21, 1910).

The faculty of Wellesley College at Commencement, 1911: (*left to right*) Eva Chandler (in profile), Vida Dutton Scudder, Margaret Pollack Sherwood, and Annie Sybil Montague.

In the 1900s, faculty became critical of the new and conformist collegiate culture, especially hair and clothing styles. The pompadour, which came in for attack, was worn by a group of students from Webb House, 1911–12.

The freshmen of Little House (1929) favored marcelled hair worn with a bandanna, a style that was all the rage in the 1920s. The faculty mocked the fashion, claiming it created the effect of a bandaged head.

The new wealth of college women in the 1920s is apparent in this view of Wellesley students in front of Founders Hall as they leave for vacation in 1924.

Professors emeriti Vida Dutton Scudder (*left*) and Mary Sophia Case, seen here in her wheelchair, ca. 1924.

Katharine Lee Bates, another professor emerita, in her room known as "Bohemia." Bates did all her writing there after the death of Katharine Coman, whose portrait can be seen on the desk.

Ellen Hayes, Wellesley's most radical professor, seen in her garden after her retirement.

The pioneers lived on through disciples. Katharine Canby Balderston, class of 1916, went on to receive her Ph.D. in English from Yale. She spent her entire academic career at Wellesley, where she held the Martha Hale Shackford Chair in English. Here Balderston is seen teaching Shakespeare to a class of seniors in 1957.

Part IV

The War Within, the War Without

Challenges to Community, 1900 – 1930

12

Melancholy Mother
Faculty-Student Clashes

*Our highest hopes are all coming gloriously true. It is like reading
a page of one of Grimm's fairy tales. The fearsome toads of those
early prophecies are turning into pearls of radiance before our
very eyes.*

*Now, women who have been to college are as plentiful as
blackberries on summer hedges.*

—M. Carey Thomas, "Present Tendencies in Women's
College and University Education," 1908

*The college girl of the period . . . comes in increasing numbers
from the well-to-do, materialistic class. She . . . goes to college for
"the life." The faculty is obviously out of place in this projected
dreamland of youth and mirth and beauty.*

—Katharine Lee Bates, "The College Girl of the Period," 1902

In 1908, boasting of the remarkable success of women's higher
education, M. Carey Thomas took note of the changing public perception of college women. Whereas her generation had been igno-
miniously labeled "fearsome toads," the new college woman was
rapidly becoming a fashionable pearl. The pioneer band of college
women had been so successful in weathering the dangerous experiment that in the twentieth century college attendance for women
was not a sacerdotal and strange experience but a socially sanctioned endeavor. Elizabeth Hazelton Haight of Vassar commented

in 1917 that unlike the "stern pioneers," many women now "wear all their . . . learning lightly like a flower."[1]

Nowhere was this success more visible than at Wellesley College. In spite of doubts about their scholarly abilities, scorn at their petticoat government, and substantial financial duress, the Wellesley faculty had achieved hegemony in their educational institution and were capable of attracting new students. But therein lay a paradox. As more socially acceptable women entered college, the staunch pioneers at Wellesley were as troubled by their success as they might have been had they failed. They viewed the increasing numbers of college girls as a grim fairy tale indeed, one that tolled death to the dedication they deemed requisite for the intellectual life and that signaled the spread of a disease they feared—dilettantism. For women faculty, the camaraderie with students and the shared commitment to social service began to erode.

For nearly the first two decades of the twentieth century, the Wellesley faculty found themselves caught in a web of contradictions that are explicable only if we understand the tensions particular to women faculty at the women's colleges. These select few women scholars had built their identities on ideals of renunciation; they had advocated a set of educational ideals that called upon women to sacrifice social life and even marriage to a career that served the community. Surveying the Wellesley scene from 1900 to 1920, they lamented that too many young women were attending college merely for what was termed "the life"—socializing in exclusive societies or participating in extracurricular activities such as dramatics or glee club.

This growing gulf between faculty and students was not unique to Wellesley, however. In 1895, the *Smith College Quarterly* worried that the prevalence of social events endangered Smith's intellectual culture. In 1908, Abby Leach cautioned that the women's colleges had to cope with "the influx of large numbers of girls, attractive, with social advantages and plenty of money, but from homes where study is looked upon as something burdensome and uninteresting and delight in learning and in books is almost inconceivable." Leach added scornfully, "Amusement is the demand of the hour." On midwestern campuses, too, a new social type emerged—"the butterfly," who went to college to make her debut. With an abundance of money, clothing, and leisure, such students made the university "a stalking ground." Their coarse conduct undercut the academic dignity of the campus.[2]

Men's colleges were also afflicted. At Princeton, Woodrow Wilson noted that "the rivalry between the life and the work of the student generally results in the victory of the life." These tensions also characterized Johns Hopkins, where faculty and student conviviality lasted but a decade before disintegrating.[3]

During this period the Wellesley faculty were increasingly subjected to attacks by male critics who denounced the women's colleges for producing a class of intellectual women who were not marrying and hence were committing race suicide. In 1908, G. Stanley Hall, of Clark University, denounced the "glorified spinster" ideal of M. Carey Thomas and other women's college presidents and faculty who upheld scholarship, economic independence, and career. May Cheney, secretary of the Western Association of Collegiate Alumnae, astutely commented that "the very success of the movement, which amounts to a great social and intellectual revolution affecting one-half the human race, has roused men to resist its progress."[4]

Like Sisyphus, the Wellesley faculty found themselves engaged in a continuous struggle to maintain their conception of the central purpose of the women's college—intellectual pursuits. But the more they accentuated intellectual ideals and denounced the squandering of women's energies in purely social activities, the more both their own students and their male opponents castigated them. Hemmed in by these contradictions, the faculty had little hope of winning either the war within or the war without.

In "The College Girl of the Period," written in 1902, Katharine Lee Bates suggested the nature of the problem. A new type of college woman known as the "society girl"—more materialistic in her concerns and probably wealthier than previous generations of students—had arrived. A perturbed faculty looked on as this new type threw herself into the increasing array of social events that detracted from serious study. Additionally, the faculty bridled at the erosion of their authority, in spite of having consented to student self-government. As yet another controversial academic issue, Bates pinpointed the elective system, which had allowed for both more choice and more laxity in the college curriculum.[5]

Teachers and students were not always in disagreement, however. The new society girl, and the associated social exclusiveness that marred a theoretically democratic community, troubled segments of both the faculty and the student body. Even so, faculty-student clashes did increase between 1900 and 1925. The growing gap between faculty and students can be explained in part by a perceived shift in the socioeconomic background and life-style of students, which spilled over into changes in student culture.

Historians have not irrefutably demonstrated a change in the socioeconomic background of students, but several have noted that in the period 1900–20, New England colleges became enclaves for the wealthy and the highly educated. David Allmendinger argues that by 1910 a new class of students attended the women's colleges. Internal evidence also indicates these economic changes. As early as 1895 President L. C. Seelye of Smith commented that each year wealthy girls "are more largely represented." President James Taylor of Vassar complained of a "great wave of self-indulgence, coincident with great wealth . . . which is undermining the spirit of scholarship."[6]

In a 1917 survey of 3,636 college women who had graduated between 1869 and 1898, the Association of Collegiate Alumnae found that in the eastern colleges, 23.7 percent, or almost one-fourth, of the students came from families whose income was over $5,000. Two-thirds of the fathers were businessmen or professionals whose median annual income was $2,042. In 1886, the average annual income in the United States was $453.[7]

The college women of the 1900s did not really represent a new class of women; after all, a few of the faculty women, namely, Vida Scudder and Margaret Sherwood, came from upper-middle-class backgrounds. What was significant is how the new wave of students and their families chose to spend their income. During the Progressive Era, the life of the middle class was transformed. The work week declined and leisure grew. Chain stores opened and the choice of goods exploded. Institutions of commercial leisure, such as parks, saloons, and sports, were cheap and legitimate. Social and psychological changes ensued. The world of the producer had been based on the values of self-denial and achievement; the world of the consumer was based on immediate gratification and indulgence.[8]

Economists of the day described the enormous increase in wealth that had created a large leisure class with an income of more than five thousand dollars a year. Critics saw the new middle class as lacking the restraint and strength of character of the older, thriftier, and more industrious middle class. An "asceticism in economics," enunciated by academic economists and sociologists, decreed that the genteel cultural stance of the old middle class was dying. Significantly, all of these economists saw women as particularly imperiled by prosperity.[9]

When the Wellesley faculty fumed over the society girl, dilettantism, the lessening of academic values, and the rise of the extracurricular, they were reflecting a larger socioeconomic and ideological discussion that raged within the middle class. At Wellesley, the virtues of character, and, in particular, symmetrical womanhood, seemed endangered by the new materialism of the society girl. This discussion encapsulates the dilemma that materialism posed—the challenge of hard work, discipline, and achievement.

The faculty had come of age before luxury tempted the middle class in America. Unattracted by materialism, they spent money modestly—on books, travel for research, or additional schooling. These traditional attitudes, as Daniel Horowitz labels them, were challenged and changed by advocates of comfort. After 1900, the definition of the salaried middle class hinged not only on income and occupation but also on a style of life. The new middle class valued clothes, recreation, and books. They deemed respectable anything that distinguished them from the working class. One of their hallmarks was the investment they made in their children's education. Ironically, it was the success of the experiment in higher education that produced tensions in women's collegiate culture. In the eyes of the faculty, the rush to the colleges by the daughters of the new middle class was a mixed blessing.[10]

The Debate over Societies

The old clubs and societies, such as Microscopical and Shakespeare, never rivaled one another. They did not seek to recruit Wellesley women on popularity. But the six societies of the 1890s (Agora, Alpha Kappa Chi, Phi Sigma, Shakespeare, Tau Zeta Epsilon, and Zeta Alpha) did compete for membership. Their meetings, held in houses constructed solely for that purpose, on land granted them by the college, were strictly private and included secret initiation rites, all of which led to exclusivity and rivalries.[11]

Throughout the 1890s and into the 1900s, students expressed to parents their feelings about the impact of societies on the student body. In May 1896, Mary Gilson wrote her parents that upon her arrival she had been mistaken in believing that a democratic spirit prevailed at Wellesley: "I *never* saw such a place for snobby cliques. I don't mean I am treated badly for I am not but I notice it every day. It is a shame, too, for we are all here, or ought to be, for the same purpose. Here a person counts for *absolutely nothing* unless she is a Society girl."[12] According to Gilson, only the literary and political societies, Shakespeare and Agora, were democratic. Because of the jealousies between society and nonsociety girls, Gilson believed that the societies should be banned. She was troubled by the differences in wealth on campus and the advantages of the socialite. "It is no wonder Wellesley girls have the reputation of greasy grinds, for we have to work so hard while we're here that we can scarcely go anywhere. . . . Unless you're rich and can go to the shore in the summer you [are forced to just] lie around."[13]

In 1903, Katharine Lee Bates indicted Wellesley's societies. Their stated purpose, promotion of friendship and community, could be better achieved by other means. Although it was not the intention of the societies "to purchase their own pleasure with the coin of others' pain," rivalry for new members resulted in this offense. Societies cost their members the opportunity to base their friendships on intellectual and artistic grounds rather than on material wealth and social background.[14]

Between 1909 and 1910, as the reformation of societies became a college-wide issue, the *Wellesley College News* ran a series of student and faculty editorials on the subject. Calling for their abolition, Sarah Baxter, class of 1911 and a society member, accused them of creating a harmful and misleading class distinction and of draining energy away from academics. Imogene Kelly agreed, underscoring the hypocrisy of distinctions "in a college that plumes itself on its democracy." Emma Hawkridge, class of 1910, retorted that even without societies, Wellesley would develop cliques. "Certain kinds of girls demand a social criterion—if they don't have one, they will build another." Excoriating societies for fostering snobbishness, another member of the class of 1910 complained that "certain chosen ones are allowed to wear attractive little pins which show them to be members of this or that set." Soon the wearing of pins to distinguish society girls became a major source of dissatisfaction, and some societies offered not to wear pins in public.[15]

Professor Margarethe Müller criticized the lucky two hundred society women who reaped prestige not as a reward for high scholarship but "because they perchance might be sisters, cousins, and agreeable acquaintances of some of the pigs in clover." Professor Mary Case warned that antagonisms in the student body were growing and that any decrease in the cooperative spirit "would shatter the unique and priceless jewel of our Wellesley life."[16]

In 1910 President Hazard appointed a committee of students and faculty to study the situation and organized an Inter-Societies Congress, with the request that students acquiesce to the new rules it issued. Eventually membership in the societies was limited to fifty students each, selected from the senior and junior classes only. An Applications Committee of the Inter-

Society Council, composed of faculty and students, appointed by the dean, and weighted toward the faculty, considered all applications, evaluated them for academic standing, and then issued the invitations.[17]

The faculty was pleased that the societies submitted to these new regulations with an unselfish community spirit. Professor Mary Calkins commended them for sharing some of their privileges and renouncing others. In 1912, Grace Coyle, perhaps in an effort to counter an increasingly negative public image, explained to her mother that "the society girl is not the Wellesley ideal." Yet in spite of changes this new type of college woman did exist.[18]

Many students in the 1900s worried about the rising costs of attending Wellesley. Letters home commonly request more funds and also demonstrate the guilt some students felt over the required expenditures of college life. After money for food, lab fees, and books had eaten into her budget, Mary Gilson wrote to her parents: "I wish money grew on trees. Here I am dead broke." She closed her letter by saying: "So sorry. Maybe I can make something next summer." She lamented again at the end of year: "I have class dues and society dues. . . . It seems perfectly awful to think of the money I spend and yet I don't spend a fourth so much as my room-mate and Lucy, etc." She vowed not to return to Wellesley if her education was causing her parents financial hardship, lamenting, "It is awful that girls are such an expense."[19]

In 1910, the poem "Pay Day," sung as a dirge, appeared in the *Legenda*. Crying "Broke, broke, broke," the student goes on to bemoan her plight:

> Oh, well for the millionaire's child
> As she pays for her *College News,*
> I can't afford to have it so,
> My roommate's I peruse.[20]

Many students felt pinched by the costs of college life. In February 1900 Betsy Manwaring wrote home: "Now I am sorry to say more money is necessary, I don't know where it goes, for I certainly don't waste it—haven't been in town—where it does fly—at all; but there have been lots of expenses." She went on to enumerate: books, a carriage ride to a faculty party, class dues, writing paper, the laundry bill.[21] In 1911 Dorothy Walton wrote her family: "Behold the check cometh today and relieved me of my desperate straits. I have lived on nothing for the past week, with four cents in the bank! I didn't even dare to go to church on Sunday."[22]

The cost of attending Wellesley did increase in the 1900s. When Wellesley opened, tuition and board amounted to $250. By the late 1880s this figure had increased to $350 because of the costs of new laboratories, equipment, and faculty. By 1904, the tuition had reached $450, in part to cover the expense of housekeeping services, which had replaced domestic work done by students. Zella Wentz commented on the new regime: "We have to make our own beds but the maids sweep and dust and everything else."[23]

In addition to students' perceptions there is other evidence of a growing differential in the economic background of students attending women's colleges. A sample of Wellesley College student budgets, compiled in 1907, reflects a spectrum of financial situations. Girls living on a modest budget relieved some costs of board by doing domestic chores. (See table 9.) Wealthier students lived in other residences. Their clothing and travel expenses were double or triple those of the more modest group. Interestingly, the difference in expenses for books and stationery was far less drastic. Not displayed are the budgets of another, even wealthier group of young women whose expenses totaled $1,000 to $1,400.[24] Other studies done of student budgets at women's colleges show similar economic variations. In a study entitled "The Budgets of Smith College Girls," published in 1916, F. Stuart Chapin, a sociology professor at Smith, found a large variation in the expenditures of students from different economic classes, suggesting that some undergraduates could afford to be extravagant, particularly with clothing or travel expenses. Moreover, Chapin's figures reveal that of 384 students surveyed more than 20 percent had annual expenditures equal to the salary of an average instructor or assistant professor. Thus, some students were not only wealthier than their fellow students but also better off than many of the faculty.[25]

The Wellesley faculty prided themselves on simplicity, especially in dress. Yet clothing became an extremely important element in the new Wellesley student culture. Mary Gilson, sensitive to the indebtedness she was incurring to her parents, tried to restrict her wardrobe. Nonetheless, her letters reveal the fashion standard set by the wealthier students. In October 1897 she wrote her mother: "I wish you would not bother about a new dress for me Christmas [sic]. I would *rather* have a simple dark, rich silk waist, any kind you choose. Really, I need *nothing* more." Gilson had hardly worn a green suit she had purchased, because she was saving it for spring. The suit was just like one made by a well-known tailor in Boston, for a girl who is "*very wealthy* (a Milwaukee brewer's daughter, so you may imagine)." She was pleased that her short coat would match the styles of all

Table 9

Samples of Budgets for Wellesley Students, 1907

Group 1 (Modest)[a]			
Tuition	$175.00	$175.00	$175.00
Board and lodging	125.00	125.00	125.00
Clothes	50.00	50.00	187.80
Travel	30.00	70.00	9.60
Extra food	3.22	7.00	12.85
Laundry	3.11[b]	2.00[c]	11.20
Books and stationery	20.50	8.00	40.00
Flowers	.71	.25	—[d]
Dues	2.15	3.70	—
Charity	3.65	12.00	—
Incidentals	26.66	52.05	12.55
Total	$440.00	$505.00	$574.00
Group 2 (Wealthy)			
Tuition	$175.00	$175.00	$175.00
Board and lodging	275.00	275.00	275.00
Clothes	100.00	215.00	175.00
Travel	100.00	15.00	28.00
Extra food	5.00	12.00	47.16
Laundry	30.00	8.00	45.00
Books and stationery	25.00	40.00	40.00
Flowers	—	2.00	4.00
Dues	—	28.00	—
Charity	—	5.00	10.00
Incidentals	75.00	25.00	54.84
Total	$785.00	$800.00	$854.00

Source: Adapted from Alice Walmsley, "The Cost of Wellesley College Life," *Wellesley Magazine* (Nov. 1, 1907): 46. Walmsley estimated that of the Wellesley College students surveyed, 10 percent lived modestly on $600 or less, while 80 percent fell into the wealthier group living on about $900 (52). She also displayed the budgets of two groups of even wealthier students who spent between $1,000 and $2,000. The latter group, however, is negligible, consisting of barely 1 percent of students (47, 50).

[a]Fiske and Eliot Cottages were dorms where students did the housework, thus containing cost.

[b]Cost of sending laundry home.

[c]Cost of doing laundry at school.

[d]Student could not estimate the expense; incidentals includes these expenses.

"the swell tailors." A month later she asked for a new underskirt, adding that "a bright red imitation moiré seems to be quite the go, and they don't cost so much as silk." She noted that "all the girls borrow my golf cape horribly. They admire it so." One week later she requested a new waist for Christmas, "but that is . . . all I need. You see I have nothing for a reception or anything of that sort."[26] As a consequence of the new emphasis on fashion in collegiate culture, many of the old guard felt "obviously out of place."[27]

The Problem of Social Life

In the 1890s, Wellesley students themselves started to debate the issue of social life. One editorial in the *College News* asked rhetorically whether there were more than a few Wellesley women "who live in such a whirl of excitement that they have no time to think." A newspaper satire about two phantoms, named "Wicked Sociability" and "Melancholy Studiosity," suggested that rather than be at cross-purposes, these two spirits could be united, to the betterment of a student. In a 1906 edition of *College News* one writer argued: "We are girls before we are students; let us not sacrifice all gracious charm and tender womanly spirit to an increase of book knowledge. Let college also be a place for learning how to live."[28]

Throughout the early 1900s, undergraduates were assailed by a bewildering variety of opportunities and demands—academic, social, and humanitarian—and by conflicting ideals of culture. It was considered priggish to take academic work seriously, and prigs were scorned.[29] Other terms of denigration developed for those who studied too much. A bit of student doggerel from 1906 scathed:

> The Sharks and Grinds of Spotless
> Land
> Are the ones who thoroughly under-
> stand
> That whoever you are, (or) wherever
> you grew,
> You must strive for the Faculty Point
> of View.[30]

Another rhyme, "The Hunting of the Shark," noted that sharks were known for getting work done ahead, studying long hours, aspiring to Phi Beta Kappa, and displaying overt ambition.[31]

The establishment of a new grading system that rewarded those with highest honors by naming them as Durant Scholars caused "A Lament" to appear in the 1902 *Legenda*:

> But now—a few are honored much
> And we are left behind,
> We know we cannot equal such
> No matter how we grind.[32]

Student letters confirm that many were average students who had trouble with academics. Betsy Manwaring, a very ambitious student, wrote home that she had to help her classmates: "One poor child is frightened over Latin, and runs in to get me to translate a sentence. . . . Mae Rice wept in my room the other day over German and English. . . . The girl next to me is frantic about German, and the one beyond her, over French. The girls around me are getting blue and discouraged over their work. Several of them have had notes from some of their teachers."[33]

Dorothy Walton struggled with the course work throughout her college years. Her letters home reveal the changing collegiate culture. As a freshman in 1911 she lamented, "I never felt so absolutely stupid in my life as I have here. They expect an awful lot of you." She resolved to work harder but added ruefully that "I'ze lit [sic] in the middle of a bunch of sharks and I'm just a plain every day minnow." Walton wrote that her usual routine was "the flunks and once in a while, a great while indeed, a brilliant recitation." She lost weight worrying about "all those teachers gabbing about the grades." Confessing that she and all of her friends had received notice that unless they improved their academic performance they would be requested to leave college at year's end, she concluded that her group had brains "but . . . we just don't know how to use them." Still, the many distractions available lured her; studying French literature was dry when compared to talking with a friend or attending Glee Club.[34]

Student Government

By the turn of the century, students not only formed and joined myriad extracurricular activities but wanted to govern these activities themselves. In principle, this desire accorded with the faculty's ideology of symmetrical womanhood, as students could thereby develop the skills necessary to govern and lead. Also, the advent of student government at Bryn Mawr made

Wellesley students conscious of their own lack of authority over nonaca-
demic affairs. Students soon began to criticize the faculty for their omnipo-
tent control of student conduct. The class of 1900 poetically mocked—and
acknowledged—faculty power:

> Because of her age and her cunning, because of her grip and
> her paw,
> In all that the law leaveth open, the word of the head here is
> law.[35]

Wellesley students accepted and admired the faculty's learnedness and
experience. They never, in all their criticism, suggested replacing women
professors with males. Yet the equality and intimacy that existed at one level
of student-faculty relationships led to resentment and disaffection when faculty exerted control of student affairs.

In 1901 the trustees and faculty of Wellesley College granted student
self-government, thereby imposing on students responsibility for their conduct. The president and faculty, however, retained power over all athletic
events, all societies, society houses, clubs, and publications. The authorities of the college pledged to support the student association and in return
asked that the student government cooperate with the president and faculty to maintain a high standard of scholarship and social life. Nonetheless,
disputes arose. In 1910 the Academic Council convulsed over reckless student behavior that damaged the new library and other college and town
property. The Student Government Association was called upon to reform
radically its disciplinary code. The faculty constituted a Committee on Non-
Academic Interests to supervise the growing number of student organizations. In 1911, students petitioned to have a representative on this faculty
committee. President Pendleton rejected the petition, declaring that it was
not permissible for students to make policy on social life.[36]

By 1911, the proliferation of student organizations led the Academic
Council, in consultation with students, to limit memberships in student
organizations. The number of memberships allowed is astonishing: students
could join seventeen clubs and one of six societies, and act in eight dramatic plays per year![37]

In spite of this liberal policy, conflicts continued between faculty and
students. In 1912, Grace Coyle documented a clash over the recitation
schedule. The faculty announced that classes would meet daily, morning
and evening, with the exception of Saturday evening and Sunday. Formerly

no classes had been scheduled on Mondays, allowing students to leave the campus on Sundays. Now they would have to work on Sunday. Coyle wrote: "It is really tragic but its object is to promote 'intensive scholarly work.'" By November 1912, Coyle recorded that the student body was "wild with impotent rage" and "ripe for actual riot" because the Committee on Non-Academic Interests had, in addition, decided to cut the extracurricular program drastically. She wailed to her mother, "They treat us like 3-year olds." President Pendleton tried to restrain the faculty committee, but, Coyle concluded, "I think that those old groups of fossilized human flesh that are heads of departments sit on her all the time."[38] In February 1913, the Academic Council finally agreed to allow student government representatives to help monitor extracurricular activities; students had won a voice, but the faculty still had the final say.

Faculty Complaints

In 1904, the faculty skit for Barnswallows, the dramatic association of the college, mocked the docile student body:

> The faculty sedate and grave
> One night an entertainment gave,
> To make some fun for everyone,
> And please the girls at Wellesley.
> . . . .
> 'Tis true they sometimes go to sleep,
> When lectures wax a bit too deep,
> 'Tis true they sometimes read or sew
> When recitations prove too slow.
> Yet when we try to play the fool
> For one brief evening out of school,
> What keen, attentive rapturous faces! O!
> O what a pity 'tis not always so![39]

Ironically, the faculty, who were all-powerful in the eyes of students, felt under siege. In 1902, Katharine Lee Bates declared that her colleagues were lost in what had become a "dreamland of youth and mirth and beauty" that left little room for intellectual endeavors. The pioneer college woman, Bates asserted, "was stoop-shouldered, perhaps, and deficient in social ease, but she took her mind seriously." In contrast, the contemporary collegian "comes in ever increasing numbers from the well-to-do, materialistic class. She is well grown, well dressed, athletic, radiant." Nearly scornful, Bates declared: "Critical of individuals, by no means overawed by fame and learning, she is intellectually submissive."[40]

Stunned but intent upon reconciling herself to this new social type, Bates took heart that a few students still pursued scholarly ideals. Expressing a glimmer of hope for the new lighthearted and light-headed college woman, Bates speculated that the butterfly would be influenced by her more scholarly peers rather than by her teachers.[41]

In the early 1900s many Wellesley faculty besides Bates criticized collegiate culture. Martha Hale Shackford declared in 1903 that any fears that college women would be lost in excessive study "have vanished in the face of the deliberate attention paid to the amusements of college life." The "heroic mood" of the pioneers had ceased, "threatened as we are with a generation of athletic students, almost too calm under the pressure of academic life." In 1906, Mary Calkins admitted to alumnae of her alma mater, Smith College, that many women students of the day were dilettantes who had discarded as old-fashioned the idea that one studied in college and prepared for a career.[42]

Dilettantism also prompted Margaret Sherwood to write an article entitled "The Ideal College" for *Wellesley Magazine*. Women's higher education admittedly did promote fellowship among students and did stir'revolt against self-centered individualism; still, Sherwood prayed that the gods might grant a greater commitment to intellectual life to the influx of students coming solely for the social dimensions of college. Sherwood warned that a "tidal wave of frivolity" was sweeping the women's colleges, leaving opponents of women's education smugly satisfied. Obviously angry at the dilution of collegiate standards, Sherwood reminded her readers that the fate of the college was in their hands. Sherwood advised women seeking only to socialize to go elsewhere: "If she longs for dramatic activity, is there not a stage? If she yearns for the trapeze, is there not the circus? Will she not leave our beloved college what it was intended to be, a place for training in the mind?"[43]

Sherwood's scorn derived from the lofty sense the pioneer generation ascribed to attending college and from the deep responsibility they felt to prove women worthy of intellectual endeavor. "It was a hard battle that was fought at the outset to win for women the opportunity for advanced education," she wrote. The contemporary college girl seemed eager to abandon the battlefield. For Sherwood, the "real woman's college as an intellectual factor was disappearing, retreating." She was unsure as to the sources of dilettantism among college women. Perhaps it was "American restlessness or as many men have said, the feminine mind invariably tends to lose itself in details." Given such pervasive evidence of anti-intellectualism, enemies of higher education for women seemed well armed.[44]

As a remedy for this condition, Margaret Sherwood suggested more time to think and to work. Intellectual intercourse should be conducted between friends during quiet walks along the river in the late hours of the night. She invoked the great men of Oxford who examined political, ethical, philosophical, and literary topics through informal discussion, a style the Wellesley faculty emulated in its intellectual life. Sherwood concluded her essay with a sobering exhortation: more than libraries or money or laboratories, "we need an awakened sense of the spiritual import of our endeavor, and we need, we need bitterly, a race of students who care supremely for the things of the mind."[45]

Angry alarms about the "woman question" swirled in the air in the early 1900s. Women were being blamed for a new moral and social laxity, for divorces, and for remaining unmarried. The faculty often tried to calm the public, who worried about the vulgarity and defiance of the new breed of college women. Still, in dealing with college girls every day, the faculty formed definite opinions on their behavior.

Ellen Hayes voiced many of the Wellesley faculty's worries in her *Letters to a College Girl,* published in 1909. Her readers were an elite, free to learn what they pleased and to marry only if they wished, but, Hayes grumbled, "Some day it will be well worth your while to set to work and find out how it comes that you are thus fortunate." The pioneers who had endured much in expanding women's higher education were not only being taken for granted but were in peril of being forgotten. Hayes's foreword in her book reveals her sentiments:

> Thoughts that great hearts once
> broke for, we
> Breathe cheaply in the common air.[46]

Until 1910, the faculty had sporadically sniped at female dilettantism and the distractions of social life within the college culture. Around that time, however, some besieged faculty began to focus more openly on the problems they confronted. In an article entitled "The Girl Who Should Not

Go to College," written in 1910 for *Ladies' Home Journal*, Professor Laura Lockwood attempted to dissuade parents from sending certain types of daughters to college.[47]

Lockwood's taxonomy is sobering even today. Many a young woman petted and praised in preparatory school went to college believing that almost without effort she would be the star of her peers and the pick of her professors. Crushed to find that she was not the only bright student around, she was unable to adjust to the competition. Even so, there was some hope for such women. Those who came for the pleasant round of social activities or succumbed to the incessant extracurricular events were really doing themselves and the college a disservice. But the most pathetic figures were the girls who were either too dull or too complacent for original thinking. Lockwood advised these "shallow imitators" to find some other place to spend their youth.

Lockwood also carped about the negative effects of higher education on women's health. She warned that the college girl who lived in a large dormitory rarely had enough quiet time for personal pursuits; she had to accommodate noise, hastily served meals eaten with many other girls, and frequent interruptions when she studied. Some girls' health could suffer under these conditions. Although Lockwood did not argue that study ruined women's health, she was treading on dangerous turf by invoking the image of the invalid college woman, an image made popular by male physicians who opposed higher education for women. Lockwood's view was a reversal of that held in the 1880s and 1890s, which usually stressed the positive effects of collegiate life on women's health. Now, however, as the symmetrical woman gave way to the society woman, faculty like Lockwood argued against college life for everyone.[48]

By 1912 Margaret Sherwood, who had defended women earlier, was writing in more truculent tones about the perils of conformity and complacency. In "The Apotheosis of the Commonplace," written for *Scribner's* magazine, she fulminated against the conventionality of young women, likening them to lambs who run in a pack. She asked: "Why is there so little individuality in their tastes as to hats, hose, slang, fiction, social ideals, art, literature, and cosmic philosophy?" With only half-shrouded humor she noted that women adopted silly styles en masse: "We have lived down the marcel wave; we are living down the pompadour; what can help us in living down the puffs?" What was worse, students mimicked one another in intellectual viewpoints and in literary and aesthetic tastes. Sherwood caustically derided the "ridiculous fillet that most of them are wearing, and that gives my class-room the appearance of an assemblage of broken and bandaged heads." She deplored college women's conventionality, their lack of individuality, and their predilection for the commonplace, concluding angrily that only mediocrity was in abundance.[49]

A year later, Sherwood published her most scathing appraisal of contemporary education. College professors had become "the showmen of the intellectual life; we must wind up this toy and that, and set it going to stir their jaded young minds. Ours the song and dance; ours the tired feet and tired minds in trying to furnish mental amusement for the young." Sherwood could not contain her disgust at the failure of progressive education: "It is for us to put the young through their paces, not for them to put us, nor is it well for them to sit torpidly at Judgment while their elders perform."[50]

Eventually, these complaints against unprepared and unmotivated college women culminated in the adoption of new admission standards by several of the women's colleges, including Wellesley in 1917. The revised criteria were based not simply on certification but on exams by the College Board and on character testimonials given by secondary teachers. The attention to character was an attempt to weed out the nonserious students; and those who did not score well on exams were encouraged to go to vocational school.[51]

The faculty were still writing about college women in the 1920s. Interestingly, however, their tone had changed, and they had again become optimistic about young women. Although the flapper and the vamp caused shrill comment elsewhere, the faculty found merit in the new generation. The faculty had become like grandmothers (even Vida Scudder used the term); they had mellowed and for the most part they defended their granddaughters. Moreover, in the post–World War I period American society seemed bent on returning to normalcy and abdicating social reform. In this changed cultural climate, the Wellesley faculty clung to the hope that college women would uphold, as Margaret Sherwood put it, "the one success in life . . . to serve one's generation and, through this, the future."[52]

In the 1920s, Margaret Sherwood resigned herself to the amusements and the recreations of the American college. She had not, however, lost all the old irony. She would not claim that intellectual achievement was the singular aim, or sole benefit, of college; tens of thousands of students refuted that notion. Citing English statesmen, Sherwood declared the greatest benefit of college life to be friendship. She even tried to interpret athletics positively, hoping they would train women in teamwork and democracy. No longer was her image of college life charged with dissonance.[53]

Sherwood was not alone in making peace with her Wellesley students. In the late 1920s and continuing into the 1930s, Vida Scudder claimed that it was normal for elders to be disconcerted by the younger generation. Scudder blamed the war for the escalation of mild shock into outcries of distress. Although she refused to paint a rose-colored picture—there were, after all, "noisy girls, vulgar girls, girls clever and unpleasant"—most of these "granddaughters" are "much like their mothers." They relished intellectual activities, asked good questions, and still valued social reform.[54]

In a 1929 essay entitled "A Pedagogic Sunset," Scudder observed that every professor who wrote for the popular magazines was expected either to denounce or defend the new generation. For her part, "in spite of lip stick, of 'petting parties,' of immunity to shock . . . I find the girls of today . . . as morally fastidious, as clean-minded and clean-living, as were their mothers." Her chief discouragement was the docility of her students: "They follow their professor like little sheep; and, while a lamb is supposed to be an endearing object, a sheep is not. They persist in giving one's own thoughts back to one." Scudder accepted the modern college woman, but like her colleagues, she opposed pandering to students who came to college merely for the life. In her view, these women were "failures" who had "[lost] their chance. . . . I have no words to say how little the fact concerns me." She preferred to concentrate on students who were serious about ideas. As if consoling herself, she proclaimed, "It is a glorious thing to be a teacher!" She clung to this line and found new challenges.[55]

The Great Depression made college women of the 1930s serious and intent on finding a vocation. President Pendleton, upon retiring in 1936, spoke of these changes, noting that attending college had once been "a crusade with banners" and that her generation had experienced the "thrill of being pioneers." After a decade of docile students, she found the Depression-era college girls more interesting to teach. By then, young women were studying the social sciences, economics, sociology, psychology, and history. Also, in 1936, after a brief return to the classroom, Vida Scudder wrote that although young women with bobbed hair and lipstick appeared "like young vampires to my old fashioned eyes . . . within the clothes and behind the lipstick they seemed exactly like the girls of forty years before; a little more serious perhaps, and quite as nice." As for Scudder herself, in becoming a teacher again, she was like "an old war horse rejoicing in the battle."[56]

13

The Race-Suicide Syndrome
Marriage Rates and Birthrates of College-Educated Women

Separate colleges for women . . . are from the viewpoint of the
eugenist an historic blunder.

—Roswell H. Johnson and Bertha Stutzmann,

"Wellesley's Birth-Rate," 1915

Mr. Johnson's claims about "excessive limitation of the students'
opportunities for social life" [as a cause of race suicide] sounds, to
those who know the large amount of social life in women's
colleges, as if it were made about a college on Mars.

—Laura Lockwood, "College Women as Wives

and Mothers," 1916

In 1915, Wellesley College became the focus of a heated debate that
had been brewing since 1900—namely, the issue of low marriage
rates for college-educated women. Ironically, during the era when
the Wellesley faculty were worrying about a decline in college
women's intellectual commitment and their excessive desire for
social life, detractors vociferously attacked women's higher education for being too feminist and encouraging celibacy among college women. In responding to one attack, Professor Laura Lockwood declared incredulously that anyone who visited Wellesley
College would hardly find what critics termed "a dry desert of ster-
ile intellectuality." Abby Leach was equally astonished: "Foolish

indeed are they who see in mental growth and profound study a menace to the race; the danger is and always has been in the direction of vanity, love of luxury, emotionalism, sensationalism."[1]

By 1905, educated women attended college in search of marriage as well as careers. Indeed, marriage rates were on the rise. Yet, paradoxically, critics mounted their most forceful attack on college-educated women and spinster faculty during this period. Wellesley College and its all-female faculty seemed to threaten middle-class cultural norms.

The charge of race suicide was merely the latest in a long list of criticisms lodged by opponents of women's higher education. In 1901, M. Carey Thomas astutely noted that "college women have . . . successfully met and silenced all the *a priori* objections to college education," only to face a new insidious argument. Indeed each generation of college-educated women confronted a specific set of attacks. Thomas herself recalled being "haunted . . . by the clanging chains of that gloomy little specter, Dr. Edward H. Clarke's *Sex in Education.*" Alarmed by Clarke's predictions that college training would irreparably damage women physically, she was relieved to learn from her mother that Clarke had exaggerated the dangers of an intellectual life. "Still," she wrote later, "we did not *know* whether colleges might not produce a crop of just such invalids."[2] But by the turn of the century, women *did* know. Between 1900 and 1915 their attendance in college quadrupled; in addition, they were winning a disproportionate number of Phi Beta Kappa keys. In spite of this progress—or more pointedly, because of it—critics began attacking the women's colleges as "modern nunneries" that were creating an "anticonnubial class."[3]

The theory concerning the physical evils of education propounded in the 1870s was now replaced by the "birthrate question." During the 1900s, complaints about higher education for women became more sociological: the fear was that elite, highly educated women seemed to be scorning the family and favoring independence and careers. These attacks were harder to counter, because the critics maintained that women rejected marriage and reproduction out of personal choice, not out of biological deficiency brought about by higher education. Still, these criticisms were clearly connected to earlier ones—they were, as Abby Leach succinctly put it, "old foes with new faces."[4] Several shifts in middle-class culture had occurred to make women students and single women faculty the center of criticism.

Marriage Rates of Female College Graduates, 1870–1900

In the late nineteenth century, celibacy was accepted as a healthy social condition. Women who refrained from marriage, especially to gain an education and to teach, were not only tolerated but praised. This philosophy is evident in the 1874 rebuttal issued by Mary Tyler Peabody Mann to Dr. Edward Clarke's "vulgar attack upon the noble army of unmarried women, who are often in the respectable ranks of 'spinsterism' . . . out of self-respect, and because their ideal of the marriage state is far beyond that of the average woman." Mann denounced the plethora of unsatisfactory marriages in America and the corruption of marriage. She held high the preferred state of single blessedness, proclaiming: "I believe it is a fact that the higher the state of civilization and refinement, the more unmarried women there are." Single blessedness was in force a quarter of a century later, leading the prominent author Charlotte Perkins Gilman to state: "The educational, religious, charitable, philanthropic, reformatory, and generally humanitarian work of this age, is largely done by single women."[5]

In spite of this feminist ideology, the first study of marriage rates of college-educated women, published in 1885 by the Association of Collegiate Alumnae (ACA), found that only 27.8 percent were married, setting off alarms throughout educated society. By 1890, the first defenses of the so-called celibacy of alumnae were in print.[6]

Millicent Shinn, in an article entitled "The Marriage Rate of College Women," found that ACA alumnae, especially those from women's colleges, had low marriage rates. Yet she asserted that celibacy signified the desire for "congenial marriage" and a eugenically better parenthood. College women could stay single because they had income from work. Furthermore, higher education did not cause celibacy; rather, college women taught predominantly in girls' schools and lacked the opportunity to meet men.[7] In a response to Shinn, entitled "College Women and Matrimony Again," Frances Abbott was more ambivalent, underscoring the point that the Vassar alumnae in Shinn's sample were still of marriageable age. In a bittersweet caveat of the supposed immutability of low marriage rates, she asserted: "Most of the Vassar graduates are not yet dead, and while there is life there is hope!" Yet Abbott was also positive about the refusal to marry, interpreting celibacy as a sign of woman's economic emancipation: "I do not say that the majority of marriages in the past have been mercenary, but as women increase in financial independence the time may come when contracts of that sort may be eliminated altogether."[8]

The marriage rates of college alumnae received nationwide attention. Even in the face of low marriage rates, however, the editors of the *Nation* did not blame higher education. They believed instead that women who had not expected to marry attended college; hence, college-oriented women self-selected out of the marriage market. Moreover, the editors argued that educated women *were* marrying and that they uplifted their unions. This explanation demonstrates how prevalent the liberal critique of conventional middle-class marriage had become by the 1890s.[9] In 1901 *Outlook* magazine also defended college women. The editors refused to attack higher education, because new studies demonstrated that there were only minor differences in the marriage rates of women of the same social class, *with* or *without* college degrees. This finding led to the conclusion that college women's intellectual and economic independence did not drastically interfere with marriage. On the contrary, they lauded college women for choosing to marry for love rather than for economic security.[10]

Because marriage as an institution was deemed problematic, staying single was viewed as a healthy choice. In the nineteenth century women in general were stereotyped as "passionless," and single women in particular as sexless. Few critics believed that the concentration of women at educational institutions encouraged threatening or deviant sexual behavior. As we have seen, it was normal for women to have close female friends and to remain in a homosocial world.[11]

Furthermore, in the period 1870–1900 there was a strong belief in Lamarckian environmentalism—the theory that education could reshape social character. Moreover, the Darwinian evolutionary creed could be used to explain the emergence of a select few women of genius who were anomalies. Brilliant women were tolerated because they were fine social types and also because by definition there could be only a few of them. In a sense, they were dismissed as exemptions to the cultural norms governing womanhood.[12]

In discussions of surveys of college women's marriage patterns, the validity of the statistics was almost always disputed. Apologists for the women's colleges typically charged that the women sampled were not representative of the group being studied: either the samples contained too many young women who might yet marry, or the responses failed to adequately reflect the broader alumnae population, many of whom did not respond to the requisite questionnaires. Elsie Clews Parsons, an anthropologist, even cautioned against using the data collected from the ACA because the organization had many more single than married women. So overwhelming were the problems in available data that in 1909 Charles Emerick, a professor of political science at Smith, concluded that the statistics "no more establish a causal relation between marriage and higher education of women than the occurrence of rain in a certain phase of the moon proves that the latter governs the former."[13] In spite of all the cautions, defenders and detractors of women's higher education, fascinated by the advances in statistical analysis, continued to use the new methods available to them, even when the results were questionable.[14]

Cultural Explanations of Marriage Rates, 1900–1925

Whereas in 1874 the numbers of well-educated single women signaled a healthy social condition to Mary Tyler Peabody Mann, by 1900 many social critics found the statistics to be barometers of cultural sterility. Indeed, in 1905 President Theodore Roosevelt would agree with Mann's equation of refinement and civilization with celibacy yet would denounce this social phenomenon as "race suicide." For him and for many other Progressive Era educators, celibacy and small families were signs of degeneracy, not progress. The unwillingness of many highly educated members of the Anglo-Saxon race to marry and have children unleashed fears that within a generation or two this segment of society would die out. Presumably the leadership of the nation would then be left in the hands of immigrants from Central and Eastern Europe whose fertility was high but whose intellect was deemed inferior. This perception is more significant than the dip in marriage rates, for it emanated from a cultural climate that blamed women for many social, economic, and cultural changes.[15]

Several factors produced this drastic cultural shift. The nature of middle-class life had changed, and many of its values were under attack. Divorce rates increased during the Progressive Era; degeneration was a concern of fin-de-siècle America; and civilization itself seemed threatened.[16]

As early as the 1880s, August Weismann, with his germ-plasm theory of inheritance, had sounded an alarm on the thinking of Jean-Baptiste Lamarck, who almost a century earlier had focused on environmentalism and the possibility that traits acquired through education could be inherited. Even after the intellectual credence of Lamarck's proposition was damaged, American social scientists continued to embrace his theory, because it allowed for radical social progress. Both enlightenment philosophy and Lamarckian doctrine aided women's higher education. These theories elevated the role of environmental conditions and therefore mandated or made possible a belief in reform. In 1905, Gregor Mendel set forth his newly discovered laws of genetics, which stressed the biological inheritance of traits, thereby definitively challenging Lamarckian thinking.[17] By 1920, hereditarianism had triumphed. There was a new cultural climate in which eugenics and the breeding of an ideal Anglo-Saxon race were paramount. The mood shifted away from hopes of race improvement through reform and education to a campaign for better breeding.[18]

Additionally, in 1905 Freud presented his theories on sexuality. Historians have argued that this and other theories provoked new definitions of sexual behavior. Freudianism stressed marriage and the family for women, undercutting tolerance for the woman of genius who remained single. After 1905, intellectual women were stigmatized, and their deviance from the life of typical American women was viewed as suspicious. Most important, the acceptance of medicine's labeling of sexual behavior meant that female bonding previously viewed as passionless innocence was now viewed as morbid and perverse. Romantic friendships were increasingly identified as lesbian. Indeed George Chauncey, Jr., argues that the "increasing denigration of single-sex institutions and relations . . . constituted . . . a veritable 'Heterosexual Counter-revolution.'" When single women were viewed in sexualized terms, the possibility of their homosexuality challenged the heterosexual marriage norms of middle-class morality. Thus, "women's segregation and solidarity with each other took on a menacing aspect unknown in earlier generations." Even some of the Wellesley professors who lived with other women were not immune from this cultural shift. Ellen Fitz Pendleton is quoted by one student in 1910 as advising: "If you must have some object for your devotion, let it be some nice college boy, not another girl. Do live a normal life, whatever else you do."[19]

By 1910, commentators were no longer prescribing that educated women refrain from mercenary marriages. There was a new emphasis on marriage as a valuable institution, albeit a reformed one. Critics called for men to recognize women as equals in marriage and to treat them as "pals." The call for companionate marriage replaced fears of wrong wedlock.

Each of these intellectual and cultural shifts affected the discourse on the behavior of college-educated women. At their founding, women's colleges had been viewed as institutional challenges to the social and gender-based power hierarchy. Nonetheless they were deemed acceptable because middle-class culture concerned itself with providing education and careers for superfluous daughters. Women's productive labor was valued. After 1900, however, the public, concerned by the notion of spinsterhood, began to view women's colleges as convenient institutions for the revival of middle-class heterosexual marriage values. Once again in American culture, women's reproductive role was elevated.[20]

Any defense of the marriage patterns of college-educated women would have to find some way to deal with these many cultural changes, but in particular with this renewed disdain for and fear of single women. Explanations tended to draw a distinct line between the first generation of college women—the pioneers—and those who followed.

Opponents of women's colleges and their apologists agreed that a general demographic decline was characteristic of both college- and non-college-educated Anglo-Saxons, particularly in New England. They connected this trend to a host of social and economic variables, including urbanization, extended professional training that forced men to delay family life, an ideology of individualism, and the women's movement. Indeed the entire discussion of the diminishing birthrate is inextricably connected with the economic and psychological reconfiguration of the middle class. Racist fears over massive immigration also fueled the debate.

Although male sociologists pinned much of the declining birthrate on "feminism, individualism and sterilized scholarship," Emily Greene Balch pointed to the negative impact of urbanization on population growth. She saw value in a "contingent element" of single women devoting themselves to social causes and progress. In 1903, George Engelmann, a physician, explained low marriage rates in terms of a "morbid craving" for the higher economic standard governing middle-class marriage. This "strenuous, nerve-wracking" struggle for luxury made middle-class men and women delay or avoid marriage. Christine Herrick attributed the phenomenon of race suicide to the financial plight of the middle class, who, facing rising rents, did not want to expand their families. Although there is still no consensus on what caused low marriage rates and fertility control during that era, there was a new ideology about women's social and economic value, as well as a new materialism that mandated a new set of expectations in the middle class.[21]

Antifeminists minimized or dismissed all the larger social forces, focusing instead on the negative rate of replenishment of the women's college alumnae. From statistics issued by the ACA and by the individual women's colleges, detractors demonstrated that the marriage rates of college-educated American women hovered near 40 or 50 percent, whereas nationally 90 percent of the eligible population of American women married. That the statistical surveys were problematic did not seem to trouble these ardent apostles of doom. They adhered to their argument that the women's colleges were responsible for race suicide. Appalled at the success of women's colleges, they worried lest women's higher education become a universal fad.[22] Ironically, the Wellesley faculty agreed with their opponents about the faddish quality of collegiate education and its growing popularity. Both parties discussed the universalization of higher education, when, in fact, it was limited to less than 4 percent of the eligible age group. College was still a select experience reserved for the elite.[23]

It was no coincidence that the Wellesley faculty should find themselves in odd agreement with some of the diatribes hurled at them by their opponents. As members of the white Protestant Anglo-Saxon elite and as academics, they found themselves, by virtue of class and professional position, in league with their adversaries. The women faculty, no less than their male counterparts, were affected by both Darwinian evolutionary dogma and the hereditarian assumptions that permeated both scientific theories and sociological thinking within the academy in the late nineteenth and early twentieth centuries.[24] Although the faculty did not subscribe to the kind of racism and sexism that this posture commonly inspired, they were not completely immune. Emily Balch, who protested immigration restriction and defended single women, still worried that an entire class of bright professional women might remain celibate and withhold their qualitatively higher characteristics from the race.[25]

Apologists for the women's colleges tried to convince the public that the earliest college alumnae were a different breed from generations that followed them and that that first rare group of high-achieving women were destined to extinction. May Cheney of the ACA proposed that "the women who bore the brunt of social opprobrium in the struggle for intellectual emancipation exhausted themselves in this willing service to humanity." The next generation would adjust and prove that the new type of college woman was the fittest to survive.[26] This *apologia pro alma mater,* which sought to calm fears about the function of women's colleges, in the final analysis undermined the status of women faculty because it depended upon a description of the first generation's uniqueness.

Reviewing the conventional interpretations given for the low marriage rates of early alumnae, Professor Charles Emerick claimed that when women's higher education was an innovation, only those women brave enough to defy public opinion attended. After all, Emerick noted, "Innovators are usually conspicuous for their individuality and their aggressiveness." Women unconventional enough to attend college at that time were probably indifferent to marriage; hence men found them unappealing. But this early type of college woman was passing from the scene; in her stead came a tamer and more socially minded type. College had become a popular institution attracting women with superficial desires. No one in the Wellesley faculty community could disagree.[27]

In applying the argument of early nonconformity, however, defenders of the women's colleges were giving their opponents some potent psychological weapons. By 1920, critics and advocates agreed that the experience of the first group of college-educated women who went into the professions and who remained single was not representative of normal womanhood. This defense was at one level useful in soothing fears and dismissing doubts about the future status of women's higher education, but it also helped to mythologize the select few, and worse, it labeled them as deviant. Of course the ideology of the select few had always had this vulnerable underbelly—one was intellectually select and prized, but one stood apart and was different from ordinary women.

This desire to appease the opponents of women's colleges by emphasizing the conventionality of the collegiate experience for women suggests that there was no other direct way to counter the fact that marriage rates for college-educated women remained lower than those for the rest of the population. Mabel Newcomer, a professor of economics at Vassar, found that as of the summer of 1922, of 4,424 alumnae surveyed, only 55.6 percent had married. Although Vassar women were marrying more than in previous decades and at younger ages, she noted that the total picture still deviated from the national averages.[28]

Opponents of Women's Colleges

The issue of marriage rates and race suicide was very complex. In fact some opponents of the women's colleges scorned rather than relied on the statistical evidence. In 1903, G. Stanley Hall and a graduate student, Theodate L. Smith, published an article entitled "Marriage and Fecundity of College Men and Women," in which they noted that alarms about race suicide "had become a theme for the comic papers." Hall pointed out that the birthrate of Harvard and Yale graduates had been declining since at least 1870. The large families of early graduates (1810–1870) stemmed from the fact that married women often died in childbirth and men remarried two or three times, producing large families. Hall conceded that the liberally educated class was rapidly decreasing. A decrease in the educated class, however, did not necessarily mean a general decrease in the overall population or an irreversible depopulation of the middle class, for aristocracies replenished themselves from classes below them. Hall also defended educated women, stating that even though the educated woman of the 1900s was in transition, her biological instinct for motherhood would eventually win out over the desire for a career.[29]

As psychologists and scholars, G. Stanley Hall and Theodate L. Smith recognized the social and intellectual value of celibacy. In the past, nuns and monks had devoted themselves to a life of service, and this cultural uplift had compensated for their sterility. Some communities needed individuals who sacrificed family life in order to attain extraordinary heights and to clear a path for the masses. In other words, Hall and Smith also valued the pioneers. In spite of this defense, the authors were ambivalent about middle-class higher education. They believed new ideals needed to be taught because typically higher education weakened men's and women's motivation for marriage. For women especially, "the apple of intelligence has been plucked at perhaps a little too great cost."[30]

More was at stake, however, in this discussion than the failure of college-educated women to marry and reproduce. The real fear was that male dominance would be eclipsed. Hugo Münsterberg voiced his alarm that newly minted female Ph.D.'s would seek university professorships. He believed that economic conditions favored the professional woman who was single and could accept a low salary. As a result, "women will enter as competitors in every field where the labour does not require specifically masculine strength. So it has been in the factories, so in the schools and so, in a few decades, it may be in the universities." Although in 1904 Münsterberg acknowledged with relief that "professional chairs for the most part belong to men," he still worried over the ultimate feminization of American culture. "The triumph in . . . competition is no honour if it consists in bidding under the market price." Like other professional men, Münsterberg was anxious to divorce himself from the cheapening effect that feminization had on the status of any profession.[31]

By 1908, even G. Stanley Hall sharpened his attack. Both allured and repelled by the new woman, Hall wrote that "many of these bachelor women are magnificent in mind and body, but they lack wifehood and yet more — motherhood." Deeply worried that women wanted to be like men, Hall noted that woman's new freedom and fame had produced a reversal of woman's aims, that they had come to reject the home for the office. He thought it "pathetic" that women graduates sought "some cause, movement, occupation, where their glorious capacity for altruism and self sacrifice can find a field." Viciously attacking single women faculty, he demanded "an end of this ghostly, scholastic, pedantic philosophy of disenchantment, evolved by minds cloistered away from life." Ironically, the thing that solaced G. Stanley Hall was that only a minority of women students "are infected by this strange canker of . . . scholastic philosophizing." In noting how few women were possessed by genuine intellectual ambition, he was, unbeknownst to him, in basic agreement with the Wellesley faculty.[32]

President Charles Eliot of Harvard demonstrated the same kind of ambivalence about college-educated females who pursued careers, ultimately condemning these women. For Eliot, the normal biological role of a woman—namely, motherhood—took priority over all other public roles. Only exceptional women could follow men into the professions and contribute to public life. Admitting that unmarried women who devoted themselves to service were able to achieve some motherlike fulfillment, Eliot warned nonetheless that these women "have lives less happy and less serviceable than those of their happily married childbearing contemporaries."[33]

These psychological and sociological attacks soon were coupled with outcries from the eugenics camp. Writing in the *Journal of Heredity* in 1915, Robert Sprague, professor of economics and sociology at the Massachusetts Agricultural College, decided that "more strong men are needed on the staffs of public schools and women's colleges." He specifically denounced Wellesley College and its female faculty for not teaching "race survival as a patriotic duty." He deplored "these bachelor staffs [who] glorify the independent vocation and life for women and create employment bureaus to enable their graduates to get into the offices, schools, and other lucrative jobs."[34]

The Response to Fears of Race Suicide

During the uproar over race suicide the Wellesley faculty remained hauntingly silent, partially because their concerns centered on precisely the opposite problem: how to stem the growing tide of collegiate frivolousness and abandonment of scholarly norms. But the situation was obviously more complex. That they did not issue direct retaliatory statements or answer their opponents head-on is a telling sign of how vulnerable an unmarried female faculty felt. Others spoke for them—and perhaps they were satisfied with the merit of the defense offered by apologists. They perhaps saw the debate as a controversy of sound and fury signifying nothing.

Finally, in 1916, Laura Lockwood responded to Wellesley's critics, probably because of specific condemnation of the college. She aptly summarized the hypotheses of the critics who argued that the birthrate was low because Wellesley (1) was an exclusively female college (coeducational colleges presumably had alumnae with higher marriage rates); (2) discouraged the students from finding fulfillment in the domestic life; and (3) had a social ban on boys. Lockwood disclaimed knowledge of collegiate life between 1879 and 1888, the years from which marriage rates were being drawn, but stated, "I know the college girl of to-day, trained in a woman's college, wants to get married and wants to be efficient in her home." Lockwood was both registering the new orientation in student culture and offering a defensive posture assumed under pressure. Astutely she concluded that the causes given for college women's celibacy were based on untested theories and prejudice.[35] Lockwood showed good judgment in doubting the validity of using marriage rates of alumnae from 1879 to 1888 in discussions of marriage patterns in 1915. The marriage rates at the women's colleges were actually rising by 1905. (See table 10.)

To some degree, cultural lag explains the continuing vehemence of the attacks against the women's colleges. Critics had not fully assimilated the shifts that had taken place in women's higher education, and in the 1920s they were still worrying about the marriage rates of an earlier generation of college-educated women. It is also true, however, that critics were using a different set of criteria. They were measuring alumnae against a popular societal norm from which female graduates deviated. Studies show that although more college-educated women were marrying, and were marrying younger, through the 1930s, there were relatively lower marriage rates and fewer births.[36] Some critics called for Wellesley and the rest of higher education to attract more "'all-around,' 'redblooded' women [who] are the really superior type." Presumably these more marriage-minded women would have a eugenic effect and dilute the numbers of serious career-minded women who failed to marry. Thus these critics were advocating the admission of precisely the type of women that the Wellesley faculty deemed ill suited for college.[37]

By the late 1920s, Freudianism, with its emphasis on the neurotic, even perverse, components of staying single, pervaded the discussion of single-sex schools. A 1926 article entitled "The Problem of the Educated Woman" noted that the brightest college women sought a position in women's colleges. Such "schools for girls are very Adamless Edens." Gifted students were prone to imitate their "unattractive and desiccated teachers," who successfully replicated themselves by influencing women students. Here one sees the fear of the threat of lesbian seduction—if not literally, then culturally.[38]

Table 10

Marriage Rates of Alumnae at Selected Schools, 1821–1929

Troy Seminary (founded 1821)		Oberlin (founded 1833)		Mount Holyoke (founded 1837)		Vassar (founded 1865)		Radcliffe (founded 1879)	
Years	%	Years	%	Years	%	Years	%	Years	%
1821–32	87	1837–46	97.5	pre-1864	77.5	1867–71	61.9	1883–90	40.9
1833–42	83	1847–56	80.6	1864–73	72.1	1872–81	54.3	1891-1900	51.3
1843–52	80	1857–66	77.8	1874–83	57.1	1882–91	55.8	1901–10	51.1
1853–62	79	1867–76	68.3	1884–93	78.2	1892–1901	56.5	1911–20	49.6
1863–72	75	1877–86	69.1	1894–1903	52.0	1902–11	60.6		
		1887–96	60.9	1904–13	52.0	1912–21	75.0		
		1897–1906	52.6	1917–21	50.0				
		1907–16	59.5	1922–26	60.6				
		1917–21	43.7						

Table 10 (continued)

Marriage Rates of Alumnae at Selected Schools, 1821–1929

University of Michigan (founded 1870[a])		Bryn Mawr (founded 1885)		Wellesley (founded 1875)		ACA census 1917*		Mary Van Kleeck Census of Nine Colleges[b] 1918*	
Years	%	Years	%	Years	%	Years	%	Years	%
1889–93	55	1889–93	43	1884–93	49	1869–78	55.4	pre-1880	57.4
1894–1903	52	1894–1903	47	1893–1903	52	1879–88	50.3	1880–90	53.0
1904–08	52	1904–08	44	1900–09	68.3	1889–98	22.5	1890–1900	50.2
1909–18	60	1909–18	67	1910–19	75.3			1900–10	46.6
				1920–29	83.3				

Source: Adapted from Barbara M. Solomon, *In the Company of Educated Women: A History of Women and Higher Education in America* (New Haven: Yale University Press, 1986), 120.

[a]Also the year that women students were first admitted.

[b]Barnard, Bryn Mawr, Mount Holyoke, Radcliffe, Smith, Vassar, Wellesley, Wells, and Cornell.

*Year of survey.

Another critic called for married men to flood the women's college: "They will set an example of natural living. No longer will it be possible to find in one women's college 114 professors and instructors, 100 of whom were women and only two of whom ever married. It is unreasonable to expect graduates of such a nunnery to give marriage and motherhood their proper place."[39]

William Ballinger echoed this view in an article entitled "Spinster Factories." Excoriating the women's colleges for not encouraging women students to marry, he demanded changes beginning with the faculty: "Gently but firmly I would push out those whose personalities and educational ideals were not in sympathy with the well-rounded life." He advocated demolishing "all the old faculty environment that was influencing young natures into artificial channels of life."[40]

The number of married women on the Wellesley faculty was low. The two married women referred to in the press were Laura Hibbard Loomis and Elisabeth Hodder. Loomis, a literary scholar, married at age forty and commuted to New York, where her husband, Roger, taught at Columbia. Hodder, hired to teach history in 1905, was a widow.[41]

From the 1890s on, Wellesley did have a smattering of men on its faculty. One headed the music department; another was a professor of geology. In the 1910s, a few young male lecturers were recruited in English, history, and economics. By the 1930s, with such vehement criticisms of the female world, more male professors were recruited.[42]

Paradoxically, however, even though men were slowly being wooed and the marriage rates of women graduates were increasing, opponents were not appeased. The cultural climate had been so altered that any form of social deviance was considered threatening. Theories of heredity and sexuality entered the public consciousness. The eugenicists condemned single faculty women for not marrying and reproducing; and the psychologists attacked them for their possible lesbianism, suppressed sexuality, or sexual inversion.[43] That such teachers could cultivate disciples worried commentators. In the politics of the late 1920s, intellectual women were cast as social radicals who threatened the status quo. One way to erode or control their power was to "deprecate the legitimacy of their social and economic aspirations" by viewing it in sexual terms, terms that increasingly stigmatized single women. These so-called misguided feminists who cultivated in their students a refusal to marry or an ambition for careers were labeled failures or freaks. This judgment had a corrosive effect on the climate of the women's colleges for two generations to come.[44]

14

Ellen's Isle

The Crisis of Succession and the War Years

Make a man president of Wellesley and we all know what is bound to happen. Just as fast as the desirable professorships fall vacant they will be filled by men. . . . Wellesley can be proud of her well organized courses of study and her brilliant names, both past and present. Women like Mary Whiton Calkins, Vida Dutton Scudder, Katharine Lee Bates and Margarethe Müller of our present faculty need no apology, and all of us recall the stirring muster roll of those who are gone.

—"Miss Pendleton and Wellesley," 1910

When Caroline Hazard announced her resignation in 1910, the trustees appointed the first official search committee to locate Wellesley's sixth president. This national inquiry produced a variety of opinions as to whether a man or a woman should lead the prestigious college. Within Wellesley itself, however, opinion was virtually unanimous.

It was, as Angie Chapin astutely noted, "a serious and critical time in the life of the college." Chapin, a Durant appointee still actively teaching, showed keen historical insight in likening the current succession crisis to the one precipitated by Durant's death. Caroline Hazard, like Ada Howard, had become a figurehead in the presidency. Although deeply revered for her contributions to the college, the sickly Hazard was no longer able to govern it. Hazard's replacement would symbolize—and to some extent determine—the future direction of the college, just as Alice Freeman had. Notwithstanding the success of Smith and Vassar under male presidents, Chapin was adamant that a man at Wellesley's helm "would seem quite revolutionary with us." The faculty shared Chapin's concerns and her convictions. Hazard's long absences meant that her resignation entailed no real interruption of the life of the college. Nevertheless, underneath lay "a tremendous interest and very deep anxiety as to what will come next." For the faculty, the issue of gender was largely moot—they wanted Ellen Pendleton, then a dean, as president. In letters to the trustees, several faculty members stressed Pendleton's qualifications. One instructor, Edith Tufts, wrote that "the faculty are, as you know, practically a unit in their desire for Miss Pendleton." In her opinion, no outsider could understand the needs of the college as well as Pendleton. Tufts spoke for many when she asked rhetorically: "Why [have] a second-rate man when we have a first-rate woman right among us?"[1]

Pendleton graduated from Wellesley in 1886, joined the mathematics department the following year, and was a full professor when she became a dean in 1901. Because President Hazard took a year's leave of absence in 1908 owing to ill health, Pendleton assumed more and more responsibility for running the college. From 1910 to June 1911, while still dean, she again took on a leadership role. She made appointments, negotiated salaries, and gave masterly direction to Academic Council under trying circumstances. Pendleton inspired loyalty and trust among the faculty, who felt that for several years she did the work of two women and did both jobs well; she also had considerable sway with the students.[2]

Alumnae opinion was divided. A minority opposed Pendleton's nomination, believing that a man was needed to govern Wellesley. In Helen Barett Montgomery's view, "There is an academic hardness about the college that can only be broken up by a man big enough to *dominate* the college and create a new atmosphere." The majority of alumnae, however, were well satisfied with the administration of their beloved alma mater and scorned the notion of a man in the seat of authority. Pauline Durant concurred. In an interview featured by several newspapers, she predicted a "marring of the institution" if a man were appointed president.[3]

The issue had cogency beyond the confines of Wellesley. In part because it coincided with the election of Ella Flagg Young as the first woman president of the National Education Association, the controversy aroused editorial comment from newspapers across the country. In Baltimore, the *Star,* for example, supported the candidacy of a woman for president of Welles-ley, labeling as "arrant silliness" the claim that women were incapable of holding important executive positions. Citing the leadership of M. Carey Thomas at Bryn Mawr and Mary Woolley at Mount Holyoke, the *Baltimore Star* urged the "progressive women of New England to resist the slur on their sex and oppose the reactionary sentiment that was reflected by the Trustees' desire to appoint a man."[4]

The trustees' decision came in 1911: they appointed Ellen Fitz Pendle-ton as president. By so doing they not only upheld the ideal of Wellesley but validated its reality following Henry Durant's death. In announcing their decision, the trustees revealed the factors they had weighed most heavily. They had decided that to abandon Wellesley's traditional policy of having a woman president "would be considered a severe blow to those who are in favor of the higher education of women." The appoint-ment of a man as Wellesley's president "would be saying to all the world that no woman could be found to carry on the succession of women presidents."[5]

The faculty were overjoyed. Ellen Pendleton was both a daughter of Wellesley and one of them. To some, Pendleton had been a student; to oth-ers she had been a mathematics teacher; to all, she was a colleague and a friend. Angie Chapin emphasized the point at Pendleton's inauguration: "It is no stranger whom we hail today as our academic leader." She then cata-logued Pendleton's virtues: "In both official and personal relations we have come to know her as a woman with a cool head and a warm heart, coura-geous and unselfish, free from petty ambition and from thirst for popularity and praise." The appointment of Pendleton meant that Wellesley's "petticoat government," under which the college had grown and prospered despite doleful predictions to the contrary, had withstood a critical challenge. The faculty rejoiced at the installation of Pendleton because it represented both a vindication of Durant's vision of a women's academic community and a reaffirmation of their Adamless Eden.

Anna Phillips, a classmate of Pendleton's, captured the community's exhilaration in a poem praising the new regime:

> Dear to us this spot so fair, so fair,
> Dear is Ellen on the throne,
> For we're sisters of the Queen,
> Ellen's Isle is all our own.[7]

The sense of stability and reaffirmed tradition that accompanied Pendleton's accession to the presidency reigned all too briefly. In March 1914 a fire consumed College Hall, for many the very symbol of Wellesley. The faculty women who lived there lost all of their worldly goods; and the departments of geology, physics, and zoology, all their equipment. Twenty-eight recitation rooms, all the administrative offices, twenty departmental offices, the assembly hall, and the study hall were destroyed. Fortunately, no one died or was injured. Vida Scudder strained to interpret the calamity as a blessing: "A utopia in heaven or on earth destitute of sharp tests is forlorn to contemplate."[8]

In spite of its disastrous impact, the fire "kindled a flame of friendliness and community spirit reigned in that hour." To Florence Converse it seemed that faculty members acted like "bees mending an injured hive." Vida Scudder bravely reminded all that the college consisted of people, not buildings. Those who had lost everything—Ellen Burrell, Mary Case, Grace Davis, Elizabeth Fisher, and Sophie Hart—began to recover by sharing residences and offices with others. With cheerful courage and without loss of academic prestige, the faculty continued its work in quickly built temporary quarters, jokingly labeled the "Hen Coop." Vida Scudder wrote to Alice Van Vechten Brown in Europe of the great intellectual loss: "Emily Balch lost all of her lecture notes of her five courses. Fräulein Müller her choice annotated books. We as a department lost all of our records, but that is little enough compared to most. The general destruction silences one. We all cling together so!"[9]

By common consent the community claimed that the cause of the fire was unknown, even though it was general knowledge that Professor Marian Hubbard's incubator for beetles had started it with an electrical fire. But because Hubbard was depressed over the loss of twenty years of research, her friends were eager to absolve her of the blame.[10]

The fire that devastated College Hall was an eerie prelude to the much larger conflagration that engulfed Europe that autumn. World War I, remarked Vida Scudder, "was not only a world event of the first magnitude; it was also an interior event to every one then living. No one emerged from those war years quite the same person as entered them."[11]

Patriotism versus Pacifism

In a community composed of so many social activists, it was only natural that World War I would have deep implications for the faculty's sense of shared purpose. Group patriotism was one response. In April 1917, President Pendleton was among eight presidents of women's colleges who sent a message to President Wilson that "the settlement of international difficulties by war is fundamentally wrong. . . . [Yet] in a world crisis such as this it may become our highest duty to defend by force the principles upon which Christian civilization is founded." Within Wellesley, twenty-three senior faculty women signed a statement agreeing with President Wilson's decision to break diplomatic relations with Germany. The group affirmed that Wilson had "taken the only course consistent with self-respect." Germany, they felt, would be responsible if the United States was drawn into the war. Believing it the duty of loyal citizens to serve their government, these women proclaimed their determination to make sacrifices to protect liberty and honor. The signatories asserted that the president would be justified in recommending to Congress the most extreme measures to protect the United States.[12]

This war mentality would eventually engulf all of Wellesley. In July 1917, President Pendleton and the faculty announced their plan for mobilizing the college. The main thrust was aimed at making students physically fit and psychologically prepared for loyal citizenship. Undergraduates were forced to adopt a regimen that called for rising at 6:30 A.M., retiring at 10:30 P.M., attending chapel regularly, maintaining a minimum weight, taking a daily bath, behaving quietly in the dormitories, and volunteering for social service. A flag ceremony was instituted, requiring members of the freshman class to raise the flag in the morning to the tune of the "Star Spangled Banner" and members of the senior class to lower the flag at night to the accompaniment of Katharine Lee Bates's "America the Beautiful."[13]

As in other women's colleges, the war was viewed as an opportunity for women to gain training in fields formerly reserved to men. This brought a heightened excitement to the era. A Committee on Patriotic Service, consisting of faculty and President Pendleton, was formed to dispense information about the progress of the war. In October 1917, under the auspices of the Wellesley College War Relief Organization, the administration announced that the faculty would offer a series of war emergency courses. The Wellesley College physician, Dr. Katharine Raymond, offered medical courses. Various faculty taught courses in business and government. Julia Orvis gave history lectures on the struggle between autocracy and democracy in Europe during the previous one hundred years. Margaret Ferguson, head of botany, offered lectures on food production and conservation and organized the Wellesley War Farm, an experimental agricultural program.[14]

Yet the war also generated friction within the community, because several faculty members adamantly disagreed with the policies of Woodrow Wilson. In 1917 Margarethe Müller returned from Germany filled with rage against England. She thereupon undertook to indoctrinate members of the faculty not convinced of the righteousness of her country's cause. Müller, however, misread the sympathies of her colleagues. Her missionary zeal shocked and angered the community. During this time the number of students studying German fell precipitously, dropping from 160 out of 449 freshmen in 1916 to 15 out of 321 in 1919. Although Müller continued to teach with dignity and in a conscientious manner, her experience during the war years left her embittered and lonely.[15]

Partly as a response to Müller's German sympathies, and also because of a small pacifist segment within the faculty, the college issued a memorandum in March 1918 explaining the trustees' views on faculty loyalty: "Loyalty to the aims of the nation as expressed by President Wilson is as necessary for the fullest service of the teacher as of the soldier." Although the trustees acknowledged that some faculty might be of foreign nationality and that others might not be in sympathy with the war aims of the United States, they warned that those members who continued to accept college service were bound by certain rules, which included not conspiring with disloyal persons, not engaging in public discussions unsympathetic to the war, and avoiding all hostile or offensive expressions concerning the United States in talks with students. In return, the trustees pledged to continue the employment of faculty who scrupulously observed the regulations.[16]

Also in March 1918, the Committee on Patriotic Service began meeting more often to stem the growth of pacifism inside the college. Led by Alice Van Vechten Brown, the faculty were enlisted to serve on several patriotic committees. Brown was to lead pro-war talks with students after dinner. Margaret Sherwood was in charge of a committee to abstract war literature. Martha Hale Shackford headed the committee to disseminate war publications.[17]

By 1918 the internal war effort at Wellesley was in high gear. A Wellesley College War Council, made up of President Pendleton, faculty members, students, and alumnae, superseded all previous war-related groups. The council coordinated all existing organizations with the college and took on financial activities such as war chests and the selling of Liberty Bonds. More educational work was offered; for example, the original course of historical lectures delivered by Julia Orvis was enlarged and became more aggressively patriotic. The War Council also supervised the Wellesley Red Cross Auxiliary. Hundreds of alumnae and instructors volunteered for service in France.[18]

The pro-Ally sentiment so characteristic of the Wellesley faculty was shared by academics on hundreds of college campuses in the United States. Loyalty to the nation assumed precedence over intellectual criticism or neutrality. In *Mars and Minerva*, Carol Gruber argues that war service was a natural extension of the service ideal that motivated academics during the Progressive Era. Also, the war heightened professors' sense of familial loyalty and obligation to their institutions. Certainly this was true at Wellesley. But according to Gruber, allegiance to the war also resulted from a lack of solidarity and low morale among faculty. She concludes that professors who had formed strong collegial bonds might have resisted outside pressures to conform to war aims. Wellesley, of course, was a cohesive community, a fact that made war mobilization easy and exciting. Yet it is also true that, unlike professors in other colleges, the Wellesley faculty did not fall mute on the question of academic freedom. They recognized that the college was violating this right when it threatened to temper the free speech of the pacifists, the most notable of whom was Emily Greene Balch.[19]

The Issue of Academic Freedom

Emily Greene Balch was a highly respected faculty member whose pacifist views caused dissension and self-examination among the faculty. Vida Scudder confessed to Balch that "a horrid little militant germ in me has held me away from full fellowship with some of my dearest friends, while my fairly marked though not absolute pacifist tendencies separate me from others." Scudder felt disgraced and bewildered that she was for once on the side of the majority; she lamented that she could not share Balch's pacifism.[20]

Katharine Lee Bates debated Balch at length on the issue, a debate enlivened by memories of comradeship and shared friends. Bates had lived with the deceased Katharine Coman, Balch's mentor, and the three had been close friends. Bates, in a letter addressed to "Katharine's dear Emily and mine," explained that she saw the war not as an international dispute but as a "mad out break of ferocity." She did not believe that Coman would have been a pacifist like Balch. Bates concluded: "Of course I honor your conscience,—but conscience has to be tempered with wisdom or it becomes fanaticism."[21]

In 1915, Emily Balch took an active role in trying to bring about an early peace. Having been granted an official leave in 1916–17, she joined the American delegation to the International Congress of Women at The Hague. As an envoy, she visited the neutral Scandinavian countries and Russia. In 1916 she took part in the International Committee on Mediation in Stockholm and in 1917 helped found the Emergency Peace Federation. She made newspaper headlines because of her presence at mass meetings and demonstrations that included not only pacifists but socialists and Bolsheviks. Although soft-spoken and coolheaded, Balch was viciously attacked in the press for her participation in pacifist meetings. The New York *Evening Sun* of May 31, 1917, accused her of sedition and treason.[22]

Because of this publicity, Balch extended her sabbatical another year, taking an unpaid leave for 1917–18. She was sensitive to the unpopularity of her position and did not want to exacerbate tensions at the college. In the early part of 1918 Balch wrote to President Pendleton that she wanted to return to Wellesley. Pendleton expressed her cordial desire that she do so. The trustees, however, seized on the excuse that Balch's five-year appointment was at an end (she had been teaching for twenty years) and decided to investigate whether she should be reappointed. In March 1918, Balch recorded in her journal: "It is to be decided whether the Trustees will reappoint me, my 'loyalty' being in question. . . . I want to do what is right both with reference to my own best service such as it is and to the general cause of freedom and especially 'academic freedom.'"[23]

Emily Balch, as well as several of her Wellesley colleagues, understood the ominous undertone of the trustees' investigation. Fourteen Wellesley women were members of the American Association of University Professors (AAUP), a newly formed professional organization that aimed to codify principles of academic freedom and tenure. The war years had impelled the AAUP to form Committee A, the Committee on Academic Freedom in Wartime. Between 1916 and 1921 the committee studied and publicized several such cases.[24]

On April 3, 1918, Emily Balch, who was living in New York City, wrote to Ellen Pendleton to clarify her position. She did not disavow her membership in several of the more radical peace organizations but tried to clarify their import and goals. She also defined her own position. She admitted to hating Junkerism and militarism. At a time when patriotism had a special hold on the nation, it was painful to be obliged to forego work toward international peace, which she presumed was the aim of the country. Nonetheless, Balch was unable to reconcile war with the teachings of Christ. She informed Pendleton that if she returned to teach at Wellesley, she would not dampen campus patriotism or carry on propaganda for her own pacifist views. She offered to drop out of most of the organizations to which she belonged once she resumed her regular college duties. She warned Pendleton, however, that it was "very dangerous in a democracy for citizens—day laborers or professors . . . —to feel that they are controlled in their decision as to joining or not joining a (legal) political organization by considerations as to retaining their opportunity to work."[25]

Balch was not alone in her pacifism or in her struggle for academic freedom. Mary Whiton Calkins informed Balch that she had written to President Pendleton requesting that she convey to the trustees Calkins's complete agreement with Balch's socioeconomic and pacifist views. Calkins stressed that she would offer to resign if the trustees did not reappoint Balch.[26]

The trustees temporized and in late April 1918 decided to postpone their decision. Katharine Lee Bates expressed her reaction to Balch: "Of course I regret, with many, many more of your Wellesley friends and champions, the action of the trustees, though I see their point of view. I do not share it, believing that your mind and soul are of inestimable value to Wellesley even though your views would naturally make you inactive in war-service." Bates added that the postponement had been announced at Council, but an effort was being made to keep the matter from the press. Vida Scudder had suggested a newspaper campaign, but Pendleton warned that such publicity would harden the trustees against Balch. Bates added that the faculty community was writing letters of support and that in a "white heat of indignation" the economics department had signed a statement of appreciation of Balch that "should make your dear heart glow."[27]

Alice Youngman, an instructor in economics, was so aggrieved over the trustees' indecision that she felt impelled "to give up college teaching forever." Youngman wrote to Balch that a "hideous intolerance" was rampant at the college: "We cannot—will not take this outrage passively, but we are hoping that [in] another year the madness will have subsided and you will return." She hoped that a general strike could be organized but felt that such direct action would be difficult among "this inert mass of teachers."[28]

Another young faculty member in English, Agnes Perkins, resented the injustice done to Balch and felt that Wellesley was losing what for her had been its most valued asset—its sense of justice and fairness. Perkins expressed what was uniformly felt by the faculty—that Ellen Pendleton was a victim of the trustees, who represented the "unthinking prosperous world." Yet Perkins could not deny that within the college community the faculty were "swinging so far towards senseless, fire eating, reasonless war spirit that I fear for our own balance. The president keeps her head, I think—Miss Waite [Dean of the College] is hopeless." Perkins informed Balch that the entire economics department had met at Vida Scudder's home to sign a statement of support drafted by Eliza Kendrick of the biblical history department. In late April heads of every department voiced support for Balch by signing the statement.[29]

Emily Balch was herself in conflict over the situation. Even though she recognized that the trustees had breached her academic freedom, she was extraordinarily reluctant to have her friends start a crusade in her defense. Balch's genteel, ladylike upbringing and her self-effacing manner hindered her from making an issue of the treatment she had received. She wrote to Katharine Lee Bates: "I am rather troubled that my friends are stirring in the matter. . . . I thought Miss Pendleton would know that I should not desire it, but I suppose that that is beside the point. I feel as if I could not bear to be made a bone of contention."[30]

Balch was reluctant to return to Wellesley, especially if a large number of trustees, and perhaps students, were against her. She had been sent an article from the Wellesley College News in which students expressed the view that a pacifist should be permitted to remain in college only "if she is silent and inactive in her belief." In their opinion, pacifism was akin to a pro-German stand, and any attempt to "convert others" was "treasonable." She believed that she would be "miserable and ashamed and self-conscious and ineffective" in such a climate. Dreading the zest of her friends, Balch still continued to walk a perilous tightrope—she would not stop them from arguing her case on the basis of academic freedom but felt that "there should be no protest and no canvassing" about her "as a person." She asked Bates rhetorically: "Is that thinskinnedness—or something else?"[31]

Although many of the Wellesley faculty did not share Balch's absolute pacifism, they did indeed share a concern over academic freedom and a hope that Balch would not be removed from their ranks. The more outspoken radical faculty tried not to let the matter pass quietly; but they also tried not to make so public a demonstration as to offend Balch or sway the trustees against her. Vida Scudder, writing to Balch in May 1918, felt that

Emily "couldn't expect the people who know your value to the college not to express themselves at this juncture." Scudder felt that the time would soon come when Balch would have to consent to some publicity for the sake of what she represented: "The real issue is of course freedom." Still, Scudder too succumbed to the climate at Wellesley. She believed that a proper preliminary act was the signed statement from Balch's department and colleagues, which expressed to the trustees the sense of Balch's value.[32]

In December 1918 nearly seventy faculty members requested her reinstatement. In spring 1919, however, the trustees took final action and chose not to reappoint her. Katharine Lee Bates informed Balch that the vote had been close. Pendleton and all of the alumnae trustees had voted for Balch's reappointment; three businessmen had apparently swayed the decision. This change in composition of the board is important. Earlier, when Vida Scudder had launched a campaign against accepting tainted money from the Rockefellers, she had been protected partly because Horace Scudder, her liberal uncle, was a board member. Even as late as 1912, when Scudder and Ellen Hayes were involved in the radical strikes at the factory in Lowell, the board resisted public outcry that the two faculty members be terminated. Of course, pacifism was a different issue, but Balch's case reflects the new conservatism of the Board of Trustees.[33]

In the end, ten faculty members, headed by Eliza Kendrick, sent a letter to the trustees asking for the reasons behind the Balch termination. This statement was eventually signed by fifty other faculty members. In response, the trustees met with faculty in the College Chapel to thrash out the question. It was a dramatic moment for all who attended. George Herbert Palmer, representing the trustees (Alice Freeman Palmer had died in 1902), claimed that no faculty member had the right to reappointment and that the college could "find a better person for the position." Many faculty protested this attitude, among them Adelaide Locke, Katharine Lee Bates, and Elizabeth Kendall. Locke declared: "If the trustees persist in a policy like this they will fill Wellesley College with a faculty of nonentities."[34]

The faculty failed in their concerted effort to sway the trustees, but they did put on record in the *Alumnae Quarterly* a statement testifying to Balch's worth as a scholar and teacher and lamenting her loss to the college. Several faculty, most notably Katharine Lee Bates, did not sign this statement. Bates believed that a future reconciliation between Balch and the trustees might be possible and that signing the statement would irritate the trustees and perhaps solicit a counterappeal by unsympathetic faculty members. In informing Emily Balch of the trustees' decision, Ellen Fitz Pendleton assured her that "you will always have many warm friends who will be interested in seeing you at Wellesley as often as possible." Mary Calkins, who did not carry out her promise to resign in sympathy, wrote to Balch, "Wellesley misses you increasingly and some of it will never cease hoping to have you again."[35]

Emily Balch refused to call upon the AAUP to investigate her case, although advised to do so by James Cattell, a Columbia professor who had been dismissed in a similar case.[36] At times, Balch believed that the trustees would change their minds. From May through August 1919 she remained silent and courted the idea of returning to Wellesley. In September, however, while in Geneva, she wrote President Pendleton a bitter letter that reveals her pain and anger:

> A friend has sent me clippings from Boston papers quoting, as I remember it, the Wellesley Alumnae Quarterly as saying that I had resigned. I want naturally to clear up this misunderstanding. Not only did I not resign but I have never received any explanation of the decision of the Trustees not to reappoint me after my many years of service (since 1896). In the ordinary course my five year appointment as full professor, which expired with the year 1917–1918, would, as I understand it, have been followed by appointment for an indefinite period and I should have been entitled to the usual Carnegie pension on my retirement.[37]

Balch notified Pendleton that she had been questioned by Alice Pearmain, a member of the Board of Trustees, on her political views and wondered why the trustees would have considered knowledge of her personal beliefs pertinent to their decision. She claimed that with the exception of a brief discussion of her pacifist views the previous year, she had been given no opportunity to talk with the trustees. Balch demanded that Pendleton make public her letter and correct the misunderstanding about her presumed resignation. She also asked for a formal statement from the trustees as to why they were cutting short her years of service.[38]

This letter stunned Pendleton and many of Balch's friends. Like Balch, they had come to believe that ladylike behavior and a genteel social code should temper conflict. Mary Calkins wrote that the letter "seems to me just not to sound like you." Calkins also felt uncomfortable with Balch's attack on Pearmain: "Of course I see why you refer to it [Pearmain's inquisition]—

but I wonder if you could include any reference to the kindly, tho' mistaken intent of the questioning."[39]

Balch's colleagues did not know how to handle her rebuke. In the end, she withdrew her demand for explanations and left it to the members of her department to decide whether to clarify her dismissal to the public. In February 1920 she wrote to Alice Youngman that she appreciated the generous attitude of her old colleagues in the department and their effort to sustain a liberal college climate. Balch, perhaps feeling guilty, explained the mood she was in when she wrote her protest letter. She believed that the college was trying to ease the pain of her dismissal and that the administration was trying to convince the public that she had left on her own initiative. She deplored this effort to spare the reputation of the institution and to keep everything running smoothly. She once again recoiled from asking for a public explanation, believing that any statement that the trustees might make would stress her incompetence or absences. Already vulnerable, she feared that a public airing of her professional past would hurt her personally. Although she wanted to aid the cause of academic freedom, she became convinced that the battle for freedom "had rolled so far to the right . . . that it would be pointless to attempt to advance objections." She also had the impression that many who were working to secure her reappointment were doing so out of a desire to clear Wellesley's record and not because they wanted her back. Emily Balch felt guilty about bothering her colleagues and "making a vast deal of pother over small affairs in this day when our civilization is in the melting pot."[40]

This interlude during World War I is a telling example of how the exigencies of war affected the Wellesley community. In terms of mobilization and consensus, many of the faculty rallied easily and found ways to provide their students with new vocational opportunities. The Balch case, however, suggests that the forces of conservatism ultimately prevailed, in terms of institutional interests as well as behavioral codes for women. If Balch had not been so unsure of herself—if she had shown more resistance—the outcome might have been different.

15

The Old War Horses

World War I had challenged the communal ethos of the Wellesley faculty. Vida Scudder described its wake: "On the surface, our Wellesley life flowed serene, clear, and not without sparkle; but there were dark undercurrents." Scudder felt submerged by a "surging flood of disillusion" brought on by the postwar climate of normalcy and the retreat from prewar progressivism. Many of her friendships with women who held diverse political views on the war had been strained, some never to be the same. Characterizing the 1920s, Scudder wrote: "There is a worse type of Depression than the economic."[1]

Scudder's words have been used to write an obituary for the professional woman of the 1920s. Although Scudder admitted in her autobiography that by the early 1930s she felt strengthened and renewed, Jessie Bernard, in her book *Academic Women*, hinges her interpretation of the postwar era on Scudder's lament. Bernard argues that by the 1920s the élan of the pioneers had dissipated and that academic women ceased to function as role models for their students. The pioneers, she maintains, were rejected by a new generation of sexually emancipated women, interested more in private fulfillment through marriage than in public achievement. But judging from the experience of the Wellesley faculty during these decades of change, women's experience was far more complex.[2]

The Wellesley faculty continued to teach and have an effect on students throughout the 1920s and into the late 1930s. The group was characterized not by disillusionment but by continued idealism and activism. For many, teaching meant a "protection against that haunting sense of futility and uselessness" caused by old age. Although fewer students emulated the private lives of the faculty by remaining single or entering into Wellesley marriages, they continued to respect these powerful women and to view them as intellectual models. In addition, these faculty were still able to stir up the younger generation on issues of national importance, such as trade unionism or the defense of Sacco and Vanzetti.[3]

The influence of a professor like Vida Scudder clearly continued. In 1922, Vice-President Calvin Coolidge, writing in the *Delineator*, branded Wellesley as a "hotbed of radicalism." He particularly criticized Scudder for her course in Social Ideals in English Literature and denounced her affiliation with the Intercollegiate Socialist Society. Coolidge also decried Mary Calkins, noting parenthetically that "(she is said to have voted for Debs for president)" and condemning her for believing in the "creed of Internationalism." Responding to Coolidge's charges in an editorial in the *Wellesley College News*, students found his article inaccurate, farfetched, misleading, and undignified. One student wrote thankfully of "the privilege of thinking for ourselves in a place where 'there is a Mary Calkins' and where Vida Scudder continues to carry on her 'demoralizing and destructive' work of seeking to make a modern fact of Christ's teaching of the brotherhood of man."[4]

In the era following World War I, there were many signs of political and social activism on the part of both students and faculty at Wellesley. In 1924, Vida Scudder organized students into a Robert M. La Follette study group to analyze the current political situation. Scudder also became a member of the National Committee on Academic Freedom, formed by the American Civil Liberties Union to fight for the right of students to hear radical speakers. Katharine Lee Bates, a staunch supporter of the League of Nations, organized a John W. Davis Club with the slogan "A New Day with Davis." Sophie Hart tried to unite students of all nationalities in the study of internationalism and contemporary political currents. Ellen Hayes, who had retired from teaching in 1916, continued to influence students and faculty through a radical monthly magazine called the *Relay*, which she printed privately in her home.[5]

As in earlier eras, however, the Wellesley community continued to have its frictions, one of which developed between senior faculty and up-and-coming junior professors. Until 1920, younger faculty had generally showed a willingness to accept the game of loving despotism. They were loyal to their mentors because the rules of the academic game demanded it and because the social intimacy of the group made it expedient. But as early as 1909 there were signs that this exclusive circle of professors was no longer assimilating junior faculty. That year Caroline Hazard recognized the generational splits within the faculty community and announced that Academic Council would absorb the Faculty, a body of assistant professors and instructors consigned to passing regulations regarding students' social life. Yet even in the newly enlarged Council, junior faculty remained awed by the wit of the senior professors and intimidated by their elders' sometimes "acrimonious debate."[6]

In retrospect, the plight of the junior faculty at Wellesley can be seen as a microcosm of the larger problems that beset the profession as a whole. In 1910, Professor Guido Hugo Marx wrote a paper that Charles Huberich presented to the Association of American Universities, entitled "The Problem of the Assistant Professor." In it he called attention to the depressing financial and psychological state of the assistant professor and condemned not only their low pay but the tendency of senior professors to look upon the lower ranks as "intellectual valets."[7] (See table 11.)

With the retirement of the first early Durant appointees in 1916, these larger issues were finally tackled at Wellesley. Prompted by the appointment opportunities these retirements provided and by the restlessness of the junior faculty, President Pendleton initiated a study of the autocratic head-of-department system. According to junior faculty, departmental heads were making too many decisions about course requirements and library budgets. Fearful of voicing criticism of departmental policies, the subordinate staff stifled their convictions, conforming to the dictates of the head.

In response to this criticism, Pendleton issued a plan that called for a chair instead of a departmental head. The duties of the chair were to preside over and guide discussions and to execute the will of the majority. Departmental meetings were to be governed by a democratic departmental committee composed of senior, associate, and assistant professors. Every opportunity was to be given for questions, suggestions, and protest. To get her plan adopted, Pendleton established a faculty committee composed of Eliza Kendrick, Eleanor Gamble, Alice Waite, and Sophie Hart. In the end, the faculty committee agreed with most of the proposed changes, adding that the chair should remain an office of dignity. Moreover, they agreed that the departmental chair should not go to "young Turks" chosen on the basis of their business ability or energy.

The reports of both the president and the faculty stressed the advantages

Table 11

Average Faculty Salary by Rank

at Selected Colleges and Universities, 1908

Institution	Professor	Associate Professor	Assistant Professor	Instructor
Bryn Mawr	$2,500	$2,000	$1,500	$1,000
Elmira	1,000	—	—	—
Smith	2,150	—	1,690	1,168
Vassar	2,896	—	1,690	1,000
Wellesley	1,900	—	1,350	1,000
Amherst	2,853	1,700	1,566	1,225
Harvard	4,413	3,600	2,719	1,048
Johns Hopkins	3,184	—	1,344	725
Oberlin	1,941	—	1,250	850
Williams	2,714	2,100	1,730	1,045
Yale	3,500	—	2,000	1,400
Top 100 Avg.	2,500	2,250	1,750	1,250

Source: Adapted from Barbara Heslan Palmer, "Lace Bonnets and Academic Gowns: Faculty Development in Four Women's Colleges, 1875–1915" (Ph.D. diss., Boston College, 1980), 328, table 4. Palmer drew her data from a 1908 study done by the Carnegie Foundation for the Advancement of Teaching of 100 institutions in the U.S. and Canada that paid over $45,000 in annual faculty salaries. Elmira fell into the next group of 54 colleges, which paid between $10,000 and $45,000 (Carnegie Foundation for the Advancement of Teaching, *The Financial Status of the Professor in America and in Germany*, bull. 2 [New York: Putnam's, 1908], v). In the original Carnegie study, the missing data were not explained. Omissions may indicate that the position did not exist at that institution or that the data were not reported.

of the new structure. All members of the staff would gain self-respect by being able to have a voice in policy, thereby creating contentment and loyalty. Presumably the distribution of responsibility would foster cooperation. With more responsibility each member could be trained to deal with important as well as minor issues. In their own self-interest, senior professors noted that their valuable time as teachers and researchers was often consumed taking care of tasks that could be distributed within the department. In spite of this liberalization of the departmental structure, many of the old department heads stayed on, because the reports recommended that they not be dislodged.[8]

Thus, even this new policy failed to diminish the autocratic power of departmental heads. In the 1920s and 1930s, young instructors keenly felt their lack of power. They were unimpressed with the "little Bismarcks" who were loath to leave their entrenched positions. Many felt that the departments at Wellesley had become ingrown. Katharine Balderston, a 1916 alumna of Wellesley who joined the English department, remembered that the "instructors were really repressed. You never opened your mouth. You weren't supposed to." To let off steam and to gain a forum, the instructors in 1920 formed an organization of their own, the Instructors' Association. Balderston recollected that they felt they were making "great strides . . . countering the feeling that we had no share, no hand in the shaping of the teaching policies of the college." Yet "the older women thought we were being very fresh, very brash." A crackdown by the senior faculty on what they saw as an "outrageous instructors' insurrection" and a threat to their power forced the junior faculty to disband the association, leaving them powerless once again.[9]

Lucy Wilson, another junior faculty member in the 1920s and later dean of the college, also recalled that life for the instructors was "pretty grim": "You see, there were still all these war-horses as heads of departments and, believe me, they knew how to lay down the law for everybody that worked for them. They didn't do it so much with the students as they did it with the young instructors, but they certainly did know how. They were dedicated women—absolutely. And they expected the young instructors to come up with similar devotion to work—they just expected it—and I think some of the younger generation of course rebelled and went off somewhere else. Others mitigated the situation as best they could."[10]

Helen Lockwood was one of those who rebelled and left, following a conflict with Sophie Hart, chair of the composition department. Upon hearing of a vacancy at Barnard, Lockwood wrote to the college and asked to be considered a candidate, because "I am fed up with Wellesley and its hostility between Composition and Literature departments." When offered a chance to teach at Vassar, Lockwood accepted, provoking Hart's wrath. Eventually, Hart smoothed things over by stating that the college and she thought a woman should aim for promotion and the highest title possible; since Vassar was offering Lockwood that opportunity, she should be encouraged and entitled to take it. Professor Elisabeth Hodder, however, protested Lockwood's departure: "It troubles me that all the good young ones leave the college."[11]

Dorothy Weeks recalled that as a young instructor in physics she felt excluded from the "old crowd." When she made the mistake of sitting at a senior faculty table for lunch, she incurred the coldness and near wrath of Anna McKeag. The glare from McKeag taught her to never make such a mistake again.[12]

The tensions at Wellesley did not dissipate until most of the old war horses finally retired or died. Frictions were muted somewhat by the fact that some young faculty in the 1920s felt close to a few of their sponsors among the old guard. Thus Katharine Balderston admired Martha Hale Shackford, who in turn took a maternal attitude toward Balderston's career. Shackford, herself overshadowed by the giants in her department (at the age of sixty she described herself as their junior), acted as a liaison between them and the generation of the 1920s. In a similar fashion, Eleanor Gamble was the warm and friendly spirit of the philosophy department who fostered the careers of incoming faculty women.[13]

Academic Council was a nightmare for many of the junior faculty in the 1920s. President Pendleton was "queen" and demanded clarity from contributors; she was known to "pick off" anyone who was not well spoken. An informal protocol prohibited younger faculty from speaking out at Council. Lucy Killough, who was an economics instructor in 1929, remembered being told about a young man who had had the "temerity to rise and speak in Academic Council" after being there only a very short time. "There was a great deal of talk around—the nerve of anybody speaking the first year at Wellesley and getting up and talking at Academic Council!"[14]

By the late 1930s and 1940s, senior faculty seemed less daunting. In fact, in 1936, when Vida Scudder was invited to dine with the new president, Mildred McAfee, she felt like a "proud grandmother of Wellesley." By that time the incoming faculty may have perceived the remaining war horses as "amazing individuals." One instructor found them "noble, hard-working, elderly women" with a "deadly single-minded devotion to Wellesley." Another, a zoology instructor, stood in awe of the "exceptional women [in zoology]—strong-minded, but with tremendous interests in their fields and in the department." But the record shows that the junior faculty of the 1920s paid a heavy price for the subservience demanded of them by their formidable seniors—in the form of nervous breakdowns and stymied careers.[15]

Even at an advanced age, however, some of the old guard did not soften. Elizabeth Jones recalled that Marian Hubbard was "a grandmotherly sort of person really. . . . She didn't give the impression of being—aggressive, but she was aggressive. When she made up her mind to do something, that was it." Agnes Abbot noted that Alice Brown was always head, never chair, of art. Abbot described Brown as intimidating and imperious. According to Abbot, Brown could not give up the reins of power and retired gradually, giving up one set of duties after another while holding on to her title as long as possible. Although Sophie Hart claimed that she was retiring in 1937 to make way for young blood, she also resented any hint that she was leaving because of frail health or old age.[16]

It was only when the older members of the faculty community retired fully that the younger ones felt free to speak. Elizabeth Jones remembered the feeling of emancipation in the 1940s: "We were very much the same age and spoke our minds. . . . There was far more discussion in Council than there had ever been before. . . . People felt freer." To the old war horses this new generation could at times seem "conventional."[17] Sally Loomis, class of 1928, who had studied under the old guard and returned to teach English in 1949, also thought that the climate in the 1940s was tame. She wrote a poem entitled "Wellesley Twenty Years after by a Woman from Mars," which compared her pioneering teachers to her contemporaries:

> Gone too the giants of the faculty, the spit-in-your
> eye women,
> The feuders, *à faire trembler les jeunes, les institutrices*
> *et les élèves*
> Pioneers, O Pioneers!
> Gone are the rosy-fingered idealists, the suffragettes,
> the peace women,
>
> . . . .
> Those who were young then and cowed, are the old ones
> now,
> And cowed, serving time to their pensions.
> No one can know everything now,
> There is no synthesis but there are no feuds, just a
> pallid politeness,
> Pomp and prestige, power and protection,
> Magnificent feminine gothic.[18]

In a sense it was only natural that the old war horses would want to hold onto their power, for they had built the college and considered it their own. It was their family, their inheritance, their progeny. Moreover, they had had

opportunities and privileges rarely granted to women at coeducational institutions.[19]

In spite of their high status within the Wellesley community, the vanguard took note of and were depressed by the changes in the status of
women in the academy at large. The signs were everywhere. Florence Converse, who lived with Vida Scudder and was involved in the settlement
movement, was struck by the turn of events. In presenting the results of a
1914 questionnaire done for the College Settlements Association, Converse
reported a novel finding: respondents believed that the economic plight of
the colleges and the settlement movement could best be solved by hiring
male professors who could "vitalize [the] subjects of sociology [and] economics." Katharine Lee Bates, who in her youth had hoped that education
would ultimately liberate women and gain for them intellectual equality
with men, noted in 1928 that at the customary meeting of the Authors
Club, "the men, for the first time in my experience of the Club did all the
talking. Not a woman peeped!" In 1926, Sarah Frances Whiting, writing the
history of the physics department, commented bitterly that the gains made
by the first generation of women in the American Physical Society were
gradually being eroded. She noted that although her generation had successfully gained entry into the all-male smokers, women were once again
being excluded.[20]

Notwithstanding these challenges, the Wellesley faculty did not lose
their importance as role models, nor did they suffer a wholesale diminution
of power on campus. They were also not completely submerged by pes-
simism. Teaching still brought them fresh contact with young people and
kept them in touch with what Vida Scudder termed the excellent. It was
true, she acknowledged, that hers had become a "disillusioned generation,"
forced to witness the defeat of the causes they had sponsored. Yet, from her
vantage point in 1937, the year she published her autobiography, *On Journey*, Scudder understood that "amazing complacencies" had been destroyed
and the old Victorian idealism replaced with a sense of reality. Always keen
to see the world as it was, she found this change in social outlook gratifying.
For Scudder, the impending spectacle of World War II made her feel the
imminence of Armageddon. She clung idealistically to the notion of future
revolutions and yearned once again for battle. Indeed, so permanent a rebel
was Scudder that she did "not wish to be a consciously successful person,
or even witness the complete outward triumph of my cause."[21]

In a similar tone, Margaret Sherwood wrote in 1936 that her generation had been confronted with developments that were full of promise as well as discouragement. She noted that idealism, which had been at the core of late Victorian philosophy, had been tarnished. Her generation had lost the assurance of constant progress, of steady evolution in institutions and in human beings. Sherwood found evidence of the erosion of that faith in much of modern literature, composed, she thought, by rootless minds, a "wailing wall of masculine youth." While recognizing this shift in social ideals, Sherwood remained fundamentally an idealist and an optimist, even with the host of unsolved national and international problems confronting the world: "I think that, in spite of discouragements, that faith in which we went out into our world fifty years ago is a true one. . . . Only, growth is slower, difficulties greater than we knew then." Fifteen years later, in 1951, Sherwood still avowed that "in spite of the fact that in many ways the world seems rushing to ruin, I have faith in the future, the long-time future. If formulas are breaking and hard-and-fast creeds are vanishing . . . I find in people I have known, in friends, neighbors, people I hear about enough of goodness, heroism, and aspiration to save the race."[22]

Vida Scudder also noted that youth was attracted to the "formulae of negation." Like Sherwood, she balked not at the independence of youth and their defiance of restraint but at something much worse: "Mere parrot chatter, faint echoes of simian critics among the magazines." Whereas she had once tried to set minds free from convention and orthodoxy, by the 1930s she was attempting to keep them loyal to tradition—though not because she had become more conservative.[23] Likewise, in 1942 a basically optimistic Sophie Hart wrote to social reformer Mary Gilson, who had been her student: "You have the highest privilege in the world, that is, to sow seeds of liberal ideas in class groups. . . . You impress me as being impatient that people cling to their old prejudices, seem unwilling to weigh new ideas on their merits. But . . . to be able to work with people, to establish good fellowship among people, and then to persuade, to stand by one's guns, not to express contempt for those who do not see eye to eye with one,—this I regard as a goal of supreme value."[24]

Yet the old war horses were not spared all bitterness and frustration. Rebels to the end, they still yearned to be the vanguard. They began to feel eclipsed not so much by junior faculty or students as by a changing culture in which they appeared to be no more than Victorian survivors. A changing sexual morality and their own advancing age, in the face of an overwhelming emphasis on youth, caused these women to feel marginal.

Vida Scudder reflected ironically that Victorian cries over "Sex in Education" turned out to be "a less serious concern than 'sex' in almost anything else" in the culture. Although Scudder admitted that the works of Freud and Jung contributed to a new analysis of social reality, she did not understand why modern America paid so much attention to sex. Moreover, an unmarried woman's life, she explained, was "not dull nor did it lack romance." She admitted her lack of sexual fulfillment, defined in the twentieth century as heterosexuality, but only because she deferred to the authority of psychologists, not from any sense of personal inadequacy. She continued to believe that "married life . . . is terribly impoverished, for women."[25]

Emily Balch also defended the unmarried professional women of her generation. She explained that two generations of professional women had lived "completely celibate lives with no sense of its being difficult or of being misunderstood." Now, as older women, they were reserved about their past, perhaps "willing to admit that it has been a serious loss, certainly, to have missed what is universally regarded as the highest form of woman's experience." (Here she means heterosexual love.) She found no evidence, however, that they were abnormal, as the Freudian psychologists were then labeling career women. Of her peers she wrote that they were strong and resilient and had aged in a mellow fashion; "they are neither excessively repelled nor excessively attracted to that second-hand intimacy with sexuality which modern science and modern literature so abundantly display." Balch found it strange to read interpretations of life in novels, plays, and psychological treatises that made sex the center of social life and presented art and religion as "mere camouflaged libido." Such "imperious claims of sex" obscured the contributions of a generation of unmarried career women.[26]

In the 1920s, Freudian psychology assailed women's colleges, making a woman's biology her destiny. Women came under increasing pressure to marry, although some tried to reconcile marriage and career. Still, the conflict of generations at Wellesley was muted. Some students turned away from their professors, but many continued to aspire to the faculty's intellectual standards. However, neither women faculty nor students directly addressed the students' new desire for marriage and careers. In the 1930s and 1940s, "an unexamined dilemma became a conflict."[27]

Yet even this frustration over a changing sexual morality, a morality that would by the late 1940s castigate career women as abnormal spinsters, took second place to the bitterness these women felt over being eclipsed as pioneers. This was particularly true for Scudder—always more feisty and assertive than the others. Protesting the so-called inflexibility of age, Vida Scudder balked at the idea that her generation could no longer be identified with progress. She declared: "I know that I am still open to new ideas. But I find myself treated politely as a survival." Young Ph.D. candidates who came to consult Scudder about the history she had watched provoked her to say: "I do not altogether relish regarding myself as an historical relic." She confessed: "I can't recognize myself as the sober person of elder years, endowed with the sad sanity of age." Reflecting in 1937 on the impending world crisis, she felt "no longer among the shock troops." Scudder lamented: "It is hard to be summoned away as the battle rages. . . . One does not like to be called from the play before the climax comes. A pity; I rebel at times."[28]

Emily Balch, like Scudder, complained at times that old age is "duller than ditch-water." But Balch also saw value in aging and was fascinated by it: "To live to be old is a strange and deeply interesting experience. In some ways I find it the best part of life." Growing old was not rewarding, however, when one did not feel valued by the younger generation. She nonetheless challenged her contemporaries to adjust to an epoch of "plastic change" and to face change with courage.[29]

At Wellesley old age became yet another communal experience, and academic women became pioneers once again—this time facing the new frontier of aging. The group, whose mean age at death was seventy-eight years, remained quite healthy, active in social causes, and involved in their work and in the college. Margaret Sherwood wrote a novel, and Mary Case produced a scholarly study of Hegel—both at the age of eighty-six. The communal quality of their aging was significant. Vida Scudder noted: "I am not called to solitude; there are still contemporaries to enjoy." Scudder lived in a household of "old women," including Mary Alice Willcox and Florence Converse. Willcox's niece recalled their domestic routine of having breakfast and lunch together and then retiring to rest and read. Later they met for dinner, the scene of lively political discussions, especially about Russia and the Cold War.[30]

The intellectual norms of this community allowed these women to maintain indomitable spirits. The admiration of former students and the challenge of new ones with whom they "click delightfully" allowed them to counter feelings of uselessness. Vida Scudder acknowledged that the "loyalty of my Wellesley daughters . . . touches me deeply, deeply . . . and strengthen[s] me to go forward into old age with a glad and tranquil heart." Like other members of the Wellesley faculty community, Scudder found thinking itself a source of the "final victory of life." Margaret Sherwood echoed this, asserting that "one must never yield to passivity, to ceasing to create if one is to avoid old age."[31]

The opportunity to keep teaching allowed several women to face old age with grace. Almost blind, almost deaf, and confined, as always, to a wheelchair, Mary Case was still teaching in her seventies. Several students found the aged Case a provocative teacher, and her lectures, read aloud by students before she appeared in the classroom, sparked uninhibited comments. She was particularly concerned with student attitudes toward war. Eager to learn something new every day, she had a Wellesley student read the *New York Times* and *Time* magazine to her. The young woman was amazed: "She always had a curious mind—this was a great influence on me."[32]

Even in a nursing home, Case was avidly interested in learning. She had nurses recite poetry to her so that she could memorize a poem a week. She composed a poem of her own, entitled "The Last Victory," which reads in part:

> Foes I have met undaunted. Pain and strife
>   were ministers of life.
> I greeted danger as one greets a friend.
> Hopes died, but fears died with them. All my heart
>   leaped to the hero's part.
> So I were true, what need of other end?
> But now—to feel my courage faint and fall;
>   To know death's grim, sure call,
> Nor flash aquiver with exultant thrill;
> Though unaffrayed, to sink in mute dismay,
>   O'erwhelmed with shadows—Yea
> Even mine own faltering I can face, and will.[33]

Case hoped to live to be ninety-six. She died at ninety-nine.[34]

At the age of ninety-six, Elizabeth Kendall finally responded to her niece's pleas and went to live with her in England. The *Boston Herald* reported that Miss Kendall's "one regret about the voyage was that her 10 o'clock bedtime rule prevented her from watching the midnight dancing."

Fellow passengers reported that on a rough day of sailing she was one of the few who remained on deck.[35]

The academic women of Wellesley had spent their youths and adulthoods together, and together they embraced old age and even death. As Margaret Sherwood wrote to her old friend Elizabeth Kendall: "The road seems long as one draws nearer the end, long and a bit lonely. It is good to have footsteps chiming with one's own, and to know that a friend in whom one has a deep and abiding trust is on the same track, moving toward the same goal." Echoing these sentiments, an aged Vida Scudder wrote to a former student, herself elderly: "I am sorry for your long winter of illness. It is hard for me to think of you, and Florence, and my other 'girls' as elderly women, but Time Marches On. Miss Balch told me last evening that she woke up a night or two ago, laughing incredulously, because she was an old woman! We agreed that age was really just a joke." In the final analysis, old age never diminished the esprit of this community. In 1953, over sixty years after the formation of the group, Martha Hale Shackford wrote to a former student that she and Margaret Sherwood were able "to make a call upon Miss Scudder who, you know, is exceedingly lame and also deaf. Florence Converse was there too. I wish you could have seen the meeting,—with our friends sitting up together on the sofa very much themselves in spite of Time."[36]

For the academic women of Wellesley, the "old memories (of past struggles and disagreements and alliances)" forged an unbreakable bond. When in 1927 Professor Emerita Vida Scudder delivered an address on college teaching, she noted that "cooperation in group life was its highest privilege." She admitted that there wei 'obstacles to full fellowship . . . [and] weary moments" when "fellowship was a sham. But at our best we know that it is a triumphant reality. We meet the challenge of our privilege with gayety and courage, and with sense of the dramatic fascination there is in our task of living together. And through accelerations and retards, through concessions and slow innovations, we do move on."[37]

Moving on inevitably meant a final parting with friends, and the loss made those who were left behind draw even closer together. In 1921, six years after Katharine Coman's death, Katharine Lee Bates wrote Elizabeth Kendall: "I do not often let tears come in these late years—if one should begin to weep for joy and beauty gone, when could the weeping cease?" Within a decade, Bates herself was dead. In 1935, her old mentor and friend

Louise Manning Hodgkins wrote Caroline Hazard: "I miss Katharine inexpressibly."[38]

In learning of Katharine Lee Bates's death, Vida Scudder wrote to Louise Manning Hodgkins: "With her, the old Wellesley passes away; but yet not really. . . . It lives on, secret and potent; and the ideals held by you teachers here in the early years are transmuted into living power." For these women, Wellesley was a world where weeping and laughter went on till the last member of the group was gone.[39]

16

Eden's End?
Epilogue

The tradition exists on a good many campuses that once upon a

time the women were genuinely scornful of mere men,

disinterested in associating with them, conscious of superiority to

them! Present undergraduates find that hard to credit, but there is

considerable evidence that there was such a period.

   —Mildred H. McAfee Horton, "Segregation and
      the Women's Colleges," 1937

The pioneers are gone, and who is to take their places?

   —Mary McCarthy, "The Vassar Girl," 1951

By the 1930s, the history of the struggle for women's higher education and the flowering of separate women's colleges began to be converted into a legend with mythic qualities. At the same time, however, this extraordinary epic seemed to have little contemporary value. Indeed, in her 1936 inaugural address, Mildred McAfee Horton, Wellesley's seventh president, asserted that before accepting the presidency, she had to consider whether she was wasting her energies on an "obsolete institution" marked by "seclusion, isolation, segregation, and cloistered aloofness."[1]

Defending the women's colleges, President Horton denied their obsolescence and correctly connected Wellesley's founding with the pioneering wave of the women's rights movement. Yet her assessment of the relevance of this feminism to educated women in the 1930s reveals startling changes in attitudes toward separatism and special female values. Of the movement for women's rights based on separatism, Horton said, "Let us hope that day is past. The women's colleges had their share in it, and it was probably an era through which we had to go." Students in the 1930s, she argued, attended women's colleges partly because they no longer offered an isolated female milieu. Women came not "to mingle exclusively in feminine society, nor to collect arguments to prove women's equality or superiority. That argument is deader on a woman's campus than almost any place else in American society!"[2]

The separatism that had been crucial to feminism and Wellesley's development became anathema to feminist thinking in the 1930s. Women's homosocial culture gave way to a new heterosocial and heterosexual ideal where women sought acceptance in the male world on the basis of sameness and equality.[3]

This new avatar of the women's movement explains why President Horton sought to make Wellesley more socially attractive and more intellectually prestigious by hiring men. She vigorously pursued President Pendleton's efforts to upgrade the Wellesley faculty, initiated in 1916 after the Board of Trustees endorsed having more men on the faculty.[4] Katharine Lee Bates informed Margaret Sherwood that "there has been some stir here" over "the policy of increasing, at higher rates (wages) if necessary, the number of men." At a dinner with emeriti, "there was some more excellent speaking. Miss Pendleton says she does *not* mean to bring in 'men as men.'"[5]

But Mildred McAfee Horton wanted Wellesley to include men, "probably the more the merrier." Because Wellesley's salaries could not compete with those in the men's colleges, however, it was hard to draw topflight men. Horton admitted that it was easier to recruit superior women scholars because they had few employment options. Nonetheless, she hired men because it was "healthier to have the faculty nearly even." She believed that "if we could introduce some regular family life into the picture that was a healthier state of affairs than a too exclusively female community."[6] Elisabeth Hodder felt this policy produced "too many men employed as teachers."[7]

There had been a tremendous backlash against single faculty women in the 1930s. During the Depression, hostility toward economically independent professional women rose. Also, the medical world continued to proclaim love between women abnormal. Theories of congenital homosexuality lost ground to environmental explanations of this behavior, as medical and lay writers focused on the social causes of homosexuality, indicting the family and the schools. Critics denounced sex-segregated colleges because they congregated young adults in what one termed "a homosexual atmosphere." With heterosexual companionate marriage becoming increasingly the popular ideal, institutions that segregated women came under suspicion.[8]

At Wellesley President Horton criticized the single woman teacher who loved to attend undergraduate dances, who got terribly excited over the social life of students, and who encouraged girls to drop in to talk about trivialities. She warned that "absorption by a faculty in its students or in the college itself is perilous." The intense female world, once so prized, was now suspect.[9]

Lucy Killough, who came to Wellesley in the 1920s, bridging the old and new guard, remembered arriving to find "a lot of noble, hard working, elderly women." After that, the faculty composition changed: "There were more men which in a sense, was too bad," because the male professors were not as integrated into the community.[10] The policy, sustained through the Margaret Clapp presidency (1949–66), dimmed Henry Durant's vision of protected professorial posts for women. One of the few "happy hunting grounds" for academic women slowly shrank.[11]

Men did not dominate as the heads of department; those who were hired were usually young and easily intimidated by the giants. The appointment in 1916 of Edward Curtis, an Americanist, into a department of women Europeanists was seen as radical, but fortunately Curtis was "sufficiently easy going to survive among a department of able, strong-minded and rather divided members, all women."[12]

President Horton recognized the dominance of the old war horses and reminisced that when "a nice boy in the English department" came to see her about the administration's attitude toward men, she was nonplussed to learn that each man on the faculty was treated as either a favorite or a drudge. Male faculty felt beleaguered. During the 1940s, males at Wellesley met in an informal "male defense league."[13] Horton strove to change this milieu: "We were struggling all the way through to get more men on the faculty."[14]

At the other women's colleges, men had long dominated. But again, this was a troubled endeavor. At Vassar, where, from its founding, one-fourth of the faculty and nearly all of the departmental heads were men, this created enormous tensions. A faculty insurrection in 1915, led by Lucy Salmon, had forced President James Taylor to resign. Taylor burned all his papers before leaving and bequeathed his successor, Henry Noble McCracken, a loaded revolver! The "sex antagonisms" McCracken had to deal with were so severe that he had to split three departments and temporarily chair another to get them to function. Little wonder that McCracken viewed the creative, radical women professors at Vassar as "dangerous women all of them."[15]

In 1937, Mount Holyoke replaced President Mary Woolley with Roswell Ham, triggering a major controversy. Dorothy Kenyon spoke for many alumnae when she said that, ideally, merit alone should be considered— even though gender was definitely a factor at men's colleges. She posed a trenchant question: "Has anyone ever seriously suggested a woman for the Presidency of Harvard? Does anyone in his (or her) senses seriously contend that a woman (any woman, no matter how brilliant) would ever have a chance at it? The idea is funny, it is hard to say why, because the idea of a man as president at Mount Holyoke is not funny at all." She caught the significance of the Holyoke transition: "One door of opportunity for a woman has been closed and no other door is likely to open to take its place. The field of opportunity is narrowed for women and there is no compensating gain."[16]

At Smith College, President William Allan Neilson fretted that the women faculty did not understand his policy of recruiting men and promoting them more often than women. So restrictive was this policy that several departments were left without any women. One emeritus professor lamented that "in the future there will be no Women Faculty in Academic Departments in Smith College, if this decrease continues."[17]

The growing employment of men at women's colleges seriously impinged on the labor market for academic women. Although women applied for posts at the best universities in the country, they were rarely hired. A 1954 study of Radcliffe Ph.D.'s found that almost all who had attained the rank of full professor taught at women's colleges. Indeed, the Seven Sisters employed one-third of all full professors in the study. Lower ranks were also disproportionately represented on women's campuses. Attitudes and policies that preferred men thus severely curtailed the number of positions open to academic women.[18]

By the mid-1950s, men had replaced women faculty in many departments across the nation. Virginia Gildersleeve, dean of Barnard, decried the "cruel and unwholesome discrimination" against single women for academic and administrative positions. She attributed this bias to "certain less

responsible psychologists and psychiatrists of the day" who devalued spinster teachers as "'inhibited' and 'frustrated.'" But, Gildersleeve implored,
"why drive them away from a profession which for generations has been
natural and congenial to them? The tendency today to regard celibate teachers as frustrated . . . threatens deprivation to many children and hardship to
women who, like those of past centuries, could give talents and whole-
hearted devotion to the teaching profession."[19]

Gildersleeve rued the thirty-year deterioration in women's opportunities
for professorships and vainly hoped that male and coed colleges could be
persuaded to recognize that young people needed to be taught by both
sexes. She sadly reported that in 1952 an outstanding junior at a top university, when asked whether she had any women professors, responded,
"No, I haven't. I never thought of a woman professor. I don't believe I
should like to study under one."[20] How different from the esteem once
bestowed upon the stalwarts!

Attitudes and policies toward professional women narrowed throughout
the 1950s and early 1960s. In the era of the Cold War, any form of social
deviance was threatening. Homosexuality was deemed not only a sexual
perversion but a political subversion. At the same time, as marriage and the
family became a national ideal, married career women came under attack.
"Experts" touted the idea that academic women, in marrying more, demonstrated less career commitment.[21]

In her book *Academic Women*, Jessie Bernard argued that academic
women were voluntarily withdrawing from the labor market. She did not
consider discrimination a factor, however, because the women's colleges,
and Wellesley in particular, had never been prejudiced against academic
women. But, in fact, Wellesley was not immune to homophobia, the search
for prestige, and the need to raise standards.[22]

Even the brightest of women, with the deepest commitment to women's
higher education, could erroneously conclude that there were too few
bright women in the academic labor market. Faye Wilson, who came to
Wellesley in the 1940s, arrived to find a history department with one male
in it. By the 1950s it was about half men and half women. Wilson
explained: "There was no active effort to seek men instead of women, but
that is the way it turned out. History in many graduate schools tends to be
a man's subject." She did not attribute this tendency to prejudice or discrimination, although she did observe that the pursuit of a Ph.D. was difficult for women, because they had to fund themselves.[23]

The ideology of professionalism and merit seemed to convince many women that objective standards did prevail, "even while they saw it travestied in practice."[24] In this era women were struggling to combine marriage and teaching careers, yet they were often stopped by roadblocks created by the very universities that had admitted them as graduate students. Few scholarships for women existed, disbelief in women's seriousness of purpose was pervasive, hiring and promotion policies were blatantly pro-male, and part-time academic positions were nearly nonexistent.[25] Rules concerning nepotism kept wives from teaching in the same departments or even the same universities as their husbands. The women's colleges that did hire women who were married were often geographically removed from the urban universities where their husbands worked.[26]

By the mid-1960s, taking a Ph.D. had become an even more isolating and alienating experience for many women than it had been in the past. Designed by and for males, the Ph.D. process took little note of a woman's life. Without a community of like-minded women scholars, women had to find personal solutions to career crises. To get a degree meant facing incredible obstacles. Yet in the era of the feminine mystique, women blamed themselves for failure. A study done at Radcliffe in 1965 reveals that graduate women were suffering problems as a group but that they personalized their problems, whether psychological, financial, or emotional. Those who married during the Ph.D. program and had children or who moved away from Cambridge felt alienated and cut off from the scholarly resources. One introspective respondent termed this group the "forgotten category." Many criticized the Harvard-Radcliffe Ph.D. program for the sink-or-swim attitude of advisers who never wanted to see their students, or chapters in a dissertation, until the thesis was completed. One woman was actually told, "Here you don't get an education but an association with brilliant men."[27] A doctoral candidate in French literature, concerned about the hiring policies of universities, wondered how "to convince Deans and Department heads that a part time woman with specialized training—i.e., a Harvard Ph.D.— is an asset to their department and not just depriving them of half a full-time man."[28]

This discrimination operated despite an ostensible dearth of talent. Overtly universities courted academics during this era because of shortages associated with the Korean War or brought on by a booming postwar economy that lured bright young men and women who once would have become college professors into industry or business. The American Associ-

ation of University Women did try to develop a national program to induce
mature women with or without a Ph.D. to retrain for academic employment, but the posts envisioned were positions at two-year colleges or part-
time jobs in urban centers so that married women could be near their husbands.[29] Only with the reawakening of the women's movement were the
barriers to women's employment in colleges and universities directly
addressed. From the 1930s well into the 1960s, no remedies existed for the
victims of sex discrimination in academe.[30]

The attack on academic women was successful—in particular, the attack
on single academic women. Mary McCarthy, a Vassar graduate, sensed this
shift. In 1951, she praised the emeritae but lamented their passing: "What is
missing is a certain largeness of mind, an amplitude of style, the mantle of
a calling, a sense of historical dignity."[31] By the 1970s, women's colleges and
women college professors were denigrated. Alumnae of the Seven Sisters
excoriated their alma maters. Nora Ephron mocked Wellesley's "Samaritan"
ideals and spinster deans. To her, Wellesley College was as significant as "a
perfume factory is to the national economy."[32] Other women intellectuals
shared this attitude. To many women undergraduates, women faculty were
unenviable "eccentrics." A Wellesley undergraduate transferred to the newly
coeducational Yale, stating, "My own personal dislike is women professors.
I avoid them whenever possible."[33]

The process by which women of ideas are marginalized, devalued, and forgotten is a complex one. Disregard for women's intellect has been long-
standing. From the 1790s and the early Republican era, intellectual women
were deemed anomalies and discredited. Female learning had long been
associated with "pedantry and masculinity." Even the women scholars at
Wellesley, who were privileged to gain the "liberty of thought," were often
plagued by a sense of oddness.[34] Their community lessened their marginality and buffered them from isolation. Ironically, however, this all-female
community has itself been stigmatized.[35] Women's intellectual contributions in curriculum building, in scholarship, in writing textbooks, and in
teaching have just begun to receive wide historical appreciation.[36]

Some historians have argued that women's colleges were compromised
from the start by an ideology of domesticity and later by a focus on teaching
as opposed to research. In reality, during the Progressive Era the women's
colleges, like the liberal arts men's colleges, had many functions. The distinctions between college and university were often blurred. Thus, it is

wrong to castigate women's colleges and to denigrate their worth. Academic women prized research; in spite of heavy teaching duties and poorly equipped departments, many women produced first-rate work.[37] The Wellesley faculty believed that research served society and humanized learning. Few today accept such an advocacy role for the professoriat. Since the 1920s, the academy has favored "objective standards" in research and discouraged reform-minded professors. Thus, the careers of women devoted to reform service have suffered, and the values they espoused have been scorned.[38]

Moreover, the social climate that had promoted reform and sponsored the select few eventually succumbed to a homophobic backlash and an alarm over eugenics. Women's reproductive roles rather than their intellectual capacities were deemed worthwhile. Educated women searched for ways to reconcile marriage and careers. With no public policy, and little institutional sympathy for the female life course, academic women found themselves "inside the clockwork of male careers."[39]

Yet the impact of the pioneers on Wellesley, which lingered well into the 1960s, must be acknowledged. Disciples of the first and second generations of faculty women continued to teach the subjects and to preach the values of their mentors. Betsy Manwaring, class of 1902, wrote in 1946 of her pride that as a member of the English department she had helped to launch several women on writing careers. She also observed wryly that she had lost quite a few to diapers.[40] The careers of women in Manwaring's generation, however, contained none of the patina of the pioneers. The research university dominated during their lifetimes. Middle-class culture castigated the single life and carped at women's career ambitions. Unlike their mentors, the later generations never experienced exemption from society's norms. When in due course they were asked to summarize their achievements, many were ashamed and resisted fame even more forcefully than had their teachers.

Looking at women as a force in history, as Mary Beard suggested, requires a new lens.[41] Previous historical analyses have used paradigms derived from male experience in higher education and intellectual life. Historians have faulted women for their flaws and failures, yet women scholars fought hard to expand women's intellectual life and civic roles.[42] The Wellesley faculty were woman-centered not only in their private lives but in their public roles. They wrote and taught about women's history, women's literary contributions, and women's status. They remained remarkably aware of women's past oppression and of the need for women's higher education. They believed that education would transform women's consciousness and revolutionize their social and cultural roles. This creed connects them to other Progressive thinkers, such as John Dewey and Mary Follett.[43]

The faculty extolled the claims of community and made citizenship an explicit goal. They spoke not of women's rights but of women's responsibilities. They socialized students for work, culture, and reform. More women participated in public life during the Progressive Era than ever before. College-educated women reformers created a "female dominion" at the federal level in, for example, the Children's Bureau. The rank and file of the social settlement movement came, in particular, from Wellesley.[44]

Because they felt privileged to become scholars, the Wellesley academics overestimated what higher education could do to effect political and social change for women. Thus, their elitist cultural values constrained their capacity to attack systematically the discrimination that stymied women in the professions. But the faculty's concern for a woman's life course, their belief in a psychology of women that emphasized women's strengths, and their ethic of caring makes them important precursors of contemporary feminist scholars. Indeed, in their feminist pedagogy and philosophy, they were creating a classroom climate that we value today as the best of women's studies.[45]

When women are placed at the center of history, their values, their consciousness, and their culture achieve a different meaning and significance. Analyses of a woman's world and its connective cultural tissue are rare. The extraordinary outpouring of emotion in poems, notes, letters, songs, pageants, and pictures has often been treated as feminine (and therefore deemed worthless and sentimental) or ignored altogether. Cultural and interdisciplinary studies are few.[46] Women's language—the discourse of affections, loyalties, and love—has been virtually silenced. But this too is woman's history. The decline of public feminism in the 1920s was due not only to the winning of the vote and the waning of suffrage energies but to the erosion of this separatist women's culture.[47]

The community at Wellesley represents an achievement of no small moment. Their subculture and the professional and personal networks they sustained not only recall the value of separatism but remind us that the competitive, bureaucratic academic model once had an alternative.

Academic life at Johns Hopkins was tragic because an unbreachable gulf existed between isolated, specialized researchers. Men there found it extremely difficult to get to know fellow faculty members. A senior professor lamented that "we only get glimpses of what is going forward in the minds and hearts of our colleagues. We are like trains moving on parallel tracks. We catch sight of some face, some form that appeals to us, and it is gone."[48] How different from Wellesley, where the academic women wrought a world that touched every woman in every aspect of her life and gave a sense of belonging to an all-embracing whole.

The Wellesley faculty created a vibrant community and an enduring institution. For her one-woman newspaper of the 1920s, the *Relay,* Ellen Hayes wrote a column called "Jane Austen Returns"; in it she pictured Austen walking around England, commenting on the changes and continuities in women's lives in the one hundred years since she had written her novels. Should Ellen Hayes gather Katharine Lee Bates, Katharine Coman, Vida Scudder, Emily Balch, and Margaret Sherwood and walk the Wellesley campus today, they would find many changes: a curriculum that aims to be multicultural, a Women's Studies Department, and more tolerance for different sexual preferences. Noting these changes, they would also find still standing the Jewett, Gamble, and Sherwood Windows, Pendleton Hall, the Hallowell Gardens, and the Horton Faculty Club. There are endowed chairs for Katharine Lee Bates, Elizabeth Kendall, and Sophie Hart, as well as a Katharine Coman Professorship. Wellesley alone of the colleges mentioned here has had only women presidents. One of its daughters, Hillary Rodham Clinton, is working to shape a new health policy for the nation. This legacy is due to the pioneers and to the liberal arts college that provided a rich and professionally pivotal milieu at a time when the research university denied them careers. At Wellesley, the faculty flourished in what they called their Adamless Eden. Their community cannot be re-created, but like all Edens, it compels us still.[49]

Abbreviations

AC	*An Academic Courtship: Letters of Alice Freeman and George Herbert Palmer, 1886–1887* (Cambridge: Harvard University Press, 1940)
AFP	Alice Freeman (Palmer)
ALS	autograph letter signed (file)
Annals	*Wellesley Annals* (1882–91), events of the year summarized by student annalists
BAAUP	*Bulletin of the American Association of University Professors*
CH	Caroline Hazard
Courant	*The Courant*, college edition (1888–89), weekly newspaper published by students, faculty, and alumnae
CUL	Carl A. Kroch Library, Division of Rare and Manuscript Collections, Cornell University, Ithaca, N.Y.
CW	Carla Wenckebach
DAB	*Dictionary of American Biography*, 22 vols. (New York: Scribner's, 1928–58, suppl. 1973)
ECM/BT	Executive Committee Minutes, Board of Trustees, Wellesley College
EFP	Ellen Fitz Pendleton
EGB	Emily Greene Balch
EKK	Elizabeth Kimball Kendall
EM	Elizabeth Manwaring
EPH	Ethel Puffer (Howes)
FBF	Faculty Biographical File
GHP	George Herbert Palmer
HL	Houghton Library, Harvard University, Cambridge, Mass.
HM	Helen Merrill
HS	Horace Scudder
HUA	Harvard University Archives, Harvard University, Cambridge, Mass.
JACA	*Journal of the Association of Collegiate Alumnae*
JM	Jeannette Marks
KC	Katharine Coman
KLB	Katharine Lee Bates

LMH	Louise Manning Hodgkins
LMN	Louise McCoy North
LSM	Louise Sherwood McDowell
MAW	Mary Alice Willcox
MB	Mary Bliss
MBT	Minutes of the Board of Trustees, Wellesley College
MCF	Margaret Clay Ferguson
MHCA	Mount Holyoke College Archives, Mount Holyoke College, South Hadley, Mass.
MHS	Martha Hale Shackford
MG	Mary Barnett Gilson
MMH	Mildred McAfee (Horton)
MPS	Margaret Pollock Sherwood
MSC	Mary Sophia Case
MWC	Mary Whiton Calkins
NAW	*Notable American Women, 1607–1950,* vols. 1–3, ed. Edward T. James and Janet Wilson James (Cambridge: Harvard University Press, 1971)
NAW:MP	*Notable American Women: The Modern Period,* vol 4., ed. Barbara Sicherman and Carol Hurd Green (Cambridge: Harvard University Press, 1980)
OCA	Oberlin College Archives, Oberlin, Ohio
RCA	Radcliffe College Archives, Radcliffe College, Cambridge, Mass.
SCA	Smith College Archives, Smith College, Northampton, Mass.
SCPC	Swarthmore College Peace Collection, Swarthmore College, Swarthmore, Pa.
SFW	Sarah Frances Whiting
SH	Sophie Hart
SJ	Sophie Jewett
SL	Arthur and Elizabeth Schlesinger Library on the History of Women in America, Radcliffe College, Cambridge, Mass.
TOI-CNH	transcribed oral interview, Centennial Historian, Wellesley College
TS	typescript signed
UPA	University of Pennsylvania Archives, Philadelphia, Pa.
VCL	Special Collections, Vassar College Libraries, Poughkeepsie, N.Y.

VDS	Vida Dutton Scudder
WAM	*The Wellesley Alumnae Quarterly* (Oct. 1916–Aug. 1924)
	The Wellesley Alumnae Magazine (Oct. 1924–Aug. 1930)
	The Wellesley Magazine (Oct. 1930–Oct. 1948)
	The Wellesley Alumnae Magazine (Dec. 1948–July 1952)
	Wellesley Alumnae Magazine (Nov. 1952–Fall 1964)
	The Wellesley Alumnae Magazine (Jan. 1965–July 1965)
	Wellesley Alumnae Magazine (Nov. 1965–winter 1979)
	Wellesley (spring 1979–present)
WCA	Wellesley College Archives, Wellesley College, Wellesley, Mass.
WCN	*Wellesley College News* (1901–), newspaper featuring campus events, editorials, humor, photographs
YUA	Manuscript and Archives, Yale University Library, Yale University, New Haven, Conn.

Notes

Introduction

1. VDS, *On Journey* (New York: Dutton, 1937), 108, 110. Bates contributed to the initial plan to found Denison House but was never active in the settlement house movement.

2. Ibid., 182–83.

3. Calvin Coolidge, "Enemies of the Republic: Are the 'Reds' Stalking Our College Women?" *Delineator,* June 1921. The term "war horses" is from Lucy Wilson, TOI-CNH, 15, WCA.

4. The pioneer faculty are generally defined as the generation born in the 1860s and 1870s, who assumed their academic posts in the 1880s and 1890s and who dominated the college through the 1920s. Ellen Burrell wrote of the "bonds of Wellesley" in a letter to President Mildred McAfee (Horton), Nov. 16, 1938, "The History of the Department of Mathematics," math dept., WCA.

5. Florence Converse, "Here Was Fellowship," dedicated to VDS, in Converse, *Collected Poems* (New York: Dutton, 1937); Vida Scudder rejoiced that she was not "called to solitude" but instead lived with her companion, Florence Converse, and Mary Alice Willcox in a "household of old women" (VDS, *On Journey,* 402).

6. The following works helped me understand the concept of community: Rosabeth Moss Kanter, *Commitment and Community: Communes and Utopias in Sociological Perspective* (Cambridge: Harvard University Press, 1972); Robert A. Nisbet, *The Quest for Community: A Study in the Ethics of Order and Freedom* (New York: Oxford University Press, 1953); Laurence R. Veysey, *The Communal Experience: Anarchist and Mystical Communities in Twentieth-Century America* (Chicago: University of Chicago Press, 1978); Patricia A. Graham, *Community and Class in American Education, 1865–1918* (New York: Wiley, 1974); Martin Duberman, *Black Mountain: An Exploration in Community* (New York: Doubleday, 1973). On women's communities in literature, see Nina Auerbach, *Communities of Women: An Idea in Fiction* (Cambridge: Harvard University Press, 1978).

7. Daniel T. Rodgers, "In Search of Progressivism," *Reviews in American History* 10, no. 4 (December 1982): 113–32; Rodgers provides a good summary of the historiographic dialogue on the meanings of progressivism. See also Robert M. Crunden, *Ministers of Reform: The Progressives' Achievement in American Civilization, 1889–1920* (New York: Basic, 1982); Clyde Griffen, "The Progressive Ethos," in *The Development of An American Culture,* ed. Stanley Coben and Lorman Ratner (Englewood Cliffs, N.J.: Prentice Hall, 1970), 120–49; Noralee Frankel and Nancy Shrom Dye, eds., *Gender, Class, Race, and Reform in the Progressive Era* (Lexington: University Press of Kentucky, 1991); Linda K. Kerber and Jane Sherron DeHart, eds., *Women's America: Refocusing the Past,* 3d ed. (New York: Oxford University Press, 1991), 241.

8. On academics and the reform ethos, see Mary O. Furner, *Advocacy and Objectivity:*

273

A Crisis in the Professionalization of American Social Science, 1865–1905 (Lexington: University Press of Kentucky, 1975). Furner argues that male academics abandoned reform in favor of objectivity in order to preserve their status in the academy.

9. Estelle Freedman, "Separatism as Strategy: Female Institution Building and American Feminism, 1870–1930," *Feminist Studies* 5, no. 3 (Fall 1979): 512–29. Currently under consideration by historians is the value of studying a separate women's culture. Nancy Hewitt, e.g., finds fault with the concept of sisterhood and separatism in "Beyond the Search for Sisterhood: American Women's History in the 1980s," *Social History* 10, no. 3 (Oct. 1985): 299–321. Others see the effectiveness and primacy of separatism. Gerda Lerner argues that such worlds reveal not only "the separate occupations, status, experiences, and rituals of women but also their consciousness" (Lerner, "Placing Women in History," in *The Majority Finds Its Past: Placing Women in History* [New York: Oxford University Press, 1979], 158). See also Lerner's survey of the social conditions that have nurtured women intellectuals: "Female Clusters, Female Networks, Social Spaces," in *The Creation of Feminist Consciousness: From the Middle Ages to 1870* (New York: Oxford University Press, 1993), 221–32. She concludes that most women "whether by choice or for want of an alternative . . . removed themselves from the marriage-market"; that most accomplished their "significant work in the single state"; and that "what mattered most was the existence of some female audiences or support network" (224). For an innovative interpretation of the changing meanings attributed to woman's sphere, see Linda K. Kerber, "Separate Spheres, Female Worlds, Woman's Place: The Rhetoric of Women's History," *Journal of American History* 75, no. 1 (June 1988): 9–39.

10. VDS, "The Privileges of a College Teacher," *WAM* 11, no. 6 (Aug. 1927): 327–29.

11. Dorothy Weeks, class of 1916 and an instructor of physics in 1928–29, used the term "Wellesley marriages" in an oral interview I conducted in 1980. A good summary of the discussion on the history of sexuality is provided by Martha Vicinus, "'They Wonder to Which Sex I Belong': The Historical Roots of the Modern Lesbian Identity," *Feminist Studies* 18, no. 3 (Fall 1992): 467–98; Annamarie Jagose, "Way Out: The Category 'Lesbian' and the Fantasy of the Utopic Space," *Journal of the History of Sexuality* 4, no. 2 (Fall 1993): 264–87; Leila J. Rupp, "'Imagine My Surprise': Women's Relationships in Mid-Twentieth Century America," in *Hidden From History: Reclaiming the Gay and Lesbian Past*, ed. Martin Duberman, Martha Vicinus, and George Chauncey, Jr. (New York: Meridian, 1989), 395–410.

12. Virginia Woolf, *A Room of One's Own* (New York: Harcourt, Brace and World, 1929).

13. Barbara Welter, "The Cult of True Womanhood, 1820–1860," *American Quarterly* 18, no. 2 (Summer 1966): 151–74.

14. KLB, "Wellesley's Fifty Golden Years of Achievement: The Purposeful Women Who Reared the College from Struggling Babyhood to Glorious Womanhood and the Men Who Aided Them," *Boston Evening Transcript,* May 16, 1925: 1, 8.

15. The standard institutional literature is too vast to summarize. One interesting study of fifty-eight male faculty who taught moral philosophy in northern colleges before the Civil War is Wilson Smith, *Professors and Public Ethics: Studies of Northern Moral Philosophers Before the Civil War* (Ithaca: Cornell University Press, 1956). James McLachlan notes that there is "an astonishing gap" in the literature on the academic profession (McLachlan, "The American College in the Nineteenth Century: Toward a Reappraisal," *Teachers College Record* 80, no. 2 [Dec. 1978]: 298 n. 27); Patricia A. Graham, "So Much to Do: Guides for Historical Research on Women in Higher Education," *Teachers College Record* 76, no. 3 (Feb. 1975): 421–29; Geraldine Jonçich Clifford, "'Shaking Dangerous Questions from the Crease': Gender and American Higher Education," *Feminist Issues* 3, no. 2 (Fall 1983): 3–62; Thomas L. Haskell, *The Emergence of Professional Social Science: The American Social Science Association and the Nineteenth-Century Crisis of Authority* (Urbana: University of Illinois Press, 1977), deals mainly with men but has helped shape my thinking. I have been influenced as well by Burton J. Bledstein, *The Culture of Professionalism: The Middle Class and the Development of Higher Education in America* (New York: Norton, 1976), which links higher education with middle-class values but focuses on male presidents.

16. Richard Hofstadter, *Academic Freedom in the Age of the College* (New York: Columbia University Press, 1955); Stanley M. Guralnick, "Sources of Misconception on the Role of Science in the Nineteenth Century American College," *Isis* 65, no. 228 (Sept. 1974): 352–66; Stanley M. Guralnick, "The American Scientist in Higher Education, 1820–1910," in *The Sciences in the American Context: New Perspectives,* ed. Nathan Reingold (Washington, D.C.: Smithsonian Institution Press, 1979), 99–141; Dorothy Ross, *The Origins of American Social Science* (Cambridge: Cambridge University Press, 1991). Margaret W. Rossiter revolutionized our understanding of the contributions of women scientists in *Women Scientists in America: Strategies and Struggles to 1940* (Baltimore: Johns Hopkins University Press, 1982). Two recent and important revisionist studies of the "old time" college are Louise L. Stevenson, *Scholarly Means to Evangelical Ends: The New Haven Scholars and the Transformation of Higher Learning in America, 1830–1890* (Baltimore: Johns Hopkins University Press, 1986); and W. Bruce Leslie, *Gentlemen and Scholars: College and Community in the "Age of the University," 1865–1917* (University Park: Pennsylvania State Press, 1992). They deal only with male faculty.

17. See, e.g., Allen F. Davis, *American Heroine: The Life and Legend of Jane Addams* (New York: Oxford University Press, 1973); Christopher Lasch uses Addams as one model in *The New Radicalism in America, 1889–1963: The Intellectual as Social Type* (New York: Random House, 1965). See also Barbara Sicherman, *Alice Hamilton: A Life in Letters* (Cambridge: Harvard University Press, 1984); Ann J. Lane, *To Herland and Beyond: The Life and Work of Charlotte Perkins Gilman* (New York: Pantheon, 1990); and Larry Ceplair, ed., *Charlotte Perkins Gilman: A Nonfiction Reader* (New York: Columbia University Press, 1991); Susan P. Conrad, *Perish the Thought: Intellectual Women in Romantic America, 1830–1860* (Secaucus, N.J.: Citadel Press, 1978), examines women intellectuals in the antebellum period.

18. Welter, "The Cult of True Womanhood, 1820–1860"; while concluding that Victorian values victimized women, Welter stressed that women might manipulate the social code by upholding morality not only at home but in the public realm. See also Glenda Gates Riley, "The Subtle Subversion: Changes in the Traditionalist Image of American Women," *The Historian* 32, no. 2 (Feb. 1970): 210–27; Karen J. Blair, *The Clubwoman as Feminist: True Womanhood Redefined, 1868–1914* (New York: Holmes and Meier, 1980).

19. Jill Ker Conway, "Perspectives on the History of Women's Education in the U.S.," *History of Education Quarterly* 14 (Spring 1974): 1–12. In *Beyond Separate Spheres,* Rosalind Rosenberg argues that this is too bald a conclusion. Some academic women, trained in psychology and sociology at coeducational research institutions such as Chicago, did challenge sexual stereotyping; but this feminist inquiry, she claims, could not occur in the milieu of a woman's college. Rosalind Rosenberg, *Beyond Separate Spheres: Intellectual Roots of Modern Feminism* (New Haven: Yale University Press, 1982); in a book review, Helen Lefkowitz Horowitz dissents, praising the high intellectual quality of the women's colleges (Horowitz, "Integrating Women in Intellectual History," *American Quarterly* 36, no. 4 [Fall 1984]: 575–80).

20. Sheila M. Rothman, *Woman's Proper Place: A History of Changing Ideals and Practices, 1870 to the Present* (New York: Basic, 1978), 39; Elaine Kendall, *Peculiar Institutions: An Informal History of the Seven Sister Colleges* (New York: Putnam's, 1975).

21. The conventional interpretation of the Gilded Age as a "dark age" for feminist reform is found in Aileen S. Kraditor, *The Ideas of the Woman Suffrage Movement, 1890–1920* (New York: Doubleday, 1971); Sally Gregory Kohlstedt presents a different interpretation in "Maria Mitchell: The Advancement of Women in Science," *New England Quarterly* 51 (Mar. 1978): 39–63, esp. 40 n. 3. Geoffrey Blodgett begins a revisionist approach to the Gilded Age in "A New Look at the Gilded Age: Politics in a Cultural Context," in *Victorian America,* ed. Daniel Walker Howe (Philadelphia: University of Pennsylvania Press, 1976), 95–108; see also Louise L. Stevenson, *The Victorian Homefront: American Thought and Culture, 1860–1880* (New York: Twayne, 1991).

22. If we are to understand the women faculty at Wellesley, we must separate style from deed. Many genteel, educated, middle-class nineteenth-century American women became social radicals. See Willie Lee Rose, "American Women in Their Place," *New York Review of Books,* July 14, 1977, 3–4; Rose, "The Emergence of the American Woman," *New York Review of Books,* Sept. 15, 1977, 19–32.

23. Anne Firor Scott, "The Ever-Widening Circle: The Diffusion of Feminist Values from the Troy Female Seminary, 1822–1872," in *Making the Invisible Woman Visible* (Urbana: University of Illinois Press, 1984), 64–88; Joan Wallach Scott, "Women's History as Women's Education," in *Women's History as Women's Education* (Northampton, Mass.: Smith College, 1985), 23–38; Joyce Antler, *Lucy Sprague Mitchell: The Making of a Modern Woman* (New Haven: Yale University Press, 1987); Rossiter, *Women Scientists in America*; Barbara Miller Solomon, *In the*

Company of Educated Women: A History of Women and Higher Education in America (New Haven: Yale University Press, 1985); Rosenberg, *Beyond Separate Spheres*; Ellen Fitzpatrick, *Endless Crusade: Women, Social Scientists, and Progressive Reform* (New York: Oxford University Press, 1990); Lynn D. Gordon, *Gender and Higher Education in the Progressive Era* (New Haven: Yale University Press, 1990). Until recently women's intellectual history in the early republic and antebellum era has received far more serious attention than has the post–Civil War era. See Linda K. Kerber, *Women of the Republic: Intellect and Ideology in Revolutionary America* (Chapel Hill: University of North Carolina Press, 1980); Mary Beth Norton, *Liberty's Daughters: The Revolutionary Experience of American Women, 1750–1800* (Boston: Little, Brown, 1980); Mary Kelley, *Private Woman, Public Stage: Literary Domesticity in Nineteenth-Century America* (New York: Oxford University Press, 1984). On the formation of a new social type of womanhood, see Carroll Smith-Rosenberg, "The New Woman as Androgyne: Social Disorder and Gender Crisis, 1870–1936," in *Disorderly Conduct: Visions of Gender in Victorian America* (New York: Knopf, 1985), 245–96.

24. Furner, *Advocacy and Objectivity*; Dorothy Ross, "The Development of the Social Sciences," in *The Organization of Knowledge in Modern America, 1860–1920*, ed. Alexandra Oleson and John Voss (Baltimore: Johns Hopkins University Press, 1979), 107–38; Dorothy Ross, *The Origins of American Social Science*.

25. Two historians who emphasize locating American intellectuals and their discourse within a particular social context are David A. Hollinger, "Historians and the Discourse of Intellectuals," in *In the American Province: Studies in the History and Historiography of Ideas* (Bloomington: Indiana University Press, 1985), 130–51; and Thomas Bender, "The Cultures of Intellectual Life: The City and the Professions," in *New Directions in American Intellectual History*, ed. Paul K. Conkin and John Higham (Baltimore: Johns Hopkins University Press, 1979), 181–95.

26. See Joan Jacobs Brumberg and Nancy Tomes, "Women in the Professions: A Research Agenda for American Historians," *Reviews in American History* 10, no. 2 (June 1982): 275–96; see also Elizabeth Scarborough and Laurel Furumoto, *Untold Lives: The First Generation of American Women Psychologists* (Ithaca: Cornell University Press, 1987); Penina Migdal Glazer and Miriam Slater, *Unequal Colleagues: The Entrance of Women into the Professions, 1890–1940* (New Brunswick: Rutgers University Press, 1987); Mary Ann Dzuback, "Professionalism, Higher Education, and American Culture: Burton J. Bledstein's *The Culture of Professionalism*," *History of Education Quarterly* 33, no. 3 (Fall 1993): 381; for a study of academic women who functioned in isolation and the toll that this marginality took on their lives and careers, see Geraldine Jonçich Clifford, ed., *Lone Voyagers: Academic Women in Coeducational Institutions, 1870-1937* (New York: Feminist Press, 1989). In *Beyond Separate Spheres*, Rosenberg also stresses the costs of isolation and marginality to academic women whose careers at the research universities cut them off from feminist communities.

27. Rayna Rapp, "Review Essay: Anthropology," *Signs* 4, no. 3 (Spring 1979): 513.

28. The differences in discourse between the antebellum women's benevolent and

reform organizations and the post–Civil war generation are discussed in Lori D. Ginsberg, *Women and the Work of Benevolence: Morality, Politics, and Class in the Nineteenth-Century United States* (New Haven: Yale University Press, 1990); see also Mary P. Ryan, *Womanhood in America: From Colonial Times to the Present* (New York: Franklin Watts, 1983), 208–10.

29. When President Hazard retired in 1910, rumors spread that she was to be replaced by a man. Alumnae and faculty cried out, "What and spoil our 'Adamless Eden'?" ("Man to Rule Wellesley? No! Say Graduates Here," *Evening Newspaper* [Minneapolis, n.d., probably 1910], Hazard Scrapbook, 1910 [pertaining to resignation], CH Papers, WCA).

30. VDS, *On Journey,* 135–53.

1
Incipit Vita Nova

1. Ernestine Giddings to "Dear Mary," Aug. 21, 1875, Class Activities, class of 1879, WCA.
2. Announcement of *Wellesley College Calendar,* Dec. 1874, 2, WCA.
3. Alice Hackett, *Wellesley: Part of the American Story* (New York: Dutton, 1949), 60.
4. Edward Abbott, "Wellesley College," *Harper's* 53, no. 315 (Aug. 1876): 321; Lyman Abbott, "Wellesley College," *Christian Union,* June 9, 1880. See also Henry H. Tilley, "Wellesley College for Women," *Washington Chronicle,* Nov. 14, 1875.
5. "A Woman's College," *Boston Daily Advertiser,* Oct. 28, 1875; J. H. W., "The Women's University," *New York Times,* Jan. 4, 1889.
6. LMN, "Speech for '79 and the Trustees at Semi-Centennial," 2, Unprocessed LMN Papers, WCA; also LMN, "A Wellesley Retrospect," *WAM* 14, no. 2 (Dec. 1929): 54–56.
7. Thomas Wentworth Higginson, "Experiments," in *Common Sense about Women* (Boston: Lee and Shepard, 1882), 199.
8. Laurel Thatcher Ulrich, "Vertuous Women Found: New England Ministerial Literature, 1668–1735," *American Quarterly* 28 (Spring 1976): 19–40.
9. Barbara Welter, "The Cult of True Womanhood, 1820–1860," in *Dimity Convictions: The American Woman in the Nineteenth Century* (Athens: Ohio University Press, 1976), 31–41. See, e.g., Susan Phinney Conrad, *Perish the Thought: Intellectual Women in Romantic America, 1830–1860* (Secaucus, N.J.: Citadel Press, 1978).
10. Linda K. Kerber, *Women of the Republic: Intellect and Ideology in Revolutionary America* (Chapel Hill: University of North Carolina Press, 1980).
11. Conrad, *Perish the Thought;* David F. Allmendinger, "Mount Holyoke Students Encounter the Need for Life-Planning, 1837–1850," *History of Education Quarterly* 19 (Spring 1979): 27–47.
12. On the common school movement, see Stanley K. Schultz, *The Culture Factory: Boston Public Schools, 1789–1860* (New York: Oxford University Press, 1973); Carl F. Kaestle, *Pillars of the Republic: Common Schools and American Society, 1780–1860* (New York: Hill and Wang, 1983).

13. John Raymond, "The Demand of the Age for a Liberal Education for Women and How It Should Be Met," in *The Liberal Education of Women:The Demand and the Method,* ed. James Orton (New York: Barnes, 1873), 27–58. Raymond found the vanguard of women's rights to be too radical; but he shrewdly noted that "extremists always precede and herald a true reform." After such a revolt, those who followed might "gather whatever of fruit it may have shaken from the tree of truth" (50). John M. Greene to Sophia Smith, Jan. 7, 1868, Beginnings of Smith College, Folio of Documents assembled by John M. Greene, SCA.

14. Edward H. Clarke, *Sex in Education, or a Fair Chance for the Girls* (Boston: Osgood, 1873).

15. I discovered that Henry Durant, Edward Clarke, and Thomas Wentworth Higginson were in the same graduating class at Harvard. See class of 1841, Bachelors of Arts Graduates, Quinquennial Catalogue of Harvard University, 1636–1930, HUA.

16. SFW, Memorial Service for Henry Durant, Oct. 1894, 23; SFW, Notes for Speeches and Addresses (1894–1916), SFW Papers, WCA. Florence Morse Kingsley, *The Life of Henry Fowle Durant: Founder of Wellesley College* (New York: Century, 1924), 193–94.

17. *La vita nuova,* or *The New Life,* is an autobiographical work by Dante in verse and prose. See MHS, *An Introduction to Dante's* The New Life (Natick, Mass.: Suburban Press, 1959).

18. Eliot praised those women's colleges that "appointed men to all professorships" and was therefore critical of Wellesley (1879 Smith College commencement address, as quoted in L. Clark Seelye, *The Early History of Smith College, 1871–1910* [Boston: Houghton Mifflin, 1923], 48). See also Thomas Wentworth Higginson, "Which College?" *Woman's Journal,* Feb. 26, 1876.

19. Mary Barnett Burke, "The Growth of the College," WAM 34, no. 3 (Feb. 1950): 179; Ada L. Howard, "Reminiscences of Henry Fowle Durant," 12, Ada L. Howard Papers, WCA.

20. Margaret E. Taylor and Jean Glasscock, "The Founders and the Early Presidents," in *Wellesley College, 1875–1975: A Century of Women,* ed. Jean Glasscock (Wellesley: Wellesley College, 1975), 2–3. See also Frances W. Knickerbocker, "Ripley, Sarah Alden Bradford," *NAW.*

21. Florence Converse, *Wellesley College: A Chronicle of the Years 1875–1938* (Wellesley: Hathaway House, 1939), 13–14. See also Michael Grossberg, "Institutionalizing Masculinity: The Law as a Masculine Profession," in *Meanings for Manhood: Constructions of Masculinity in Victorian America,* ed. Mark C. Carnes and Clyde Griffen (Chicago: University of Chicago Press, 1990), 133–51.

22. Henry Durant, *The Influences of Rural Life* (Boston: Norfolk Agricultural Society, 1860), 17–18.

23. On Pauline Durant see "Centennial of YWCA Honored by Library," *Boston Public Library News* 7, no. 4 (1955): 2; "Mrs. Pauline A. Durant Dead," *Boston Transcript,* Feb. 13, 1917; Founders Papers, Pauline A. Durant, WCA.

24. The connection between the rhetoric, ideology, and goals of the women's rights

movement and those of the movement for higher education has never been adequately pursued. If one subscribes to Ellen DuBois's thesis that feminism did not die in the 1870s, one might persuasively argue that the movement for women's higher education in the late nineteenth century was a legacy of the women's rights movement of 1840–70. See *Feminism and Suffrage: The Emergence of an Independent Women's Movement in America, 1848–1869* (Ithaca: Cornell University Press, 1978). Interestingly, Durant, as a lay evangelist minister who encouraged women to rebel against restrictive sentimental womanhood to demand more intellectual public roles, is a cultural type at variance with the ministers presented by Ann Douglas in *The Feminization of American Culture* (New York: Knopf, 1977).

25. *Mount Holyoke Journal,* entry for Nov. 28, 1867, MHCA; Taylor and Glasscock, "Founders," 8.

26. Durant, *The Influences of Rural Life,* 8. I obtained information on Eben Horsford from Andrew Fiske, TOI-CNH, WCA. Fiske is Eben Horsford's great-grandson. See also Taylor and Glasscock, "Founders," 18–21.

27. On pre–Civil War communitarian efforts, see John L. Thomas, "Romantic Reform in America, 1815–1864," *American Quarterly* 17, no. 4 (Winter 1965): 656–81; and Ronald G. Walters, *American Reformers, 1815–1860* (New York: Hill and Wang, 1978). Both scholars emphasize a diminution of reform spirit after the Civil War. A recent revisionist study that supports my interpretation is Robert S. Fogarty, *All Things New: American Communes and Utopian Movements, 1860–1914* (Chicago: University of Chicago Press, 1990). Standard accounts treat the period as bereft of feminism; see Aileen S. Kraditor, *The Ideas of the Woman Suffrage Movement, 1890–1920* (New York: Doubleday, 1971), 4. A challenge to this interpretation is Sally Gregory Kohlstedt, "Maria Mitchell: The Advancement of Women in Science," *New England Quarterly* 51 (Mar. 1978): 39–63, esp. 40 n. 3.

28. Henry Durant, *The Spirit of the College* (a sermon, probably delivered Sept. 23, 1877) (Boston: n.p., 1890), 3, Founders File, WCA.

29. *Wellesley College Calendar,* 1876–77. The Browning Room contained a copy of the poem "Aurora Leigh"; it is still in the library.

30. Wellesley College Circular to Parents, June 1, 1876, WCA. Durant's diet reforms were no doubt influenced by Eben Horsford, who invented a number of health foods and advertised them in the college newspaper. For a discussion of the ideals of nineteenth-century health reformers and how these affected the role of women, see Regina Morantz, "Making Women Modern: Middle Class Women and Health Reform in Nineteenth-Century America," *Journal of Social History* 10, no. 4 (June 1977): 490–507. See also Bruce Haley, *The Healthy Body and Victorian Culture* (Cambridge: Harvard University Press, 1978). Wellesley College Circular to Parents and Students, Aug. 1, 1878, and Aug. 1, 1879, WCA.

31. Abbott, "Wellesley College."

32. C. Stuart Gager, "Wellesley College and the Development of Botanical Education in America," *Science* 67 (Feb. 17, 1978): 171–78; Joan Burstyn, "Early Women in Education: The Role of the Anderson School of Natural History," *Journal of Edu-*

cation 159, no. 3 (Aug. 1977): 50–64. The library is described in the *Washington Chronicle* (Washington, D.C.), Nov. 14, 1875, clipping file, WCA.

33. SFW, "The Department of Physics," *WCN,* Feb. 22, 1911, 6.

34. Information on Sarah Glazier can be found in HM, "The History of the Department of Mathematics," math dept., 8–10, WCA. I obtained biographical information on Glazier and Storke from the Vassar College Archives. Sarah Glazier's letters written during her undergraduate years are in Constance Mayfield Rourke, ed., "Some Vassar Letters," *Vassar Quarterly* (May 1922): 153–63. Susan Hallowell and SFW FBF, WCA. See also Gladys Anslow, "Whiting, Sarah Frances," *NAW.* Information on Ada Howard can be found in Ada L. Howard Papers, WCA.

35. Mary Russell Bartlett, "Wellesley Revisited," *WAM* 9, no. 6 (Aug. 1925): 316.

36. Because these regulations were printed with a grey cover, they were known to generations of students as "The Grey Book" (WCA).

37. KLB, as quoted in Taylor and Glasscock, "Founders," 17.

38. Converse, *Wellesley College,* 26.

39. *Wellesley Magazine* (a literary magazine published between 1892 and 1921; not to be confused with the *Wellesley Alumnae Magazine*), 1895–96, 167–68, WCA; Hermann R. Muelder, "Whiting Hall: The Preservation of History," *The Knox Reporter* 1, no. 5 (Mar. 1977): 2; Ada L. Howard Papers, WCA. According to Sarah Gold Hayden, class of 1879, whose mother had been a roommate of Ada Howard's at Mount Holyoke, Howard doubted her fitness for the presidency and had to be persuaded by Henry Durant to accept the position (Sarah Gold Hayden, "Recollections and Impressions of Wellesley College, 1877–79, or Days of '79 at Wellesley," 2, class of 1881, WCA). Hackett, *Wellesley,* 69.

40. Frances Robinson Johnson to her mother, Jan. 9, 1876, and Feb. 4, 1877, class of 1879, Frances Robinson Johnson Papers, WCA.

41. Converse, *Wellesley College,* 37; Charlotte Conant, as quoted in Hackett, *Wellesley,* 69. See also Sarah Gold Hayden, "Recollections and Impressions," 6, class of 1881, WCA.

42. Ambia C. Harris, notebook, 1877–88, class of 1879; Mary Ella Whipple, notebook, 1873–89, class of 1879, WCA.

43. Estelle M. Hurll, "Professor Lord and Old Wellesley," *WAM* 5, no. 1 (Oct. 1920): 1. Lucia Grieve, diary entry, Sept. 6–7, 1882, vol. 9, class of 1883, Lucia Grieve Papers, WCA. For another view of the "two strong opposing elements" of women faculty, see Mary A. Burnham to "My dear Mrs. Lord," Sept. 11, 1875, TS, botany dept. scrapbook (1875–1946), WCA.

44. MBT, Nov. 16, 1875, discusses the role of visitors to the college who evaluate classes under the auspices of the Executive Committee, WCA. See "An Act to Change the Name of Wellesley Female Seminary, 1873," in *Acts of Incorporation, Deeds of Gift, and Statutes of Wellesley College* (Boston: Frank Wood, 1885), 5. The college was authorized to grant degrees in Feb. 1877. HM, "The History of the Department of Mathematics," math dept., 9, WCA.

45. Frances Robinson Johnson to her mother, June 4, 1876, class of 1879, Frances Robinson Johnson Papers, WCA.

46. Frances Robinson Johnson to her mother, Thursday, n.d. (June 15, 1876), class of 1879, Frances Robinson Johnson Papers, WCA.

47. Frances Robinson Johnson to her mother, June 11 and 18, 1876, class of 1879, Frances Robinson Johnson Papers, WCA.

48. Bessie Capen to Mr. Durant, Aug. 1, 1876, Correspondence with Trustees, Unprocessed Records of the Board of Trustees, WCA. On the envelope Mrs. Pauline Durant scribbled: "Miss Capen's insolent letter from Berlin resigning."

49. Frances Robinson Johnson to her mother, June 14, 1876, class of 1879, Frances Robinson Johnson Papers, WCA.

50. Barbara M. Solomon, "Freeman, Alice," *NAW*.

51. Hackett, *Wellesley*, 68; Carrie Park Harrington to "My Dear Sophie and Papa," Nov. 6, 1881, class of 1883, Carrie Park Harrington Papers, WCA. LMH diary entry, Oct. 9, 1881, Unprocessed LMH Papers, WCA.

52. Emily Murdock Dawley to "Dear Flo," Nov. 14, 1881 (about Ada Howard she said: "Nothing can be worse than the past reign"), class of 1883, WCA; Florence Floyd Merriam to "Dear Mama," Nov. 16, 1881, class of 1885, Florence Floyd Merriam Papers, WCA.

53. History of the Class of 1882, quoted in Hackett, *Wellesley*, 70. Emily Murdock Dawley to "Dear Flo," Nov. 14, 1881, class of 1883, WCA; ECM/BT, Minutes, June 1, 1882, WCA.

54. Hackett, *Wellesley*, 70, and "Class History of 1885," 4, WCA. Emily Murdock Dawley to "Dear Flo," Nov. 14, 1881, class of 1883, WCA. Lucia Grieve, diary entries, Nov. 14, 17, 1881, vol. 7, class of 1883, Lucia Grieve Papers, WCA. Carrie Park Harrington to "My Dear Soph and Papa," Monday morning (Nov. 21, 1881), Nov. 22 postmark on back of envelope, class of 1883, WCA. Ada Howard was given a financial subsidy raised as a voluntary gift by alumnae and transmitted to her by Pauline Durant each year to save her from destitution. She is buried in Woodlawn, a cemetery in the town of Wellesley (Hackett, *Wellesley*, 70–71; MBT, Nov. 5, 1885, WCA).

2

Alice Freeman and Young Wellesley

1. Barbara Miller Solomon, "Palmer, Alice Elvira Freeman," *NAW*; as quoted in Margaret E. Taylor and Jean Glasscock, "The Founders and the Early Presidents," in *Wellesley College, 1875–1975: A Century of Women*, ed. Jean Glasscock (Wellesley: Wellesley College, 1975), 27. In her autobiography Vida Scudder used the term "Young Wellesley" to portray this era (*On Journey* [New York: Dutton, 1937], 99 and throughout chap. 1). Scudder borrowed the phrase from the title of a poem by Katharine Lee Bates, which was reprinted in *On Journey* (98).

2. Vassar College, founded in 1865, suffered a confusion of purposes by the 1880s. Cf. Debra Herman, "College and After: The Vassar Experiment in Women's Education, 1861–1924" (Ph.D. diss., Stanford University, 1979). Sage College, the women's college of Cornell, similarly experienced a shift from a pioneering mentality and mission in the mid-1880s and early 1890s. See Charlotte Williams

Conable, *Women at Cornell: The Myth of Equal Education* (Ithaca: Cornell University Press, 1977), esp. chap. 4. Under Alice Freeman, Wellesley's renewed intellectual vigor precipitated the extraordinary social and intellectual activism that characterized the college in the 1890s.

3. Taylor and Glasscock, "Founders," 24; alumna quoted in GHP, *Life of Alice Freeman Palmer* (Boston: Houghton Mifflin, 1908), 154; hereafter cited as *Life of AFP.*

4. KLB, "An Intimate Study of a Rare Woman," *The Congregationalist and Christian World,* May 16, 1908, 650. My ideas about leadership styles in communes have been crystallized by Laurence R. Veysey, *The Communal Experience: Anarchist and Mystical Communities in Twentieth-Century America* (Chicago: University of Chicago Press, 1978); and by Rosabeth Moss Kantor, *Commitment and Community: Communes and Utopias in Sociological Perspective* (Cambridge: Harvard University Press, 1972). Leila S. McKee to Miss Perkins, Feb. 5, 1903, Correspondence, AFP Papers, WCA.

5. GHP, *Life of AFP,* 160, 331.

6. Ibid., 332, 139. CH, "Personal Recollections of AFP," in *From College Gates* (Boston: Houghton Mifflin, 1925), 208.

7. GHP, *Life of AFP,* 20–21; AFP, "Why I Am an Optimist," Apr. 5, 1902 (unidentified clipping), General (continued), AFP Papers, WCA.

8. GHP, *Life of AFP,* 33.

9. Ibid., 21.

10. Ibid., 36.

11. Barbara Welter, "Coming of Age in America: The American Girl in the Nineteenth Century," in *Dimity Convictions: The American Woman in the Nineteenth Century* (Athens: Ohio University Press, 1976), 17.

12. On women and the evangelical conversion experience, see Joan Jacobs Brumberg, *Mission For Life: The Story of the Family of Adoniram Judson* (New York: Free Press, 1980), esp. 79–81; Joan Jacobs Brumberg, "Zenanas and Girlless Villages: The Ethnology of American Evangelical Women, 1870–1910," *Journal of American History* 69, no. 2 (1982): 347–71; and Nancy F. Cott, *The Bonds of Womanhood: "Woman's Sphere" in New England, 1780–1835* (New Haven: Yale University Press, 1977), 139–40. GHP, *Life of AFP,* 62.

13. AFP, *Why Go to College?* (Boston: Crowell, 1897), 13; GHP, *Life of AFP,* 43. AFP, "Three Types of Women's Colleges," in GHP and AFP, *The Teacher: Essays and Addresses on Education* (Boston: Houghton Mifflin, 1908), 322–23.

14. Barbara Welter, "The Merchant's Daughter: A Tale from Life," in Welter, *Dimity Convictions,* 42–56.

15. Alice Freeman had several marriage offers and finally did marry an older man. In her role as Wellesley president she successfully dealt with Henry Durant, Eben Horsford, Charles Eliot, Andrew White, William Rainey Harper, James Angell, and William Tucker. There are parallels with Emma Willard's managerial talents. See Anne Firor Scott, "What, Then, Is the American: This New Woman?" *Journal of American History* 65, no. 3 (Dec. 1978): 679–703.

16. The idea of a "family claim" on a bright daughter is set forth by Jane Addams,

"The Subjective Necessity of Social Settlements," in *The Social Thought of Jane Addams*, ed. Christopher Lasch (New York: Bobbs-Merrill, 1965), 28–44.

17. Dorothy Gies McGuigan, *A Dangerous Experiment: One Hundred Years of Women at the University of Michigan* (Ann Arbor: Center for Continuing Education of Women, 1970), 31–34, 71–72.

18. AFP, "Three Types of Women's Colleges," 321.

19. McGuigan, *A Dangerous Experiment,* 72.

20. The description of the QC (Quadrantic Club) comes mainly from Lucy Salmon, as quoted in Louise Fargo Brown, *Apostle of Democracy: The Life of Lucy Maynard Salmon* (New York: Harper, 1943), 50. See also AFP to Lucy Salmon, Nov. 1, 1874, file 42, AFP Papers, University of Michigan Archives. Angie Chapin, a professor of Greek at Wellesley, was also an undergraduate at Michigan and a member of the QCs (Brown, *Apostle of Democracy,* 58). Dress reform was another subject taken up by the QCs. A photo of the QCs, with information on their accomplishments, appeared in the *Michigan Alumnus*, May 10, 1941, 402. On Freeman's reorganization of the YMCA, see Kate Upson Clark, "AFP," *Ladies' Home Journal*, n.d. (probably 1902).

21. University of Michigan Ladies Library Association Centennial Message, 1876, copied from Michigan Historical Collection, AFP Papers, WCA. I thank Wilma Slaight for bringing this document to my attention.

22. AFP, "Three Types of Women's College," 323.

23. AFP, *Why Go to College?* 13.

24. Harriet Bishop, as quoted in McGuigan, *A Dangerous Experiment,* 73.

25. KLB, "Wellesley's Fifty Golden Years of Achievement: The Purposeful Women Who Have Reared the College from Struggling Babyhood to Glorious Womanhood and the Men Who Have Aided Them," *Boston Evening Transcript,* May 16, 1925, 8.

26. GHP, *Life of AFP,* 67, 69, 71. See also AFP to Lucy Andrews, Apr. 5, 1875, ALS, WCA; in this letter Freeman discusses the fifty-two-year-old bachelor who pursued her.

27. GHP, *Life of AFP,* 74, 75–76, 77.

28. Ibid., 88. George Palmer recalled that as Alice lay dying, she murmured Stella's name (91).

29. Alice Payne Hackett, *Wellesley: Part of the American Story* (New York: Dutton, 1949), 78; GHP, *Life of AFP,* 103. The various offers to teach at Wellesley are recorded in the retrospective joint diary of AFP and GHP, AFP Papers, WCA.

30. The faculty recognized that Freeman had had an unusual opportunity to advance her career: "Few women have had her opportunity and few have met with her success" (Testimonial of the Faculty of Wellesley College to President Freeman [handwritten MS], Dec. 1, 1887, President's Office Files, WCA).

31. KLB, "Wellesley's Fifty Years of Achievement," 1.

32. GHP, *Life of AFP,* 96, 160–61; see Lucia Grieve diary, June 23, 24(?), 1882, vol. 8, class of 1883, Lucia Grieve Papers, WCA.

33. GHP, *Life of AFP,* 113. For the correct dating of Freeman's lung hemorrhage, I

have relied on Ruth Bordin, *Alice Freeman Palmer: The Evolution of a New Woman* (Ann Arbor: University of Michigan Press, 1993).

34. Carrie Park Harrington to her family ("My Beloved Family"), Wednesday afternoon (n.d., probably Nov. 1881), class of 1883, Carrie Park Harrington Papers, WCA. Harrington astutely noted: "Miss Freeman is aware of her own prestige and is a mite of a toady."

35. Carrie Park Harrington to her family ("My Dear Soph and Papa"), Nov. 22, 1881, class of 1883, Carrie Park Harrington Papers, WCA.

36. Alice Freeman's conversation with Henry Durant is quoted in Lyman Abbott, "Snap-shots of My Contemporaries," *The Outlook,* Aug. 24, 1921, 644; GHP, *Life of AFP,* 160.

37. Leila S. McKee to Miss Perkins, Feb. 5, 1903, Correspondence, AFP Papers, WCA.

38. Abbott, "Snap-Shots of My Contemporaries," 645.

39. GHP, *Life of AFP,* 102.

40. Emily Orr Clifford, "Wellesley in the Eighties," *WAM* 31, no. 2 (Dec. 1946): 105.

41. GHP, *Life of AFP,* 162. For another student's example of Freeman's control, see Clara Capron to her family, Oct. 28, 1883, class of 1887, Correspondence of Clara Capron, WCA.

42. Mary C. Wiggin, class of 1885, as quoted in Florence Converse, *Wellesley College: A Chronicle of the Years 1875–1938* (Wellesley: Hathaway House, 1939), 128. Alice Freeman lived in a presidential suite in the newly built Norumbega Hall for only one year, 1886–87.

43. Faculty information was obtained from the *1942 Record Number of the Wellesley College Bulletin* (Wellesley: Wellesley College, 1942). This bulletin lists the Officers of Instruction and Administration, 1874–1942. Information on the group of Michigan alumnae who taught on the Wellesley faculty is taken from SFW, "Faculty Dinner in Honor of Professor Coman," *WCN,* May 15, 1913, 5–6; Mary B. Jenkins, "Michigan Women at Wellesley," *WAM* 10, no. 2 (Dec. 1925): 57–59; Converse, *Wellesley College,* 46.

44. KLB, "Wellesley's Fifty Years of Achievement," 8; GHP, *Life of AFP,* 117.

45. MAW, "Willcox Family Life," 60, folder 16, box 1, 14/10/504, Walter F. Willcox Papers, CUL.

46. Glasscock and Taylor, "Founders," 17; VDS, *On Journey,* 94, 103–04; Margarethe Müller, *Carla Wenckebach: Pioneer* (Boston: Ginn, 1908), 225.

47. Müller, *Carla Wenckebach,* 245–46. See KC FBF, WCA; Hackett, *Wellesley,* 80.

48. Glasscock and Taylor, "Founders," 26.

49. Robert E. Koehane, "Barnes, Mary Downing Sheldon," *NAW;* Allen F. Davis, "Coman, Katharine," *NAW;* Müller, *Carla Wenckebach,* 243.

50. Article 3, Section 3: Academic Council, *Acts of Incorporation, Deeds of Gift, and Statutes of Wellesley College* (Boston: n.p., 1885), 25, WCA.

51. Vassar College, in contrast, did not eliminate the preparatory department until 1888. See Stephen Clement, "Aspects of Student Religious Life at Vassar College, 1861–1914" (Ph.D. diss., Harvard University, 1977); Winifred Lowry Post, *Pur-*

pose and Personality: The Story of Dana Hall (Wellesley: Dana Hall School, 1978); E.T., "Sarah Porter Eastman" (Boston: n.p.), June 6, 1930, Sarah Porter Eastman FBF, WCA; see also Julia A. Eastman FBF, WCA; Marion Pelton Guild, "Historical Sketch of Wellesley College," in George Bush, The History of Higher Education in Massachusetts (Washington, D.C.: GPO, 1891), 431–32.

52. Cf. Kathryn Kish Sklar, Catharine Beecher: A Study of American Domesticity (New Haven: Yale University Press, 1978); Elizabeth Alden Green, Mary Lyon and Mount Holyoke: Opening the Gates (Hanover: University Press of New England, 1979). Alice Freeman, "The Influence of Women's Education on National Character," Proceedings of the American Institute of Instruction (1885): 171. See also AFP, Why Go to College? 21–22.

53. AFP, "The Influence of Women's Education," 172–73; AFP, Why Go to College? 31. For Jane Addams's ideas on the role of college women in settlements, see "The Subjective Necessity for Social Settlements" (1892), in The Social Thought of Jane Addams, ed. Lasch, 28–43. See also VDS, "The Relation of College Women to Social Need," JACA, 2d ser., no. 30 (Oct. 24, 1890): 1–16.

54. AFP, "Dear Graduates of Mt. Holyoke Seminary," in Semi-Centennial Celebration of Mount Holyoke Seminary, 1837–1887, ed. Sarah Locke Stow (South Hadley, Mass.: Mount Holyoke Seminary, 1888), 137–38.

55. See esp. Marion Talbot's eulogy of AFP: "AFP as a Member of the Association of Collegiate Alumnae," in Alice Freeman Palmer: In Memoriam (Boston: Association of Collegiate Alumnae, 1903), 9–12; the other eulogies are also important, esp. Samuel Capen's (18–20). On the International Institute for Girls in Madrid, see Elizabeth Putnam Gordon, Alice Gordon Gulick: Her Life and Work in Spain (New York: Revell, 1917).

56. GHP, Life of AFP, 166.

57. SFW, "The Wellesley Spirit," Sept. 26, 1915, unpub. MS, SFW Papers, WCA.

58. The term "perilous transition" is used by GHP in a letter to AFP, May 8, 1887, rpt. in AC, 169.

3

The Perilous Transition

1. GHP to AFP, Jan. 24, Feb. 6, 1887, in AC, 100–01, 104–07. The president of the college was made a member of the Board of Trustees by vote of the trustees (MBT, June 5, 1884, WCA).

2. AFP to GHP, Apr. 4, Apr. 1, Apr. 24, 1887, in AC, 155, 156, 160; GHP to AFP, Apr. 21, 1887, in AC, 156–57.

3. GHP to AFP, May 8, 1887, in AC, 169.

4. One history, for example, erroneously interprets Freeman's marriage and resignation as signaling her abandonment of both her career and her commitment to the college (cf. Roberta Frankfort, Collegiate Women: Domesticity and Career in Turn-of-the-Century America [New York: New York University Press, 1977]). A new biography of AFP focuses more attention on her as a "new woman" and highlights her leadership role in women's higher education even after her marriage (Ruth Bor-

din, *Alice Freeman Palmer: The Evolution of a New Woman* [Ann Arbor: University of Michigan Press, 1993]).

5. Florence Converse, *Wellesley College: A Chronicle of the Years 1875–1938* (Wellesley: Hathaway House Bookshop, 1939), 60; *Annals, 1887–1888,* 5, WCA. Helen Shafer was acting president from Dec. 21, 1887, until June 7, 1888, when she was made president of Wellesley (MBT, Nov. 3, 1887, June 7, 1888, WCA).

6. Marion Pelton Guild, "Historical Sketch of Wellesley College," in George Bush, *History of Higher Education in Massachusetts* (Washington, D.C.: GPO, 1891), 437; Marion Pelton Guild, "President Shafer's Official Career," *Wellesley Magazine* 2, no. 5 (Feb. 24, 1894): 238.

7. MAW, "Willcox Family Life" (typescript of family history), 62, folder 16, box 1, 14/10/504, Walter F. Willcox Papers, CUL.

8. The new faculty appointed in 1888 were: Adeline Hawes (Latin), Ellen Fitz Pendleton (mathematics), and Vida Dutton Scudder (English); in 1889, Katharine Edwards (Greek), Sophie Jewett (English), Margaret Pollock Sherwood (English), and Margarethe Müller (German); in 1890, Charlotte Bragg (chemistry), Julia Irvine (Greek), Margaret Jackson (Italian), Helen Webster (comparative philology), and Eliza Ritchie (philosophy); in 1893, Sophie Hart (English), Helen Merrill (mathematics), and Margaret Clay Ferguson (botany); in 1894, Elizabeth Fisher (geology) and Marian Hubbard (zoology).

9. KLB, "Wellesley's Fifty Golden Years of Achievement: The Purposeful Women Who Have Reared the College from Struggling Babyhood to Glorious Womanhood and the Men Who Have Aided Them," *Boston Evening Transcript,* May 16, 1925, 8.

10. Cf. Robert Fletcher, *A History of Oberlin College: From Its Foundation through the Civil War,* 2 vols. (Oberlin, Ohio: Oberlin College, 1943); *Courant,* Sept. 1888, WCA.

11. "Mr. Durant's Last Words" (copied by Marion Pelton Guild from Pauline Durant's manuscript), ALS, WCA.

12. Cf. Ellen Hayes's column "Our Outlook," *Courant,* Sept. 1888–Sept. 1889, WCA; Arthur Mann, *Yankee Reformers in the Urban Age: Social Reform in Boston, 1880–1900* (Cambridge: Harvard University Press, 1954), 203–04.

13. For a discussion of the debate over sex roles within the academy, see Rosalind Rosenberg, *Beyond Separate Spheres: Intellectual Roots of Modern Feminism* (New Haven: Yale University Press, 1982); Flavia Alaya, "Victorian Science and the 'Genius' of Woman," *Journal of the History of Ideas* 38, no. 2 (Apr.–June 1977): 261–80; Cynthia E. Russett, *Sexual Science: The Victorian Construction of Womanhood* (Cambridge: Harvard University Press, 1989); Aileen S. Kraditor, *The Ideas of the Woman Suffrage Movement, 1890–1920* (New York: Columbia University Press, 1965), esp. 4.

14. Anne Eugenia Morgan, FBF, WCA; Robert Fletcher, *A History of Oberlin College*; Anne Eugenia Morgan, "Speech on the Fortieth Anniversary of the First National Women's Rights Convention," *The Woman's Journal,* Jan. 1891, 41.

15. Margarethe Müller, *Carla Wenckebach: Pioneer* (Boston: Ginn, 1908), 62.

16. AFP to CW, Jan. 6, 1889, ALS, WCA.

17. Marion Pelton Guild, "Notes for the Possible Use of Mrs. Durant's Possible Biographer," enclosed with Marion Pelton Guild to EFP, Feb. 15, 1936, 6, ALS, WCA; also MBT, May 24, Nov. 6, 1890, and Feb. 5, 1891, WCA.

18. Dorothy Burgess, *Dream and Deed: The Story of Katharine Lee Bates* (Norman: University of Oklahoma Press, 1952), 85, 90; Marion Pelton Guild, "Notes for the Possible Use of Mrs. Durant's Possible Biographer," 8, ALS, WCA.

19. Diary of HS, Dec. 16, 1890, HS Papers, HL.

20. See ECM/BT, Jan. 23, 1884, May 20, 1885, WCA. See also HM, "The History of the Department of Mathematics," math dept., WCA; Ellen Hayes, *Letters to a College Girl* (Boston: Ellis, 1909), 19–20; Barbara Heslan Palmer, "Lace Bonnets and Academic Gowns: Faculty Development in Four Women's Colleges, 1875–1915" (Ph.D. diss., Boston College, 1980), esp. chap. 6, "Where the Ladies Reigned: Faculty Development at Wellesley College, 1875–1915," 291–92.

21. Margaret E. Taylor and Jean Glasscock, "The Founders and the Early Presidents," in *Wellesley College, 1875–1975: A Century of Women*, ed. Jean Glasscock (Wellesley: Wellesley College, 1975), 43; *President's Report, 1892*, WCA.

22. Julia Irvine's FBF gives some details (WCA). On Irvine's mother, see Clifton J. Phillips, "Thomas, Mary Frame Meyers," *NAW*; Norma Kidd Green, "Brackett, Anna Callander," *NAW*.

23. ECM/BT, Nov. 13, 1890, WCA; AFP to GHP, May 22, 1890, letters between GHP and AFP, WCA. Many of the letters between AFP and GHP in WCA are copies of the originals, which are housed in the Houghton Library, at Harvard University; there are also some original letters in WCA.

24. Virginia Onderdonk, "The Curriculum," in *Wellesley College,* ed. Glasscock, 122–48.

25. *President's Report, 1892,* WCA.

26. Taylor and Glasscock, "Founders," 41.

27. Diary of HS, Feb. 23, Feb. 25, 1891, box 6, HS Papers, HL.

28. AFP had conceived the idea of a deanship for Wellesley as early as 1885. See GHP to AFP, Friday morning, Sunset Rock (July[?] 1886); Mary Claflin to GHP, Aug. 6, 1886, enclosed with GHP to AFP, Aug. 8, 1886, letters between GHP and AFP, WCA.

29. KLB, "Wellesley's Fifty Years of Achievement," 8.

30. Already in 1890, AFP stated: "Now is the time for Wellesley to pass from college to university" (Alice Hackett, *Wellesley: Part of the American Story* (New York: Dutton, 1949), 128. *President's Report, 1896,* and MBT, 1899, WCA.

31. Converse, *Wellesley College,* 57, 60.

32. Harriet Manning Blake, "I Remember—the Lady of the Greek Tongue," *WAM* 9, no. 4 (Apr. 1925): 168. Pauline Durant had been treasurer since 1881 (see Board of Trustee Minutes, Nov. 9, 1881, WCA). She resigned the position on Mar. 27, 1895, and was replaced by Mr. Alpheus Hardy, a businessman (*President's Report, 1895,* WCA).

33. MSC, "An Appreciation of President Irvine," Sept. 1943, handwritten addendum,

Julia Irvine Papers, WCA. Because there was no official tenure policy, Case must be referring to the loyalty some trustees evinced toward some senior professors.

34. MAW, "Willcox Family Life," 63–64, folder 16, box 1, 14/10/504, Walter F. Willcox Papers, CUL. In one sense, Helen Shafer's appointment of seventeen junior faculty had already changed the nature of the institution, but Irvine's purge of senior faculty was considered more dire because it was overt.

35. Taylor and Glasscock, "Founders," 52.

36. Eliza Kendrick, *A History of Bible Teaching at Wellesley College* (1932, ed. by her colleagues 1950), 16, biblical history dept., WCA.

37. *President's Reports,* 1894–1896, WCA.

38. William H. Willcox to LMN, Feb. 3, 1899, ALS, WCA; Julia Irvine sadly reported the loss of Margaret Maltby in her *President's Report* of 1895, WCA. See Agnes Townsend Wiebusch, "Maltby, Margaret," *NAW.*

39. The thirteen full professors at Wellesley in 1890 were: Angie Chapin, Katharine Coman, Elizabeth Denio, Susan Hallowell, Ellen Hayes, Louise Manning Hodgkins, Frances Ellen Lord, Anne Morgan, Margaret Stratton, Helen Webster, Carla Wenckebach, Sarah Frances Whiting, Mary Alice Willcox.

40. Webster's appointment is discussed in MBT, May 10, 1890. Criticism of the summer school is found in ECM/BT, Mar. 24, 1897, 116, WCA.

41. MAW to Marian Hubbard, Dec. 2, 1927, Unprocessed MAW Papers, WCA.

42. For the purposes of this study, only fifteen women who reached the rank of associate and senior professors by 1910 are included in "incoming faculty." The compendiums used to determine distinguished achievement are: *American Men of Science* (1906, 1910, 1920, 1927, 1933); *DAB* (20 vols., 6 suppls.); *NAW* and *NAW:MP; The Part Taken by Women in American History* (1912, rpt. 1972); *Principal Women of American* (1932); *Who Was Who in America* (vols. 1–3, 1943).

43. MAW, "Willcox Family Life," 64, folder 16, box 1, 14/10/504, Walter F. Willcox Papers, CUL. Members of the Harvard faculty, who faced similar professional pressures in this same era because of the opening of Johns Hopkins University, enjoyed much better employment prospects. Robert McCaughey discusses the transformation of the Harvard faculty during this period in "The Transformation of American Academic Life: Harvard University 1821–1892," *Perspectives in History* 8 (1974): 239–332.

44. VDS, *On Journey* (New York: Dutton, 1937), 179, 184.

45. Ibid., 104; VDS, "Mary A. Willcox," *WAM* 38, no. 1 (Nov. 1953): 35.

46. HM, "The History of the Department of Mathematics," math dept., WCA; also ECM/BT, May 25, 1898, 172, WCA.

47. Estelle M. Hurll to LMN, Dec. 22, 1897, ALS, WCA; MBT, 1897, WCA.

48. Taylor and Glasscock, "Founders," 52; KLB, "Wellesley's Fifty Years of Achievement," 8. Irvine returned to Wellesley only once, in 1913, at the invitation of President Ellen Pendleton, to fill a sudden vacancy in the French department.

49. Pauline Durant to LMN, Dec. 22, 1898, ALS, WCA.

50. EFP, "Wellesley, Past and Present," *WAM* 14, no. 6 (Aug. 1930): 412. Hazard first met Horace Scudder at Houghton Mifflin, where, as a literary critic, he assessed a manuscript she had submitted. James Angell was a friend of the family. He and her father had been classmates at Brown. See Hazard autobiography, pp. 3–5, ser. 5, CH, Nathanial Terry Bacon Papers, folder 15, box 111, James P. Adams Library, Rhode Island College, Providence, R.I.

51. Margaret Clapp, "Hazard, Caroline," *NAW*.

52. CH to HS, Jan. 24, 1899; HS to CH, Feb. 1, 1899; CH to HS, Feb. (?), 1899; CH to AFP, Jan. 18, 1899, CH Papers, WCA.

53. CH to HS, Jan. 24, 1899, CH Papers, WCA.

54. HS to CH, Feb. 26, 1899, CH Papers, WCA.

55. AFP to CH (n.d., probably 1899); CH to AFP, Feb. 24, Mar. 21, 1899; draft of a telegram sent by CH to Wellesley Board of Trustees, Mar. 8, 1899, CH Papers, WCA.

56. CH, "Inaugural Address," in *From College Gates* (Boston: Houghton Mifflin, 1925), 227.

57. CH, "The Illuminators" (poem), Jan. 17, 1905, in *From College Gates*, 325; see also CH, "Speech to Peace Dale Congregational Conference," May 23, 1905, CH Papers, WCA.

58. Margaret Clapp, "Hazard, Caroline," *NAW*. Her appointments were: Edith Rose Abbot (art), Caroline Breyfogle (biblical history), Eliza Kendrick (biblical history), Anna McKeag (education), Edna Moffett (history), Frances Perry (English), Ethel Puffer (philosophy), Martha Hale Shackford (English), Caroline Thompson (zoology), Roxanna Vivian (mathematics), and Natalie Wipplinger (German).

59. CH, "Address to Honor Students," in *From College Gates,* 291.

60. Florence Converse, *The Story of Wellesley* (Boston: Little, Brown, 1915), 101–02.

61. KC to CH, 1910, ALS, WCA.

62. EKK to CH, July 26, 1910, ALS; also VDS to CH, Sept. 5, 1910, ALS, WCA.

63. Adelaide Locke to CH, July 23, 1910, ALS, WCA.

4

The Family Culture of the Faculty

Epigraph: Florence Converse, *Wellesley College: A Chronicle of the Years 1875–1938* (Wellesley, Mass.: Hathaway House, 1939), 80–81.

1. Included in this study are women faculty who had been at Wellesley at least five years between 1900 and 1910 and who reached the rank of either associate or senior professor. I selected the ten-year duration to allow for a valid picture of the faculty group. To augment the social and cultural portrait, I categorized and coded qualitative data and then processed it with the Statistical Package for the Social Sciences (SPSS). For the purposes of the narrative, I have periodically included the biography of Carla Wenckebach, professor of German (1883–1902), who was very much a part of the faculty community. CH, "Tribute to KLB," *WAM,* suppl. 13, no. 5 (June 1929): 15.

2. "Niles, William Harmon," *National Cyclopedia of American Biography,* 63 vols.

(New York: James T. White, 1904), 12:481. See also "The Niles Memorial Fund" (fund-raising notice), William Niles FBF; and Hamilton C. Macdougall, Faculty Questionnaire, Macdougall FBF, WCA. Vida Scudder wrote of Charles Lowell Young, who in 1895 joined the bold pioneers of the English department: "I fear we women were a little self-conscious in those days as to our prerogatives." She noted that "his natural attitude toward us was exquisitely chivalrous; but chivalry and equal comradeship do not always agree very well" (VDS, "Charles Lowell Young," WAM 22, no. 2 [Dec. 1937]: 113–14).

3. Eleanor Gamble discusses the emeriti colony in "Anna J. McKeag," WAM 16, no. 5 (June 1932): 408.

4. Linda K. Kerber, Women of the Republic: Intellect and Ideology in Revolutionary America (Chapel Hill: University of North Carolina Press, 1980), 190–91; for literacy rates see Nancy Cott, The Bonds of Womanhood: "Woman's Sphere" in New England, 1780–1835 (New Haven: Yale University Press, 1977), 15, 101; Barbara Welter, "The Cult of True Womanhood, 1820–60" and "Anti-Intellectualism and the American Woman, 1800–1860," in Dimity Convictions: The American Woman in the Nineteenth Century (Athens, Ohio: Ohio University Press, 1976), 21–41, 71, respectively.

5. On Margaret Fuller, see Barbara Welter, "Mystical Feminist: Margaret Fuller, A Woman of the Nineteenth Century," Dimity Convictions, 145–98; Susan P. Conrad, Perish the Thought: Intellectual Women in Romantic America, 1830–1860 (Secaucus, N.J.: Citadel Press, 1978).

6. KC to Jane Addams, Aug. 8, 1912, SCPC; see Ann Douglas, The Feminization of American Culture (New York: Alfred Knopf, 1977); Mary Kelley, Private Woman, Public Stage: Literary Domesticity in Nineteenth-Century America (New York: Oxford University Press, 1983).

7. Sally Gregory Kohlstedt, "In from the Periphery: American Women in Science, 1830–1880," Signs 4 (1978): 81–97. In an exemplary essay, Linda K. Kerber traces the "range of sites" for women's intellectual history, concluding: "The theater for women's intellectual life has rarely been institutional" (Kerber, "'Why Should Girls Be Learn'd and Wise?' The Unfinished Work of Alice Mary Baldwin," in Visible Women: New Essays on American Activism, ed. Nancy A. Hewitt and Suzanne Lebsock (Urbana: University of Illinois Press, 1993), 349–380, esp. 351.

8. VDS, On Journey (New York: Dutton, 1937), 404; Mary Augusta Jordan, The Higher Education of Women (Northampton, Mass.: Association of Collegiate Alumnae, 1886), 24.

9. See Silvano Arieti, Creativity: The Magic Synthesis (New York: Basic, 1976); L. S. Feuer, The Scientific Individual: The Psychological and Sociological Origins of Modern Science (New York: Basic, 1963).

10. VDS, On Journey, 34; EGB as quoted in Mercedes M. Randall, Improper Bostonian: Emily Greene Balch (New York: Twayne, 1964), 45, 46; MAW, "Willcox Family Life," 16, 12, 24, folder 16, box 1, 14/10/504, Walter F. Willcox Papers, CUL.

11. VDS, On Journey, 21, 34. Emily Balch is another example. She always claimed

that in her life it "was not an apple but a book that did the mischief" (Randall, *Improper Bostonian,* 67, 69).

12. KLB diary, July 22, 1866; on Dec. 23, 1866, Bates recorded that she had read fifteen books by Charles Dickens (KLB diary, July 11, 1866, KLB Papers, WCA). Dorothy Burgess, *Dream and Deed: The Story of Katharine Lee Bates* (Norman: University of Oklahoma Press, 1952), 31–32. For a discussion of the significance of books to the Progressive generation of women, as well as the "female culture of reading," see Barbara Sicherman, "Reading and Ambition: M. Carey Thomas and Female Heroism," *American Quarterly* 45, no. 1 (Mar. 1993): 73–103.

13. Louise Brown, *Ellen Hayes: Trail-Blazer* (West Park, N.Y.: n.p., 1932), 21, 28; also Ellen Hayes, *Wild Turkeys and Tallow Candles* (Boston: Four Seas, 1920), 135. Hayes in turn complimented Katharine Coman for caring for books (Ellen Hayes, "In Memoriam: Katharine Coman" [text of address given at the Memorial Service for KC], Jan. 31, 1915, rpt. in *WCN,* Apr. 1915, 11, WCA).

14. Sherwood left her books to the Vassar College Library as well as a bequest for the purchase of new books (MPS, untitled typed autobiographical reminiscence [hereafter cited as Reminiscence], 7, MPS FBF, WCA). See also Dorothy Coclin McMann, "Margaret Pollock Sherwood, 1864–1955," *WAM* (Jan. 1956): 99. MWC recalls these moments in the introduction to Louise Rogers Jewett and Mary W. Calkins, eds., *The Poems of Sophie Jewett* (New York: Crowell, 1910), ix.

15. KLB, "Autobiography in Brief," KLB FBF, WCA. See a verse she wrote at the age of seven entitled "Spectacles" (KLB diary, May 7, 1866, KLB Papers, WCA). EGB, "Confessions of a Professional Woman," 6, EGB Papers, SCPC.

16. VDS, *On Journey,* 36; see also MAW, "Willcox Family Life," 35, folder 16, box 1, 14/10/504, Walter F. Willcox Papers, CUL.

17. EGB, "Confessions of a Professional Woman," 9–10, EGB Papers, SCPC; VDS, *On Journey,* 403. "Ethel Puffer Howes: In Memoriam," *Smith Alumnae Quarterly* 42, no. 2 (Feb. 1951): 93.

18. Data obtained from the Wellesley Faculty Statistical Profile run on SPSS with the assistance of George H. Ropes.

19. For child-rearing styles, see Philip Greven, *The Protestant Temperament: Patterns of Child Rearing, Religious Experience and the Self in Early America* (New York: New American Library, 1977); Barbara Welter, "The Cult of True Womanhood: 1820–1860," *American Quarterly* 18, no. 2 (1966): 151–74. Jane Addams, "The Subjective Necessity of Social Settlements," in *The Social Thought of Jane Addams,* ed. Christopher Lasch (New York: Bobbs–Merrill, 1965), 28–44; in *The New Radicalism in America, 1889–1963: The Intellectual as a Social Type* (New York: Knopf, 1965), Lasch stresses the conflict between educated women and their families. I have benefited from Barbara Sicherman's views on family culture, some of which are expressed in *Alice Hamilton: A Life in Letters* (Cambridge: Harvard University Press, 1984). See also Kirk Jeffrey, "The Family as Utopian Retreat from the City: The Nineteenth-Century Contribution," in *The Family, Communes, and Utopian Societies,* ed. Sallie TeSelle (New York: Harper and Row, 1971); and

William Hutchinson, "Cultural Strain and Protestant Liberalism," *American Historical Review* 76 (1971): 386–411.

20. I used the federal census, autobiographies, biographies, and reference encyclopedias to determine fathers' occupations. On definitions of social class in the nineteenth century see Michael Katz, "Occupational Classification in History," *Journal of Interdisciplinary History* 3 (1972): 63–88; Michael Katz, *The People of Hamilton, Canada West: Family and Class in a Mid-Nineteenth-Century City* (Cambridge: Harvard University Press, 1975); and Stuart Blumin, *The Emergence of the Middle Class: Social Experience in the American City, 1760–1900* (Cambridge: Cambridge University Press, 1989).

21. John G. Sproat, *The Best Men: Liberal Reformers in the Gilded Age* (New York: Oxford, 1968); George M. Fredrickson, *The Inner Civil War: Northern Intellectuals and the Crisis of The Union* (New York: Harper and Row, 1965); Stow Persons, *The Decline of American Gentility* (New York: Columbia University Press, 1973), esp. 39.

22. Frank H. Ristine, "Brown, Samuel Gilman," *DAB* (1929); see also *Memorial of Samuel Gilman Brown* (New York: n.p., 1886), 12, provided by the Hamilton College Archives; Agnes Abbot, "Brown, Alice Van Vechten," *NAW*. A similar case is Martha Hale Shackford's father; see Charles Burnham Shackford Papers, Bowdoin College Archives; and the entry for Shackford in H. Cleaveland, *History of Bowdoin College with Biographical Sketches of the Graduates, 1806–1876* (Boston: n.p., 1882).

23. Randall, *Improper Bostonian,* 49. Similarly, Eliza Kendrick noted that a student in her father's Sunday school class praised him as one of the "best men in the world." She informed her mother: "His reputation for 'goodness' has reached even here" (Eliza Kendrick to her mother, May 28, 1882, Eliza Kendrick Papers, WCA).

24. George M. Fredrickson, *The Inner Civil War*. MPS, Reminiscence, MPS FBF, WCA.

25. I have benefited from the analysis of James M. McPherson in *The Abolitionist Legacy: From Reconstruction to the NAACP* (Princeton: Princeton University Press, 1979), esp. 3–10.

26. Randall, *Improper Bostonian,* 33; see also Mary Simkhovitch, "Emily Balch," TS, folder A.97, Simkhovitch Papers, SL. MPS, Reminiscence, MPS FBF, WCA.

27. KC, ed., *Memories of Martha Seymour Coman* (Boston: Fort Hill Press 1913), 44–46.

28. Laurel Furumoto, "Mary Whiton Calkins (1863–1930): Fourteenth President of the American Psychological Association," *Journal of the History of the Behavioral Sciences* 15 (1979): 347; Maud Calkins to her mother, Wed. eve. (1878), "In Memoriam" album, Unprocessed MWC Papers, WCA.

29. Dr. Kendrick to Eliza (Lida) Kendrick, Sept. 15, 1881; Lida Kendrick to "My Dear Momma," June 15, 1885, Eliza Kendrick Papers, WCA; see also MAW, "Willcox Family Life," 7, folder 16, box 1, 14/10/504, Walter F. Willcox Papers, CUL.

30. Francis Balch to EGB, Mar. 8, 1896, EGB Papers, SCPC; Randall discusses Balch's path to pacifism in *Improper Bostonian;* see also Barbara Miller Solomon, "Balch,

Emily," in *NAW:MP*; Patricia A. Palmieri, "Emily Greene Balch: A Citizen of the World," in *The Nobel Peace Award from 1901 until Today* (Germany: Pacis, 1991).

31. MAW, "Willcox Family Life," 41, folder 16, box 1, 14/10/504, Walter F. Willcox Papers, CUL. Furumoto, "Mary Whiton Calkins," 348. See also Henry Durant to Marion Pelton (Guild), Sept. 20, 1880, ALS, WCA.

32. VDS, "Emily Greene Balch," 3, EGB Papers, SCPC. MAW, "Willcox Family Life," 55, folder 16, box 1, 14/10/504, Walter F. Willcox Papers, CUL.

33. Randall, *Improper Bostonian,* 392, 49, 127.

34. Francis Balch to EGB, Mar. 8, 1896, EGB Papers, SCPC; Randall, *Improper Bostonian,* 87; EGB to "Dear Papa," 1892, EGB Papers, SCPC. Death prompted some women to create an idealized father. In Vida Scudder's mind, her father, David Scudder, a learned missionary who drowned fording a river in India, was an unusual man "who feared nothing in life but intellectual stagnation" (VDS, *On Journey,* 16; VDS, *Listener in Babel* [Boston: Houghton Mifflin, 1903], 5). See also Horace E. Scudder, *Life and Letters of David Coit Scudder, Missionary in Southern India* (New York: Dutton, 1864).

35. See Jean Dietz, "Wellesley's Miss Mary Linked Dreams to Real Life," *Boston Sunday Globe,* June 17, 1962. For a similar discussion of mothers who were ambitious for their daughters, see Marjorie Housepian Dobkin, ed., *The Making of a Feminist: Early Journals and Letters of M. Carey Thomas* (Kent: Kent State University Press, 1979), 9.

36. KC, *Memories of Martha Coman,* 19; see also the Burgess biography of KLB, *Dream and Deed.* Cornelia Lee Bates, a graduate of Mary Lyon's seminary, encouraged her daughter Katharine to write and to have an academic career (Burgess, *Dream and Deed,* 33–35); information on Cornelia Lee Bates can also be found in Class of 1845 Papers, MHCA.

37. *Lucretia Hasseltine Kendall Clark* (privately printed, 1937), 7–8, EKK Papers, WCA. Dietz, "Wellesley's Miss Mary"; for another example see MHS, ed., *Whittier and Cartlands* (Wakefield, Mass.: Montrose Press, 1950).

38. Carroll Smith-Rosenberg, in "The Female World of Love and Ritual: Relations between Women in Nineteenth-Century America," *Signs* 1 (Autumn 1975): 1–29, emphasizes the close ties that developed among nineteenth-century women because of their segregation from public life. See also Cott, *The Bonds of Womanhood.* One of those women who rebelled against the female world was Emily Balch; see EGB, "The Burroughs St. House Four to Twelve" (autobiographical handwritten fragment), EGB Papers, SCPC.

39. On women's academies and social change, see Anne Firor Scott, "The Ever-Widening Circle: The Diffusion of Feminist Values from the Troy Female Seminary, 1822–72," in *Making the Invisible Woman Visible* (Urbana: University of Illinois Press, 1984), 64–88. Katharine Coman wrote Jane Addams that she and her mother had just finished reading Addams's *Twenty Years at Hull-House* together, and they agreed it showed college women "the type of living that is best worthwhile" (KC to Jane Addams, Aug. 8, 1912, SCPC); see also Allen F. Davis, *An American Heroine: The Life and Legend of Jane Addams* (New York: Oxford University Press, 1973).

40. Hayes, *Wild Turkeys,* 118, 121, 130. Ruth Wolcott Hayes, mother of Ellen Hayes, studied and taught at the Granville Female Seminary, founded by her father in Ohio; she taught Ellen botany. Cornelia Lee Bates, Katharine Bates's mother, was another seminary-trained woman who loved and studied botany. For a discussion of this early generation of amateur botanists, see Elizabeth Keeney, *The Botanizers: Amateur Scientists in Nineteenth-Century America* (Chapel Hill: University of North Carolina Press, 1992).

41. "Mary Sophia Case," *WAM* 37, no. 5 (July 1953): 306; see Case's heroic poem "The Last Victory" (Case FBF, WCA).

42. Randall, *Improper Bostonian,* 45, 31. Emily Balch had to vie with her siblings for her mother's attention. She admitted that one of the happiest periods of her life was when she had scarlet fever at age ten and was quarantined with her mother. Balch confessed that her love for her mother had an "'element of passion' in it" (Randall, *Improper Bostonian,* 44). See also Emily Balch's short story entitled "A Modern Martyr," EGB Papers, SCPC. Carroll Smith-Rosenberg argues that college-educated daughters had a psychological need for distance from their mothers ("The New Woman as Androgyne," in *Disorderly Conduct: Visions of Gender in Victorian America* [New York: Knopf, 1985)], 248–49). But the opposite could be true as well. See Linda W. Rosenzweig, "'The Anchor of My Life': Middle-Class American Mothers and College-Educated Daughters, 1880–1920," *Journal of Social History* 25, no. 1 (1990): 5–25.

43. LSM, "Margaret Hastings Jackson," *WAM* 24, no. 2 (Dec. 1939): 109 and passim. Mrs. Jackson even accompanied her daughter to the interview! GHP to AFP, May 26, 1890, letters between GHP and AFP, WCA.

44. MWC, "The Place of Scholarship in Life" (handwritten draft of an essay), n.d. (probably 1910), Unprocessed MWC Papers, WCA.

45. For letters that particularly capture Maud Calkins's dependence on her mother, see Maud Calkins to Charlotte Calkins, Feb. 27, Mar. 1, 1878, "In Memoriam" album, Unprocessed MWC Papers, WCA. Raymond Calkins, quoted in Dietz, "Wellesley's Miss Mary." Thomas Proctor, TOI-CNH, 6, WCA. Charlotte Calkins sponsored Mary's intellectual life. See, e.g., "Family Rhymes," Unprocessed MWC Papers, WCA.

46. VDS, *On Journey,* 58 (Scudder divulged that she had a "private fairy tale, wherein, disguised as a boy," she crept into Harvard); VDS, *Listener in Babel,* 7–8.

47. VDS, *On Journey,* 112, 177–78; VDS, *Listener in Babel,* 12. VDS, *On Journey,* 24. Emily Balch was similarly attached to her mother. In her eighties, Balch could still recall the "taste of my mother's milk" (EGB, "The Burroughs St. House Four to Twelve," EGB Papers, SCPC).

48. EKK to her mother, June 19, 1904, EKK Papers, WCA; Eliza Kendrick to her mother, Jan. 8, 1882, Eliza Kendrick Papers, WCA. See also KLB to her mother, quoted in Burgess, *Dream and Deed,* 84–91.

49. Cf. Carroll Smith-Rosenberg, "The Female World of Love and Ritual."

50. "Autobiography" of Anne Holmes Goodenow [Mrs. Willcox], TS, 40–41, Unprocessed MAW Papers, WCA; Walter F. Willcox to MAW, Mar. 22, July 31,

1893, 14/10/821, Walter F. Willcox Papers, CUL; "MAW: Professor Emeritus of Wellesley College," *Boston Globe*, June 7, 1953. Letters written at Wellesley from Lida Kendrick to her brother Arthur reveal how much she missed their pranks and longed to be reunited with him. She advised him to study his Greek and algebra so as to be ready should Wellesley open an annex for men (Lida Kendrick to Arthur Kendrick, Nov. 13, 1881, Eliza Kendrick Papers, WCA); see also Margaret Sherwood's discussion of her brother Sidney (Reminiscence, MPS FBF, WCA). Some letters of Sidney Sherwood, and one by MPS, can be found in the Milton Eisenhower Library, Division of Special Collections, Johns Hopkins University.

51. MAW, "Willcox Family Life," 17, 27, folder 16, box 1, 14/10/504, Walter F. Willcox Papers, CUL. See also Hayes, *Wild Turkeys*, 88, 102, 132.

52. KLB diary, Aug. 15, Mar. 31, Apr.1–3, July 12, 1866, KLB Papers, WCA.

53. VDS, *On Journey*, 23, 34–35.

54. "Autobiography" of Anne Holmes Goodenow [Mrs. Willcox], TS, 30, WCA; MAW, "Willcox Family Life," 20, Walter F. Willcox Papers, CUL. See also VDS, *On Journey*, 21, 37; MPS, Reminiscence, MPS FBF, WCA.

55. Virginia Onderdonk, "Calkins, Mary Whiton," *NAW*; Gertrude C. Bussey, "Calkins, Mary Whiton," *DAB*, supp. 1 (1944); KLB's poem "The Ivy and the Oak" is pasted into the scrapbook of Cora Stickney (Class of 1880 Papers, WCA). By the age of seven, Bates had already developed a feminist consciousness. In a poem entitled "Women" in her childhood diary, she praised women for becoming "impatient under the restraint men put upon them / So the great question of women's rights has arison [sic]" (KLB diary, Mar. 10, 1866, KLB Papers, WCA). See also Carla Wenckebach, as quoted in Margarethe Müller, *Carla Wenckebach: Pioneer* (Boston: Ginn, 1908), 79–80.

56. Louise Rogers Jewett and MWC, introd. to *The Poems of Sophie Jewett*, vii; MPS, Reminiscence, MPS FBF, WCA.

57. Hayes, *Wild Turkeys*, 68.

58. EGB, "The Burroughs St. House Four to Twelve"; Annie Balch to EGB, n.d. (probably 1899), EGB Papers, SCPC.

59. The following are examples of such professional sister–submissive sister teams: Katharine Lee Bates and Jennie Bates; Katharine Coman and Harriet Coman; Katharine May Edwards and Lena Edwards; Anna J. McKeag and Mary E. McKeag; Margarethe Müller and Elsbeth Müller; Caroline Thompson and Harriet Thompson; Alice Vinton Waite and Louise Waite; Carla Wenckebach and Helene Wenckebach; Sarah Frances Whiting and Elizabeth Whiting; Mary Alice Willcox and Nellie Willcox. In one telling diary entry, Bates wrote: "Jennie and I work like the demented over bibliography" (KLB diary, Aug. 21, 1896, KLB Papers, WCA). On Jennie Bates, see Burgess, *Dream and Deed*, 25.

60. Elizabeth Balch [Bessie] to EGB, Tuesday, n.d. (probably 1890 or 1891); Elizabeth Balch to EGB, n.d., EGB Papers, SCPC; Randall, *Improper Bostonian*, 312–13, 315; see also MAW, "Willcox Family Life," 46, folder 6, box 1, 14/10/504, Walter F. Willcox Papers, CUL (Willcox details her sister's breakdown on p. 73).

61. VDS, *On Journey,* 37–38, 3, 19. See also MAW, "Willcox Family Life," 13–14, folder 16, box 1, 14/10/504, Walter F. Willcox Papers, CUL. For information on the Willcox family members, see an untitled newspaper clipping (n.d.), MAW FBF, WCA; MAW, "Willcox Family Life," 24, CUL.

62. Randall, *Improper Bostonian,* 45, 42, 43. Agnes Balch to Erin-Go-Bragh, Apr. 22, 1947, folder B-10, Erin-Go-Bragh, SL. The Erin-Go-Bragh were a group of graduates in the class of 1886 from Miss Ireland's School in Boston; they continued to meet for reunions for over sixty-five years. There are many such examples of multiple-family sponsors.

63. MAW, "Willcox Family Life," 19–20, 54–56, folder 16, box 1, 14/10/504, Walter F. Willcox Papers, CUL; MAW, "Recollections Willcox Home Kennebunk, Maine" (abbreviated version of her longer reminiscences), 27–31, folder 6, box 1, 14/10/821, Walter F. Willcox Papers, CUL. See also MPS to Marion Bates Westcott, Apr. 17, 1937, MPS FBF. In her girlhood, Scudder was beseiged by agnosticism and tortured by skepticism. She disdained Calvinism and evangelical revivals but found Catholicism attractive because of its revolutionary social implications. Later in life she joined the Companions of the Holy Cross (VDS, *On Journey,* 43, 370–90, 416; *The Society of the Companions of the Holy Cross* [Byfield, Mass.: n.p., n.d.]). Other Wellesley faculty in the society include Eleanor Gamble and Alice Van Vechten Brown.

64. VDS, "Alice Van Vechten Brown," *WAM* 34, no. 4 (Apr. 1950): 397; Hayes, *Wild Turkeys,* 132; HM discusses Hayes in "The History of the Department of Mathematics," math dept., WCA.

65. KLB diary, June 24, 1886, KLB Papers, WCA; Burgess, *Dream and Deed,* 64.

66. On Balch, see Randall, *Improper Bostonian,* 48.

67. VDS to "Dear Head" (LMH), fall 1889, ALS, WCA; EGB as quoted in Randall, *Improper Bostonian,* 389–90; KLB to KC, Feb. 20, 1891, KLB Papers, WCA.

5

From Cinderella to Woman Scholar

1. MPS, "The Ideal of a College," *Wellesley Magazine* 15, no. 2 (Nov. 1906): 47. Florence Converse as quoted in Jessie Bernard, *Academic Women* (New York: New American Library, 1964), 31.

2. Patricia Albjerg Graham, "Expansion and Exclusion: A History of Women in American Higher Education," *Signs* 3, no. 4 (Summer 1978): 766.

3. SFW, Ellen Louisa Burrell, and MCF, "Susan Maria Hallowell: In Memoriam," *WCN* 20, no. 21 (Mar. 1912): 10–12; Joan Burstyn, "Early Women in Education: The Role of the Anderson School of Natural History," *Boston University Journal of Education* 159, no. 3 (Aug. 1977): 50–64.

4. MAW, "Willcox Family Life," 33–42, folder 16, box 1, 14/10/504, Walter F. Willcox Papers, CUL.

5. Information from undergraduate transcripts was granted by the president and trustees of Wellesley College. Other women on the faculty were also elected to Phi Beta Kappa—e.g., Margaret Sherwood was elected while at Vassar (letter to

the author from the registrar of Vassar College, April 4, 1989).

6. Ethel Dench Puffer (Howes), Mary Whiton Calkins, and Margaret Pollock Sherwood are among the Wellesley faculty who studied with William James, Hugo Münsterberg, or Josiah Royce. On Josiah Royce, see John Clendenning, *The Life and Thought of Josiah Royce* (Madison: University of Wisconsin Press, 1985). Balch's mentor, Franklin H. Giddings, is discussed in Mercedes M. Randall, *Improper Bostonian: Emily Greene Balch* (New York: Twayne, 1964), 69–72; and in Dorothy Ross, *The Origins of American Social Science* (Cambridge: Cambridge University Press, 1991), 130–31. See also Franklin H. Giddings, *Outline of Lectures on Political Economy* (Philadelphia: Ferris Bros., 1891). Vida Scudder evaluates the influence of Phelps and Clark in *On Journey* (New York: Dutton, 1937), 69. On Charles Edward Garman, see Thomas Le Duc, *Piety and Intellect at Amherst College, 1865–1912* (New York: Columbia University Press, 1946), 115–18; Scudder also has a chapter in *On Journey* entitled "Oxford Days," 115–18. Margaret Pollock Sherwood's experiences at Oxford are mentioned in Reminiscence, TS, 8, MPS FBF, WCA. Katharine Lee Bates also studied at Oxford; see Dorothy Burgess, "Oxford," in *Dream and Deed: The Story of Katharine Lee Bates* (Norman: University of Oklahoma Press, 1952), 75–83.

7. HM to "My Dear Miss Corwin," Dec. 10, 1919, HM folder, box 215; MHS folder, box 284; S. Beers to "Dear Professor Philip," n.d., in Laura Lockwood folder, box 192; MPS, box 282, Graduate School Registrar Records, YUA.

8. Information on Julia Swift Orvis is in Graduate School Records, 12/5/636, CUL; George L. Atkinson to Dean H. S. Waite, Jan. 5, 1901, in MCF, Graduate School Records, 12/5/636, CUL. See also the Graduate School Records of Katharine May Edwards and Eleanor Acheson Gamble; Alice Walton's full record is not available, but there is a one-page graduate school record card in Registrar's Records, 36/1/667, CUL.

9. EPH, "The Golden Age," *Radcliffe Quarterly* 21, no. 2 (May 1937): 15. Information on Howes is cited in Margaret W. Rossiter, *Women Scientists in America: Strategies and Struggles to 1940* (Baltimore: Johns Hopkins University Press, 1982), 44.

10. James's comment is recorded in Wolcott Calkins's log, May 28, 1895, as cited in Elizabeth Scarborough and Laurel Furumoto, *Untold Lives: The First Generation of American Women Psychologists* (New York: Columbia University Press, 1987), 46. The letter submitted by the Harvard philosophy department requesting a Ph.D. for Calkins has recently been reprinted; see Charlene Haddock Seigfried, "Archive: 1895 Letter from Harvard Philosophy Department," *Hypatia* 8, no. 2 (Spring 1993): 230–33. Carl Murchison, ed., *A History of Psychology In Autobiography* (Worcester, Mass.: Clark University Press, 1930), 1:33–34.

11. Report of the President of Yale University for the Year Ending December 31, 1891, p. 25, YUA. "Closing Remarks by Provost Pepper," University of Pennsylvania: Addresses Delivered at the Opening of the Graduate Department for Women, May 4, 1892, p. 22, UPA. I thank Maryellen C. Kaminsky, archivist at the University of Pennsylvania, for helping me locate this source.

12. Sarah Frances Whiting discusses her career in "History of the Physics Department," physics dept., WCA. On Balch, see Randall, *Improper Bostonian*, 70–101. Julia Swift Orvis to Lucy Maynard Salmon, Oct. 14, 1895, Apr. 22, 1906, May 23, 1906, Salmon Papers, VCL. Lucretia Crocker was an important mentor to Mary Alice Willcox; see MAW, "Willcox Family Life," 38–55, folder 16, box 1, 14/10/504, Walter F. Willcox Papers, CUL.

13. William De Witt Hyde, *The College Man and the College Woman* (Boston: Houghton Mifflin, 1906), 208–09.

14. Hugo Münsterberg, *The Americans* (New York: McClure, Phillips, 1904), 577, 586–88. See also Charles Thwing, *College Women* (New York: Baker and Taylor, 1894), 145–47. M. Carey Thomas, "Present Tendencies in Women's College and University Education," in *The Educated Woman in America: Selected Writings of Catharine Beecher, Margaret Fuller, and M. Carey Thomas*, ed. Barbara M. Cross (New York: Teachers College Press, 1965), 167–68. Abby Leach, "Hindrances to the Intellectual Life in College," *JACA*, 3d ser., no. 17 (Feb. 1908): 78.

15. Ellen L. Burrell, "Charlotte Fitch Roberts," *WAM* 2, no. 2 (Jan. 1918): 80–81. Between 1892 and 1915, Yale gave only 24 Ph.D.'s in chemistry; nationwide only 472 were conferred. See also Daniel Kevles, "The Physics, Mathematics and Chemistry Communities: A Comparative Analysis," in *The Organization of Knowledge in Modern America, 1860–1920*, ed. Alexandra Oleson and John Voss (Baltimore: Johns Hopkins University Press, 1979), 139–73. SH, "Conservation Work by Professor Elizabeth Fisher," *WAM* 3, no. 2 (Jan. 1919): 99–100; Virginia Onderdonk, "Calkins, Mary Whiton," *NAW*; Ann M. Hirsch and Lisa J. Marroni, "Ferguson, Margaret," *NAW:MP*.

16. KLB, "Woman as Scholar," *Chatauquan*, April 1891. VDS, *On Journey*, 426; Ellen Hayes, as quoted in Louise Brown, *Ellen Hayes: Trail-Blazer* (West Park, N.Y.: n.p., 1932), 22.

17. VDS, *On Journey*, 84, 88; VDS, "Work for Women at Oxford," pt. 1, *Christian Union* 33, no. 17 (Apr. 1886): 8. Scudder added that despite the increase in lecture courses open to women at Oxford, "some benighted professors still sturdily refuse to admit them."

18. SFW, "The Experiences of a Woman Physicist," *WCN*, Jan. 9, 1913, 1–6, esp. 4–5.

19. Randall, *Improper Bostonian*, 96.

20. Burgess, *Dream and Deed*, 78. Randall, *Improper Bostonian*, 317.

21. EPH to her mother, Nov. 2, 1895, Morgan-Howes Family Papers, SL.

22. EPH to her mother, Mar. 29, 1896, Morgan-Howes Family Papers, SL. On Münsterberg, see Jutta Spillmann and Lothar Spillmann, "The Rise and Fall of Hugo Münsterberg," *Journal of the History of the Behavioral Sciences* 29, no. 4 (Oct. 1993): 322–38.

23. EPH to her mother, Nov. 11, 1896, Morgan-Howes Family Papers, SL.

24. EPH to her mother, May 4, 1896, and undated letter, Morgan-Howes Family Papers, SL.

25. Randall, *Improper Bostonian*, 74–77. Emily Greene Balch, *Public Assistance of the Poor in France* (American Economic Association, 1893).

26. See Joyce Antler, "'After College, What?': New Graduates and the Family Claim," *American Quarterly* 32 (Fall 1980): 409–33.

27. VDS, *On Journey*, 93–94.

28. Ibid., 96, 175.

29. Randall, *Improper Bostonian*, 69; EGB to "Dear Papa," 1892, EGB Papers, SCPC.

30. Randall, *Improper Bostonian*, 87, 101.

31. Laurel Furumoto, "Are There Sex Differences in Qualities of Mind? Mary Whiton Calkins versus Harvard University, a Thirty-Seven-Year Debate" (typescript, 1976, in author's possession), 14.

32. MWC to Charles E. Garman, Jan. 1, 1889, Charles Edward Garman Papers, Amherst College Archives. Charles E. Garman to MWC, Apr. 27, 1889; Mary Augusta Jordan to MWC, Dec. 18, 1888, Unprocessed MWC Papers, WCA.

33. KLB, "A Line-a-Day" diary, Mar. 19, 1896; also Mar. 5, 1896 (italics added), KLB Papers, WCA; Burgess, *Dream and Deed*, 89–91. On this generation's use of the passive voice in personal narrative see Jill Ker Conway, ed., *Written by Herself. Autobiographies of American Women: An Anthology* (New York: Vintage, 1992), x.

34. HM, "The History of the Department of Mathematics," 51, 36, math dept., WCA. Similarly, Eliza Kendrick lamented accepting a post in a high school when she was offered a position at Grinnell College since it was "a better place to rise in" (Eliza Kendrick to "My Dear Mamma," June 15, 1885, Eliza Kendrick Papers, WCA).

35. Margarethe Müller, *Carla Wenckebach: Pioneer* (Boston: Ginn, 1908), 179.

36. Ibid., 213, 225.

37. Ibid., 209.

38. EGB, diary entry, Dec. 31, 1894, SCPC.

39. KLB, "Across the Atlantic" diary, 1894, 34, KLB Papers, WCA.

40. Burgess, *Dream and Deed*, 66, 64.

41. Christopher Lasch, "Woman as Alien," in *The New Radicalism in America, 1889–1963: The Intellectual as a Social Type* (New York: Vintage, 1965), 62–68.

42. MWC, "The Place of Scholarship in Life" (handwritten draft filed in an envelope; n.d., probably 1910), Unprocessed MWC Papers, WCA. Contemporary feminist literary and linguistic analysis probes the anxiety women writers have using the word *I*; see Joanne S. Frye, "The Subversive 'I,'" in Frye, *Living Stories, Telling Lives: Women and the Novel in Contemporary Experience* (Ann Arbor: University of Michigan Press, 1986); Sidonie Smith, *A Poetics of Women's Autobiography: Marginality and the Fictions of Self-Representation* (Bloomington: Indiana University Press, 1987).

43. MPS, "Undergraduate Life at Vassar," *Scribner's* 23, no. 6 (June 1898): 643; Randall, *Improper Bostonian*, 51.

44. VDS, "The Effect on Character of a College Education," *Christian Union* 35, no. 14 (Apr. 7, 1887): 12; EPH, "The College Girl," *Boston Transcript*, June 23, 1900.

45. KLB, "Woman as Scholar."

46. MWC, "The Place of Scholarship in Life," WCA; MWC, "Publishing and Marrying," *WAM* 7, no. 3 (May 1923): 171–78.

47. EGB, "The Education and Efficiency of Women," *Academy of Political Science* 1, no. 1 (1910): 61–71, rpt. New York: Academy of Political Science, 1910.

48. L. Clark Seelye to EPH, Apr. 29, 1908, Morgan-Howes Family Papers, SL.

49. EPH, "The Revolt of Mother," *Woman's Home Companion* 50 (Apr. 1923): 30–32. EPH, "The Golden Age," *Radcliffe Quarterly* 21, no. 2 (May 1937): 15.

50. M. Carey Thomas, "The Future of Women's Higher Education" (1913), rpt. in *The Educated Woman in America,* ed. Cross, 172.

51. EPH, "The Meaning of Progress in the Woman Movement," *Annals of the American Academy of Political and Social Science* 143 (May 1929): 14–20. Howes's negative view of celibate professional women would grow increasingly popular in the 1930s and 1940s. She predicted that the unmarried professional women would become a "race of dry, cold, warped, inhibited little creatures" (EPH, "Accepting the Universe," *Atlantic Monthly,* May 1922, 453). See also EPH, "Notes for an Address to AAUW on Continuity for the Educated Woman" (1930), where she classifies the two emerging groups of professional women as the "queen bee" and the "sexless worker" (Morgan-Howes Family Papers, SL). Howes felt that the woman who wanted to marry, "not the celibate," should be of concern to feminists. C. Todd Stephenson, "'Integrating the Carol Kennicotts': Ethel Puffer Howes and the Institute for the Coordination of Women's Interests," *Journal of Women's History 4,* no. 1 (Spring 1992): 89–113.

52. VDS, *On Journey,* 95; VDS, *A Listener in Babel* (Boston: Houghton Mifflin, 1903), 13–22.

53. Randall, *Improper Bostonian,* 117; Burgess, *Dream and Deed,* 83. Information on Margaret Sherwood was obtained from the diary of KLB, "A Line-a-Day" diary, Nov. 18, Nov. 21, Nov. 23, 1893, KLB Papers, WCA; MAW, "Willcox Family Life," 19, folder 16, box 1, 14/10/504, Walter F. Willcox Papers, CUL.

54. EPH, "Accepting the Universe," 444.

6

Even Blue Stockings Have to Be Darned

Epigraph: KLB, handwritten untitled speech (n.d.), 7–8, Manuscripts of Speeches, KLB Papers, WCA.

1. Ibid., 8. Marjorie Hope Nicholson, "Scholars and Ladies," *Yale Review* 19 (Summer 1930): 794, italics added. I recognize that this image of the woman scholar is as much about cultural conceptions of womanhood as it is about salary.

2. M. Carey Thomas, "The Future of Woman's Higher Education" (1913), rpt. as "Marriage and the Woman Scholar," in *The Educated Woman in America: Selected Writings of Catharine Beecher, Margaret Fuller, and M. Carey Thomas,* ed. Barbara M. Cross (New York: Teachers College Press, 1965), 174. As early as 1884, while visiting Wellesley, M. Carey Thomas enthusiastically declared: "Not a man's influence is seen or felt. . . . The devotion to study of these girls and women profs. in this Princesslike community of Wellesley is more devoted than elsewhere" (M. Carey Thomas to Mary E. Garrett, May 3, 1884, reel 15, M. Carey Thomas

Papers, Bryn Mawr College Archives. I thank Barbara Sicherman for this reference).

3. MAW, "Willcox Family Life," 64, folder 16, box 1, 14/10/504, Walter F. Willcox Papers, CUL.

4. Henry Durant to "Dear Sir" (Dr. Azel Ames), Nov. 11, 1874, ALS, WCA. This policy was reaffirmed in the ECM/BT, May 8, 1891, WCA.

5. Helen Sard Hughes, "The Academic Chance," *JACA* 12, no. 2 (Jan. 1919): 52. *Compensation in Certain Occupations of Women Who Have Received College or Other Special Training* (Boston: Wright and Potter, 1896), 29.

6. Kate Holladay Claghorn, "The Problem of Occupation for College Women," *JACA*, ser. 2, no. 66 (1897): 221.

7. William R. Harper, "The Educational Progress of the Year 1901–1902," *Educational Review* 24 (Oct. 1902): 262.

8. Christine Ladd-Franklin, "Endowed Professorships for Women," *JACA*, ser. 3, no. 9 (Feb. 1904): 56–57.

9. Margarethe Müller, *Carla Wenckebach: Pioneer* (Boston: Ginn, 1908), 219. Kate Edelman to "My Dear Mrs. Randall," May 28, 1957, "Balch Project," ser. 2, box 2, Mercedes Randall Papers, SCPC.

10. Susan Kingsbury, "Economic Efficiency of College Women," *JACA*, ser. 3, no. 20 (Feb. 1910): 9–10, 19–20.

11. Money problems plagued Wellesley. In 1881, Henry Durant, as treasurer, recorded that Wellesley had insufficient funds for raising salaries. MBT, June 21, 1881, 80–81; Pauline Durant expressed her anger over the paucity of bequests: "I felt so sorry to see Ex. Governor Morgan's money divided between Harvard, Yale and Amherst and Williams and not one cent for Wellesley." Pauline Durant to Eben Horsford, Feb. 13, 1883, Eben Horsford Papers, WCA; see also ECM/BT, Dec. 13, 1899. In the 1920s, Wellesley joined with other women's colleges to issue a plea for more funds; EFP et al., "The Question of the Women's Colleges," *Atlantic Monthly* (Nov. 1927): 577–84.

12. Transcripts of letters regarding Maria Mitchell's and Alida Avery's fight with the Trustees of Vassar College over salary, Maria Mitchell Papers, VCL. Mary Emma Byrd is discussed in Bessie Z. Jones and Lyle G. Boyd, *The Harvard College Observatory: The First Four Directorships, 1838–1919* (Cambridge: Harvard University Press, 1971), 414.

13. Elizabeth Hazelton Haight, "Pleasant Possibles in Lady Professors," *JACA* 11, no. 1 (Sept. 1917): 12–13.

14. Claghorn, "The Problem of Occupation for College Women," 223.

15. Teachers Salaries, 1879–80, Trustee Ledger, Treasurers Files, WCA. Rachel Speckman, M.D., the resident physician (1884–94), was paid $1,000 and given a room, MBT, June 24, 1884, 145. The $1,500 figure was still a benchmark for senior professors in 1885. The president's salary was set at $3,000 and a home, to be raised to $4,000 in 1887–88, ECM/BT, Oct. 21, 1885, WCA. Discussions of salary also appear in MBT, Nov. 5, 1888, 176–77. The calculation of $200 in lieu of board is discussed in MBT, June 2, 1887, 218, WCA. In 1884, Junius W.

Hill, the newly hired professor of music and director of the School of Music, was given a salary of $3,000 (MBT, June 5, 1884, WCA). This salary probably reflects the unusual number of duties that the college required of the music program director, including organizing recitals and concerts (*Wellesley College Calendar*, 1886, 11). In 1897 the School of Music was eliminated, and course work changed to the department of music.

16. ECM/BT, Jan. 3, 1900, 50, WCA. The Executive Committee Minutes of Feb. 28, 1900, show that Mary Calkins earned $1,700 and Ellen Hayes $1,800 (59). In 1902, for example, Margaret Ferguson, a Ph.D. in botany, had a starting salary of $1,100; Roxanna Vivian, a Ph.D. in mathematics, began at $1,000 (Amy Tanner, "The Salaries of Women Teachers in Institutions of Collegiate Rank," *JACA*, ser. 3, no. 15, spec. bull. [Nov. 1907]: 24). In 1881, a survey of seventy-six women doctors reported their average yearly income was $2,907 (Rachel L. Bodley, Valedictory Address to the Twenty-Ninth Graduating Class of the Women's Medical College of Pennsylvania [Philadelphia: n.p., 1881], 7. It is important to note that this sample is small. I thank Regina Morantz Markell-Sanchez for this reference).

17. Susan Kingsbury, "Committee on Academic Appointments," *JACA*, ser. 4, no. 1 (Jan. 1911): 22; "The Salary of the College Woman," *The Independent* 65 (July 9, 1908): esp. 88–92. On women's slow rate of promotion through the academic ranks, see Marion O. Hawthorne, "Women as College Teachers," *Annals of the American Academy of Political and Social Science* 143 (May 1929): 149–51.

18. VDS, *On Journey* (New York: Dutton, 1937), 178; MPS, Faculty Questionnaire, FBF, WCA. KLB, "Autobiography in Brief," KLB Papers, WCA; see also Dorothy Burgess, *Dream and Deed: The Story of Katharine Lee Bates* (Norman: University of Oklahoma Press, 1952), 101.

19. ECM/BT, Oct. 23, 1895, 55, WCA; *President's Report*, 1897, 19, WCA.

20. Müller, *Carla Wenckebach*, 240–41, 279–80.

21. Several studies from the 1890s through the 1920s demonstrated the falsity of this assumption. See *Compensation in Certain Occupations of Women*; this study revealed that 41 percent of the women surveyed contributed to the support of others. Of the teachers who responded, 37 percent helped support others. See also Second Report of Committee W on the Status of Women in College and University Faculties, *BAAUP* 10, no. 7 (1924): 65–73; Emilie Hutchinson's 1929 survey of 1,025 women with Ph.D.'s underscored that more than two-thirds of the respondents had had dependents either during or after graduate work, while "an undeniably heroic" 25 percent of these women had been entirely responsible for the support of others at some point during their careers (Emilie J. Hutchinson, *Women and the Ph.D.*, published as the *Institute of Women's Professional Relations Bulletin*, no. 2 [Greensboro, N.C.: North Carolina College for Women, 1929], 14, 90–91). Tanner, "The Salaries of Women Teachers," 23.

22. Katharine May Edwards, Helen Merrill, and Eliza Kendrick, Wills, WCA. Julia Swift Orvis took care of her cousins into their old age; see "Julia Swift Orvis Died March 16," *The Townsman* (Wellesley, Mass.), Mar. 24, 1949.

23. Burgess, *Dream and Deed*, 100.

24. The Shackford bequest was to be made into the "M. A. Cartland Shackford Fund," the income of which was to be used for a female college graduate (not limited to Wellesley) who wished to study medicine (MHS, Wills, WCA). Elizabeth Whiting was employed on the administrative staff of the college but also had to have been supported by her sister, Sarah. Elizabeth eventually received a substantial inheritance of her own, and in 1927, when Sarah died, Elizabeth deeded her share of her sister's legacy to Wellesley (Sarah Frances Whiting, Wills, WCA). When Mary Calkins died in 1930, she left one-fourth of her estate, amounting to approximately $4,000, to the college (MWC, Wills, WCA). In 1955, her brother, Grosvenor Calkins, deeded $10,000 to Wellesley, to be used for a Mary Whiton Calkins Professorship or for a scholarship by the departments of philosophy and psychology.

25. Margaret Hastings Jackson to "Dear Sir" (James Dean, treasurer), Feb. 23? (1931), Treasurer's Office Files, WCA. James Dean to "My Dear Miss Jackson," Mar. 13, 1931, Wills, WCA.

26. Margarethe Müller's plight is revealed in several letters between her and the Wellesley College cashier, Evelyn A. Monroe, found in Miscellaneous, Carnegie Retiring Allowances, Margarethe Müller, Unprocessed Assistant Treasurer's Files, WCA. Susan Hallowell was another faculty member in "extreme need" after retirement. She was voted special grants by the trustees; see ECM/BT, Dec. 9, 1908, WCA. An American academic woman in the South asked rhetorically: "I wonder if I shall be content, when I get too old to teach, and am spending my days in—well, say a poor house. For that is almost the only place a school teacher can hope to end her days" (letter of Corinne Lacey to Mary Elizabeth [Mamie] Jenkins, Jan. 9, 1923, as quoted in Sally Brett, "A Different Kind of Being," in *Stepping Off the Pedestal: Academic Women of the South,* ed. Patricia A. Stringer and Irene Thompson [New York: Modern Language Association, 1982], 15).

27. Frank Stricker, "American Professors in the Progressive Era: Income, Aspirations, and Professionalism," *Journal of Interdisciplinary History* 19, no. 2 (Autumn 1988): 236 and 231–57. See also W. Bruce Leslie, "When Professors Had Servants: Prestige, Pay, and Professionalization, 1860–1917," *History of Higher Education Annual* 10 (1990): 19–30; studying nineteenth-century male faculty at four colleges, Leslie finds them well paid. He argues that expansion of lower-paid junior ranks caused income disparities and concludes that faculty exaggerated the relative decline in salaries.

28. Stricker, "American Professors in the Progressive Era," 235–36; see also Guido Hugo Marx, "The Problem of the Assistant Professor," *Journal of Proceedings and Addresses of the Association of American Universities* 11 (1910): 17–47.

29. Stricker, "American Professors in the Progressive Era," 248, esp. n. 31; see also Frank Stricker, "An American Middle Class Meets the Consumer Age: Peixotto's Rational Professor in the 1920s," *Amerikastudien/America Studies* 34 (1990): 311–31, esp. 314; F. Stricker, "Economic Success and Academic Professionalization: Questions from Two Decades of U.S. History (1908–1929)," *Social Science History* 12, no. 2 (Summer 1988): 143–70.

30. KLB, signature next to her name on payroll ledger, 1901–02, Business Manager Financial Records, WCA; also Tanner, "The Salaries of Women Teachers," 23, MBT, 1886–1915, WCA. There were many examples of requests that were denied. See, for example, Miss Emerson who requested more salary for chairing Latin as well as teaching her regular load and Hebrew (MBT, Feb. 17, 1886); Carla Wenckebach's request for $500 for board and lodging was denied (ECM/BT, May 2, 1900, WCA).

31. MBT, Apr. 20, 1916, app. 2, 392; Wellesley Salaries as They Will Stand in 1918–19, salary chart enclosed with MBT, Mar. 8, 1917, 455. See also app. J, 391, WCA. For a discussion of the recruitment of men and the relationship to raised salaries see chap. 16, "Eden's End."

32. "The Confessions of a Woman Professor," The Independent 55 (Apr. 1903): 957.

33. Ibid., 954–56.

34. Carrie Harper, "A Feminine Professorial Viewpoint," Educational Review 46 (June 1913): 47–48. Hawthorne, "Women as College Teachers," 153. Disparities in the academic salaries of men and women of the same rank were reported in numerous other studies. See, e.g., "Opportunities and Salaries of Women in the Teaching Profession in Nebraska," JACA 13, nos. 5–6 (Mar.–Apr. 1920): 10–13; John H. McNeely, Salaries in Land-Grant Universities and Colleges, pamphlet no. 24 (Washington D.C.: Office of Education, November 1931).

35. Scheme, Matured and Adopted by the Trustees in 1886, on the Basis of a Bequest Made to Wellesley College in 1878 (Cambridge: John Wilson, 1886), WCA; paid leaves went only to department heads. Susan Hallowell, "really needing rest and change," was the first professor granted this sabbatical, ECM/BT, Feb. 17, 1886, WCA. She deferred it until 1887–88, ECM/BT, Mar. 10, 1886. In 1902, all full professors were deemed eligible for sabbatical leave on half-salary. This privilege was not extended to associate and assistant professors until 1929 (Ella Keats Whiting, "The Faculty," in Wellesley College, 1875–1975: A Century of Women, ed. Jean Glasscock [Wellesley: Wellesley College, 1975], 102).

36. Horsford first sought permission to furnish the faculty parlor from the Executive Committee of the Board of Trustees, Mar. 24, 1888, WCA. The Faculty Parlor is discussed in MHS and Edith Harriet Moore, eds., College Hall (privately printed, n.d.), 8. Courant, Sept. 28, 1888, 2, WCA.

37. Müller, Carla Wenckebach, 218, 252–53.

38. VDS, On Journey, 108.

39. Charlotte Conant, letter to her family, Oct. 17, 1880, as cited in Martha Pike Conant et al., A Girl of the Eighties: At College and at Home (Boston: Houghton Mifflin, 1931), 104. See also EM, "I Remember Wellesley: An Arrival at Wellesley in 1898," WAM 31, no. 1 (Oct. 1946): 29–30. On serving arrangements, see "Notice to Faculty about Service at Tables," Domestic Department, WCA; a chart of seating arrangements can be found in "Dinner 1913–14," College House Book, 1913–14, WCA.

40. In 1891 Mary Alice Willcox wrote to Professor Frances Lord, acting president, for permission to "live outside College limits" (MAW to Frances Lord, Mar. ?, 1891,

ALS, WCA). On Mar. 11, 1891, the trustees voted to grant the request (ECM/BT, WCA). The new faculty residence policy is in President's Report, 1900, 4, WCA. Alumna Lucy Wilson recalled that "it was a great thing for seniors to be invited to [Hazard's] house to dinner. That had never happened before" (Lucy Wilson, TOI-CNH, 12, WCA).

41. Scudder did finally buy a house in the town of Wellesley. Pictures of the Scudder home and household are pasted into the WCA copy of *On Journey*.

42. Lucy Wilson, TOI-CNH, 12, WCA. After the fire that destroyed College Hall, Case lived in Stone Hall.

43. Mabel M. Young, "Helen Abbot Merrill," *WAM* 16, no. 5 (June 1932): 406.

44. Emily F. Wheeler, "Households of Women," *Critic*, Aug. 24, 1889, 88–90, esp. 90; see also the retort to Wheeler by M. A. Jordan, "To the Editors of the Critic," *Critic*, Sept. 21, 1889, 137–38; Alumna, "Should Women's Colleges Provide Homes?" *Critic*, Nov. 2, 1889, 221–22; Kate Morris Cone, "To the Editors," *Critic*, Nov. 2, 1889, 222. Helen Lefkowitz Horowitz, *Alma Mater: Design and Experience in the Women's Colleges from Their Nineteenth-Century Beginnings to the 1930s* (New York: Knopf, 1984), 179–97. Horowitz does recognize the role that salaries played in determining residency patterns (187). Katharine Lee Bates was among those who delayed moving off campus because of financial problems; see Burgess, *Dream and Deed*. On-campus services provided by the college eased the burden of personal and domestic chores. For example, faculty were allowed to use the medical services of the resident female doctor; see Dr. Emily Jones, FBF, WCA. "Dr. Katharine Piatt Raymond, College Physician: A Few Tributes from Those Whom She Has Helped," *WAM* 9, no. 5 (June 1925): 259–61.

45. The department of rhetoric, for example, employed a married woman, Mrs. Manly. Her husband taught rhetoric at Wellesley for seven years as well. On the appointment of Mr. and Mrs. Manly, see ECM/BT, 1884–85; on Ralza Morse Manly, see *Manly Family Newsletter* (privately published) 3, no. 1 (Apr. 1984): 5, WCA. The college wished Alice Freeman to stay on after her marriage to George Herbert Palmer. The invitation to George Herbert Palmer to share the presidency with his wife is documented in the Trustees Minutes and the Palmers' correspondence (AFP Papers, WCA).

46. Statement of Normal Salary and Workload for Faculty, CH (1899–1910) Folder, President's Office Files, WCA.

47. KLB, handwritten untitled speech (n.d.), Manuscripts of Speeches, KLB Papers, WCA.

48. Ladd-Franklin, "Endowed Professorships for Women."

49. Louise Pound, "The College Woman and Research," *JACA* 14, no. 2 (Nov. 1920): 31–34; Haight, "Pleasant Possibles in Lady Professors," 13.

50. Helen Sard Hughes, "College Women and Research Again," *JACA* 14, no. 4 (Jan. 1921): 88–90; see also Helen Sard Hughes, "Can Women Make Good?" *School and Society* 2, no. 36 (Sept. 4, 1915): 336–44.

51. Louise Rogers Jewett and MWC, introd. to *The Poems of Sophie Jewett* (New York: Crowell, 1910), xii–xiii.

52. KLB, "Autobiography in Brief," KLB Papers, WCA; also KLB to Grace Cook Kurz, Jan. 25, 1921, KLB Papers, WCA.

53. "Half a Century of Wellesley," *Ladies Home Journal*, June 1925, 89; VDS to KLB, Aug. 6, 1919, ALS, WCA. This pattern was repeated throughout the college. Many women put off pet projects until retirement. Margarethe Müller initially considered retiring in 1908 to do some creative work she had been wanting to do for more than fifteen years. She was ready to foreit her Carnegie Foundation pension because she did "not wish to sell my soul for a mess of potage—however welcome" (Margarethe Müller to CH, Autumn 1908 and Oct. 16, 1908, ALS, WCA). In the end Müller waited until 1923 to retire. She never completed her manuscript. "Distress and disillusionment" marked her later years (Henrietta Littlefield, "Margarethe Müller," WAM 18, no. 3 [Feb. 1934]: 250). She died in Germany in 1934.

54. Alice Robertson to EFP (Zoology Department Report), 1912–13, zoology dept., WCA. EGB, diary entry, Apr. 15, 1900, EGB Papers, SCPC.

55. Bruce Fink, "A Memoir of Clara E. Cummings," *The Bryologist* 10, no. 3 (May 1907): 38–39.

56. MCF to Ella Keats Whiting, Mar. 17, 1948, MCF Papers, WCA.

57. MPS to Miss Bradstreet, May 4, 1935, MPS FBF, WCA. MAW to Miss Whiting, Mar. 27, 1948, MAW FBF, WCA; see also Willcox, Faculty Questionnaire, MAW FBF, WCA.

58. LMH to MHS, Nov. 12, 1924, ALS, WCA.

59. EGB (Ambition), EGB Papers, SCPC. EGB ("I am no princess . . ."), EGB Papers, SCPC. Balch wrote to Mary Simkhovitch about all the festivities that accompanied her winning the Nobel Prize for Peace: "It is a curious experience to be so treated as an important person and I hope I shall not come home spoiled." She then apologized for "writing so much about myself" (EGB to Mary Simkhovitch, Apr. 23, 1948, Unprocessed Simkhovitch Papers, SL).

60. MAW, "Willcox Family Life," 73–77, folder 16, box 1, 14/10/504, Walter F. Willcox Papers, CUL.

61. Laurel Furumoto, "Are There Sex Differences in Qualities of Mind?: Mary Whiton Calkins versus Harvard University, a Thirty-Seven-Year Debate" (typescript, 1976, in author's possession), 42–43. There was a professional side to her reluctance to go to Columbia as well. She believed she would be shackled with courses outside her speciality. It is arguable whether Mary Calkins would have achieved a larger reputation had she had Ph.D. students at Columbia.

62. MAW to Marian Hubbard, Dec. 2, 1927, MAW FBF, WCA.

63. Margaret W. Rossiter, "Women's Colleges: The Entering Wedge," Rossiter, *Women Scientists in America: Struggles and Strategies* (Baltimore: Johns Hopkins University Press, 1982), 23.

64. For more information on distinguished achievers and levels of activism, see Patricia A. Palmieri, "In Adamless Eden: A Social Portrait of the Academic Community at Wellesley College 1875–1920" (Ed.D. diss., Harvard, 1981), table 15, p. 416.

65. VDS, *On Journey,* 298; Scudder also wrote: "If there is any happier game than

building a house, I have failed to play it" (272). Alice Walton speaks of her house as her "fascinating plaything" (Alice Walton to Alice Van Vechten Brown [1914], College Hall Fire, WCA). See also correspondence between MCF and MB, which chronicles the establishment of Ferguson's new home (MCF Papers, WCA).

7
The Bonds of Wellesley

Epigraph: Ellen Burrell to MMH, Nov. 16, 1938, "History of the Department of Mathematics," math dept., WCA.

1. M. Margaret Ball, TOI-CNH, 2, WCA. *Legislation of Wellesley College,* 1908; "Academic Council"; "The Faculty," WCA; see also Ella Keats Whiting, "The Faculty," in *Wellesley College, 1875–1975: A Century of Women,* ed. Jean Glasscock (Wellesley: Wellesley College, 1975), 98–99; MBT, Feb. 11, June 10, 1910, WCA. Laurence R. Veysey argues that "departmental dictatorships" were characteristic of academe in the 1880s (Veysey, *The Emergence of the Modern University* [Chicago: University of Chicago Press, 1965], 320–24).

2. E. Elizabeth Jones, TOI-CNH, 11, WCA; art was another department that had very few meetings. Agnes Abbot, TOI-CNH, 13, WCA; see also HM, "History of the Department of Mathematics," 42, math dept., WCA.

3. VDS, *On Journey* (New York: Dutton, 1937), 123; VDS, "Katharine Lee Bates, Professor of English Literature," *WAM* (suppl.) 13, no. 5 (June 1929): 5; HM, "History of the Department of Mathematics," 42, math dept., WCA. Margarethe Müller, "German at Wellesley College," address delivered at the fifty-ninth annual meeting of the New Hampshire Teachers' Association, fall 1912 (privately printed, 1913), 4–5, WCA.

4. HM, "History of the Department of Mathematics," 41–58, math dept., WCA; Agnes Abbot, TOI-CNH, 5–6, WCA.

5. MHS, "The Centenary of Katharine Lee Bates," 3, KLB Papers, WCA.

6. KLB to "My Dear Poet" (Josephine Preston Peabody), Nov. 4, 1908, KLB Papers, WCA.

7. Katharine Balderston, TOI-CNH, 17; Lucy Wilson, TOI-CNH, 15, WCA; VDS, *On Journey,* 220.

8. KLB to LMH, July 1, 1885, KLB Papers, WCA.

9. KLB to LMH (n.d., probably spring 1889), KLB Papers, WCA.

10. KLB to LMH, Nov. 19, 1886, and Thursday (1889); KLB to LMH, Dec. ?, KLB Papers, WCA.

11. KLB to "Dear Cheer-Up" (LMH), Mar. 2, 1916, KLB Papers, WCA; KLB to LMH (letter dictated to and signed by Louise R. Hicks), Mar. 6, 1929, KLB Papers, WCA.

12. VDS to LMH, July 6, 1887, ALS; VDS to LMH, Aug. 26, 1887, ALS; VDS to LMH, Sept. 9, 1887, ALS, WCA.

13. VDS to LMH, Dec. 26, 1889, ALS, WCA.

14. VDS to LMH, fall 1889, ALS, WCA.

15. VDS to LMH (a note scribbled on the back of a calling card), n.d., ALS, WCA.

16. VDS to LMH, May 29, 1928, ALS, WCA. SJ to LMH, Aug. 23, 1890, ALS, WCA.

17. Sophie Jewett to KLB, Nov. 27, 1889, ALS, WCA.

18. KLB to JM, Dec. 16, 1901, KLB Papers, WCA. VDS to JM, May 11, 1902, ALS, WCA.

19. Historian Margaret W. Rossiter finds that women who failed to inspire protégées sometimes considered themselves failures. Rossiter, "Women's Education: The Entering Wedge," in *Women Scientists in America: Struggles and Strategies to 1940* (Baltimore: Johns Hopkins University Press, 1982); Helen French, "Charlotte Almira Bragg," *WAM* 13, no. 5 (June 1929): 287–88; Helen French FBF, WCA.

20. Eleanor Gamble to "Dear Girls," Dec. 1889, class letter, class of 1889, 9, WCA.

21. Calkins counted converting Gamble to her personalist theory of self-psychology as one of the "greatest triumphs of her life" (Eliza Hall Kendrick, "Eleanor Acheson McCulloch Gamble," *WAM* 18, no. 1 [Oct. 1933]: 2); Calkins mentions Gamble in her autobiographical entry in Carl Murchison, ed., *A History of Psychology in Autobiography* (Worcester, Mass.: Clark University Press, 1930), 1–35.

22. MCF, "Susan Hallowell," *Botanical Gazette* 53, no. 4 (Apr. 1912): 346–47; on "grandfather clauses" (here "grandmother clauses") that protect mentors, see William Goode, "Community within a Community: The Professions," *American Sociological Review* 22 (1957): 194-200; MCF to CH, Jan. 20, 1910, ALS, WCA; MB to MCF, Wednesday (n.d., probably 1911), MCF-MB Correspondence, MCF Papers, WCA.

23. Alice Ottley, like her aunt, got her B.A. from Cornell in 1904. She received her M.A. from Wellesley in 1906 and her Ph.D. in 1921 from the University of California. She spent her entire academic career at Wellesley and inherited the direction of the Ferguson greenhouses and gardens. See *1942 Record Number of the Wellesley College Bulletin*, "Officers of Instruction and Administration" (Wellesley: Wellesley College, 1942); see also Alice Ottley FBF, WCA.

24. In this letter, Bliss admitted that her relationships with students were often unwise, a defect due to a "tendency in my nature to love people intensely." (Indeed, she wrote of loving Ferguson "with all my heart.") MB to MCF, Dec. 18, 1909; MB to MCF, Apr. 25, 1916, MFC-MB Correspondence, MCF Papers, WCA.

25. In return for such devotion, Ferguson helped to publish Bliss's papers and recommended her for fellowships and postgraduate study. MB to MCF, Nov. 5, 1916, Oct. 29, 1920, and n.d. (probably 1912); MCF to "My Dear Professor Kendrick," Jan. 17, 1921, MCF-MB Correspondence, MCF Papers, WCA.

26. MAW to Marian Hubbard, Dec. 2, 1927, Willcox FBF, WCA.

27. Agnes Abbot, TOI-CNH, 36, WCA.

28. Elizabeth L. Broyles, TOI-CNH, 2, WCA.

29. MAW to Marian Hubbard, Dec. 2, 1927, Willcox FBF, WCA; MAW, "Willcox Family Life," TS, 60, folder 16, box 1, 14/10/504, Walter F. Willcox Papers, CUL; E. Elizabeth Jones, TOI-CNH, 8–9, WCA.

30. HM, "History of the Department of Mathematics," math dept., 42, 52, WCA.

31. Agnes Abbot, TOI-CNH, 17, WCA,

32. Lucy Killough, TOI-CNH, 25, WCA. E. Elizabeth Jones, TOI-CNH, 1, WCA.

33. Florence Converse, *Wellesley College: A Chronicle of the Years 1875-1938* (Wellesley: Hathaway House Bookshop, 1939), 98.

34. Allen F. Davis, "Coman, Katharine," *NAW*; on Scudder, see Alice Payne Hackett, *Wellesley: Part of the American Story* (New York: Dutton, 1949), 123; information on Hayes was obtained from *The Class of 1878* (n.p.: Oberlin College, 1913), OCA.

35. VDS, *On Journey,* 110; Mercedes M. Randall, *Improper Bostonian: Emily Greene Balch* (New York: Twayne, 1964), 82; *Second Annual Report of the College Settlements Association* (New York: Brown and Wilson, 1892), 9. See also John P. Rousmaniere, "Cultural Hybrid in the Slums: The College Woman and the Settlement House, 1889–1894," *American Quarterly* 22 (1970): 45–66.

36. See Marion Talbot and Lois K. M. Rosenberry, *The History of the American Association of University Women, 1881–1931* (Boston: Houghton Mifflin, 1931). The Vineyard Shore School Papers are located in the Helen Lockwood Papers, VCL; see also Louise Brown to "Dear Friends," May 1930, Vineyard Shore School for Women Workers in Industry Papers, A76, folder 307, SL; Ellen Hayes to "Dear Ben" (Benjamin Hayes), June 21, 1930, Archives of the Granville Historical Society, Granville, Ohio. I thank Flo Hoffmann for helping me locate this letter.

37. VDS, *On Journey,* 181.

38. VDS to "The Board of Trustees of Wellesley College," 1900, ALS, WCA; MPS to VDS, May 1900, ALS, WCA. This tactic of individual appeals to the board was advised by Horace Scudder, Vida's uncle, who counseled his niece throughout this entire episode (HS to VDS, May 1, 1900, ALS, WCA). Confirmation that Emily Balch considered resigning can be found in EGB, diary entry, Apr. 15, 1900, EGB Papers, SCPC; VDS, *On Journey,* 182–83.

39. MPS, *Henry Worthington, Idealist* (New York: Macmillan, 1899). Scudder deals with the topic in her semiautobiographical novel, *A Listener in Babel* (Boston: Houghton Mifflin, 1903).

40. MAW to VDS(?), 1900, ALS, WCA. In this letter, Willcox criticizes the University of Chicago for not renewing the contract of Bemis, a young faculty member, because of his antimonopolistic economic views. The affair caused an outpouring of public sentiment against Chicago. See Laurence R. Veysey, *The Emergence of the Modern University,* 368.

41. VDS, *On Journey,* 182, 188, 184. See also "Strife within the IWW," *Boston Evening Transcript,* n.d. (probably Mar. 1912), Hayes FBF, WCA.

42. VDS, *On Journey,* 189–90.

43. Ibid., 427, 183–84; VDS to CH, Mar. 25, 1900, and three other letters written during 1900 on file with this letter, VDS Papers, WCA; see also VDS, "Academic Freedom," *The Century Magazine* (1916), rpt. in VDS, *The Privilege of Age: Essays Secular and Spiritual* (New York: Dutton, 1939), 107–26.

8
A Colony of Friends

Epigraph: VDS, *On Journey* (New York: Dutton, 1937), 219.

1. Eleanor Gamble, "An Open Letter," *WAM* 11, no. 1 (Oct. 1926): 7; see also Louise Rogers Jewett and MWC, introd. to *The Poems of Sophie Jewett* (New York: Thomas A. Crowell, 1910); information on Ellen Hayes and Katharine Coman was obtained from "Katharine Coman," TS (n.d.), Coman FBF, WCA; *1942 Record Number of the Wellesley College Bulletin,* "Officers of Instruction and Administration" (Wellesley, Wellesley College, 1942).

2. The mean age of the senior faculty in 1900 was thirty-seven. Mary Haskell, "Professor Wenckebach's Relation to Her Students," *Wellesley Magazine* 11, no. 4 (Feb. 1903): 160; "Tribute to Miss Kendall," EKK FBF, WCA; Eleanor Gamble used the term *colony* in writing about the professors emeriti who lived in Wellesley Village, but it applies equally well to the faculty community as a whole. Gamble, "Anna McKeag," *WAM* 8, no. 4 (June 1932): 6.

3. On the intricacies of group identity, see Harold Isaacs, "Basic Group Identity: The Idols of the Tribe," in *Ethnicity: Theory and Experience,* ed. Nathan Glazer and Daniel P. Moynihan (Cambridge: Harvard University Press, 1975), 32.

4. VDS to LMH, Dec. 29, 1910, ALS, WCA; 1916 Recorded Reminiscences of Wellesley and two readings by former faculty members. Edna Moffett is one of the voices heard on "Wellesley College 1902–1938," Collection of Phonograph Records, WCA.

5. Geraldine Gordon, TOI-CNH, 15, WCA.

6. VDS to JM, June 11, 1899, ALS, WCA; Ellen L. Burrell to LMN, June 4, 1899, ALS, WCA; MPS, "Old Trails," in *Familiar Ways* (Boston: Little, Brown, 1917), 175–93. MHS wrote: "In Wellesley . . . every hole is taken. There are too many single women here occupying large houses." MHS to MG, Dec. 28, 1948, class of 1899, MG Papers, WCA.

7. KLB, "Sophie Jewett: The Passing of a Real Poet" (untitled newspaper clipping), SJ FBF, WCA. On the cult of the pastoral in the late nineteenth century, see Leo Marx, *The Machine in the Garden: Technology and the Pastoral Ideal in America* (New York: Oxford University Press, 1964).

8. For information on one such compound, see Anna Jane McKeag, "Mary Frazier Smith," *WAM* 18, no. 1 (Oct. 1933): 6–9.

9. MPS, "Gardens Real and Imagined," in *Familiar Ways,* 100, 110. On the relationship between women and landscape values, see Vera Norwood, *Made from This Earth: American Women and Nature* (Chapel Hill: University of North Carolina Press, 1993), esp. chap. 4.

10. MPS, *Familiar Ways,* 191–92.

11. Marion Pelton Guild to Birdie Ball Morrison, Dec. 6, 1930, class of 1880, WCA. See also Scudder's eulogy of Sophie Jewett: "Our fellowship extends into the Heavenly Country and is part of the life eternal." VDS, "Memorial Address" (for SJ), *Wellesley Magazine* 18, no. 2 (Nov. 1, 1909): 43.

12. *President's Report,* 1910, 3, WCA.

13. MPS to JM, June 29, 1910, ALS, WCA. In 1949, at the age of eighty-six, Margaret Sherwood wrote a novel whose title, *Pilgrim Feet* (Wakefield, Mass.: Montrose Press, 1949), showed the depth and durability of Jewett's influence. VDS, "Memorial Address" (for SJ), 43.

14. KC, "Last Days," in *Memories of Martha Seymour Coman,* ed. KC (Boston: Fort Hill Press, 1913), 99.

15. Mary B. Jenkins, "Elizabeth Kimball Kendall: 1855–1952," *WAM* 37, no. 1 (Nov. 1952): 24; MPS to EKK, Dec. 2, 1945, EKK Papers, WCA.

16. KLB to EKK, Jan. 23, 1918, EKK Papers, WCA.

17. Balch's valentine to Kendall appears in her volume of poetry, *The Miracle of Living* (New York: Island Press, 1941), 41–42. Katharine Lee Bates called Coman her "Joy of Life" in a poem of that title included in *Sigurd Our Golden Collie and Other Comrades of the Road* (New York: Dutton, 1919), 215; see also Bates's devotional poetry to Coman after Coman's death, in *Yellow Clover: A Book of Remembrance* (New York: Dutton, 1922). The gossip about Shackford is from Geraldine Gordon, TOI-CNH, May 20, 1971, 28, WCA.

18. Carroll Smith-Rosenberg, "The Female World of Love and Ritual: Relations between Women in Nineteenth-Century America," *Signs* 1 (Autumn 1975): 1–29; Nancy Sahli, "Smashing: Women's Relationships before the Fall," *Chrysalis,* no. 8 (Summer 1979): 17–27.

19. Blanche Wiesen Cook, "Female Support Networks and Political Activism: Lillian Wald, Chrystal Eastman, Emma Goldman," *Chrysalis,* no. 3 (1977): 48, 43–61; Cook, "Women Alone Stir My Imagination: Lesbianism and the Cultural Tradition," *Signs* 4 (Summer 1979): 718–40; cf. Lee Chambers-Schiller, "Miss Marks and Miss Woolley: A Review," *Frontiers* 4, no. 1 (1979): 73–75; Carroll Smith-Rosenberg, "The Female World of Love and Ritual"; Lillian Faderman, *Surpassing the Love of Men: Romantic Friendship and Love Between Women from the Renaissance to the Present* (New York: William Morrow, 1981). Terry Castle is a literary scholar who echoes Blanche Cook. See *The Apparitional Lesbian: Female Sexuality and Modern Culture* (New York: Columbia University Press, 1993), esp. "A Polemical Introduction: Or, the Ghost of Greta Garbo," 1–20.

20. Lillian Faderman, *Odd Girls and Twilight Lovers: A History of Lesbian Life in Twentieth-Century America* (New York: Columbia University Press, 1990), 4, 6, 112. Today, Faderman argues that for younger women "not even a sexual interest in other women is absolutely central to the evolving definition of lesbianism" (5).

21. See, e.g., Estelle B. Freedman, "Missing Links," *Women's Review of Books* (Oct. 1991): 15–17; George Chauncey, Jr., "From Sexual Inversion to Homosexuality: The Changing Medical Conceptualization of Female 'Deviance,'" in *Passion and Power: Sexuality in History,* ed. Kathy Peiss and Christina Simmons (Philadelphia: Temple University Press, 1989). For a provocative approach which suggests that all women-centered behavior can be charted on a lesbian continuum, see Adrienne Rich, "Compulsory Heterosexuality and Lesbian Existence," *Signs* 5, no. 4 (Summer 1980): 631–60. Ann Ferguson, Jacquelyn N. Zita, and Kathryn Pyne Addelson, "On 'Compulsory Heterosexuality and Lesbian Existence': Defining the

Issues," in *Signs* 7, no. 1 (Autumn 1981): 158–99; Sharon O'Brien, "'The Thing Not Named': Willa Cather as a Lesbian Writer," *Signs* 9, no. 4 (Summer 1984): 576–99; Leila Rupp, "'Imagine My Surprise': Women's Relationships in Mid-Twentieth Century America," in *Hidden from History: Reclaiming the Gay and Lesbian Past,* ed. Martin Duberman, Martha Vicinus, and George Chauncey, Jr. (New York: Meridian, 1990), 398, 408. In an oral interview I did with eighty-eight-year-old scientist Dorothy Weeks, who lived at Wellesley with physicist Louise Sherwood McDowell, Weeks emphatically denied that their forty-year relationship was lesbian. She called it a loving friendship characterized by kissing goodnight, sharing a home, and vacationing together (Weeks, class of 1916, interview with author, Feb. 1978). Nina Maglin would argue that such reluctance to self-identify as lesbian is due to reticence or the negative labeling of such relationships. I feel we have to respect Weeks's interpretation. Maglin, "Vida to Florence: Comrade and Companion," *Frontiers* 4, no. 3 (Fall 1979): 13–20.

22. Weeks, class of 1916, interview with author, Feb. 1978; Margarethe Müller called herself the "most intimate friend" of Carla Wenckebach (*Carla Wenckebach* [Boston: Ginn, 1908], 252).

23. We must be careful not to create a monolith in terms of sexual attitudes or behaviors. Emily Greene Balch, e.g., could not reciprocate the declared love of another woman, claiming that she remained "a virgin in my emotions" (Mercedes M. Randall, *Improper Bostonian: Emily Greene Balch* [New York: Twayne, 1964], 396). Martha Vicinus notes that "a lesbian identity did not result from economic independence or from an ideology of individualism or from the formation of women's communities, although all these elements were important for enhancing women's personal choices" (Vicinus, "'They Wonder to Which Sex I Belong': The Historical Roots of the Modern Lesbian Identity," *Feminist Studies* 18, no. 3 (Fall 1992): 472. On a modern lesbian community, see Elizabeth Lapovsky Kennedy and Madeline D. Davis, *Boots of Leather, Slippers of Gold: The History of a Lesbian Community* (New York: Routledge, 1993); also Esther D. Rothblum and Kathleen A. Brehony, eds., *Boston Marriages: Romantic but Asexual Relationships among Contemporary Lesbians* (Amherst: University of Massachusetts Press, 1993).

24. VDS, *On Journey,* 220.

25. VDS to JM, Jan. 29, 1898, July 30, 1899, Aug. 20, 1899, ALS, WCA; VDS to LMH, May 29, 1928, ALS, WCA; see also Nina Bauer Maglin, "Early Feminist Fiction: The Dilemma of Personal Life," *Prospects: An Annual of American Cultural Studies* 2 (1976): 167–91; Maglin, "Vida to Florence: Comrade and Companion," *Frontiers* 4, no. 3 (Fall 1979): 13–20; Judith Schwartz, "Yellow Clover: Katharine Lee Bates and Katharine Coman," *Frontiers* 4, no. 1 (Spring 1979): 59–67.

26. VDS to JM, Sept. 18, 1953, ALS, WCA. Scudder's will, dated Dec. 27, 1943, is in the WCA. Article 7 discusses the disposition of her home.

27. KLB, diary entry, Mar. 25, 1897; KLB to KC, Feb. 24, 1891, KLB Papers, WCA.

28. See KLB diary entry, Sept. 4, 1907: "First sleep in the Scarab." Then, Sept. 14, 1907: "Katharine arrived . . . with Sigurd, both as dear as life." Diary

(1897–1911), KLB Papers. KC to KLB (note scribbled on the back of a letter from Bates), 1915, Unprocessed KC Papers, WCA.

29. Bates explained the process of preparing the poems to Elizabeth Kendall: "I have read through, during these past three years, all her [Coman's] letters to me and mine to her in one quarter century of friendship—destroying as I read,—for I could not leave them for careless hands to destroy." KLB to EKK, July 16, 1921, EKK Papers, WCA.

30. Caroline Hazard praised Bates's *Yellow Clover* (CH to KLB, Apr. 25, 1922, ALS, WCA); VDS to KLB, Apr. 19, 1922, ALS, WCA. Jane Addams to KLB, May 9, 1922, ALS, WCA.

31. KLB to Abbie Farwell Brown, 1926, Brown Papers, SL; Bates's "Last Will and Testament," WCA.

32. CH, "At Eight and Twenty," CH Papers, WCA.

33. CH to KLB, Oct. 1905, KLB Papers, WCA.

34. CH to KLB, July 2, 1905, KLB Papers, WCA.

35. KLB to CH, Dec. 18, 1905, KLB Papers, WCA.

36. CH to KLB, Dec. 28, 1905, KLB Papers; CH to KLB, Jan. 14, 1906, KLB Papers, WCA.

37. KLB to CH, Mar. 22, 1910; Nov. 1, 1910, KLB Papers, WCA.

38. CH to KLB, May 21, 1911, KLB Papers, WCA.

39. KLB to CH, Jan. 30, 1915, KLB Papers, WCA.

40. KLB to CH, Aug. 24, 1926, Feb. 3, 1929, KLB Papers, WCA.

41. VDS to SFW, Apr. 8, 1948, ALS, WCA; KLB to CH, Feb. 3, 1928, KLB Papers, WCA.

9

Symmetrical Womanhood and the Claims of Community

Epigraph: VDS, "The Effect on Character of a College Education" (pt. 1), *The Christian Union* 35, no. 14 (Apr. 7, 1887): 12.

1. Ibid.; (pt. 2), *The Christian Union*, 35, no. 15 (Apr. 14, 1887): 12; VDS, "The Educated Woman as a Social Factor" (pt. 3), 35, no. 16 (Apr. 21, 1887): 12–13.

2. Lee Chambers-Schiller, *Liberty, A Better Husband: Single Women in America, the Generations of 1780–1840* (New Haven: Yale University Press, 1984).

3. See, e.g., David F. Allmendinger, "Mount Holyoke Students Encounter the Need for Life Planning, 1837–1850," *History of Education Quarterly* 19 (Spring 1979): 27–47; Thomas Woody discusses "Superfluous Women" in *A History of Women's Education in the United States*, 2 vols. (New York: Science Press, 1929), 2:1–5. Katharine Coman also comments on the employment prospects for superfluous women in "Transition in the Industrial Status of Women," *Wellesley Magazine* 1, no. 4 (Jan. 14, 1893): 175.

4. Susan B. Anthony, "Homes of Single Women," in *Elizabeth Cady Stanton–Susan B. Anthony: Correspondence, Writings, Speeches*, ed. Ellen Carol DuBois (New York: Schocken, 1981), 148. Kate Gannett Wells, "The Transitional American Woman," *Atlantic Monthly*, 46 (Dec. 1880): 819. Marjorie Housepian Dobkin, ed., *The Mak-*

ing of a Feminist: Early Journals and Letters of M. Carey Thomas (Kent, Ohio: Kent State University Press, 1979), 238–39.

5. Jane Addams, "The Subjective Necessity of College Settlements," in *The Social Thought of Jane Addams*, ed. Christopher Lasch (New York: Bobbs-Merrill, 1965), 38; EGB, "Citizenship in College," *Wellesley Magazine* 9, no. 5 (Feb. 21, 1901): 229–30.

6. Burton J. Bledstein, *The Culture of Professionalism: The Middle Class and the Development of Higher Education in America* (New York: Norton, 1976).

7. William Leach, *True Love and Perfect Union: The Feminist Reform of Sex and Society* (New York: Basic, 1980), discusses the health-related ideal of symmetry; Julia Ward Howe, ed., *Sex and Education: A Reply to Dr. E. H. Clarke's 'Sex in Education'* (Boston: Roberts Bros., 1874); Anna Julia Cooper, an African-American educator, employs the term as well; see Cooper, "The Higher Education of Women," in *Afro-American Women Writers, 1746–1933: An Anthology and Critical Guide,* ed. Ann Allen Shockley (New York: New American Library, 1988), 215.

8. Carroll Smith-Rosenberg and Charles Rosenberg, "The Female Animal: Medical and Biological Views of Woman and Her Role in Nineteenth-Century America," *Journal of American History* 60 (Sept. 1973): 332–56; Linda K. Kerber, *Women of the Republic: Intellect and Ideology in Revolutionary America* (Chapel Hill: University of North Carolina Press, 1980).

9. George E. Peterson, *The New England College in the Age of the University* (Amherst: Amherst College Press, 1964). SH, "Relation of College Experience to Present Social Demands," *JACA,* ser. 3, no. 18 (Dec. 1908): 56.

10. VDS, "The Relation of College Women to Social Need," *JACA,* ser. 2, no. 30 (Oct. 24, 1890): 2–3. For a discussion of the intellectual and social roots of settlement workers, see Mina Carson, *Settlement Folk: Social Thought and the American Settlement Movement, 1885–1930* (Chicago: University of Chicago Press, 1990). Mary Woolley, who left Wellesley in 1900 to become president of Mount Holyoke, shared this outlook. She believed there was boundless opportunity for college women in social work if women acquired a "more symmetrical training and development" (Mary Woolley, "Inaugural Address," *The Mount Holyoke,* inauguration number, 1901, 10–11).

11. VDS, "The Educated Woman as a Social Factor," 13; VDS, *On Journey* (New York: Dutton, 1937), 64; VDS, "The Privileges of a College Teacher," *WAM* 11, no. 6 (Aug. 1927): 329.

12. John Higham, "The Reorientation of American Culture in the 1890s," in *Writing American History: Essays on Modern Scholarship* (Bloomington: Indiana University Press, 1970), 90.

13. See Jean B. Quandt, *From the Small Town to the Great Community: The Social Thought of Progressive Intellectuals* (New Brunswick: Rutgers University Press, 1970). On cultural organicism, see Morton White, *Social Thought in America: The Revolt Against Formalism,* expanded ed. (Boston: Beacon, 1957).

14. On domesticity as a hallmark of the middle class in the nineteenth century, see Stuart M. Blumin, *The Emergence of the Middle Class: A Social Experience in the*

American City, 1760–1900 (New York: Cambridge University Press, 1989); Mary Ryan, *Cradle of the Middle Class: The Family in Oneida County, New York, 1790–1865* (New York: Cambridge University Press, 1981); Karen J. Blair, *The Clubwoman as Feminist: True Womanhood Redefined, 1868–1914* (New York: Holmes and Meier, 1980).

15. Assessments that treat women's higher education as reenforcing the ideology of domesticity include Sheila M. Rothman, *Woman's Proper Place: A History of Changing Ideals and Practices, 1870 to the Present* (New York: Basic, 1978); and Roberta Frankfort, *Collegiate Women: Domesticity and Career in Turn-of-the-Century America* (New York: New York University Press, 1977). A more revisionist approach is Joyce Antler, "Culture, Service, and Work: Changing Ideals of Higher Education for Women," in *The Undergraduate Woman,* ed. Pamela J. Perun (Lexington, Mass.: Heath, 1982), 22.

16. KLee (KLB), "The American Heroine," *Boston Evening Transcript,* July 21, 1879, in Scrapbook, 1876–85, KLB Papers, WCA.

17. VDS, "Womanhood in Modern Poetry," *Poet-Lore* 1, no. 10 (Oct. 15, 1889): 451, 450.

18. EPH, "The College Girl," *Boston Transcript,* June 23, 1900, in Florence Ellery Scrapbook, class of 1888, 148–49, WCA. A parallel argument by another philosophy professor at Randolf-Macon Woman's College is C. S. Parrish, "Women's Problems," *Independent* 53 (Oct. 31, 1901): 2582–85. She also issues a call for "symmetrical development" (2585).

19. VDS, "The Effect on Character of a College Education," pts. 1 and 2, p. 12.

20. Palmer reminded her audience that men had their profession, giving them a means to grow old with dignity. AFP, *Why Go to College?* (Boston: Crowell, 1897), 16–19.

21. VDS, "Clara French," *Courant,* Oct. 19, 1888, 1.

22. EPH, "The College Girl."

23. VDS, *On Journey,* 64; KLB, "Investing in an Education," *The Interior,* Aug. 12, 1897, in Scrapbook, 1894–99, 28–29, KLB Papers; KLB, "The Women's Colleges of our Country," *American Agriculturist,* Jan. 1892, in Scrapbook 1886–94, 52, KLB Papers, WCA.

24. VDS, "The Educated Woman As a Social Factor."

25. Ibid.

26. VDS, "Womanhood in Modern Poetry," 461. Much of Scudder's thinking foreshadows contemporary feminist "standpoint theory" that defines a feminist epistemology. See, e.g., Nancy M. Hartsock, "The Feminist Standpoint," in *Discovering Reality: Feminist Perspectives on Epistemology, Metaphysics, Methodology, and Philosophy of Science,* ed. Sandra Harding and Merrill Hintikka (Boston: Reidel, 1981); and Ann Garry and Marilyn Pearsall, eds., *Women, Knowledge, and Reality: Explorations in Feminist Philosophy* (Boston: Unwin Hyman, 1989); EGB, "Citizenship in College," 232.

27. EGB, "Citizenship in College," 232; VDS, "The Educated Woman as a Social Factor," 13. It is interesting to compare Scudder's discussion of ethics with contem-

porary feminist philosophers. See, e.g., Alison M. Jaggar, "Feminist Ethics: Projects, Problems, Prospects," in *Feminist Ethics*, ed. Claudia Card (Lawrence: University Press of Kansas, 1991), 78–104; see also Woolley, "Inaugural Address," 13–14, where she too argues that women's capacity for intuition and sensitivity would "not be despised, only held in check."

28. Historians Paula Baker and Lori Ginsberg both argue that by the 1880s and 1890s there was a transformation in women's culture and in political culture. Baker concludes that political culture was domesticized: liberal individualism was now coupled with a sense of social responsibility and a call for collective social action. Woman's culture was redefined as well. The woman's sphere of private domestic concerns was devalued. The public sphere, heretofore reserved for men, became an acceptable arena for women (Paula Baker, "The Domesticization of Politics: Women and American Political Society," *American Historical Review* 89, no. 3 [June 1984]: 620–48; Lori Ginsberg, *Women and the Work of Benevolence: Morality, Politics, and Class in the Nineteenth-Century United States* [New Haven: Yale University Press, 1990], 209 and chap. 6). Ginsberg provides an elegant class and gender analysis of women's work for benevolence in the antebellum era. I disagree, however, that after the 1860s the rhetoric of female benevolence and the ideology of separatism gave way to "the standard represented by men" (209). The Wellesley faculty believed that the rule of masculine efficiency could be reworked by women into a new public morality that hinged on feminine values to produce social activism. This interpretation of the post–Civil War generation is shared by Sarah Stage in "The Perils of Post-Feminism: Gender, Class and Female Benevolence," *Reviews in American History* 19, no. 4 (Dec. 1991): 511–16; Victoria Bissell Brown, reviews of *Women and the Work of Benevolence* and *Endless Crusade, The Historian* 54, no. 1 (Autumn 1991): 157. See also Kathleen D. McCarthy, *Women's Culture: American Philanthropy and Art, 1830–1930* (Chicago: University of Chicago Press, 1991); Anne Firor Scott connects the women's colleges, the social sciences, and reform in "Women's Voluntary Associations: From Charity to Reform," in *Lady Bountiful Revisited: Women, Philanthropy, and Power*, ed. Kathleen D. McCarthy (New Brunswick: Rutgers University Press, 1990), 35–54.

29. VDS, "The Educated Woman as a Social Factor"; see also EGB, "What's Hecuba to Me or I to Hecuba?" *Wellesley Magazine* 15, no. 4 (Jan. 1, 1907): 143–53. Kathryn Kish Sklar argues that this "moral vision" is central to middle-class women's political culture and the creation of the American welfare state (Sklar, "The Historical Foundations of Women's Power in the Creation of the American Welfare State, 1830–1930," in *Mothers of a New World: Maternalist Politics and the Origins of Welfare States*, ed. Seth Kovan and Sonya Michel [New York: Routledge, 1993], 68, 79–80 n. 4).

30. Margaret Stratton, "The Aims and Best Conditions of College Life," *Wellesley Prelude*, no. 26 (Apr. 19, 1890): 364 (the *Wellesley Prelude*, a weekly published between 1889 and 1892, succeeded the *Courant*, adding editorials and other

expressions of student opinion to the format). SH, "Relation of College Experience to Present Social Demands," 55.

31. KLB, "The College Girl of the Period," *Boston Transcript,* June 14, 1902, in Scrapbook, 1900–09, 26–27, KLB Papers.

32. VDS, "The Effect on Character of a College Education," pt. 2; SH, "Relation of College Experience to Present Social Demands," 56.

33. KLB, "College Girls," *Wellesley Magazine* 4, no. 4 (Jan. 18, 1896): 185; KLB, introd. to *Wellesley: The College Beautiful,* ed. Mary Bingham Hill and Helen G. Eager (Boston: n.p., 1894), 13 ("It is, in a word, the spirit of service . . . by which all Wellesley achievement is quietly meted"). MPS, "Undergraduate Life at Vassar," *Scribner's* (June 1898): 643–60; EPH, "The College Girl."

34. SH, "Relation of College Experience to Present Social Demands," 55.

35. EGB, "Citizenship in College," 227.

36. Ibid., 228–29.

37. CH, commencement address, in *From College Gates* (Boston: Houghton Mifflin, 1925), 246; CH, "College Women and the Church," in *From College Gates,* 76.

38. VDS, "The Effect on Character of a College Education," pt. 2; SH, "Relation of College Experience to Present Social Demands," 58.

39. Nancy F. Cott, *The Bonds of Womanhood: "Woman's Sphere" in New England, 1780–1835* (New Haven: Yale University Press, 1977).

40. For a comprehensive history that demonstrates how educated women utilized associations to contribute to progressive reform, see Anne Firor Scott, *Natural Allies: Women's Associations in American History* (Urbana: University of Illinois Press, 1991).

41. KC, "The Wellesley Alumnae as Social Servants," *Wellesley Magazine* 13, no. 2 (Nov. 1904): 41–48; this effort was not limited to social science faculty; see also the views of Roxanna Vivian, professor of mathematics, in "Educational Currents," *Wellesley Magazine* 18, no. 9 (June 1910): 399.

42. KLB, "Woman as Scholar," *Chatauquan,* Apr. 1891, in Scrapbook, 1886–94, 42–43, KLB Papers, WCA.

43. EGB, "Citizenship in College," 231. VDS connected "the impulse of gratitude toward the community" to the creation of the college settlement movement (VDS, "The College Settlements Movement," *Smith College Monthly,* May 1900, 447). See also Ellen Hayes, *Letters to a College Girl* (Boston: George H. Ellis, 1909), 65–66.

44. Standard accounts stress that the women's colleges were silent on suffrage because, as educational experiments, they were already on the defensive and could not afford to support the cause. See, e.g., Mabel Newcomer, *A Century of Higher Education for American Women* (New York: Harper and Row, 1959), 18, 225; Barbara Miller Solomon, *In the Company of Educated Women: A History of Women and Higher Education in America* (New Haven: Yale University Press, 1985), 111–14. The entire subject of suffrage at the women's colleges deserves reexamination.

45. VDS, "The Educated Woman as Social Factor," 12; EGB, "Citizenship in College," 229.

46. E.g., Ellen A. Hayes, "Women and Political Duties," *Courant*, Nov. 30, 1888, WCA. Address presented by Professor Mary W. Calkins at the College Evening of the thirty-eighth annual convention of the National American Woman's Suffrage Association, Baltimore, Feb. 8, 1906, rpt. *The Woman's Journal*, Mar. 10, 1906, MWC FBF, WCA; "Equal Suffrage League," *WCN*, Jan. 26, 1910, 15–18; "Books on Suffrage," *WCN*, Apr. 6, 1910, 5, WCA; List of Officers, Women's Suffrage League, *Legenda*, 1909, 88, WCA; KC, "The Department of Economics," *WCN*, Mar. 1, 1911, 4; Mary Woolley, "The Civic Responsibility of the College Woman," *JACA* 7, no. 1 (Jan. 1914): 15–16; see also M. Carey Thomas, as quoted in Rothman, *Woman's Proper Place*, 131.

47. KLB, "Editor of the Lewiston Journal" (letter dated Aug. 9, 1917), KLB Papers, WCA. See also the poem "To an Anti-Suffragist," which spoofs the opponents of the vote for women (Aug. 7, 1915, KLB Scrapbook, Oct. 1909–16, vol. 5, KLB Papers, WCA).

48. Theodore Roosevelt, "Social Evolution," in *American Ideals and Other Essays Social and Political* (New York: Putnam's, 1897), 327–28.

49. William De Witt Hyde, *The College Man and the College Woman* (Boston: Houghton Mifflin, 1904), 203, 209–10.

50. G. Stanley Hall, *Adolescence: Its Psychology and Its Relation to Physiology, Anthropology, Sociology, Sex, Crime, Religion, and Education*, 2 vols. (New York: Appleton, 1904), 2:646, 619; interestingly Hall agreed with Vida Scudder: "The old cloistral seclusion and exclusion is forever gone and new ideals are arising" (612). He argued, however, for a curriculum that favored sexual differences and strengthened the domestic ideals of motherhood (617). Potential changes in the ideal of womanhood threatened the ideals of manhood. See E. Anthony Rotundo, *American Manhood: Transformations in Masculinity from the Revolution to the Modern Era* (New York: Basic, 1993), esp. chaps. 9 and 10.

51. See Peterson, *The New England College in the Age of the University*, 31–32; William Leach provides an important discussion of "organic symmetry" in *True Love and Perfect Union*, 323–46.

52. Peterson, *The New England College in the Age of the University*, 38–39; Stow Persons, *The Decline of American Gentility* (New York: Columbia University Press, 1973). See Burton J. Bledstein, *The Culture of Professionalism*, esp. "The Man of Character," 146–58. My approach in this chapter has been much influenced by Bledstein's pathbreaking psychosocial interpretation of the creation of character as fundamental to the development of a middle-class mentality, as well as his linking higher education to the culture of professionalism.

53. VDS, "The Effect on Character of a College Education," pt. 1; KLB, "The Women's Colleges of Our Country," 52, KLB Scrapbook, 1886–94, KLB Papers, WCA.

10

Adventures in Pedagogy

Epigraph: Florence Converse, *Wellesley College: A Chronicle of the Years 1875–1938* (Wellesley: Hathaway House, 1939), 87.

1. The title of this chapter is taken from Vida Scudder's autobiography *On Journey* (New York: Dutton, 1937), 119–32; Barbara M. Cross, ed., *The Educated Woman in America: Selected Writings of Catharine Beecher, Margaret Fuller, and M. Carey Thomas* (New York: Teachers College Press, 1965), 149; Frederick Rudolf, in *The American College and University: A History* (New York: Random House, 1962), concludes that "Vassar, Smith and Wellesley in quick succession [used] the classical curriculum that was on the brink of collapse in the old men's colleges" (169). John Brubacher and Willis Rudy, in *Higher Education in Transition: A History of American Colleges and Universities, 1636–1968* (New York: Harper and Row, 1968), 7, argue that the women's colleges "slavishly" followed the men's college curriculum; the same interpretation is found in George Schmidt, *The Liberal Arts College: A Chapter in American Cultural History* (New Brunswick: Rutgers University Press, 1957), 141. Even Mabel Newcomer, while giving credit to the innovative science curriculum produced by the women's colleges, dismisses the rest as "a safe imitation of those of the men's colleges" (Newcomer, *A Century of Higher Education for American Women* [Washington, D.C.: Zenger, 1959], 87).

2. The disparagement of the women's college curriculum is part of a larger devaluation of women's contributions to the life of the mind in the United States. For the significance of curriculum reform to the contemporary feminist transformation of the academy, see, e.g., Elizabeth Kamarck Minnich, *Transforming Knowledge* (Philadelphia: Temple University Press, 1990); concerning the preconditions for a radical pedagogy, see Jennifer M. Gore, *The Struggle for Pedagogies: Critical and Feminist Discourses as Regimes of Truth* (New York: Routlege, 1993), 34–35, 6–7; Henry A. Giroux, *Teachers as Intellectuals: Toward a Critical Pedagogy of Learning* (Granby, Mass.: Bergin and Garvey, 1988).

3. Bliss Perry discusses the Harvard English department during the same period in *And Gladly Teach: Reminiscences* (Boston: Houghton Mifflin, 1935); KLB, "The Department of English Literature," *WCN*, Jan. 25, 1911, 4; VDS, "Katharine Lee Bates, Professor of English Literature," in *In Memoriam, Katharine Lee Bates*, suppl. to *WAM* 13, no. 5 (June 1929): 6.

4. KLB to KC, Feb. 28, 1891, KLB Papers, WCA; Eva Phillips Body, "Katharine Lee Bates, Poet-Teacher," *English Journal* (college ed.) 20, no. 6 (June 1931): 461.

5. Gamaliel Bradford, "English Drama Seminar, 1924–1925," as quoted in Body, "Katharine Lee Bates," 461–62. MHS, "The Centenary of Katharine Lee Bates," KLB Papers, WCA.

6. Florence Converse, "Bates, Katharine Lee," *DAB*, suppl. 1 (1944); Richard Cabot, as quoted in Dorothy Burgess, *Dream and Deed: The Story of Katharine Lee Bates* (Norman: University of Oklahoma Press, 1952), 48–49.

7. KLB, "The Remonstrance," in *America the Beautiful and Other Poems* (New York: Thomas Y. Crowell, 1911), 90–92; Laura Loomis, as quoted in VDS, "Katharine Lee Bates, Professor of English," 6–7. Bliss Perry characterized the isolation felt by members of the English department at Harvard during this era: "Here was a brilliant array of prima-donnas, each supreme in a chosen role. . . . But it was difficult for a stranger to discover any common denominator of their activities. . . . I

remember that a colleague in English said to me gloomily: 'We *have* no real Department, and never have had'" (Perry, *And Gladly Teach,* 243).

8. VDS, *On Journey,* 127–28, 189; VDS, *Social Ideals in English Letters* (Boston: Houghton Mifflin, 1898; rpt. 1923); KLB to Miss Brown, Apr. 23, 1912, KLB Papers, WCA.

9. MG, *What's Past Is Prologue* (New York: Harper and Row, 1940), 12; Maynard Force, as quoted in JM, *The Life and Letters of Mary Emma Woolley* (Washington, D.C.: Public Affairs Press, 1955), 48; VDS, *On Journey,* 122.

10. VDS, *On Journey,* 121–22; VDS, "A Pedagogic Sunset," in *The Privilege of Age: Essays Secular and Spiritual* (New York: Dutton, 1939), 90.

11. Scudder talks about liaison courses in *On Journey,* 130; Maynard Force, as quoted in JM, *Life and Letters of Mary Emma Woolley,* 48; MG, *What's Past Is Prologue,* 13; Harriet Sampson, "Vida Dutton Scudder," *WAM* 11, no. 6 (Aug. 1927): 337; Ruth Hurwitz, "Coming of Age at Wellesley," *Menorah Journal* 38 (Fall 1950): 230.

12. Jessie Bernard, *Academic Women* (New York: Meridian, 1974), 5; Hurwitz, "Coming of Age at Wellesley," 230; VDS, *On Journey,* 130.

13. JM, *Life and Letters of Mary Emma Woolley,* 47–48; Burgess, *Dream and Deed,* 99.

14. MPS FBF, WCA. Some of Sherwood's novels are: Elizabeth Hastings [Margaret Sherwood], *An Experiment in Altruism* (New York: Macmillan, 1895); MPS, *The Princess Pourquoi* (Boston: Houghton Mifflin, 1907); MPS, *The Worn Doorstep* (Boston: Little, Brown, 1916). See also Dorothy Cochlin McCann, "Margaret Pollock Sherwood, 1864–1955," *WAM* 40, no. 2 (Jan. 1956): 99; Sally Loomis, alumna, class of 1928, interview with author, June 28, 1980.

15. MHS, Wellesley College Alumnae Association Questionnaire, Oct. 1, 1941, Alumnae Biographical File, WCA; Katharine Balderston, TOI-CNH, 17, WCA.

16. Thomas Proctor, "Laura Emma Lockwood—In Memoriam," *WAM* 41, no. 3 (Mar. 1957): 157; Jeannette Bailey Cheek, class of 1928, interview with author, June 20, 1980.

17. "Memorial Meeting for Sophie Chantal Hart," Jan. 23, 1949, 6, TS, SH FBF, WCA; Geraldine Gordon, TOI-CNH, 24, WCA; of Frances Melville Perry, the other teacher of composition, we know very little. One student reminisced that Perry "pushed [one] to the limits of capabilities, by never accepting anything but the best" (personal communication with a former student of Frances Melville Perry [who asked to remain anonymous], University of Arizona, Sept. 24, 1979).

18. See M. Elizabeth Tidball and Vera Kistiakowsky, "Baccalaureate Origins of American Scientists and Scholars," *Science* 193 (1976): 646–52. Wellesley granted the M.A. in English through its graduate department. See KLB, "Graduate Work: English Literature Department," *WCN,* Dec. 5, 1912, 5–6.

19. Barbara P. McCarthy, "Greek and Latin at Wellesley," *WAM* 33, no. 1 (Oct. 1948): 12–16.

20. Ibid., 14; Jean Glasscock, postscript to *Wellesley College, 1875–1975: A Century of Women* (Wellesley: Wellesley College, 1975), 474. I obtained information on Chapin's courses from the *Wellesley College Calendar, 1879–1919.* Florence Shirley Marden, "Katharine May Edwards," *WAM* 11, no. 6 (Aug. 1927): 338–39.

"In Memoriam, Angie Sybil Montague," *WCN,* Mar. 14, 1914, 7; C[aroline] R[ebecca] F[letcher], "Alice Walton," *WAM* 17, no. 5 (June 1933): 434.

21. Katharine Edwards's hostility toward the Latin department is discussed in Glasscock, *Wellesley College,* 474; Alice Walton, "Adeline Belle Hawes: Professor of Latin Literature—Emeritus," *WAM* 10, no. 1 (Oct. 1925): 15; A. Berthe Miller, "Caroline Rebecca Fletcher, Professor of Latin," *WAM* 20, no. 6 (Aug. 1936): 436. Dorothy M. Robathan, "Caroline R. Fletcher: Professor Emeritus of Latin," *WAM* 37, no. 4 (May 1953): 239.

22. Henrietta Littlefield, "Margarethe Müller," *WAM* 18, no. 3 (Feb. 1934): 249–50. Wipplinger was described as "remarkable" by Sally Loomis. Loomis recalled that: "Even though I was not fluent in German, Wipplinger didn't put me down; rather she put me up in a way. She took my remarks and made more of them" (interview with author, June 28, 1980).

23. Margarethe Müller, *Carla Wenckebach: Pioneer* (Boston: Ginn, 1908); Mary Haskell, "Professor Wenckebach's Relation to her Students," *Wellesley Magazine* 11, no. 4 (Feb. 1903): 160.

24. Robert E. Keohane, "Barnes, Mary Downing Sheldon," *NAW.*

25. Allen F. Davis, "Coman, Katharine," *NAW;* Elizabeth Wallace, class of 1884, describes Coman in *The Unending Journey* (Minneapolis: University of Minnesota Press, 1952), 58; Scudder talks about Coman in *On Journey,* 110.

26. See Louise Fargo Brown, *Apostle of Democracy: The Life of Lucy Maynard Salmon* (New York: Harper and Bros., 1943), 99. Sarah H. H. Walden, "Julia Swift Orvis," *WAM* 25, no. 5 (June 1941): 413–14. Because she felt the college bookstore was lacking, Orvis organized the Hathaway House Cooperative Bookstore. She also ran a small faculty club on Curve Street (Geraldine Gordon and Agnes F. Perkins, "Julia Swift Orvis Died March 16," *The Townsman* (Wellesley, Mass.), Mar. 24, 1949, clipping in Orvis FBF, WCA).

27. Anna J. McKeag, "Edna Virginia Moffet," *WAM* 22, no. 4 (Apr. 1938): 296–98.

28. Mary Beltzhoover Jenkins, "Elizabeth Kimball Kendall: 1885–1952," *WAM* 37, no. 1 (Nov. 1952): 24–25. Information on the books Kendall wrote with others can be found in Allen F. Davis, "Coman, Katharine," *NAW;* see also EKK, Radcliffe College Admissions Form, Nov. 7, 1898; EKK, Radcliffe Alumnae Information Questionnaire, May 21, 1928, 1934, and 1940 Alumnae Information Survey, Alumnae Biographical File, RCA; information on Kendall's course of study at law school was provided by the Registrar, Boston University, School of Law.

29. Jenkins, "Elizabeth Kendall," 24; EKK, *A Wayfarer in China* (Boston: Houghton Mifflin, 1913).

30. Molly Dewson to "My Dear Teacher" (EKK), July 29, 1951, EKK Papers, WCA. An inscription by Dewson in a two-volume typed transcript of her book *An Aid to the End,* which described Dewson's political role in helping Franklin D. Roosevelt, reads: "Given to Wellesley College in memory of my most stimulating teacher (EKK, June 13, 1952, WCA; original in FDR Library, Hyde Park, N.Y.). Susan Ware, *Partner and I: Molly Dewson, Feminism, and New Deal Politics* (New Haven: Yale University Press, 1987), 21. Ware states that Dewson left five thou-

sand dollars to Wellesley—her largest bequest—for a lecture series in Kendall's name (268 n. 17). It is currently administered by the Department of Political Science.

31. On economics at Harvard during this period, see Robert L. Church, "The Economists Study Society: Sociology at Harvard, 1891–1902," in *Social Sciences at Harvard, 1860–1920: From Inculcation to the Open Mind*, ed. Paul Buck (Cambridge: Harvard University Press, 1965), 18–91.

32. The description for Coman's course on political economy is listed in the *Wellesley College Calendar*, 1883, 1887; see the course entitled Statistical Study of Certain Economic Problems, *Wellesley College Calendar*, 1895–96, 1896–97. Joan M. McCrea, "Katharine Coman: A Neglected Economist," paper presented at the History of Economics Society, University of Illinois, Champaign-Urbana, May 25, 1979, in author's possession and in KC FBF, WCA.

33. Besides helping to found Denison House Settlement in Boston, she was active in the Consumer League of Massachusetts and the Women's Trade Union League. Consumer League of Massachusetts, Appeal Letters (1906–30) in B24/27, SL. The Massachusetts League predated the national organization and was vital to its workings. Mary Heaton Vorce remembered that: "The liberal spirit of Massachusetts played a major role in building the National Consumer's League." Vorce, "The Watchdog," 38. MS in National Consumer's League File, B2, SL. Denison House records are also in SL. For Coman's influence on Laughlin and Dewson and for a summary of their careers, see Ruth Sargent, "Laughlin, Gail," *NAW:MP*; Paul C. Taylor, "Dewson, Mary Williams," *NAW:MP*; and Ware, *Partner and I*, 20–31.

34. Harriet Rice to KC, June 1913, Unprocessed KC Papers, WCA.

35. Kate Edelman to Mercedes Randall, May 28, 1957, Mercedes Randall Papers, SCPC; Mercedes Randall, *Improper Bostonian: Emily Greene Balch* (New York: Twayne, 1964), 107–23.

36. Both the course on immigration and social economics are described in the *Wellesley College Calendar*, 1907–08; see also EGB, *An Outline of Economics* (Cambridge, Mass.: Cooperative Press, 1899). See also Barbara Miller Solomon, "Balch, Emily Greene," *NAW:MP*.

37. The syllabus for Consumption Economics is located in EGB Papers, SCPC.

38. Randall, *Improper Bostonian*, 110, 111.

39. Mary A. Wyman to Mercedes Randall, May 1, 1953, Randall Papers, SCPC; Kate Edelman to Mercedes Randall, May 28, 1957, Randall Papers, SCPC.

40. Kate Edelman to Mercedes Randall, May 28, 1957, Randall Papers, SCPC.

41. James McLachlan, "American Colleges and the Transmission of Culture: The Case of the Mugwumps," in *The Hofstadter Aegis: A Memorial*, ed. Stanley Elkins and Eric McKitrick (New York: Knopf, 1974), 184–207.

42. Anna Mathieson, "Mary Sophia Case: 1854–1953," *WAM* 37, no. 5 (July 1953): 308–09; Case's courses are listed in the *Wellesley College Calendar*, 1890–91, 1900–01.

43. Laurel Furumoto, "Mary Whiton Calkins (1863–1930): Fourteenth President of

the American Psychological Association," *Journal of the History of the Behaviorial Sciences* 15 (1979): 346–56; Furumoto, "Mary Whiton Calkins (1863–1930)," *Psychology of Women Quarterly* 5, no. 1 (Fall 1980): 55–68; Furumoto, "The College Laboratory: Promoting the Scholarly and Scientific Ideal," paper presented at the annual meeting of Cheiron (The International Society for the History of Behavioral and Social Sciences), Ottawa, June 1975, 3–9, in author's possession. Gertrude C. Bussey, "Calkins, Mary Whiton," *DAB,* suppl. 1 (1944).

44. MWC, *The Persistent Problems of Philosophy* (New York: Macmillan, 1907).

45. Furumoto, "Mary Whiton Calkins: Fourteenth President of the American Psychological Association"; Helen Cook Vincent, "Miss Calkins as a Teacher," *WAM* 14, no. 5 (June 1930): 312; MWC, "The Relation of College Teaching to Research," *JACA,* 4th ser., no. 2 (Mar. 1911): 79.

46. Vincent, "Miss Calkins as a Teacher," 312; Lucy Wilson, TOI-CNH, 51, WCA.

47. In fact, Puffer and Calkins were graduate students together. Puffer, however, elected in 1902 to take a Radcliffe Ph.D., while Calkins held out unsuccessfully for one at Harvard. E.N.H., "Ethel Puffer Howes, 1891: In Memoriam," *Smith Alumnae Quarterly,* 42, 2 (Feb. 1951): 93; "Howes, Ethel Puffer," *Principal Women of America,* 1 (1932); Ethel D. Puffer, *The Psychology of Beauty* (Boston: Houghton Mifflin, 1905). Puffer's doctoral thesis, entitled "Studies in Symmetry," was later published as part of the Harvard Psychological Studies.

48. I have traced the development of the education department from the *Wellesley College Calendar,* 1875–1900. See also Anna J. McKeag, "The Department of Education," *WCN,* Feb. 8, 1911, 5–6.

49. E[leanor] G[amble], "Anna J. McKeag," *WAM* 16, no. 5 (June 1932): 407–08. Clark University was nationally recognized as an educational center for child study. William Henry Burnham was a leader in the field of child development. See Bernard G. DeWulf, "William Henry Burnham," *DAB,* suppl. 3 (1941–45).

50. Margaret W. Rossiter, *Women Scientists in America: Struggles and Strategies to 1940* (Baltimore: Johns Hopkins University Press, 1982), 26.

51. Margaret W. Rossiter, *Women Scientists in America*; James M. Cattell, ed., *American Men of Science* (New York: Science Press, 1906, 1910, 1920, 1927, 1933).

52. C. Stuart Gager, "Wellesley College and the Development of Botanical Education in America," *Science* 67 (Feb. 17, 1928): 171–78; *Wellesley College Calendar,* 1877–78. Susan Hallowell is discussed in Joan Burstyn, "Early Women in Education: The Role of the Anderson School of Natural History," *Boston Journal of Education* 159, no. 3 (Aug. 1977): 60–64. Elizabeth Wallace, who later became an English professor at the University of Chicago, recalled that her "first experience of the joy of original research came in Hallowell's botanical library" (Wallace, *The Unending Journey,* 58).

53. Special students were those admitted to study but who were not degree candidates. Teachers sometimes studied as special students. A certificate was granted to those completing certain requirements. See, "Admission of Special Students," *Wellesley College Calendar,* 1890–91, 20–21, WCA; Ann M. Hirsch and Lisa J. Merroni, "Ferguson, Margaret Clay," *NAW:MP.*

54. Cummings later attended the University of Zurich but received no graduate degree. Bruce Fink, "A Memoir of Clara Eaton Cummings," *Bryologist* 10, no. 3 (May 1907): 37–41; Cummings entry, in Cattell, ed., *American Men of Science*.

55. MAW to Marian Hubbard, Dec. 2, 1927, MAW FBF, WCA. Willcox's connections in the scientific community read like a roll call of *Who's Who*. Trained in a teacher's course given by Alpheus Hyatt, a student of Louis Agassiz, Willcox also spent two summers at Alexander Agassiz's Newport, Rhode Island, laboratory. She attended Newnham College, in Cambridge, England, where she studied under the physiologist Sir Michael Foster. She also worked with the embryologist Sir Francis Balfour and the anatomist Joseph Lister. She studied for her Ph.D. at Zurich with Dr. Arnold Lang. See David R. Lindberg, "Mary Alice Willcox, 1856–1953," *Tenth Annual Report of the Western Society of Malacologists* (Dec. 14, 1977): 16–17.

56. On course listings in zoology, see *Wellesley College Calendar*, 1895–96; MAW, "Willcox Family Life," 58, folder 16, box 1, 14/10/504, Walter F. Willcox Papers, CUL.

57. Alice V. Waite, "Caroline Burling Thompson," *WAM* 16, no. 2 (Feb. 1922): 102; Mary E. Collett, "An Impression of Caroline Burling Thompson," *WAM* 6, no. 2 (Feb. 1922): 103; T[homas] E. S[nyder], "Caroline Burling Thompson," *Science* 55, no. 1411 (Jan. 13, 1922): 40–41.

58. *Wellesley College Calendar*, 1876–77, 1877–78. By 1879–80 there were seven systems of courses offered. The largest were the General College Course for Honors in Mathematics; The Course for Honors in Modern Languages; The Scientific Course; The Five Years' Musical Course; The Five Years' Art Course. See *Wellesley College Calendar*, 1878–79, 14. The Scientific Course was intended for those who wished to pursue in depth the "natural, physical and mathematical sciences and the modern languages." Candidates studied French and German in lieu of Greek. See "The Scientific Course," *Wellesley College Calendar*, 1881–82, 18.

59. Ellen L. Burrell, "Charlotte Fitch Roberts," *WAM* 2, no. 2 (Jan. 1918): 80–81.

60. Helen S. French, "Charlotte Almira Bragg," *WAM* 13, no. 5 (June 1929): 287–88; *Wellesley College Calendar*, 1889–90.

61. Charlotte Almira Bragg to EFP, departmental report, June 19, 1913, Reports to the President (1912–13, 1926–44), chemistry dept., WCA; M. K. Seikel to Miss Whiting, Nov. 25, 1955, chemistry dept., WCA; Carole B. Shmurak and Bonnie S. Handler, "'Castle of Science': Mount Holyoke and the Preparation of Women in Chemistry, 1837–1941," *History of Education Quarterly* 32, no. 3 (Fall 1992): 315–42.

62. For information on domestic science, see the *Wellesley College Calendar*, 1892–97; Ellen Fitzpatrick, "For the 'Women of the University': Marion Talbot, 1858–1948," in Geraldine Jonçich Clifford, *Lone Voyagers: Academic Women in Coeducational Institutions, 1870–1937* (New York: Feminist Press, 1989), 85–124; see also Lynn D. Gordon, "Co-Education on Two Campuses: Berkeley and Chicago, 1890–1912," in *Woman's Being, Woman's Place: Female Identity and Vocation in American History*, ed. Mary Kelley (Boston: Hall, 1979), 171–95.

63. Gladys A. Anslow, "Whiting, Sarah Frances," *NAW*. Whiting went to the Institute of Technology and took a course in woodwork, including the use of the lathe. She then convinced Eben Horsford to donate money for a lathe at Wellesley, where she offered a course in woodwork and the construction of instruments. With a mixture of pride and humor Whiting presented Horsford with a box made of black walnut in appreciation of his sponsorship, complete with a list of the twenty tools she had used in making it. In the bottom was a satin sachet with his initials embroidered on it, as proof that she could still use the "woman's tool." SFW, "History of the Physics Department of Wellesley College from 1878–1912" (1926), physics dept., WCA.

64. Grace Davis, who earned a B.A. and M.A. at Wellesley, helped Whiting teach these classes. Davis's specialty in physics was meteorology; along with Whiting she was one of the first scientists in the country to make X-rays. Lucy Wilson, "Grace Evageline Davis, Professor of Physics," *WAM* 20, no. 6 (Aug. 1936): 435–36.

65. Anslow, "Whiting, Sarah Frances"; Ellen Hayes, "Our Observatory," *Wellesley Magazine* 9, no. 2 (Nov. 1900): 82–87. Dorris Hoffleit, "Cannon, Annie Jump," *NAW*; Bessie Z. Jones and Lyle G. Boyd, *Harvard College Observatory: The First Four Directorships, 1839–1919* (Cambridge: Harvard University Press, 1971), 405.

66. Mary Louise Brown, class of 1893, did graduate study at Cornell and was a science teacher at Dana Hall School from 1904 to 1927 (Louise Brown, *Ellen Hayes: Trail-Blazer* [n.p., 1932], 25). In one of her letters home, Mary Gilson noted that "Miss Hayes who wrote the Trig, is too expectant of us." Nonetheless, she added that her friend, Georgia Rolph, who previously hated math had Hayes and "has fallen in love with it now. She says she has to work hard in it but Miss Hayes makes it so interesting." MG to "My dear mother," May 24, 1896, class of 1899, MG Papers, WCA.

67. Ellen Burrell to HM, Aug. 7, 1917, math dept., WCA. Ellen Burrell gathered her lecture notes in geometry and had them privately printed (Burrell, "The Number System" and "Synthetic Projection Geometry," privately printed class notes, Ellen Burrell Papers, WCA). Ellen Hayes had her lecture notes printed and produced four books: Hayes, *Algebra for High Schools and Colleges* (Boston: Cushing, 1897); *Calculus with Applications: An Introduction to the Mathematical Treatment of Science* (Boston: Allyn and Bacion, 1900); *Elementary Trigonometry* (Boston: Cushing, 1896); *Lessons on Higher Algebra* (Boston: Cushing, 1894). Helen Merrill also published; see HM, *Mathematical Excursions: Side Trips along Paths Not Generally Traveled in Elementary Courses in Mathematics* (Norwood, Mass.: Norwood Press, 1933; New York: Dover, 1957); Helen A. Merrill and Clara E. Smith, *Selected Topics in College Algebra* (Norwood, Mass.: Norwood Press, 1914). Roxanna Vivian, another Wellesley alumna, class of 1894, taught mathematics from 1901 to 1927, when she "tendered a forced resignation." She states that at fifty-six years of age and with no pension, the college terminated her. See untitled TS in Vivian Alumnae Biographical File, WCA. The Executive Committee Minutes reveal that "there had been criticism of Miss Vivian's work" and that if reduction of staff was

required she "would not be reappointed after June 1928." In light of this decision, Vivian resigned "at once" (ECM/BT, Oct. 3, 1927, WCA).

68. Rosalind Rosenberg criticizes the women's colleges for falling victim to stereotypes about women's biological inferiority and secondary social status; see Rosenberg, "The Academic Prism: The New View of American Women," in *Women of America*, ed. Carol R. Berkin and Mary Beth Norton (Boston: Houghton Mifflin, 1979), 318–41. Florence Howe, on the other hand, criticizes the women's colleges curriculum for equating women with men (Howe, "Women's Education: Its History and Future," *Radical Teacher* 15 [1980]: 27–31).

69. M. Carey Thomas, "Old Fashioned Disciplines," *JACA* 10, no. 9 (May 1917): 589. Thomas warned that women's colleges were "threatened by a terrible foe at the gates—a wolf in sheep's clothing" (590). They needed to resist calls to provide practical courses in domestic science or stenography, for example.

70. MWC, *Smith Alumnae Quarterly* (Feb. 1915): 79. Joseph Jastrow, "A Study of Mental Statistics," *New Review* 5 (1981): 559–68; MWC, "Community of Ideas of Men and Women," *Psychological Review* 3 (Jan. 1896): 430.

71. Ellen Hayes, "Women and Scientific Research," *Science* 32 (Dec. 16, 1910): 864–66; see also Ellen Hayes, *Letters to a College Girl* (Boston: George H. Ellis, 1909), 20. M. Carey Thomas similarly argues that women of genius are "crushed by their unfavorable environment" (Thomas, "Present Tendencies in Women's College and University Education," rpt. in *The Educated Woman in America,* ed. Cross, 169).

72. VDS, "The Privileges of a College Teacher," *WAM* 11, no. 6 (Aug. 1927): 329.

73. Hurwitz, "Coming of Age at Wellesley," 221.

11

Daughters of My Spirit

Epigraphs: VDS to "My own darling Mary" (MG), Aug. 23, 19??, class of 1899, MG Papers, WCA; and Tree Day Oration, class of 1888, Wellesley College, WCA.

1. KLB, "Tribute to Miss Kendall and Miss Chandler" (informal farewell), May 23, 1920, 4, EKK FBF, WCA. EM to her parents, Oct. 2, 1898, EM Papers, WCA.

2. *Annals,* 1883–84, 4, WCA.

3. Annie D. Rhea, "Woman," *Annals,* 1883–84, 9, WCA.

4. Tree Day Oration, class of 1888, Wellesley College, 20–21, WCA.

5. There is extensive information on the class of 1888 in the WCA; on Breckinridge, see Ellen Fitzpatrick, *Endless Crusade: Women, Social Scientists, and Reform* (New York: Oxford, 1990). Class of 1888, thirtieth reunion booklet, 1918, WCA.

6. Sarah Woodman Paul, "College Societies," *Courant,* Jan. 25, 1889, 2, WCA; Edith Metcalf, "Phi Sigma, 'Though Dead, Yet Speaketh,'" *Courant,* Feb. 1, 1889, 2.

7. Constitution, Microscopical Society Records, WCA; S. F. Clarke, "Duties of Microscopical Society" (handwritten note), Dec. 8, 1884, in notebook with Constitution and membership list; "Subject Darwin," Notice of a Monthly Meeting, Microscopical Society, Jan. 15 (1883); "Informal Address on the Advantages for Scientific Work in Cambridge, England," by Professor Willcox, Notice of a

Monthly Meeting, Mar. 7 (1884); LSM to Professor Simon H. Gage, Apr. 13, 1942, Microscopical Society Records, WCA.

8. Microscopical Society Secretaries' Book, Apr. 17, 1886, 41, 43, Microscopical Society Records, WCA. *Courant* (Wellesley, Mass.), Apr. 22, 1886, cited in Microscopical Society Secretaries' Book, 44; Emily Orr Clifford, "Wellesley in the '80s," *WAM* 31, no. 2 (Dec. 1946): 106.

9. Allen F. Davis, *Spearheads for Reform: The Social Settlements and the Progressive Movement, 1890–1914* (New York: Oxford, 1967). VDS, *On Journey* (New York: Dutton, 1937), 135–50.

10. VDS, "Report of Electoral Board," *First Annual Report of the College Settlements Association* (New York: Republic Press, 1890), 13.

11. *Second Annual Report of the College Settlements Association*, 1891. There were twelve Wellesley faculty members. Vassar had a group of ten student subscribers; Bryn Mawr, six; the Annex (later Radcliffe), twelve. Thirty-three Wellesley students became subscribers to the CSA in 1890. Only Smith, with forty-two student memberships, exceeded that number.

12. *Annals,* 1889–90, WCA. Constitution of the Wellesley Alumnae Chapter of the College Settlements Association, CSA, WCA. Also Caroline L. Williamson, "Six Months at Denison House," *Wellesley Magazine* 3, no. 5 (Feb. 9, 1895): 233–39.

13. John Rousmaniere, "Cultural Hybrid in the Slums: The College Woman and the Settlement House," *American Quarterly* 22 (Spring 1970): 45–66.

14. "The Consumer's League," *Wellesley Prelude* 1, no. 35 (June 21, 1890): 494. Reference to the founding of the Wellesley branch of the National Consumers' League is in the Student's Handbook (1903, 25, Christian Association, WCA).

15. S. T., "The Spectator," *Wellesley Magazine* 8, no. 7 (Apr. 1900): 398; "The Consumers' League," *WCN,* Jan. 30, 1902, 1; see also "Mrs. Kelley and the Consumers' League," *WCN,* Dec. 9, 1903, 1; "The Consumers' League and Mrs. Kelley," *WCN,* Mar. 2, 1904, 1; "Annual Meeting of the Consumers' League," *WCN,* Mar. 16, 1904, 4.

16. MG, *What's Past Is Prologue* (New York: Harper and Bros., 1940), 14–15.

17. Mary Cross Ewing, "The Agora Society at Wellesley College," TS; and Constitution and Bylaws of the Agora, Agora Society Records, WCA. The Agora Society is discussed in the *Legenda* (the student yearbook for the graduating class), 1894, 122, WCA.

18. Agora Society Program, House of Commons, Agora Society Records, Feb. 15, 1896, WCA.

19. "The Political Campaign," *Agora* (newsletter), Feb. 1901, Agora Society Records, WCA. Debates were very important. See, e.g., "Points Made by the Different Speakers Greatly Appreciated" (on the Boston central labor union), *Globe,* Feb. 28, 1898, Agora Scrapbook, WCA; Child Labor Debate, Agora Society, Apr. 2, 1907, Agora Society Records, WCA. This political behavior fits that described by Michael McGerr in "Political Style and Women's Power, 1830–1930," *Journal of American History* 77, no. 3 (Dec. 1990): 864–85.

20. "Our Boys," class of 1894, tenth reunion booklet, 1904, WCA. See also *Annals,*

1884–85, 2, on women's right to vote in a student government election: "For once college women had an equal chance with their fellow college men."

21. "Our Play" column of the *Agora* [newsletter], Feb. 1901, Agora Society Records, WCA.

22. Geraldine Gordon, TOI-CNH, 31, WCA.

23. LSM to "My Dear Mother," Oct. 18, 1896, Unprocessed LSM Papers, WCA.

24. EM to "My Dear Mother and Father," Oct. 24, 1898, EM Papers, WCA; on May 14, 1899, she reported that "Miss Hart and I talked about books." On the "female culture of reading" in this generation, see Barbara Sicherman, "Reading and Ambition: M. Carey Thomas and Female Heroism," *American Quarterly* 45, no. 1 (Mar. 1993): 73–103.

25. EM to "My Dear People" (parents), Oct. 16, 1898; Manwaring commented: "Miss Bates is said to be one of the most intellectual of all the faculty. . . . She's also one of the favorite faculty among the girls" ("My Dear Father and Mother," Feb. 12, 1899); again, "I long to see my double" (EM to "My Dear Mother," Feb. 15, 1899, EM Papers, WCA).

26. Draft of article for *WAM* by an alumna, 3, Alumnae, class of 1895, WCA; Grace Cook Kurz, "Facing the Fiftieth—A Reunion Message," *WAM* 33, no. 4 (Apr. 1949): 264. Composite of class of 1896, Class Book, 1896, 85, WCA.

27. MG to "Dearest father," June 10, 1897; MG to "Dearest father and mother," June 17, 1894; MG to "My dearest home folks," May 10, 1897, class of 1899, MG Papers, WCA. Elizabeth Manwaring similarly told her parents that it would be "far from pleasant" to have men attend political rallies on campus (Oct. 28, 1900, EM Papers, WCA).

28. *Annals*, 1883–84, 3, WCA.

29. EM to "My Dear Father and Mother," Nov. 6, 1898, EM Papers, WCA.

30. Mary Rosa to "Dear Mother," Nov. 11, 1912, class of 1914, WCA.

31. Mary Cookingham, "Bluestockings, Spinsters and Pedagogues: Women College Graduates, 1865–1910," *Population Studies* 38 (Nov. 1984): 360. The distinct ethos of the pioneers is discussed in Jill Ker Conway, *The First Generation of American Women Graduates* (New York: Garland, 1987).

32. Barbara Sicherman, "College and Careers: Historical Perspectives on the Lives and Work Patterns of Women College Graduates," in *Women and Higher Education in American History: Essays from the Mount Holyoke College Sesqui-Centennial Symposia*, ed. John Mack Faragher and Florence Howe (New York: Norton, 1988), 141; see also Peter R. Uhlenberg, "A Study of Cohorts Life Cycles: Cohorts of Native Born Massachusetts Women, 1830–1920," *Population Studies* 23 (Nov. 1969): 407–20; Peter R. Uhlenberg, "Cohort Variations in Family Life Cycle Experience of U. S. Females," *Journal of Marriage and the Family* 16 (May 1975): 284–92; Alison Mac-Kinnon, "Interfering with Nature's Mandate: Women, Higher Education, and Demographic Change," *Historical Studies in Education* 1, no. 2 (Fall/Autumn 1989): 219–37.

33. "Twenty-Five" and "The Call," reunion booklet (1913); see also "Pluck and Luck = '94," poem written by a member of the class of 1894, Twentieth Reunion Booklet (1914), WCA.

34. "Alumnae Notes," *WCN*, Oct. 5, 1904, 7; see "The Outcome," in Decennial Reunion Booklet, class of 1894, WCA.

35. Fifteenth Reunion Booklet (1897), class of 1882 (handwritten), 6, class of 1882 records, WCA.

36. Class of 1907, Tune: "I've a Little Pink Pettie from Peter," songsheet (n.d., 1907?), class of 1907 programs (1906–07), WCA.

37. William L. O'Neill, *Divorce in the Progressive Era* (New Haven: Yale University Press, 1967); Elaine Tyler May, *Great Expectations: Marriage and Divorce in Post-Victorian America* (Chicago: University of Chicago Press, 1980); Glenda Riley, *Divorce: An American Tradition* (New York: Oxford University Press, 1991).

38. KLB to "Dearest of Editors" (Edith Tufts), Aug. 4, 1889, KLB Papers, WCA. Bates often criticized marriage in her stories. See, e.g., KLB, "An Interlude," *Sunday Republican*, Feb. 27, 1887 (pasted in KLB scrapbook, vol. 1, 1876–81), 25–27, WCA.

39. KLB to "My dear Anna" (Anna Stockbridge Tuttle), July 20, 1901, KLB Papers, WCA.

40. KLB to "My dear May" (Mary Russell Bartlett), Jan. 3, 1910, KLB Papers, WCA.

41. Statistics on women graduate students at the University of Chicago are given in Marion Talbot, "The Women of the University," in *The President's Report, 1892–1902* (Chicago: University of Chicago Press, 1902). I found statistics on Wellesley graduates attending Cornell in Dean's Report, "The Graduate Department," app. 11, p. 13, CUL; see also Ben Franklin Stambaugh, Jr., "The Development of Postgraduate Studies at Cornell: The First Forty Years, 1868–1908," app. 1, pp. 256–331 (Ph.D. diss., Cornell University, June 1965, CUL). Many Wellesley College alumnae were members of the Cornell Women Graduates' Association. The constitution, minutes, and fund-raising information of this association are in CUL.

42. Class Prophecy of '96, class of 1896, in The Classbook of 1896, 88–99, WCA.

43. EM to "Dear People" (her parents), Oct. 9, 1898; EM to "My dear Mother," Oct. 23, 1899, and Feb. 26, 1900; EM to "My Dear Father," Oct. 2, 1899: "They consider me quite a favorite with the teachers." Katharine Lee Bates cultivated another would-be writer when she encouraged Miriam Vedder; see KLB to Miriam Vedder, June 19, 1915, KLB Papers, WCA.

44. LSM to "Dear Mamma," Oct. 28, 1894, Unprocessed LSM Papers, WCA.

45. Sally Loomis, class of 1928, interview with author, June 28, 1980.

46. MG, *What's Past Is Prologue*, 20.

47. MG to "Dearest mother," Oct. 8, 1910, class of 1899, MG Papers, WCA.

48. MG to "Dearest Agnes," Oct. 11, 1910; MG to "Dearest Agnes," Oct. 29, 1910; Boston Socialist Headquarters, "What is Socialism? Socialism! Votes For Women!!" Flyer for a Meeting of the Socialist Party, class of 1899, MG Papers, WCA.

49. MG to "My darling mother," Dec. 5, 1910, class of 1899, MG Papers, WCA.

50. MG to "Dearest mother and father," Oct. 2, 1911 ("I love the trade school girls . . . who are up against it and are preparing for work"), class of 1899, MG Papers, WCA.

51. MG to "Dearest mother," Apr. 4, 1912, class of 1899, MG Papers, WCA.

52. VDS to "Mine Precious 'Methodist Deaconess'" (MG), Mar. 27, 1939, class of 1899, MG Papers, WCA.

53. SH to "Dearest Mary" (MG), Jan. 18, 1942; VDS to "My Precious Mary," Sept. 12, 1947, and July 25, 1949, class of 1899, MG Papers, WCA.

54. Ruth Sargent, "Laughlin, Gail"; Louise M. Young, "Sherwin, Belle"; and Paul C. Taylor, "Dewson, Mary Williams (Molly)," *NAW:MP*. See also Susan Ware, *Partner and I: Molly Dewson, Feminism, and New Deal Politics* (New Haven: Yale University Press, 1987). Material on Grace Coyle can be found in her alumna biographical file and in the Coyle Correspondence, class of 1914, WCA; information on Dr. Connie Guion is available at CUL.

55. The meaning of careers for women between 1890 and 1920 has been the subject of much historical debate. Although most college-educated women entered teaching, there were new careers carved in social service, medicine, and law. This was the case at Wellesley. In an earlier article, I detailed the problems associated with deriving vocational commitment from alumnae surveys and criticized the devaluing of "female careers" (Patricia A. Palmieri, "Paths and Pitfalls: Illuminating Women's Education History," *Harvard Educational Review* 49, no. 4 [1979]: 534–41). I disagree with the low rates of employment for graduates of Wellesley cited in Roberta Frankfort, *Collegiate Women: Domesticity and Career in Turn-of-the-Century America* (New York: New York University Press, 1977), table 9:60 and 58–61; Frankfort calculates those who entered teaching by 1908 at only 21 percent. From data collected in 1900, however, I calculate that 43 percent of Wellesley alumnae taught. A 1918 Wellesley in-house vocational survey states that 50 percent of the alumnae entered teaching. See "Report of the Sub-Committee Appointed to Investigate the Question of Vocational Courses at Wellesley College," Bureau of Occupations, WCA; also "Supplementary Report of the Subcommittee Appointed to investigate the Question of Vocational Courses at Wellesley College," presented to the Trustee-Faculty Committee, May 9, 1924, Bureau of Occupations, WCA. A 1915 survey of almost 17,000 alumnae found that 70% had been gainfully employed, 83% of these in teaching. See Mary Van Kleeck, "A Census of College Women," *JACA* 11, no. 9 (May 1918): 557–91. By 1930, the Wellesley Personnel Bureau calculated that the women graduates entering teaching had dropped to about 30%, probably because more alternatives were opened to them. The faculty had endorsed, indeed help create, these new career paths. Alice Perry Wood, "What Do Alumnae Do?" *WAM* 14, no. 5 (June 1930): 320–22; Hélène Kazanjian Sargeant, "Genus: Alumnae; Species: Wellesley," *WAM* 49, no. 1 (Nov. 1964): 12–17, reports that of alumnae surveyed, 83 percent had been employed; see also Pamela J. Perun and Janet Giele, "Life after College: Historical Links between Women's Education and Women's Work," in *The Undergraduate Woman*, ed. Pamela J. Perun (Lexington, Mass.: Heath, 1982), 375–98; Margaret Dollar, "The Beginnings of Vocational Guidance for College Women: The Women's Educational and Industrial Union, the Association of Collegiate Alumnae, and Women's Colleges" (Ph.D. diss., Harvard Graduate School

of Education, 1992), supports my interpretation. See also Barbara Sicherman, "College and Careers."

56. VDS to MG, handwritten card, n.d., St. John's Day, class of 1899, MG Papers, WCA.

12
Melancholy Mother

Epigraphs: M. Carey Thomas, "Present Tendencies in Women's College and University Education," *Educational Review* 25 (Jan. 1908): 68, 66, rpt. in *The Educated Woman in America: Selected Writings of Catharine Beecher, Margaret Fuller, and M. Carey Thomas*, ed. Barbara M. Cross (New York: Teachers College Press, 1965); and KLB, "The College Girl of the Period," *Boston Transcript*, June 14, 1902, LKB Scrapbook, 1900–09, KLB Papers, WCA.

1. Thomas, "Present Tendencies in Women's College and University Education," *Educational Review* 25 (Jan. 1908): 64–85, rpt. in *The Educated Woman,* 162; Elizabeth Hazelton Haight, "Pleasant Possibles in Lady Professors," *JACA* 11 (Sept. 1917): 15.

2. Abby Leach, "Hindrances to the Intellectual Life in College," *JACA,* 3d ser., no. 17 (Feb. 1908): 79; Mary Bidwell Breed, "The Control of Student Life," *JACA,* 3d ser., no. 18 (Dec. 1908): 61–62.

3. Laurence R. Veysey, *The Emergence of the American University* (Chicago: University of Chicago Press, 1965), 298, 295; the entire section "The Gulf between Students and Faculty" (294–302) is pertinent; W. Bruce Leslie, *Gentlemen and Scholars: College and Community in the "Age of the University," 1865–1917* (University Park: Pennsylvania State University Press, 1992), esp. chap. 9.

4. G. Stanley Hall, "The Kind of Women Colleges Produce," *Appleton's,* Sept. 1908, 319. May S. Cheney, "Will Nature Eliminate the College Woman?" *JACA,* 3d ser., no. 10 (Jan. 1905): 2.

5. KLB, "The College Girl of the Period"; Helen M. Olin makes a remarkably similar complaint about the University of Wisconsin in *Women of the State University* (New York: Knickerbocker Press, 1909).

6. David Allmendinger, Jr., "History and the Usefulness of Women's Education," *History of Education Quarterly* 19 (Spring 1979): 119; Seelye, as quoted in Helen Lefkowitz Horowitz, *Alma Mater: Design and Experience in the Women's Colleges from their Nineteenth-Century Beginnings to the 1930s* (New York: Knopf, 1984), 148; Taylor, as quoted in Olin, *Women of the State University,* 210. Ellen Cushman, class of 1901, who had entered in 1893 and graduated after taking time out, commented on the changes in the incoming students of 1900: "They were much more sophisticated and had much more money" (Cushman, TOI-CNH, 2, WCA). Horowitz dates the entrance of a new clientele in the 1890s (147); Lynn D. Gordon disagrees. Gordon sees students between 1890 and 1920 as more homogenous by social class (Gordon, *Gender and Higher Education in the Progressive Era* [New Haven: Yale University Press, 1990], 5).

7. The fathers who were businessmen and professionals were represented as follows:

merchants and dealers, 20.8 percent; farmers, 10.9 percent; clergymen, 9.1 percent; manufacturers, 7.7 percent; lawyers, 6.7 percent; physicians, 4.3 percent; and teachers, 3.6 percent. Bankers, agents, bookkeepers, editors, brokers, and contractors represented 2 percent or less (*A Preliminary Statistical Study of Certain Women College Graduates* [Bryn Mawr: Association of Collegiate Alumnae, 1917], 22). A 1927 study reported that fathers of women attending private women's colleges earned more than fathers of students attending men's colleges (O. Edgar Reynolds, *The Social and Economic Status of College Students* [New York: Teachers College, Columbia University, 1927], 23). In the 1920s the median income of parents for the women's colleges was $5,140; for the men's, $4,889 (Colin Burke, *American Collegiate Populations: A Test of the Traditional View* [New York: New York University Press, 1982], table 5.8, p. 228). Burke concludes that by the 1920s the older, representative New England liberal arts colleges had become "enclaves for the wealthy and the sons and daughters of the highly educated" (229).

8. Daniel Horowitz, *The Morality of Spending: Attitudes toward the Consumer Society in America, 1875–1940* (Baltimore: Johns Hopkins University Press, 1985); Stanley Lebergott, *The Americans: An Economic Record* (New York: Norton, 1984). The cultural implications of this shift to a modern consciousness of self are discussed by Warren I. Susman, "Personality and the Making of Twentieth-Century Culture," in *Culture as History: The Transformation of American Society in the Twentieth Century* (New York: Pantheon, 1973, rpt. 1984), 271–85.

9. Simon Patten, "The Crisis in American Home Life," *The Independent* (Feb. 17, 1910): 342–46; Patten saw this shift as weakening the socioeconomic status of the salaried class, whose incomes ranged from $1,000 to $3,000. J. Laurence Laughlin, "Women and Wealth," *Scribner's* 49, no. 2 (Feb. 1911): 199–206. Scott Nearing's views are discussed in Daniel Pope, "American Economists and the High Cost of Living: The Late Progressive Era," *Journal of the History of the Behavioral Sciences* 17 (1981): 83; Frank Stricker, "An American Middle Class Meets the Consumer Age: Peixotto's Rational Professor in the 1920s," *Amerikastudien/American Studies* 34 (1990): 322.

10. Daniel Horowitz, *The Morality of Spending,* xxi–xxiv, 95. A study published in 1912 by Martha B. Bruère and Robert W. Bruère, *Increasing Home Efficiency* (New York: Macmillan, 1912), showed that among middle-class families one-third of businessmen spent their surplus income on education, books, and recreation; this study is discussed in Horowitz, 87–108, esp. 95.

11. Two of the original literary societies established in 1876—Zeta Alpha and Phi Sigma—were abolished in 1881. Some faculty charged that the burdens of extra literary work detracted from course work. In 1889, however, students successfully pressured the administration to reestablish societies. Maryette Goodwin, class of 1887, "The Society Question Renewed," *Prelude,* Nov. 23, 1889, 147–48. Cora Stickney, class of 1880, "The Early Societies," *Courant,* Feb. 8, 1889, 2; Sarah Woodman Paul, class of 1881, "College Societies," *Courant,* Jan. 25, 1889, 2; Angie Lacey Peck, class of 1890, "The Intellectual Need," *Courant,* Feb. 1,

1889, 2. The college retained ownership of the land on which the societies' houses are built.

12. MG to "My dear mother," May 24, 1896, class of 1899, MG Papers, WCA.

13. MG to "Dearest folkses," Nov. 22, 1897, MG to "Dearest father and mother," Nov. 9, 1896; MG to "Dearest father and mother," Oct. 3, 1897, class of 1899, MG Papers, WCA; Zella Wentz complained to her father that the girls at her table "talk of nothing but 'our summer homes in Canada,' our 'homes in Chicago,' 'Newport' and 'Long Island'" (Zella Wentz to "Dear Dad," Sept. 26, 1901, class of 1905, Wentz Papers, WCA).

14. KLB, "The Smoldering Question," *Wellesley Magazine* (Jan. 1, 1905): 133; see also Ruth Bradford, Nov. 14, 1905, diary of 1904–05 (senior year), class of 1905, WCA.

15. Sarah Baxter, "Can the Existence of Societies at Wellesley Be Justified?" *WCN*, Nov. 24, 1909, 1; Imogene Kelly, "Free Press," pt. 1, *WCN*, Dec. 1, 1909, 4; Emma Hawkridge, "Free Press," pt. 1, *WCN*, Dec. 1, 1909, 4–5; "Free Press," pt. 2, unsigned statement by a member of the class of 1910, *WCN*, Dec. 15, 1909, 5. On the decision to restrict the wearing of society pins, see Phi Sigma letter, n.d., Material from Reorganization of Societies, 1910, Shakespeare Society, WCA; Zeta Alpha, letter containing notes of meeting, Nov. 22, 1909, Material from Reorganization of Societies, 1910, Shakespeare Society, WCA.

16. Margarethe Müller, "The Burning Question," pt. 1, *WCN*, Dec. 8, 1909, 4–5; MSC, "Free Press," pt. 2, *WCN*, Jan. 12, 1910, 4–5.

17. Mary P. Ingalls, "Society Congress," *WCN*, Jan. 26, 1910, 1; "Society Congress," *WCN*, Feb. 16, 1910, 1, 4–5; Mary W. Dewson, "Society Congress," *WCN*, Mar. 9, 1910, 1, 4–5; Mary W. Dewson, "Society Congress," *WCN*, Mar. 23, 1910, 1; CH to "My Dear Miss Ellison," n.d., Material from Reorganization of Societies, 1910, Correspondence, Shakespeare Society, WCA. "Inter-Societies, Rules, and Resolutions, Wellesley College, 1910," Material from Reorganization of Societies, 1910, Resolutions and Reports, Shakespeare Society, WCA.

18. MWC to the Board of Society Presidents, May 25, 1910, Material from Reorganization of Societies, 1910, Correspondence, Shakespeare Society, WCA; Grace Coyle to "Dearest Mother," Oct. 3, 1910, class of 1914, Coyle Papers, WCA.

19. MG, to "Dearest father and mother," Nov. 9, 1896; MG to "Dearest father and mother," June 17, 1897, class of 1899, MG Papers, WCA.

20. *Legenda*, 1910, 77; also "On My Penury," *Legenda*, 1903, 19; see also the advice to students with financial difficulties by an alumna, "Free Press," pt. 2, *WCN*, Feb. 2, 1910, 5.

21. EM to "My Dear Father," Nov. 25, 1900, EM Papers, WCA.

22. Dorothy Walton to "Family Dear," Nov. 8, 1911, class of 1915, Walton Papers, WCA.

23. Tuition figures are taken from the *Wellesley College Calender,* 1876–1906. Zella Wentz to "Dear Papa and Mamma," Sept. 18, 1901, class of 1905, Wentz Papers, WCA.

24. Alice Walmsley, "The Cost of Wellesley College Life," *Wellesley Magazine*, Nov. 1, 1907, 45, 47–49.

25. F. Stuart Chapin, "The Budgets of Smith College Girls," *Publications of the American Statistical Association* 15, no. 114 (June 1916): 149–56; see also William Bacon Bailey, "Personal Budgets of Unmarried Persons," *Yale Review* 10, no. 1 (May 1901): 70–83. Bailey gives samples of student budgets at Vassar and Smith (79). He contrasts these with budgets of Yale undergraduates. See chapter 6 for a sample faculty budget.

26. MG to her mother, Oct. 31, Nov. 22, Nov. 29, 1897, class of 1899, MG Papers, WCA; emphasis on dress is also seen in Zella Wentz to "Dear Momma," Sept. 29, 1901, class of 1905, Wentz Papers, WCA.

27. KLB, "The College Girl of the Period."

28. *Prelude,* May 10, 1890, 410; "The Two Phantoms," *Prelude,* May 10, 1890, 411; see also "Our Social Life in College," *Prelude,* Apr. 26, 1890, 379–80; J. Norris, "Free Press, I" *WCN,* Feb. 28, 1906, 7. The "Free Press" section of the *WCN* commented that recitations were being interrupted by students who burst into class late, whispered while instructors taught, and left class early (*WCN,* Feb. 7, 1906, 4).

29. "Free Press," *WCN,* Apr. 21, 1909, 6.

30. "In Spotless Land," *Legenda,* 1906, 220.

31. "The Hunting of the Shark," *Legenda,* 1906, 243; see also "To the Watchman's Pup," which mocks a student who is "chipper with the Faculty" (230).

32. *Legenda,* 1902, 52.

33. EM to "My Dear Mother and Father," Nov. 9, 1898, Dec. 4, 1898, EM Papers, WCA.

34. Dorothy Walton to "Deah Family" (notice the Easte'n accent), Oct. 19, 1911; Walton to "Dear People," Oct. 22, 1911; Walton to "Dear Family," Nov. 5, 1911; Walton to "Dear Mother," Feb. 25, 1912, class of 1915, Walton Papers, WCA.

35. "The Law is a Jumble," *Legenda,* 1900, 24.

36. See, e.g., "An Account of the Movement for Student Government at Wellesley," *Wellesley Magazine* 9, no. 9 (June 1901): 470–72. The "Free Press" section of *WCN* stated that student government aimed to succeed "where faculty rule had failed" (*WCN,* Sept. 30, 1903, 4). On damages done to property, see Wellesley College Minutes, adopted by the Academic Council, Friday, May 13, 1910 (3 pp.), Student Organizations, President's Office, WCA. The Committee on Non-Academic Interests is discussed in Joint Council Minutes (1911–17). EFP, Dec. 13, 1912, Academic Council's Committee on Non-Academic Interests, Minutes of Dec. 13, 1912, WCA.

37. "The 1911 Agreement between Students and Faculty," voted by Academic Council on May 11, 1911 (pt. 1), Joint Council, College Government (1911–17), WCA.

38. Grace Coyle to "Dearest Family," Apr. 22, 1912; Coyle to "Dearest Family," Nov. 18, 1912; Coyle to "Dear Family," May 1, 1913, class of 1914, Coyle Papers, WCA.

39. "The Faculty Barnswallows," *WCN,* Feb. 10, 1904, 1.

40. KLB, "The College Girl of the Period"; Le Baron Russell Briggs, dean of Radcliffe,

commented on this shift in his essay "At Graduation," in *To College Girls and Other Essays* (Boston: Houghton Mifflin, 1911), 41–42; Katharine Fullerton Gerould declared: "In my day, and even more, a little earlier, we tended, I think, to be *Hypatias*. . . . There was . . . a real devotion to things of the mind; a real appreciation of the privilege of study and research; a real almost spiritual, desire to be Mary and not Martha" ("Cap-and-Gown Philosophers," *Delineator* 95 [Oct. 1919]: 7).

41. KLB, "The College Girl of the Period."

42. MHS, "The Eastern Colleges for Women," *Churchman* (suppl.), Aug. 1903, no pages given, Unprocessed MHS Papers, WCA; MWC, "The Dilettantism of Modern Women," address to the Alpha Society of Smith College, Mar. 17, 1906, reported in *Smith College Monthly* (May 1906): 538–39. Marjory Stoneman Douglas, class of 1912, lambasted the changing climate that had affected even reunions: "The life of the mind, if it is recognized at all, certainly has scant place on alumnae programs or in general conversation" ("The Problem of the Colleges," *WAM* 7, no. 1 [Nov. 1922]: 4).

43. MPS, "The Ideal College," *Wellesley Magazine* 15, no. 2 (Nov. 1, 1906): 43–47, esp. 44.

44. Ibid., 45.

45. Ibid., 47.

46. Ellen Hayes, *Letters to a College Girl* (Boston: Ellis, 1909), 7. Annie Tuell, class of 1896 and a junior English professor at Wellesley, lamented that college girls perceived women professors as "a semi-fossilized formation, all devotees of bookish labor" ("The 'Grind' Peril in a Girl's College," *Scribner's* 62 [Dec. 1917]: 767).

47. Laura E. Lockwood, "The Girl Who Should Not Go to College," *Ladies' Home Journal,* Sept. 1, 1910, 26; see also Dorothy Waldo, "College or Not," in Mabelle Babcock Blake et al., *The Education of the Modern Girl* (Boston: Houghton Mifflin, 1929), 96–145.

48. Laura Lockwood, "The Girl Who Should Not Go to College."

49. MPS, "The Apothesis of the Commonplace," *Scribner's* (Mar. 1912): 378–79.

50. MPS, "Our Conspiracy against the Young," *Scribner's* (Jan. 1913): 129–31.

51. M. L. Burton, "The New Admission System of Mt. Holyoke, Smith, Vassar and Wellesley Colleges," *Education* 37, no. 5 (Jan. 1917): 290–301; Alice V. Waite, "The New Plan for Admission," *JACA* 10, no. 5 (Jan. 1917): 304–09. The revamped admission policy also ultimately resulted in the barring of many talented minorities, such as Jews and blacks. See David O. Levine, *The American College and the Culture of Aspiration, 1915–1940* (Ithaca: Cornell University Press, 1986).

52. MPS, "Should I Go to College?" *Good Housekeeping,* June 1921, 57, 134–36; see also Freda Kirchwey, "Too Many College Girls?" *The Nation* 120 (May 27, 1925): 597–98.

53. MPS, "Should I Go to College?"

54. VDS, "The College Girl's Mind" (1924), in *The Privilege of Age: Essays Secular and Spiritual* (New York: Dutton, 1939), 102–06; see also Eleanor Gamble, "The Psy-

chology of the Modern Girl," address delivered to the Association of Principals of Secondary Schools, Cleveland, Feb. 21, 1929, 1–23, Faculty Publications, WCA.

55. VDS, "A Pedagogic Sunset" (1929), in *The Privilege of Age*, 86, 88, 92–93.

56. "Girls at College Held Widening Their Interests" (interview with EFP), *New York Herald Tribune*, June 7, 1936, clippings folder, EFP Papers, WCA; VDS, *On Journey*, 131–32.

13

The Race-Suicide Syndrome

Epigraphs: Roswell H. Johnson and Bertha Stutzmann, "Wellesley's Birth-Rate," *Journal of Heredity* 6, no. 6 (June 1915): 251–52; and Laura E. Lockwood, "College Women as Wives and Mothers," *School and Society* 3, no. 62 (Mar. 4, 1916): 337.

1. Laura E. Lockwood, "College Women as Wives and Mothers," *School and Society* 3, no. 62 (Mar. 4, 1916): 335; Abby Leach, "Hindrances to the Intellectual Life in College," *JACA*, ser. 3, no. 17 (Feb. 1908): 80.

2. M. Carey Thomas, "The College Women of the Present and the Future" (n.p., privately printed), 4; M. Carey Thomas, "Present Tendencies in Women's College and University Education," *Educational Review* (1908), rpt. in Barbara M. Cross, ed., *The Educated Woman in America: Selected Writings of Catharine Beecher, Margaret Fuller, and M. Carey Thomas* (New York: Teachers College Press, 1965), 162.

3. George E. Gardner, "College Women and Matrimony," *Education* 20 (Sept. 1899–June 1900): 287.

4. Louise Michele Newman, ed., *Men's Ideas/Women's Realities: Popular Science, 1870–1915* (New York: Pergamon Press, 1985), 54–152; Leach, "Hindrances to the Intellectual Life in College," 77; see also Sue Zschoche, "Dr. Clarke Revisited: Science, True Womanhood, and Female Collegiate Education," *History of Education Quarterly* 29, no. 4 (Winter 1989): 545–69.

5. Julia Ward Howe, ed., *Sex and Education: A Reply to Dr. E. H. Clarke's "Sex in Education"* (Boston: Roberts Bros., 1874), 52, 55; Charlotte Perkins Gilman, "Superfluous Women" (1900), in *Charlotte Perkins Gilman: A Nonfiction Reader*, ed. Larry Ceplair (New York: Columbia University Press, 1991), 123; Mary Livermore, *What Shall We Do with Our Superfluous Daughters?* (Boston: Lee and Shepard, 1883); Agnes Repplier, "The Spinster," *Harper's Bazaar*, Feb. 1904, 115–20; on the changing status of spinsters see Ruth Freeman and Patricia Klaus, "Blessed or Not? The New Spinster in England and the United States in the Late Nineteenth and Early Twentieth Centuries," *Journal of Family History* 9, no. 4 (Winter 1984): 394–414. See also Barbara A. Johns, "Some Reflections on the Spinster in New England Literature," in *Regionalism and the Female Imagination: A Collection of Essays*, ed. Emily Toth (New York: Human Sciences Press, 1985), 29–64.

6. Carroll D. Wright, *Health Statistics of Female College Graduates* (Boston: Massachusetts Bureau of Labor Statistics, 1885).

7. Millicent Washburn Shinn, "ETC.," *Overland Monthly*, 2d ser., 15, no. 88 (Apr. 1890): 443–44; Shinn, "The Marriage Rate of College Women," *Century* 50 (Oct. 1895): 946–48.

8. Frances M. Abbott, "College Women and Matrimony Again," *Century* 51 (Mar. 1896): 797, 798.

9. "The Marriages of Women College Graduates," *Nation,* Apr. 4, 1890, 330–31. The *Nation* cited statistical problems with Shinn's study, correcting her figures and finding no difference in the marriage rates of graduates of women's colleges and alumnae of coeducational institutions.

10. "Marriages among College Women" (editorial), *Outlook* 69, no. 5 (Oct. 5, 1901): 256–58, esp. 258; their conclusion that it was class and not education that determined marriage rates is based on Mary Roberts Smith, "Statistics of College and Non-College Women," *Publications of the American Statistical Association,* n.s., 7 (Mar.–June 1900): 1–26. Interestingly, the editors noted the V-like trend in marriage rates that contemporary economist Mary Cookingham highlights, as discussed in chapter 11 of this book. In the late nineteenth century the institution of marriage came under attack in both England and the United States. Although staying single was not advocated, it was more acceptable than "mercenary marriages." A spate of articles on this topic appeared; see, e.g., J. H. Brown, "To Marry or Not to Marry?" *Forum* (New York) 6 (1888–89): 432–42.

11. Nancy F. Cott, "Passionlessness: An Interpretation of Victorian Sexual Ideology, 1790–1850," *Signs* 4, no. 2 (Winter 1978): 219–36.

12. See Cynthia Eagle Russett, *Sexual Science: The Victorian Construction of Womanhood* (Cambridge: Harvard University Press, 1989), 88–89.

13. Elsie Clews Parsons, "Higher Education of Women and the Family," *American Journal of Sociology* 14 (1909): 759 n. 5; Charles Franklin Emerick, "College Women and Race Suicide," *Political Science Quarterly* 24 (June 1909): 270. Emerick stated emphatically that the "lame and impotent conclusion(s)" reached by a variety of thinkers and writers would only "mar their reputations . . . and bring statistical methods into disrepute" (283).

14. Margo J. Anderson, *The American Census: A Social History* (New Haven: Yale University Press, 1988); interestingly, Francis Galton, who helped develop the methods of statistical sampling, did so from his studies on the determinants of genius. On the power of statistics, see Patricia Cline Cohen, *A Calculating People: The Spread of Numeracy in Early America* (Chicago: University of Chicago Press, 1982), esp. the conclusion.

15. Theodore Roosevelt, *Presidential Addresses and State Papers of Theodore Roosevelt,* 4 vols. (New York: P. F. Collier and Son, 1905[?]), 3:282–91; see also Frederick A. Bushee, "The Declining Birth Rate and Its Cause," *Popular Science Monthly* 63 (1903): 355–61. For a retort to Roosevelt, see Susan B. Anthony, "Reply to President Roosevelt's Race Suicide Theory," *Socialist Woman* 2, no. 16 (Sept. 1908): 6–7. A recent article reevaluates nativist fears and finds them misplaced. Actually, the overall fertility of immigrants and their children was substantially lower than that of native-born women. Second-generation (foreign) women delayed or avoided marriage (Miriam King and Steven Ruggles, "American Immigration, Fertility, and Race Suicide at the Turn of the Century," *Journal of Interdisciplinary History* 20, no. 3 [Winter 1990]: 347–70).

16. William L. O'Neill, *Divorce in the Progressive Era* (New Haven: Yale University Press, 1967); Glenda Riley, *Divorce: An American Tradition* (New York: Oxford University Press, 1991); Brooks Adams, *The Law of Civilization and Decay* (New York: Macmillan, 1896; rpt., New York: Knopf, 1971).

17. Jill Conway, "Stereotypes of Feminity in a Theory of Sexual Evolution," in *Suffer and Be Still: Women in the Victorian Age*, ed. Martha Vicinus (Bloomington: Indiana University Press, 1967); George W. Stocking, Jr., "Lamarckianism in American Social Science, 1890–1915," in *Race, Culture, and Evolution: Essays in the History of Anthropology* (New York: Free Press, 1968), 234–70. Most scholars in women's intellectual history have emphasized the negative implications of scientific thought, in particular the "brain versus uterus" controversy. See Barbara Ehrenreich and Deirdre English, *For Her Own Good: One Hundred Fifty Years of the Experts' Advice to Women* (New York: Doubleday, 1978). Theories of sex differences also devalued women as inferior intellects. See Rosalind Rosenberg, *Beyond Separate Spheres: Intellectual Roots of Modern Feminism* (New Haven: Yale University Press, 1982); Russett, *Sexual Science*. However, the positive aspects of Lamarckianism deserve more study.

18. Flavia Alaya, "Victorian Science and the 'Genius' of Woman," *Journal of the History of Ideas* 38 (Apr.–June 1977): 261–80; Mark H. Haller, *Eugenics: Hereditarian Attitudes in American Thought* (New Brunswick: Rutgers University Press, 1963); Hamilton Cravens, *The Triumph of Evolution: American Scientists and the Heredity-Environment Controversy, 1900–1941* (Philadelphia: University of Pennsylvania Press, 1978); Russett, *Sexual Science*, 159–60; Carl N. Degler, *In Search of Human Nature: The Decline and Revival of Darwinism in American Thought* (New York: Oxford University Press, 1991), esp. chap. 2; Mikuláš Teich, "The Unmastered Past of Human Genetics," in *Fin de Siècle and Its Legacy*, ed. Mikuláš Teich and Roy Porter (Cambridge: Cambridge University Press, 1990), 296–324; Alexander Graham Bell, "Is Race Suicide Possible?" *Journal of Heredity* (Nov.–Dec. 1920): 339–41. Bell's argument demonstrates the growing hostility toward celibacy.

19. Lillian Faderman, "The Morbidification of Love between Women by Nineteenth-Century Sexologists," *Journal of Homosexuality* 4, no. 1 (Fall 1978): 73–90; George Chauncey, Jr., "Female Sexual Inversion to Homosexuality: The Changing Medical Conceptualization of Female 'Deviance,'" in *Passion and Power: Sexuality in History*, ed. Kathy Peiss and Christina Simmons (Philadelphia: Temple University Press, 1989), 107; Christina Simmons, "Companioniate Marriage and the Lesbian Threat," *Frontiers: A Journal of Women's Studies* 4 (Fall 1979): 55; Pendleton, as quoted in "Miss Caroline Hazard as Wellesley's Head," *Tribune* (Providence, R.I.), Aug. 21, 1910, CH Scrapbook, 1910, WCA; see also Lillian Faderman, *Odd Girls and Twilight Lovers: A History of Lesbian Life in Twentieth-Century America* (New York: Columbia University Press, 1991), 34–36.

20. William S. Sadler, "College Women and Race Suicide," *Ladies' Home Journal*, Apr. 1922, 63; Simmons, "Companionate Marriage and the Lesbian Threat," 54–59; on the change in social behavior on campus, see Lynn D. Gordon, *Gender and Higher Education in the Progressive Era* (New Haven: Yale University Press, 1990);

Laurence R. Veysey, *The Emergence of the American University* (Chicago: University of Chicago Press, 1965).

21. EGB, discussion of Edward A. Ross, "Western Civilization and the Birth-Rate," *American Journal of Sociology* 12, no. 5 (Mar. 1907): 623–26, esp. 626, and entire article; George J. Engelmann, "Education Not the Cause of Race Decline," *Popular Science Monthly* 63 (1903): 179–80; Christine Terhune Herrick, "Concerning Race Suicide," *North American Review* 184, no. 4 (Feb. 15, 1907): 407–12; see also Alice Stevens, "Three Famous New England Colleges," *New England Magazine,* June 1906, 629; see also Kate Gannett Wells, "Why More Men Do Not Marry," *North American Review* 165, no. 1 (July 1897): 123–28; George E. Gardner, "College Women and Matrimony," 285–91; Frederick A. Bushee, "The Declining Birth Rate and Its Cause," *Popular Science Monthly* 63 (1903): 355–61; Jennifer Breay, "The Chaos of Modern Marriage" (undergraduate honor's thesis, History and Literature Program, Harvard University, 1991). For a superb cultural discussion of the race suicide phenomenon in England that underscores the difficulty in establishing causation, see Richard A. Soloway, *Demography and Degeneration: Eugenics and the Declining Birthrate in Twentieth-Century Britain* (Chapel Hill: University of North Carolina Press, 1990); Charles L. Vigue, "Eugenics and the Education of Women in the United States," *Journal of Educational Administration and History* 19, no. 2 (1987): 51–55. I thank Margaret W. Rossiter for the Vigue reference.

22. See, e.g., William L. Felter, "The Education of Women," *Educational Review* 31 (Apr. 1906): 362.

23. Patricia A. Graham, "Expansion and Exclusion: A History of Women in American Higher Education," *Signs* 3, no. 4 (Summer 1978): 766, table 1.

24. Men and women educators of the middle class sometimes saw the same cultural problems. Inevitably, however, gender divided them on solutions. For a discussion of how gender affects political and cultural discourse, see Joan Wallach Scott, *Gender and the Politics of History* (New York: Columbia University Press, 1988), esp. chap. 2, "Gender: A Useful Category of Historical Analysis."

25. EGB, "The Education and Efficiency of Women," *Annals of the Academy of Political Science* 1 (1910): 61–71.

26. May S. Cheney, "Will Nature Eliminate the College Woman?" *JACA,* 3d ser., 10 (Jan. 1905): 9.

27. Emerick, "College Women and Race Suicide," 269–83. This viewpoint was popular. See also Nellie Seeds Nearing, "Education and Fecundity," *Publication of the American Statistical Association* 14 (June 1914): 156. Amy Hewes, an economics professor at Mount Holyoke, explained that the pioneering college woman was a "'bluestocking,' more differentiated intellectually and professionally from other women" ("Note on the Racial and Educational Factors in the Declining Birth-Rate," *American Journal of Sociology* 29 [Sept. 1923]: 184); Katharine Fullerton Gerould, "Cap-and-Gown Philosophers," *Delineator* 95 (Oct. 1919): 7, 59–60. Gerould concluded that "the intellectual fire . . . has died down in the college girl. . . . But that had to come. Some of us may regret the age of the

bluestocking; but you cannot breed a yearly crop of Hypatias through many decades" (60).

28. Mabel Newcomer and Evelyn S. Gibson, "Vital Statistics from Vassar College," *American Journal of Sociology* 29 (July 1923–May 1924): 430–42; Amy Hewes also pointed to economic forces: "A Study of Families in Three Generations," *JACA* 13, nos. 5 and 6 (Mar. and Apr. 1920): 5–9.

29. G. Stanley Hall and Theodate L. Smith, "Marriage and Fecundity of College Men and Women," *Pedagogical Seminary* 10 (Sept. 1903): 275–314.

30. Ibid., 313.

31. Hugo Münsterberg, *The Americans* (New York: McClure, Phillips, 1904), 5. Such fears confirm Margaret W. Rossiter's analysis that academic men who were caught up in defining their career paths as professional rather than amateur were threatened by women (Margaret W. Rossiter, *Women Scientists in America: Struggles and Strategies* [Baltimore: Johns Hopkins Press, 1982], 73–100); see also Rosalind Rosenberg, *Beyond Separate Spheres,* chap. 2, "The Feminization of Academe."

32. G. Stanley Hall, "The Kind of Women Colleges Produce," *Appleton's,* Sept. 1908, 316–17; Hall and Smith, "Marriage and Fecundity," 313. The attack on women's colleges and spinster faculty surfaced in the popular magazines around 1910; see, e.g., Madeline Z. Doty, "What a Woman's College Means to a Girl," *Delineator* 75 (Mar. 1910): 209, 265–66, which stated that "many of the professors are merely dead and dry spinsters . . . women . . . who took a Ph.D. and then returned to their alma mater to teach without ever having lived, even for a day, the throbbing vigorous life of real women" (266).

33. Charles Eliot, "The Woman That Will Survive," *Delineator,* Aug. 1911, rpt. in Eliot, *A Late Harvest: Miscellaneous Papers Written between Eighty and Ninety* (Boston: Atlantic Monthly Press, 1924), 68–69. In contrast, Earl Barnes, who married Mary Sheldon, a former Wellesley College professor, wrote a sympathetic defense of single women: "The Celibate Women of Today," *Popular Science Monthly* 86, June 1915, rpt. in Newman, *Men's Ideas/Women's Realities,* 323–29.

34. Robert J. Sprague, "Education and Race Suicide," *Journal of Heredity* 6, no. 4 (Apr. 1915): 162; see also Roswell H. Johnson and Bertha Stutzmann, "Wellesley's Birth-Rate," *Journal of Heredity* 6, no. 6 (June 1915): 250–53. Scott Nearing praised the presumed "anti-social" individuals as really "race saviors" ("Race Suicide vs. Overpopulation," *Popular Science Monthly* 78 [Jan. 1911]: 81–83).

35. Lockwood, "College Women as Wives and Mothers," 335. Roswell H. Johnson issued a stinging rejoinder: "The Birth-Rate of College Women" (letter to the editor), *School and Society* 5, no. 128 (June 9, 1917): 678–80.

36. Mary Cookingham, "Combining Marriage, Motherhood, and Jobs before World War II: Women College Graduates, Classes of 1905–1935," *Journal of Family History* 9 (Summer 1984): 178–95; Helen Butts Correll, "The Birth Rate for Wellesley College Graduates," *WAM* 24, no. 1 (Oct. 1939): 16–17; F. Lawrence Babcock, *The U.S. College Graduate* (New York: Macmillan, 1941), 13–14. Using the 1930 census, Babcock reported that spinsterhood was still highly disproportional in the college population.

37. Howard J. Banker, "Coeducation and Eugenics," *Journal of Heredity* 8, no. 5 (May 1917): 212; "Stanford's Marriage Rates," *Journal of Heredity* 8, no. 4 (Apr. 1917): 173; "Coeducation and Marriage," *Journal of Heredity* 8, no. 1 (Jan. 1917): 43–45.

38. R. Le Clerc Phillips, "The Problem of the Educated Woman," *Harper's* 154 (Dec. 1926): 61–62; Phillips, "Cracks in the Upper Crust," *The Independent* 116 (May 29, 1926): 633–44; see also W. Béran Wolfe, "Why Educate Women?" *Forum* 81, no. 3 (Mar. 1929): 165–67, esp. 167.

39. Henry R. Carey, "Career or Maternity? The Dilemma of the College Girl," *North American Review* 228, no. 6 (Dec. 1929): 742–43; see also Carey, "Sterilizing the Fittest," *North American Review* 228, no. 5 (Nov. 1929): 519–24. Carey also connected the employment of single women to a labor market that would "limit the earning power of married men" (524).

40. Willis J. Ballinger, "Spinster Factories: Why I Would Not Send a Daughter to College," *Forum and Century* 87, no. 5 (May 1932): 304. I found a retort to this article by Suzette Morton, "Vassar College: A Typical Spinster Factory," *Miscellany News* (Vassar College), May 25, 1932, 2–4. She challenged his entire analysis, calling it "insulting to educated women and their educators." In particular, she denounced his attack on women faculty, whom he called "apostles of dull and narrow living," stating that this is "almost too ridiculous to merit an answer. . . . The women who have explored intellectual realms, who have travelled . . . do not fit Mr. Ballinger's description" (4). Unfortunately, such responses rarely got published in popular magazines.

41. See Elisabeth Hodder and Laura Hibbard Loomis, FBF, WCA.

42. Data on male faculty is obtained from trustee's minutes and from faculty biographical files. In checking the Trustee Minutes of 1880–1915 (WCA), I have found no favoritism in salaries for male instructors.

43. Using a structuralist approach to the sociology of education, Sara Delamont gives a remarkably similar list of intellectual currents that undercut the success of the pioneers: race suicide and eugenics, Freudianism, and post–World War I hedonism (Delamont, *Knowledgeable Women: Structuralism and the Reproduction of Elites* [London: Routledge, 1989], 148); Gerda Lerner posits that how society views single women is a barometer of cultural attitudes toward all women (Lerner, "Single Women in Nineteenth-Century Society: Pioneers or Deviants," *Reviews in American History* 15, no. 1 [Mar. 1987]: 94–100).

44. G. Stanley Hall, "The Kind of Women Colleges Produce," 313–19; Simmons, "Companionate Marriage and the Lesbian Threat," 57; Carroll Smith-Rosenberg similarly argues that "by constituting [The New Woman as] a sexual subject" the sexologists "made her subject to the political regulation of the state" (Smith-Rosenberg, "Discourses of Sexuality and Subjectivity: The New Woman, 1870–1936," in *Hidden from History: Reclaiming the Gay and Lesbian Past,* ed. Martin Duberman, Martha Vicinus, and George Chauncey, Jr. [New York: Meridian, 1990], 269). Linda Gordon sees the episode of race-suicide alarms as a backlash to feminism (Gordon, *Woman's Body, Woman's Right: A Social History of Birth Control in America* [New York: Penguin, 1977], chap. 7).

14

Ellen's Isle

Epigraph: "Miss Pendleton and Wellesley," *New York Evening Post,* Nov. 12, 1910.

1. Angie Chapin to LMN, Aug. 7, 1910, ALS, WCA; Edith Souther Tufts to LMN, Nov. 29, 1910, ALS, WCA; Samuel Capen to CH, July 21, 1910, WCA.

2. Angie Chapin to LMN, Aug. 7, 1910, ALS, WCA. Alice Van Vechten Brown, who lobbied for Pendleton as president, stressed that Wellesley had endured a two- or three-year "period of uncertainty," in terms of the presidency (Brown to "My Dear Mr. Capen," Apr. 14, 1911, ALS, WCA). In 1909 Hazard termed her physical ailment "gall-stone colic" (CH to Mrs. Durant, Aug. 19, 1909, ALS, WCA). Hazard's nervousness is discussed in the following letter: Angie Chapin to LMN, Aug. 7, 1910, ALS, WCA. In writing to another sister Helen, Rowland Hazard discussed Caroline Hazard's health and stated: "The situation is rather vague" (Aug. 26, 1909). On Aug. 29, 1909, in another letter to Helen, he mentions the discontinuation of medicine for the thyroid gland. These letters are in Helen Hazard Bacon correspondence, Nathanial Terry Bacon Papers, folder 11, box 113, James P. Adams Library, Rhode Island College, Providence, R.I.; on Hazard's desire to resign in 1908 and the trustees refusal to accept her resignation granting her instead a year's leave, for 1908–09, see ECM/BT, Sept. 18, 1908; ECM/BT, Nov. 13, 1908. Hazard returned to her duties in May 1909; she officially resigned in May 1910; see CH to Mrs. Durant, May 31, 1910, bound in MBT, July 12, 1910. The Executive Committee of the Board of Trustees voted Pendleton a salary of $3,000 "during the time that she is doing the work of the President, beginning August 1, 1910" (ECM/BT, Oct. 27, 1910, WCA).

3. Helen Barett Montgomery to LMN, n.d. (probably 1910), ALS, WCA; "No Man for Wellesley's Head, Declares Widow of the College Founder," *Boston Post,* July 31, 1910, Scrapbook of Clippings, 1910, CH Papers.

4. "Women as Executives," *Baltimore Star,* July 25, 1910, Scrapbook of Clippings, 1910, CH Papers.

5. EFP received the unanimous vote of the nineteen trustees present for the vote for the presidency, Report of Special Committee, Wellesley College Trustees, June 9, 1911, tipped in with MBT, WCA. Samuel Capen mentions that of the two or three absentee trustees, one "might not have voted with the rest but I know . . . she will give a most cordial and loyal support to the new President" (Samuel Capen to CH, June 10, 1911, ALS, WCA).

6. "Miss Chapin Speaks for the Faculty," *Boston Transcript,* Oct. 19, 1911; Helen Merrill, who graduated in the same class as Pendleton, sent the new president a bag of gold upon her inauguration (EFP to HM, Dec. 18, 1911, ALS, WCA); untitled newspaper clipping, *Tribune* (Providence, R.I.), Aug. 21, 1910.

7. Anna Phillips, class of 1886, "Ellen's Isle," handwritten in Scrapbook, compiled by Marion Elizabeth Stark, July 1936, EFP Papers, WCA.

8. Florence Converse, *Wellesley College: A Chronicle of the Years 1875–1938* (Wellesley, Hathaway House, 1939), 160–63. See also VDS, "The Passing of College Hall,"

Churchman, Apr. 4, 1914, 434–36; VDS, *On Journey* (New York: Dutton, 1937), 276.

9. Converse, *Wellesley College,* 168; Florence Converse to Eleana Prescott Hammond, Mar. 22, 1914, College Hall Fire, WCA; VDS, "The Passing of College Hall," 435; VDS to Alice Van Vechten Brown, Mar. 27, 1914, College Hall Fire, WCA.

10. Katharine Balderston, "The Great Fire," in *Wellesley College, 1875–1975: A Century of Women,* ed. Jean Glasscock (Wellesley: Wellesley College, 1975), 348.

11. VDS, *On Journey,* 278. She reflected: "One socialist group after another succumbed to the line of a false patriotism; the radical movement disintegrated on every side; and like many . . . during those difficult years, I had a desperate and tragic sense of 'playing a lone hand'" (285–86).

12. Converse, *Wellesley College,* 191; Faculty Minutes in Support of Wilson's Policies, War Conditions I, World War I, WCA.

13. Julia E. Moody, "The Mobilization of Wellesley College," WAM 1, no. 4 (July 1917): 234–39; Converse, *Wellesley College,* 192.

14. "List of Members," Patriotic Service Committee, Association of Officers and Instructors, Wellesley College Patriotic Service Committee (1915–21), World War I; "Wellesley College," War Emergency Courses, Oct. 16, 1917, Wellesley College Mobilization Committee (1917–18), World War I, WCA. For the impact of World War I on women's work and the women's movement, see William O'Neill, *Everyone Was Brave: The Rise and Fall of Feminism in America* (Chicago: Quadrangle Press, 1969), 169–225; Maurine Weiner Greenwald, *Women, War, and Work* (Westport, Conn.: Greenwood Press, 1980).

15. Converse, *Wellesley College,* 196–97; "Report of the Dean" (of Wellesley College), July 1920, table (unnumbered) of subjects elected by freshmen, 1916–19, p. 29; July 1, 1921, table (unnumbered) of subjects elected by freshmen, 1918–21, p. 31; also tabulated percentages showing election by freshmen, 1918–21, p. 32, all in Wellesley College President's Reports, WCA.

16. "To All Members of the Official Staff" (loyalty memorandum signed by Ellen F. Pendleton), Mar. 1918, War Activities, President's Office Files, WCA.

17. Minutes, Committee on Patriotic Service, Mar. 18, Apr. 9, Apr. 23, May 14, Sept. 27, 1918; Jan. 10, May 23, 1919; Jan. 25, 1921, Wellesley College Committee on Patriotic Service (1915–21), World War I, WCA.

18. "Report of the Wellesley College War Council," 1919, Wellesley College War Council: War Relief Committee (1918–19), World War I; EM, "Wellesley Women in War Service Overseas," WAM 3, no. 3 (Apr. 1919): 172–204.

19. Carol Signer Gruber, *Mars and Minerva: World War I and the Uses of Higher Learning in America* (Baton Rouge: Louisiana State University Press, 1975), esp. chap. 5, "Academic Freedom under Fire."

20. VDS to EGB, Jan. 17, 1917; VDS to EGB, May 18, 1918, EGB Papers, SCPC. On Scudder's posture and feelings see also, *On Journey,* 280. Interestingly, Ellen Hayes, who had nettled the administration several times in her forty years of service, was denied emeritus status in 1916. Hayes, a social radical who scorned

compromise, had not been unanimously liked by her colleagues; her socialist and pacifist views had made her "a thorn in the flesh of some members of the trustee and alumnae groups." Her case to some extent prefigures what happened to Balch. Louise Brown angrily accused Wellesley of disowning Hayes "on account of her opinions" (Brown, "They Would Burn the Brunos," in *Ellen Hayes: Trail-Blazer* [n.p., 1932], 32–33); see also HM, "History of the Department of Mathematics," 44, math dept., WCA.

21. KLB to EGB (1917?), EGB Papers, SCPC.

22. Barbara M. Solomon, "Balch, Emily Greene," *NAW:MP*; the editorial "To-Night's Pacifist Meeting," which appeared in the *Evening Sun*, is reported in Mercedes M. Randall, *Improper Bostonian: Emily Greene Balch* (New York: Twayne, 1964), 240–41.

23. Randall, *Improper Bostonian,* 246–47.

24. *BAAUP* 2, no. 1 (Mar. 1916): 44. By January 1918, twenty-seven Wellesley faculty in this study were listed as members of the AAUP. See *BAAUP* 4, no. 1 (Jan. 1918): 41. See also "General Report of the Committee on Academic Freedom and Academic Tenure," presented Dec. 31, 1915, *BAAUP* 1 (Dec. 1915): 29–39; "Report of the Committee of Inquiry on the Case of Professor Scott Nearing of the University of Pennsylvania," *BAAUP* 2, no. 3 (May 1916): 127–77; "Academic Freedom in Wartime," *BAAUP* 4, nos. 2–3 (Feb.–Mar. 1918): 29–47.

25. EGB to EFP, Apr. 3, 1918, EGB Papers, SCPC. Junkerism refers to a mindset or policy characterized by extreme militarism, nationalism, and antidemocratic views.

26. MWC to EGB, Apr. 23, 1918, EGB Papers, SCPC.

27. Bates claimed she was eager for Balch to return, because she was "a vital part of my Wellesley and of my faith in goodness." KLB to "My dear Emily," Apr. 28, 1918, EGB Papers, SCPC.

28. Alice Youngman to EGB, Thursday (?), 1918, EGB Papers, SCPC.

29. Kendrick announced to Scudder and Perkins, "I feel as if I were coming to a funeral and must join the family." Agnes Perkins to "Dearest Partner dear," Apr. 26 (1918), EGB Papers, SCPC.

30. EGB to KLB, May 8, 1918, EGB Papers, SCPC.

31. "Pacifism in College," *WCN,* Apr. 25, 1918, 2. EGB to KLB, May 8, 1918, EGB Papers, SCPC.

32. VDS to EGB, May (11) 1918, EGB Papers, SCPC.

33. KLB to "Emily Very Dear," Sept. 1, 1919, EGB Papers, SCFC.

34. MWC to EGB, Oct. 26, 1919, EGB Papers, SCPC; Randall, *Improper Bostonian,* 252; see also JM, May 21, 1919, TS, WCA.

35. MWC to EGB, Oct. 26, 1919, EGB Papers, SCPC. EFP to EGB, May 8, 1919, EGB Papers, SCPC; MWC to EGB, Oct. 26, 1919, EGB Papers, SCPC. Calkins stated, however, that she would like to be an associate of the Women's League for Peace and Freedom. She remained a rather "silent-pacifist" at Wellesley (MWC to EGB, Dec. 7, 1919, EGB Papers, SCPC).

36. The Cattell case is chronicled in the James McKeen Cattell Collection, housed in

the Special Collections, Rare Book and Manuscript Library, Columbia University Libraries; see also Carol Signer Gruber, "Academic Freedom at Columbia University, 1917–1918: The Case of James McKeen Cattell," *BAAUP* (Autumn 1972): 297–305.

37. EGB to EFP, Sept. 29, 1919, EGB Papers, SCPC.

38. EGB to EFP, Sept. 29, 1919, EGB Papers, SCPC; see Alice Pearmain to EGB, Apr. 8, 1919 for Pearmain's political viewpoint and confirmation that she had quizzed Balch (EGB Papers, SCPC).

39. MWC to EGB, Oct. 26, 1919, EGB Papers, SCPC; see also KLB to EGB, Dec. 3, 1919, which also comments that Balch's letter, critical of Permain, "wasn't like you" (EGB Papers, SCPC).

40. EGB to Alice Youngman, Feb. 1, 1920, EGB Papers, SCPC. Years later, informed that the case had been minimized in Alice Payne Hackett's semiofficial history of Wellesley and that Katharine Lee Bates had been quoted as saying that Balch was after all hired to teach economics and not pacifism, Balch quipped, "How absurd." Yet in 1925, after serving in Geneva as international secretary of the Women's International League for Peace and Freedom, Balch returned to the village of Wellesley to retire, taking her place among her emeriti friends, many of whom had tried to uphold the right of dissent on campus.

15
The Old War Horses

1. VDS, *On Journey* (New York: Dutton, 1937), 299–300. Scudder's mother died in January 1920. Although this event barely gets mentioned in her autobiography, given her close relationship, it must have deepened her psychological despondency (292).

2. Jessie Bernard, *Academic Women* (New York: Meridian, 1974), 36–37. See William H. Chafe, *The American Woman: Her Changing Social, Economic, and Political Roles, 1920–1970* (New York: Oxford University Press, 1972), reissued as *The Paradox of Change: American Women in the Twentieth Century* (New York: Oxford University Press, 1991), 104; introd. to *These Modern Women: Autobiographical Essays from the Twenties*, ed. Elaine Showalter (New York: Feminist Press, 1978, 1989); Patricia M. Hummer, *The Decade of Elusive Promise: Professional Women in the United States, 1920–30* (Ann Arbor, Mich.: University Microfilms Research Press, 1979); Frank Stricker, "Cookbooks and Law Books: The Hidden History of Career Women in Twentieth-Century America," *Journal of Social History* 10 (Fall 1976): 1–19; Dorothy M. Brown, *Setting a Course: American Women in the 1920s* (Boston: Twayne, 1987); Stanley Coban, *Rebellion against Victorianism: The Impetus for Cultural Change in 1920s America* (New York: Oxford, 1991). For the decade of the 1930s, see Susan Ware, *Holding Our Own: American Women in the 1930s* (Boston: Twayne, 1982).

3. VDS, *On Journey,* 131; Jeannette Bailey Cheek, class of 1928, interviews with author, July 1, 1991, and June 20, 1980; Virginia Onderdonk, telephone conversation with author, June 21, 1980.

4. Calvin Coolidge, "Enemies of the Republic: Are the 'Reds' Stalking Our College Women?" *Delineator* 98 (June 1921): 66; Alice Payne Hackett, *Wellesley: Part of the American Story* (New York: Dutton, 1949), 221.

5. Hackett, *Wellesley,* 221–23, 188; see also SH, "The Des Moines Student Volunteeer Convention," *Experimenter* 1, no. 5 (1920): 5–7. John W. Davis, a lawyer, served as United States solicitor general from 1913 to 1918 and as United States ambassador to England from 1918 to 1921. In 1924 he was the presidential nominee of the Democratic Party (Leslie H. Southwick, *Presidential Also-Rans and Running Mates, 1788–1980* [Jefferson, N.C.: McFarland, 1984], 468–76). KLB to LMH, Nov. 17, 1924, KLB Papers, WCA. Copies of the *Relay* are in WCA.

6. Dorothy Burgess, *Dream and Deed: The Story of Katharine Lee Bates* (Norman: University of Oklahoma Press, 1952), 118. On the merger between Academic Council and faculty, see MBT, Feb. 14, 1908, June 12, 1908, Nov. 12, 1909, WCA. Martha Hale Shackford characterized the quality of debate in Council in "Alice Vincent Waite," *WAM* 15, no. 5 (June 1931): 308.

7. Guido Hugo Marx, "The Problem of the Assistant Professor," *Association of American Universities Journal of Proceedings and Addresses* 11 (Jan. 1910): 19. The housing expenses of junior faculty at Wellesley were a particular problem. In 1910, Olive Davis, director of residences, described their plight: "Members of the Faculty were forced into the region known as 'across the tracks,' since it was the only one left in the village where rooms, large enough to live in, could be had for what the Faculty could afford to pay." A special committee was formed to construct a house on campus that would rent rooms at reasonable rates ("Report of the Director of Halls of Residency," 1910, in *President's Report,* 1910, 44).

8. Plan of Department Organization for Use as an Experiment in 1917–1918, submitted to Council Dec. 13, 1917, attached to Minutes of the Academic Council, WCA.

9. The term "little Bismarck" was applied to Carla Wenckebach, but it is an apt one for many in the Wellesley faculty group; Lucy Killough, TOI-CNH, 7, WCA; Katharine Balderston, TOI-CNH, 17, WCA; Agnes Abbot, TOI-CNH, 17, WCA.

10. Lucy Wilson, TOI-CNH, 15, WCA.

11. Helen Lockwood, two-page handwritten letter to Barnard College, n.d.; Lockwood, handwritten notes of her conversation with SH, Lockwood Papers, VCL.

12. Dorothy Weeks, class of 1916, interview with author, Feb. 5, 1978. See also the complaint of a junior faculty woman in the composition department who fled to Goucher, happy to be away from "the maddening crowd of old maids" (Anita Oyarzabal to Lockwood, Jan. 7, 1929, Lockwood Papers, VCL).

13. Pearl Strachen, "More Mature Literary Tastes Seen in College Girls of Today," *Christian Science Monitor,* June 26, 1943, MHS FBF, WCA; Lucy Wilson, TOI-CNH, 15, WCA.

14. Leland H. Jenks, TOI-CNH, 11; Lucy Killough, TOI-CNH, 12, WCA.

15. VDS to MG, Dec. 21 (1936), ALS, WCA. Lucy Killough, TOI-CNH, 20. Killough also noted that since Mildred McAfee Horton was so young, faculty didn't feel as constrained in her presence when she led Council (14); E. Elizabeth Jones, TOI-

CNH, 8; Edith Abbot, "Brown, Alice Van Vechten," *NAW*; Jeannette Bailey Cheek described the psychological costs to junior faculty (Cheek, class of 1928, interview with author, June 20, 1980). According to Sally Loomis, who was on the faculty in the 1940s, Katharine Balderston suffered this fate (Sally Loomis, class of 1928, interview with author, June 28, 1980).

16. E. Elizabeth Jones, TOI-CNH, 8; Agnes Abbot, TOI-CNH, 6, 15; SH to Betty Bradstreet Walsh, Sept. 26, 1935, SH FBF, WCA.

17. E. Elizabeth Jones, TOI-CNH, 14, WCA; MHS, 1952 Alumnae Questionnaire, Alumnae Biographical File, WCA. See also SH to MG, Jan. 18, 1942, where Hart characterizes Wellesley: "It is a much smaller, small-town community than you remember it, where most of the people are singularly conservative and intolerant of differences of opinion." She adds, "I should *not* like to be quoted as saying this" (class of 1899, MG letters from friends, WCA).

18. Sally Loomis, "Wellesley Twenty Years After by a Woman from Mars," typescript, Mar. 1949 (in author's possession). English professor Laura Hibbard Loomis echoed this conclusion in 1952, when she wrote of the weaknesses of Wellesley: "Too few outstanding personalities on Faculty" (Laura Hibbard Loomis, 1952 Alumnae Questionnaire, WCA).

19. See, e.g., Helen Sard Hughes, "The Academic Chance," *JACA* 7, no. 1 (Jan. 1919): 79–82; Ella Lonn, "Academic Status of Women on University Faculties," *Journal of the American Association of University Women* 17, no. 1 (Jan. 1924): 5–11; A. Caswell Ellis, "Preliminary Report of Committee W, on Status of Women in College and University Faculties," *BAAUP* 7, no. 6 (Oct. 1921): 26.

20. *After Twenty Five Years: A Questionnaire Re-printed from the College Settlements Association Anniversary Report* (1889–1914), compiled by Mrs. Lucius H. Thayer and Miss Florence Converse (n.p.: n.p., 1914?), 21; KLB to "Dearest my Friend" (CH), Jan. 8, 1928, KLB Papers, WCA; SFW, "A History of the Department of Physics," 15, physics dept., WCA; see also SH to MG, Mar. 21, 1933, class of 1899, MG Papers, WCA; SFW to "Dear Friends of Half a Century," Sept. 3, 1926, class of 1880, letters to class president, WCA.

21. VDS, *On Journey*, 398–400, 430.

22. MPS, "Address Given on Behalf of the Class of 1886 on the Fiftieth Anniversary of Its Graduation," 1936, Unprocessed MPS Papers, WCA. For a discussion of the losses women writers endured in this era, see the chapter entitled "The Other Lost Generation," in Elaine Showalter, *Sister's Choice: Tradition and Change in American Women's Writing* (New York: Oxford University Press, 1991), 104–26; MPS to MG, May 19, 1951, class of 1899, MG Papers, WCA. Mary Case also remained optimistic. See "Excerpts from a Round Robin Letter Written by Miss Case to Former Students of One of Her Classes," Aug. 16, 1940, Unprocessed MSC Papers, WCA.

23. VDS, "A Pedagogic Sunset," in *The Privilege of Age: Essays Secular and Spiritual*, 87–88.

24. SH to MG, 1942(?), class of 1899, MG Papers, WCA. In 1954, Emily Greene Balch also underscored that her inner life was "fed by the comradeship and inspi-

ration of others" (Mercedes M. Randall, *Improper Bostonian: Emily Greene Balch* (New York: Twayne, 1964), 432.

25. VDS, *On Journey*, 57, 212–13, and entire section. For a good general discussion, see John C. Burnham, "The Progressive Era Revolution in American Attitudes toward Sex," in *Paths into American Culture: Psychology, Medicine, and Morals* (Philadelphia: Temple University Press, 1988), 150–69.

26. Jane Addams, *The Second Twenty Years at Hull-House: September 1909 to September 1929* (New York: Macmillan, 1930), 197–98.

27. Jeannette Bailey Cheek, class of 1928, interview with author, June 20, 1980.

28. VDS, *On Journey*, 426–28, 430. A typical scathing psychological attack on feminist and professional women is Ferdinand Lundberg and Marynia F. Farnham, *Modern Woman: The Lost Sex* (New York: Harper and Bros., 1947), esp. "The Psychopathology of Feminism," 159–67.

29. Balch defined old age as the "cooling-off period of life"; EGB, "Old Age," in *Vignettes in Prose* (Philadelphia: Women's International League for Peace and Freedom, 1952), 41. Randall, *Improper Bostonian*, 443, 427, 433, 431–433; Balch saw change as "the very essence of life!" (432).

30. Margaret Sherwood's semiautobiographical novel is entitled *Pilgrim Feet* (Wakefield, Mass.: Montrose Press, 1949). The description of the Scudder household is from a typed letter written by Mrs. Anna Willcox Dwight for Jean Glasscock, ed., *Wellesley College*, filed with Unprocessed MAW Papers, WCA.

31. VDS to MG, Dec. 21 (1936), ALS, WCA; VDS to MG (1931), ALS, WCA; VDS, *On Journey*, 404. Sherwood, as quoted in Dorothy Cochlin McCann, "Margaret Pollock Sherwood: 1864–1955," *WAM* 40, no. 2 (Jan. 1956): 99; see also SH, "Expanding Discernment," in "When Teaching Stops . . . ," ed. Josephine Batchelder, *WAM* 30, no. 3 (Feb. 1946): 181–82.

32. Julia Adams Lacey to Stephanie Welch, June 27, 1979 (letter regarding MSC), Archives Donor File, WCA; see also Mary Case's 1940 address to her classmates, "The Functions of Old Age" (written for the fifty-first reunion of the class of 1889), 2, class of 1889, records, reunions, general (1889–1952), WCA; Mary Katharine Britton Henderson, TOI-CNH, 5, WCA.

33. MSC, "The Last Victory," n.d., MSC FBF, WCA.

34. Mary Katharine Britton Henderson, TOI-CNH, 5, WCA; Anna Mathiesen, "Mary Sophia Case: 1854–1953," *WAM* 37, no. 5 (July 1953): 308–09.

35. "Vermont Woman, 96, on Trip to England," *Boston Herald*, Aug. 19, 1951, EKK FBF, WCA.

36. MPS to EKK, Dec. 2, 1945. EKK Papers, WCA; VDS to JM, July 9, 1939, ALS, WCA; MHS to JM, Aug. 20, 1953, ALS, WCA. For a larger literary frame of analysis, see Anne M. Wyatt-Brown and Janice Rossen, *Aging and Gender in Literature: Studies in Creativity* (Charlottesville: University Press of Virginia, 1993).

37. Florence Converse, *Wellesley College: A Chronicle of the Years 1875–1938* (Wellesley, Mass.: Hathaway House, 1939), 258; VDS, "The Privileges of a College Teacher," *WAM* 11, no. 6 (Aug. 1927): 327.

38. KLB to EKK, July 16, 1921, EKK Papers, WCA; LMH to CH, June 7, 1935, ALS, WCA.

39. VDS to LMH, Good Friday (Mar. 29, 1929), ALS, WCA; see also CH, "To K.L.B.," *WAM* 10, no. 1 (Oct. 1925): 14.

16

Eden's End?

Epigraphs: MMH, "Segregation and the Women's Colleges," *American Journal of Sociology* 43 (July 1937): 18; and Mary McCarthy, "The Vassar Girl," in *The Humanist in the Bathtub: Selected Essays from Mary McCarthy's Theatre Chronicles, 1937–1962, and on the Contrary* (New York: Signet, 1964), 64.

1. MMH, "A Reasoned Choice: The College of Liberal Arts," *Inaugural Address* (Wellesley, Mass.: Wellesley College, 1936), 1–2, WCA.

2. MMH, "Segregation and the Women's Colleges," 18, 20. A 1928 alumna admitted that although single women faculty were still revered, she and her classmates wanted more men on the faculty: "We thought something was wrong in the larger sense to education and life if we didn't see or talk to men. Something was missing" (Jeannette Bailey Cheek, interview with author, June 20, 1980).

3. Nancy F. Cott states that women "joined in a pervasively duplicitous discourse" when they argued that profound sex differences existed between men and women in private yet were absent or irrelevant in public, where women wanted equality with men. Nancy F. Cott, *The Grounding of American Feminism* (New Haven: Yale University Press, 1989), 279.

4. MBT, Apr. 20, 1916, WCA.

5. KLB to MPS, June 10, 1916, Unprocessed MPS Papers, WCA.

6. MMH, TOI-CNH, 13, WCA; MMH, "The Faculty Member as a Cultural Force in the College," address delivered to the Association of American Colleges, Louisville, Jan. 11–13, 1939, 5, MMH Unpublished Speeches, Unprocessed MMH Papers, WCA.

7. MMH, "Faculty Member," 5; Elisabeth Hodder, 1952 Alumnae Questionnaire, FBF, WCA.

8. Lillian Faderman, *Odd Girls and Twilight Lovers: A History of Lesbian Life in Twentieth-Century America* (New York: Columbia University Press, 1991), 94; Christina Simmons, "Companionate Marriage and the Lesbian Threat," *Frontiers: A Journal of Women's Studies* 4 (Fall 1979): 54–56. John D'Emilio calls this the "new lesbian taboo" (D'Emilio, "Not a Simple Matter: Gay History and Gay Historians," *Journal of American History* 76, no. 2 [Sept. 1989]: 440).

9. MMH, "Faculty Member," 4–5. On the diminished tolerance for deviancy in the social behavior of academic women, see Patricia Albjerg Graham, "Expansion and Exclusion: A History of Women in American Higher Education," *Signs* 3, no. 4 (Summer 1978): 759–73.

10. Lucy Killough, TOI-CNH, 20, WCA.

11. One can trace the increase in the number of men on the faculty from statistical data in the president's office files. There were 20.6 men as full-time faculty in 1948–49 and 76 men in 1965–66 (table on Instructing Staff [1948–49], memo, D. Drescher to H. Anderson, Nov. 4, 1965, Officers of Instruction and Govern-

ment; table on Instructing Staff [Oct. 1952–Oct. 1964], Statistics Folders, President's Office Files, WCA; this document contains statistics on the percentage of married people on the faculty); Jessie Bernard, *Academic Women* (New York: New American Library, 1974); Willystine Goodsell, "The Educational Opportunities of American Women—Theoretical and Actual," *Annals of the American Academy of Political and Social Science* 143 (May 1929): 12. The preference for male professors in science is discussed by Margaret W. Rossiter, *Women Scientists in America: Struggles and Strategies to 1940* (Baltimore: Johns Hopkins University Press, 1982). Between 1930 and 1960 the percentage of men at Wellesley rose steadily, albeit unevenly across academic areas: in language and literature, from 6 percent (1930) to 26 percent (1960); in math and science, from 9 to 17 percent; in social sciences and history, from 29 to 59 percent; and in art and music, from 22 to 59 percent (Bernard, *Academic Women,* 54). Women represent about 60 percent of the current Wellesley faculty, exceeding other women's colleges.

12. Edward V. Gulick, "Edward Ely Curtis," *WAM* 55, no. 2 (Winter 1971): 29, Curtis FBF, WCA.

13. Horton learned of this club when her husband, Douglas, was asked to join (MMH, TOI-CNH, 12, WCA).

14. MMH, TOI-CNH, 11, WCA. The goal of her administration was to have 25 percent of the faculty male. Lucy Wilson, who had been a dean, recalled that the percentage of men on the faculty was discussed, particularly when it reached 31 percent. There was some feeling that men didn't work as hard in terms of committee work or "odd things in addition to teaching." Wilson did not necessarily share this perception (Lucy Wilson, TOI-CNH, 31, WCA). Leland H. Jenks felt that as a junior faculty male he "never got praised for anything." When he eventually become the chair of sociology, he had to mediate between women faculty who "did not jibe." Jenks felt he was treated fairly in terms of salary, but he considered Wellesley "dull" because there were so many women faculty (Leland Jenks, TOI-CNH, 10–15, WCA). In 1945, a planning committee of the Wellesley trustees reported the desire for a higher proportion of men on the faculty; therefore, increased inducements such as higher salaries, better housing, and modern research facilities were requested (Memorandum for Meeting of Executive, Building, and Postwar Planning Committees of the Trustees, Nov. 13, 1945, President's Office, WCA). In 1946, the Alumnae Council criticized the "undue number of Wellesley graduates on the faculty," adding "they should like to have more men" (Report to the Academic Council of the Meetings of the Alumnae Council, Feb. 8–11, 1946, 4, Academic Council, Minutes, 1944–46, WCA).

15. Henry Noble MacCracken, *The Hickory Limb* (New York: Scribner's, 1950), 66.

16. Dorothy Kenyon, "The Presidency of Mount Holyoke College," *Journal of the American Association of University Women* 30, no. 1 (Oct. 1936): 16–17. In 1992, Harvard picked another man, Neil Rudenstine, as president. Mount Holyoke has a woman president, Elizabeth Kennon. The University of Pennsylvania has become the first Ivy League university to be headed by a woman, Judith Rodin (William H. Honan, "Woman Is Penn President: The First in the Ivy League,"

New York Times, Dec. 7, 1993, A8). Nannerl H. Keohane, Wellesley's former president, is now president of Duke University (Denise K. Magner, "A 'Risk' Worth Taking," *Chronicle of Higher Education*, Nov. 10, 1993, A16–A17).

17. Marjorie Hope Nicholson, Oral History Interview #10, conducted by John Wieler, May 16, 1975, 273, copies of transcripts, Marjorie Hope Nicholson Papers, SCA. Nicholson makes clear that the Smith women faculty were sensitive to and complained of this policy of giving men more opportunities (Nicholson, 282); Myra M. Sampson, covering letter to Mary D. Murdock, archivist of Smith College, Sept. 25, 1970, attached to "A Report Important to the Future of Smith College: The Status of Women Faculty in Academic Departments in Smith College in 1969–70"; "The Status of Women Faculty in the Academic Departments of Smith College, Aug. 18, 1966; "Faculty of Smith College, 1875–1966"; "A Study of the Teaching Faculty of Smith College, 1956–57," Myra M. Sampson Papers, SCA. At Vassar, Sarah Blanding also favored hiring married men (Sarah Blanding, Oral History Interview, 137, CUL). In 1935, M. Carey Thomas lamented that she had not promoted more women scholars to the Bryn Mawr faculty. Humiliated by the few rewards offered to women scholars, she said: "We had not provided them with the straw with which to make bricks" (address by President Emeritus M. Carey Thomas, Nov. 2, 1935, *Bryn Mawr College Fiftieth Anniversary, November First and Second, 1935* [Bryn Mawr, Penn.: n.p., 1935], 54).

18. Radcliffe College, Committee on Graduate Education for Women, *Graduate Education for Women: The Radcliffe Ph.D.* (Cambridge: Harvard University Press, 1956), 25–39. The percentage of women faculty at selected women's colleges drastically declined from 1940 to 1960. At Smith the percentage dropped from 58.3 to 43.5; at Bryn Mawr, from 51.8 to 34.4; at Vassar, from 70.0 to 53; at Goucher, from 72.1 to 47.8; and at Wellesley, from 90.1 to 62.8 (adapted from Jessie Bernard, *Academic Women*, table 3/4, p. 55).

19. Virginia Crocheron Gildersleeve, *Many a Good Crusade: Memoirs* (New York: Macmillan, 1954), 108–09. This attitude is exemplified by Dr. Carl Binger, a resident psychiatrist at Vassar, who, concerned about the "sexual developments of undergraduates in an atmosphere of supervision by matriarchy," resigned, complaining that there were "too many unmarried women at Vassar in supervisory capacities." Binger's attack on Vassar is reported in Anne MacKay, ed., *Wolf Girls at Vassar: Gay and Lesbian Experiences, 1930–1990* (New York: Ten Percent, 1992), ix.

20. Gildersleeve, *Many a Good Crusade*, 109. Mabel Newcomer concluded her 1959 classic, *A Century of Higher Education for American Women*, with the plea that "more opportunities must be available to women on university faculties and in research institutions" (Mabel Newcomer, *A Century of Higher Education for American Women* [New York: Harper and Bros., 1959], 255). Newcomer admitted, however, that as an undergraduate she took pride in avoiding women professors (244).

21. John D'Emilio, *Sexual Politics, Sexual Communities: The Making of a Homosexual Minority in the United States, 1940–1970* (Chicago: University of Chicago Press,

1983); Donna Penn, "The Meanings of Lesbianism in Post-War America," *Gender and History* 3, no. 2 (Summer 1991): 190–203.

22. Bernard, *Academic Women,* 43; in fact, women's share of doctorates did not fall by more than 1 percent from the peak in 1928 until the 1940s. The decline was not dramatic until the early 1950s. On an absolute basis, the number of academically prepared women rose from 1920 through 1940 (Susan Boslego Carter, "Academic Women Revisited: An Empirical Study of Changing Patterns in Women's Employment as College and University Faculty, 1890–1963," *Journal of Social History* 14 (Summer 1981): 675–92); Frank Stricker, "Cookbooks and Law-books: The Hidden History of Career Women in Twentieth-Century America," *Journal of Social History* 10 (Fall 1976): 1–19; Elaine Tyler May, *Homeward Bound: American Families in the Cold War Era* (New York: Basic, 1988).

23. Faye Wilson, TOI-CNH, 1–2; Margaret Ball, TOI-CNH, 10, WCA. On the obstacles that women historians faced, see Jacqueline Goggin, "Challenging Sexual Discrimination in the Historical Profession: Women Historians and the American Historical Association, 1890–1940," *American Historical Review* 97, no. 3 (June 1992): 769–802; Joan Wallach Scott, "American Women Historians, 1884–1984," in *Gender and the Politics of History,* ed. Scott (New York: Columbia University Press, 1988), 178–98; Anne Firor Scott, ed., *Unheard Voices: The First Historians of Southern Women* (Charlottesville: University of Virginia Press, 1993); Judith P. Zinsser, *History and Feminism. A Glass Half Full: The Impact of Feminism on the Arts and Sciences* (New York: Twayne, 1993); Gerda Lerner, "A View from the Women's Side," *Journal of American History* 76, no. 2 (Sept. 1989): 446–59; Barbara Sicherman, "Looking Forward/Looking Back," *Journal of Women's History* 4, no. 3 (Winter 1993): 137–40.

24. Cott, *The Grounding of American Feminism,* 234. Many women, however, never bought the merit myth. In *Graduate Education for Women* (Radcliffe College), several saw the discrimination. One woman stated: "University teaching is still a man's game." Another noted that "I, like many other women who take their jobs seriously, would have been offered jobs in universities, had I been a man. Indirectly, this absence of offers interferes with a woman's rise in the academic world both from a professional and financial point of view" (30).

25. E.g., Professor Salome Waelsch asked her mentor why, despite an uninterrupted and highly productive scientific career at Columbia, she remained a research associate while men were climbing the academic ladder. "He told me there was no chance for advancement for me." She understood that "my femaleness was responsible" (Salome Waelsch, as quoted in Harriet Zuckerman, Jonathan R. Cole, and John T. Bruer, eds., *The Outer Circle: Women in the Scientific Community* [New York: Norton, 1991], 82–84). "A Jew, a Woman and Still a Scientist," *New York Times,* Feb. 6, 1993, 25.

26. President Pendleton, e.g., allowed couples only if they met and married after coming to Wellesley. Mary Coolidge, a Wellesley dean, revealed this policy in a response to Berenice Cronkhite (Oct. 20, 1954, Office of the Graduate Dean, Record Group 4, box 2, Alumnae Letters, RCA).

27. Betty Friedan, *The Feminine Mystique* (New York: Dell, 1963); Questionnaire for Former Members of the Radcliffe Graduate School, Office of the Graduate Dean, Record Group 4, ser. 4, box 4, RCA. Eighty-four women who had started graduate school between 1950 and 1962 offered painful but illuminating replies. The anonymity of respondents has been protected.

28. Respondents to the Questionnaire for Former Members of the Radcliffe Graduate School, Office of the Graduate Dean, Record Group 4, ser. 4, box 4, RCA.

29. Ibid.; "Highlights of the Discussion of Re-Educating College Women for College Teaching," AAUW, July 27, 1959; Eleanor Dolan to Dean J. Peter Elder, Harvard Graduate School of Arts and Sciences, Dec. 9, 1959. See, too, his response of Dec. 18, 1959, Office of the Graduate Dean, Record Group 4, ser. 2, box 2, RCA.

30. Ann Sutherland Harris, "The Second Sex in Academe," *BAAUP* 56, no. 3 (1970): 283–95; Nayda Aisenberg and Mona Harrington, *Women of Academe: Outsiders in the Sacred Grove* (Amherst: University of Massachusetts Press, 1988). Despite the modern women's movement, "academic women continue to find themselves uncomfortable in the academy" (Linda K. Kerber, "Afterword," *Personal Lives and Professional Careers: The Uneasy Balance* [College Park, Md.: Report of the Women's Committee of the American Studies Association, 1989], 30); Shirley M. Tilghman, "Science vs. Women: A Radical Solution," *New York Times,* Jan. 26, 1993, A23; and Anthony DePalma, "Rare in Ivy League: Women Who Work as Full Professors," *New York Times,* Jan. 24, 1993, 1, 23. In 1992, Caroline G. Heilbrun took early retirement from Columbia University, concluding with disgust: "Columbia will continue to be run by male professors who behave like little boys saying 'This is our secret treehouse club, no girls allowed'" (Anne Matthews, "Rage in a Tenured Position," *New York Times,* Nov. 8, 1992, 47).

31. Mary McCarthy, "The Vassar Girl," 63.

32. Liz Schneider blamed Bryn Mawr for abjuring its feminist premises and doing little to advance the cause of women's liberation (Schneider, "Our Failures Only Marry: Bryn Mawr and the Failure of Feminism," in *Woman in Sexist Society: Studies in Power and Powerlessness,* ed. Vivian Gornick and Barbara K. Moran [New York: Basic, 1971], 419–35); Nora Ephron, "Reunion," in *Crazy Salad: Some Things about Women* (New York: Bantam, 1975), 28–36. Ironically, Ephron confirmed that the beacon of scholarship was kept alive at Wellesley by "a group of elderly spinsters who believed that the only valuable role for Wellesley graduates was to go on to the only life the deans knew anything about—graduate school scholarship, teaching" (30). Ephron felt that the model for her generation was either this celibate or the housewife. In *Reinventing Womanhood* (New York: Norton, 1979), Carolyn G. Heilbrun also criticized Wellesley for ignoring career women and their problems in favor of those "graduates who pursued domestic or volunteer careers with a besotted devotion to ladylike attitudes" (18). In a more recent essay Heilbrun has noted that "many women . . . still prefer to attend all-women colleges. This has a great deal to do with the life of the mind" (Heilbrun, "The Politics of Mind: Women, Tradition and the University," in *Gender in the*

Classroom: Power and Pedagogy, ed. Susan L. Gabriel and Isaiah Smithson [Urbana: University of Illinois Press, 1990], 30).

33. Pepper Schwartz and Janet Lever, "Women in the Male World of Higher Education," in *Academic Women on the Move*, ed. Alice S. Rossi and Ann Calderwood (New York: Russell Sage Foundation, 1973), 66.

34. Dale Spender, *Women of Ideas, and What Men Have Done to Them: From Alphra Behn to Adrienne Rich* (London: Routledge and Kegan Paul, 1982); Berenice A. Carroll, "The Politics of 'Originality': Women and the Class System of the Intellect," *Journal of Women's History* 2, no. 2 [Fall 1990]: 136–63); Margaret W. Rossiter, "The ~~Matthew~~ Matilda Effect in Science," *Social Studies of Science* 23 (1993): 325–41 (Rossiter has coined the term "Matilda effect" to describe the lack of recognition accorded talented women.); Gerda Lerner, *The Creation of a Feminist Consciousness: From the Middle Ages to 1870* (New York: Oxford, 1993); Linda K. Kerber, *Women of the Republic: Intellect and Ideology in Revolutionary America* (Chapel Hill: University of North Carolina Press, 1980), 198–229.

35. See Rosalind Rosenberg, *Beyond Separate Spheres: Intellectual Roots of Modern Feminism* (New Haven: Yale University Press, 1982); Clarke A. Chambers concludes that when professional women traded their women-centered networks for the seemingly neutral bureaucratic model, they lost ground. According to Chambers, "they left behind styles and structures that had sustained and strengthened them in an earlier generation." Without their separate social space where they had lived and worked together, morale declined and "thus dissipated the strength that had come from common engagement and experience" (Chambers, "Women in the Creation of the Profession of Social Work," *Social Service Review* [Mar. 1986]: 23).

36. E.g., Mary Jo Deegan has recently appraised Katharine Coman and Emily Balch as pioneer sociologists, in "Sociology at Wellesley College, 1900–1919," *Journal of the History of Sociology* 6 (Dec. 1983): 91–115. See also Deegan, *Jane Addams and the Men of the Chicago School, 1892–1918* (New Brunswick, N.J.: Transaction, 1990); Melinda M. Ponder, "Katharine Lee Bates as Hawthorne Critic and Scholar," *Nathanial Hawthorne Review* 16, no. 1 (1990): 6–11; Ponder is working on a literary biography of Bates. The spiritual roots and the model of Scudder's and Balch's social reform ethos and activism are examined by Catherine A. Faver, "Feminist Spirituality and Social Reform: Examples from the Early Twentieth Century," *Women's Studies Quarterly* 21, nos. 1–2 (Winter 1993): 90–105.

37. For criticisms of the women's colleges for being citadels of domesticity, see Sheila Rothman, *Woman's Proper Place: A History of Changing Ideals and Practices, 1870 to the Present* (New York: Basic, 1978), 106–09; Roberta Frankfort, *Domesticity and Career in Turn-of-the-Century America* (New York: New York University Press, 1977). Margaret W. Rossiter, in *Women Scientists in America*, demonstrates that as late as 1938 Wellesley led the way in employing the greatest number of women scientists starred for the most distinguished achievement in *American Men of Science*. Louise L. Stevenson refutes the assumption that Yale was a backwater "old-time college" in the 1840s (Stevenson, "Between the Old-Time College and the

Modern University: Noah Porter and the New Haven Scholars," *History of Higher Education Annual* 3 [1983]: 39–57).

38. Peter Novick, *That Noble Dream: "The Objectivity Question" and the American Historical Profession* (Cambridge: Cambridge University Press, 1988); Mary O. Furner, *Advocacy and Objectivity: A Crisis in the Professionalization of American Social Science, 1865–1905* (Lexington: University Press of Kentucky, 1975).

39. In the late 1960s and early 1970s many women complained of being made to conform to a male career path. See Arlie Russell Hochschild, "Inside the Clockwork of Male Careers," in *Women and the Power to Change*, ed. Florence Howe (New York: McGraw-Hill, 1975), 47–80. Several feminist British scholars have argued that women's control of their reproductive capacities is a determinant of their liberation from the patriarchy. See Juliet Mitchell, "Four Structures in a Complex Unity," in *Liberating Women's History: Theoretical and Critical Essays*, ed. Berenice A. Carroll (Urbana: University of Illinois Press, 1976), 385–400; Shulamith Firestone, *The Dialectic of Sex: The Case for Feminist Revolution* (New York: Bantam, 1970); Sheila Rowbotham, *Women, Resistance and Revolution: A History of Women and Revolution in the Modern World* (New York: Vintage, 1972); Sheila Jeffreys, *The Spinster and Her Enemies: Feminism and Sexuality, 1880–1930* (London: Pandora, 1985); see also Gerda Lerner, *The Majority Finds Its Past: Placing Women in History* (New York: Oxford University Press, 1979).

40. EM, Faculty Questionnaire, Sept. 1946, FBF, WCA.

41. Mary Beard, *Woman as Force in History* (New York: Collier, 1946).

42. Penina Migdal Glazer and Miriam Slater, *Unequal Colleagues: The Entrance of Women into the Professions, 1890–1940* (New Brunswick: Rutgers University Press, 1987). More compelling is the framework of opportunity, discrimination, and compromise offered by Diana Long Hall when analyzing the careers of the women scientists at Chicago (Hall, "Academics, Bluestockings, and Biologists: Women at the University of Chicago, 1892–1932," *Annals of the New York Academy of Sciences* 323 (1979): 300–20.

43. Jean B. Quandt, *From the Small Town to the Great Community: The Social Thought of Progressive Intellectuals* (New Brunswick: Rutgers University Press, 1970).

44. Susan Ware, *Partner and I: Molly Dewson, Feminism, and New Deal Politics* (New Haven: Yale University Press, 1987); Robyn Muncy, *Creating a Female Dominion: American Reform, 1890–1935* (New York: Oxford University Press, 1991).

45. The literature on women's studies is vast. For a good overview see Elizabeth Minnich, Jean O'Barr, and Rachel Rosenfeld, eds., *Reconstructing the Academy: Women's Education and Women's Studies* (Chicago: University of Chicago Press, 1988); Susan L. Gabriel and Isaiah Smithson, eds., *Gender in the Classroom: Power and Pedagogy* (Urbana: University of Illinois Press, 1990); Leslie Miller-Bernal, "Single-Sex versus Coeducational Environments: A Comparison of Women Students' Experiences at Four Colleges," *American Journal of Education* 102, no. 1 (Nov. 1993): 23–54. On the contemporary feminist approaches to the issue of caring, see Nel Noddings, *Caring: A Feminine Approach to Ethics and Moral Education* (Berkeley: University of California, 1984).

46. An innovative book that looks at architecture to determine the configuration of women's culture is Helen Lefkowitz Horowitz, *Alma Mater: Design and Experience in the Women's Colleges from Their Nineteenth-Century Beginnings to the 1930s* (New York: Knopf, 1984); Lynn D. Gordon creatively considers a number of popular culture themes in *Gender and Higher Education in the Progressive Era* (New Haven: Yale University Press, 1990).

47. Estelle Freedman, "Separatism as Strategy: Female Institution Building and American Feminism, 1870–1930," *Feminist Studies* 15, no. 3 (Fall 1979): 514–15. Carroll Smith-Rosenberg connects the decline of feminism with the demise of "this rich and vital world of women-identified women," in Ellen Dubois, Mari Jo Buhle, Temma Kaplan, Gerda Lerner, and Carroll Smith-Rosenberg, "Politics and Culture in Women's History: A Symposium," *Feminist Studies* 6, no. 1 (Spring 1980): 63. Several contemporary feminist scholars seek to restore the power of women's friendships. See, e.g., Mary E. Hunt, *Fierce Tenderness: A Feminist Theology of Friendship* (New York: Crossroad Press, 1992); Janice G. Raymond, *A Passion for Friends: Toward a Philosophy of Female Affection* (Boston: Beacon Press, 1986).

48. Hugh Hawkins, *Pioneer: A History of the Johns Hopkins University, 1874–1889* (Ithaca: Cornell University Press, 1960), 237. Virtually without exception, historians have seen the research university as an advance over the liberal arts college. This view understates the costs of the research university, while at the same time it belittles the benefits of some liberal arts colleges. To assess accurately the relative merits and costs of each educational institution, we need to accord greater value to community. James McLachlan reviews and criticizes standard historical accounts of the "old-time" liberal arts college in "The American College in the Nineteenth Century: Toward a Reappraisal," *Teachers College Record* 80 (Dec. 1978): 287–306; Roger L. Williams, "The Not-So-Old-Time College," *History of Higher Education Annual* 12 (1992): 105–12.

49. On the subject of community, see Maurice Stern, *The Eclipse of Community* (Princeton: Princeton University Press, 1960). For a revisionist approach to the notion that community has declined in the United States, see Thomas Bender, *Community and Social Change in America* (New Brunswick: Rutgers University Press, 1978). On male intellectuals of the 1920s and 1930s and the ethos of communitarianism, see Casey Nelson Blake, *Beloved Community: The Cultural Criticism of Randolf Bourne, Van Wyck Brooks, Waldo Frank, and Lewis Mumford* (Chapel Hill: University of North Carolina Press, 1990). For over twenty-five years, sociologists, political scientists, and philosophers have been criticizing American individualism and fragmentation and calling for a renewal of the ethos of community; see, e.g., Philip E. Slater, *The Pursuit of Loneliness: American Culture at the Breaking Point* (Boston: Beacon Press, 1970); Robert N. Bellah et al., *Habits of the Heart: Individualism and Commitment in American Life* (New York: Harper and Row, 1985); Charles Taylor, *The Ethics of Authenticity* (Cambridge: Harvard University Press, 1992); Amitai Etzioni, *The Spirit of Community: Rights, Responsibilities, and the Communitarian Agenda* (New York: Crown, 1993). Women's unique

role in community building is focused upon in Gerda Lerner, "The Majority Finds Its Past," in *The Majority Finds Its Past*, 160–67; Anne Firor Scott, *Natural Allies: Women's Associations in American History* (Urbana: University of Illinois Press, 1991); Elizabeth Fox-Genovese, *Feminism without Illusions: A Critique of Individualism* (Chapel Hill: University of North Carolina Press, 1991).

Select Manuscript Collections

Bowdoin College Archives, Brunswick, Maine
    Charles Burnham Shackford, class of 1863, Alumni Biographical File
Bryn Mawr College Archives, Bryn Mawr, Pa.
    Emily Greene Balch Alumnae Bio-Files
    Class of 1889 Commencement Program
    Class of 1889 Reunion Files
Columbia University, Rare Book and Manuscript Library, New York, New York
    James McKeen Cattell Papers
Cornell University Libraries, Division of Rare Books and Manuscript Collections, Ithaca,
    New York
    Alumni Records
    Sarah Blanding, Oral History Interview
    Graduate School Records
    Mary Alice Willcox Family History (filed with Walter F. Willcox Papers)
    Women Graduates' Association Records
Dartmouth College Archives, Hanover, N.H.
    Samuel Gilman Brown Manuscripts (correspondence and manuscripts)
FBI Records, U.S. Department of Justice, Washington, D.C.
    Emily Greene Balch File
    Vida Dutton Scudder File
Harvard University Archives, Cambridge, Mass.
    Henry Durant Biographical File
    George Herbert Palmer Biographical File
    Quinquennial Catalogue of Harvard University, 1636–1930
Houghton Library, Harvard University, Cambridge, Mass.
    Katharine Lee Bates Papers
    Thomas Wentworth Higginson Papers
    Horace Scudder Papers
The Johns Hopkins University, Milton Eisenhower Library, Special Collections, Baltimore,
    Md.
    Sidney Sherwood Letters (includes a Margaret Pollock Sherwood letter)
MIT Museum Historical Collections, Cambridge, Mass.
    Betsy T. Capen Biographical File
Mount Holyoke College Archives, South Hadley, Mass.
    Cornelia Lee Bates (Alumnae File, class of 1845)
    Louise Rogers Jewett Papers
    President's Reports
    Mary Emma Woolley Papers
Oberlin College Archives, Oberlin, Ohio
    Alumni Records

College General, Class Letters

John Morgan Papers

Ohio State University Archives, Columbus, Ohio

Caroline Breyfogle Biographical File

Radcliffe College Archives, Cambridge, Mass.

Alumnae Biographical Files

Graduate Dean's Papers

Graduate Records

Rhode Island College, James P. Adams Library, Providence, R.I.

Caroline Hazard Papers (filed with Nathaniel Terry Bacon Papers)

The Arthur and Elizabeth Schlesinger Library on the History of Women in America, Radcliffe College, Cambridge, Mass.

Belle Sherwin Papers

Erin-Go-Bragh Records

Molly Dewson Papers

Morgan-Howes Family Papers (Ethel Dench Puffer Howes Papers)

Vineyard Shore School Records

Smith College Archives, Northampton, Mass.

Beginnings of Smith College (folio of documents assembled by John M. Greene)

Mary Byrd Faculty Biographical File

Bessie Capen Faculty Biographical File

Class Files

Ethel Dench Puffer (Howes) Faculty Biographical File

Institute for the Coordination of Women's Interests Records

Myra M. Sampson Papers

The Society of the Companions of the Holy Cross, Adelynrood, Byfield, Mass.

Records of the Society

Sophia Smith Collection, Smith College, Northampton, Mass.

College Settlements Association Records

Vida Dutton Scudder Papers

Stanford University Archives, Stanford University Libraries, Stanford, Calif.

History Department Records

Clelia Mosher Papers

University Course Listings

Swarthmore College Peace Collection, Swarthmore, Pa.

Emily Greene Balch Papers

Katharine Coman Letters

Mercedes Randall Papers

University of Arizona, Phoenix, Ariz.

Frances Melville Perry Biographical File

University of California, The Bancroft Library, Berkeley, Calif.

Mary Roberts Smith Coolidge Papers (filed with Dane Coolidge Papers)

University of Chicago, Joseph Regenstein Library, Department of Special Collections, Chicago, Ill.

Sophonisba Breckenridge Manuscript Autobiography
Graduate Records
Marion Talbot Papers (includes Alice Freeman Palmer Papers)
University of Michigan, Michigan Historical Collections, Bentley Historical Library, Ann Arbor, Mich.
Alumni Records
Catalogs of Courses
Eliza Mosher Papers
Alice Freeman Palmer Papers (undergraduate records and correspondence)
President's Report
Mary Alice Williams Papers
University of Pennsylvania, The University Archives, Philadelphia, Pa.
Caroline Burling Thompson Biographical File
Vassar College Libraries, Special Collections, Poughkeepsie, New York
Alumnae Materials
Faculty Materials
Helen Lockwood Papers (includes Vineyard Shore School Records)
Maria Mitchell Papers
Lucy Salmon Papers
Wellesley College Archives, Wellesley, Mass.
Academic Council and Committees
Agora Society Records
ALS File
Alumnae Autobiographical File
Board of Trustees
Bureau of Occupations
Centennial Historian: Oral History Interviews
Records of Classes (including papers of the following students)
Ruth Bradford, class of 1905
Clara Capron, class of 1887
Grace Coyle, class of 1914
Mary Barnett Gilson, class of 1899
Lucia Grieve, class of 1883
Carrie Park Harrington, class of 1883
Frances Robinson Johnson, class of 1879
Florence Floyd Merriam, class of 1885
Dorothy Walton, class of 1915
Zella Wentz, class of 1905
College Government
College Hall Fire
Department Histories and Records
Faculty Biographical Files
Faculty Members' Papers
Katharine Lee Bates Papers

Ellen Burrell Papers
Mary Whiton Calkins Papers
Mary Sophia Case Papers
Katharine Coman Papers
Margaret C. Ferguson Papers
Sophie Jewett Papers
Elizabeth K. Kendall Papers
Eliza Hall Kendrick Papers
Louise Sherwood McDowell Papers
Elizabeth Manwaring Papers
Louise McCoy North Papers
Margaret Pollock Sherwood Papers
Sarah Frances Whiting Papers
Mary Alice Willcox Papers
Faculty Publications File
Financial Records (including faculty payroll ledgers)
Founders Papers (Henry and Pauline Durant)
Eben Horsford Papers
Microscopical Society
Phonograph Collection
President's Office Files
President's Papers:
Margaret Clapp Papers
Caroline Hazard Papers
Mildred McAfee Horton Papers
Ada Howard Papers
Alice Freeman Palmer Papers
Ellen Fitz Pendleton Papers
Records of Student Societies
Treasurer's Office
Wellesley College Publications
Annals
Bylaws and Articles of Government of the College
Catalog of Courses
Circulars
Courant
Legenda
1942 Record Number of the Wellesley College Bulletin
Prelude
President's Reports
Wellesley Alumnae Magazine
Wellesley College News
Wills

World War I Records
   Mobilization Committee
   Patriotic Service Committee
Yale University Library, Manuscripts and Archives, New Haven, Conn.
   Graduate School Registrar Records

Acknowledgments

This book began as three themes scribbled on the back of a napkin handed to me by my friend George H. Ropes during a conversation we were having at a restaurant in Cambridge, Massachusetts. Since then, he has continued to offer challenges, criticism, advice, and consolation; even with his work in world hunger, he has taken time to edit several drafts of the manuscript. It is to him that I owe my greatest debt.

I wish to thank Barbara Sicherman for years of fruitful conversations about women's history and for her critical readings of this manuscript at several stages of its evolution. She also suggested the title. Patricia Albjerg Graham first encouraged me to write a book on academic women. Joseph Featherstone inspired me to attempt to write gracefully about community; equally welcome has been his friendship. Peter Filene probably does not remember his prompt and helpful letter when I initiated my research on professional women, but I do. Stephen Clement first told me that Wellesley had several single academic women to study. William Chafe just retitled and reissued *The American Woman,* but I will forever recall reaching for my original edition to reflect on his analysis of the cultural conditions that account for the rise and disappearance of the pioneering women scholars of the Progressive Era. Jessie Bernard's *Academic Women* challenged me as well.

Chuck Grench, my editor at Yale University Press, believed in this book and never flagged in his commitment to publish it. His faith in me, expressed with warm wit when my spirits sank and gentle but firm guidance, has made all the difference. Karen Gangel, my manuscript editor, strengthened the manuscript with her superb skills and kept in contact with me during its final preparation, when I was involved in moving to Denison University.

Many scholars took the time to comment on this work during its development. I am particularly grateful to Mary Roth Walsh, who provided me with an entree to Yale University Press, Mary Kelley, Jill Ker Conway, Lynn Gordon, James McLachlan, Susan Ware, Ilene Kantrov, W. Bruce Leslie, and Louise Michele Newman. Comments by Allen F. Davis on an earlier version of the manuscript produced a sensitive and sensible blueprint for changes. Joan Jacobs Brumberg's careful reading of the final draft and expert editorial suggestions were crucial. Margaret Rossiter's pathfinding research and her friendship have been of inestimable value. Ellen Fitzpatrick has encouraged me and provided unparalleled moral support. Gerald Gill has been particularly generous with his time and wise counsel. Others who have helped me clarify and refine my ideas and provided me with a community of discourse, even at a distance, are Carol Hurd Green, Joyce Antler, Rosalind Rosenberg, the late Barbara Miller Solomon, Anne Firor Scott, Susan Carter, Linda Perkins, Burton J. Bledstein, Laurel Furumoto, Marian E. Strobel, Deborah King, Elsa Barkley Brown, Mary Frederickson, Alexander Bloom, Regina Markell Morantz-Sanchez, Elizabeth H. Pleck, Debra Herman, Harold Wechsler, Jennifer Brown, David Levine, Blanche Linden, and Lynda Shaffer. Although we have only just met, over the years Frank Stricker shared with me via mail several of his published and unpublished articles. He also commented on chapter 6. Since graduate school, Sally Schwager and I have been like sisters in search of our mothers' gardens; I thank her for this comradeship, as well as for the insightful comments on several chapters.

I wish that my mother, Mildred Bonagur Palmieri, who died on January 3, 1990, could celebrate with me. She left me a small subsidy to complete my book and an infinitely more important legacy of courage. My father, Patsy J. Palmieri, helped tide me over some rough financial days in order that I might stay in academe. I wish to thank other family who encouraged me over the years, especially my brothers, Ernest and Robert; my cousin Lillian Lanzafame; and my aunt Jo Bonagur. Among the many friends who rendered support are Barbara Flynn, Cathy Ropes and Hardy Ropes, Phil Enns, Honey Weiner and Bill Lott, Vince Dixon, Peggy Darrow, James Wright, Bruce Pipes, Bruce Tucker, Christina Simmons, Joanne J. Meyerowitz, Mark Leff, Ann J. Lane, Barbara Haber, June Namais, Naomi

Miller, Mariam K. Chamberlain, Florence Howe, Terrie Epstein, Mary Tervo, Phil Cerny, Bill Hopkins, Lisa McDonnell, Kay Roberts, Karen Graves, Judith Tyson, George Patrick, Peggy Warren, Cornelia Cremens, Toni Fulginiti, and the Peltsman family.

I have accomplished this collective biography only with the guidance and assistance of a number of archivists. Chief among these is Wilma R. Slaight, Wellesley College archivist; Jean N. Berry, archives assistant at Wellesley, has been extremely helpful as well. The trustees and several presidents of Wellesley, especially Nannerl Keohane, gave me access to restricted documents. I located many manuscripts because of the assistance of a score of other archivists, some of whom I have met and some of whom I know only through correspondence. I am particularly grateful to Jane Knowles at Radcliffe College; Frances Goudy and Nancy S. MacKechnie at Vassar College; Mary Jo Pugh and Nancy Bartlett at the University of Michigan; Maryellen C. Kaminsky at the University of Pennsylvania; Kathleen Jacklin and Elaine Engst at Cornell University; Mary Trott, Margery N. Sly, and Susan Grigg at Smith College; Elaine Trehub at Mount Holyoke; Eva Moseley at the Schlesinger Library; Caroline Rittenhouse at Bryn Mawr; Bernice B. Nichols and Wendy Chmielewski at the Swarthmore College Peace Collection; the late Sally M. Wilson at Rhode Island College; and Phyllis Ball at the University of Arizona. I am deeply indebted as well to Oberlin College, Hamilton College, Bowdoin College, Brown University, Barnard College, Columbia University, Ohio State University, Stanford University, Princeton University, Yale University, Harvard University, Houghton Library, University of Chicago, Johns Hopkins University, University of Kansas, Rollins College, Elmira College, Wilson College, and Dartmouth College, all of which allowed me access to and generous use of their archives. Some local historical societies were also of help, especially the Saratoga County Historical Society, in Ballston Spa, New York, and the Granville Historical Society, in Granville, Ohio. Also of assistance was the Public Library of the City of Dover, New Hampshire. The librarians of Vassar College, Dartmouth College, the University of Cincinnati, Tufts University, Harvard University, and Denison University, especially Emily Hoffmire, have been exceedingly helpful in responding to requests for references and interlibrary loans. Three Wellesley alumnae—Jeannette Bailey Cheek, Sally Loomis, and Dorothy Weeks—granted me valuable personal interviews. Another, Diane Weeks Cavers, class of 1956, commented on a draft and discussed with me the milieu of the college during the 1950s.

During a time of depleting resources for scholars in the humanities and social sciences, I have enjoyed the sponsorship of a number of institutions. For making the research, writing, and publication of this book possible, I thank the Radcliffe Grants to Graduate Women, the Annie Ryder Fellowship of the Boston chapter of the American Association of University Women, the Woodrow Wilson Women's Studies Dissertation Fellowship, the Mary Bunting Institute Summer Fellowship, Vassar College Faculty Grants, Dartmouth College Faculty Grants, Tufts University Faculty Research Grants, the Wellesley College Center for Research on Women, the Center for Women's Studies at the University of Cincinnati, and Harvard University Research Funds for Faculty. The Spencer Foundation gave me a major grant that allowed time off from teaching to do research and writing. Nannerl Keohane and Diana Chapman Walsh provided funds for the photographs in this book through the President's Office at Wellesley College.

Early in the project, I had a special friend and typist par excellence with whom I discussed women's history. Grace Clark died before she could read the final copy, but she provided many crisp corrections, wise amendments, and sparkling wit. John Wing helped me research articles, set up my files, and smiled. Gail Patten, Maryanne Kazanjian, and Cynthia Farr Brown helped computerize the original typed version of the manuscript. Lauri Shorter spiritedly assisted me during the final stage of word processing. Susanmarie Harrington provided outstanding research assistance and subsequent enthusiasm for the project. Lisa Rudman and Janet Raiffa also helped track down arcane articles.

My students at Vassar, Dartmouth, and Tufts, where I have been fortunate to teach not only women's history but seminars in higher educational history, have encouraged me and allowed me to refine many ideas. I wish to thank especially Merle Weiner, Chris Estes Burton, Jenny Weiner, and Andrew Grief. I profited as well from my students and colleagues in the Honors Program in History and Literature at Harvard University; at Bloomfield College I am particularly indebted to Sandra Van Dyk.

The generous financial endowment of the Laura C. Harris Distinguished Visiting Professorship at Denison University, which I held in 1993–94, provided many support services, including a proofreader. I am grateful to President Michele T. Myers; Provost Charles Morris; Amy Gordon, Michael Gordon, and the other members of the history department; Mary Jane Dennison, secretary; and the members of the Women's Studies Program for their collegiality during the crucial last stages of my book. I also wish to thank Paul Elswick for computer support.

Vida Scudder aptly wrote: "The only way to know life is to share life." In becoming an academic, I have met many scholars and editors, several of whom have become good friends. There are, however, many other scholars whom I never met—part of the lost generation—whose careers were cut short owing to the disastrous job market of the last decade and whose dissertations were not published. I have nonetheless benefited from their ideas and labor.

Since the late 1970s, my intellectual life has been challenged and shaped by the history of the successes and setbacks of the Wellesley community of academic women. That my gain shall not remain private but be shared, I wish this book to reconfirm one of my favorite lines of the Tao: "To live in the hearts we leave behind is not to die."

Photo Credits

Unless otherwise noted, all photographs are courtesy of the Wellesley College Archives.

Between pages 54–55:
Alice Freeman Palmer: Photo by McCormick.
President Hazard: Photo by G. L. Abell.
Tree Day: Photo by Partridge.
Katharine Bates: Photo by Pach Bros.
Vida Scudder: Photo by Pach Bros.
Sophie Hart: Photo by Emily Stokes.
Margaret Sherwood: Photo by Partridge.
Sophie Jewett: Photo by Chas. W. Hearn.
Mary Case: Photo by Partridge.
Mary Whiton Calkins: Photo by Partridge.
Eleanor Gamble: Photo by Bachrach.
Katharine Coman: Photo by Notman.
Denison House: Courtesy of the Arthur and Elizabeth Schlesinger Library on the History of Women in America, Radcliffe College.
Sarah Whiting: Photo by Notman.
Caroline Thompson: Photo by Bachrach.
Ellen Pendleton: Photo by Marceau.
Between pages 180–81:
Carla Wenckebach and Margarethe Müller: Photo by Knackstedt and Näther.
Vida Scudder and Florence Converse: Photo by Henry Bowen Brainerd.
The German Table at College Hall: Photo by Seaver.
Biology class of Mary Alice Willcox: Photo by Seaver.
Martha Hale Shackford in physiology class: Photo by Partridge.
Agora Society: Photo by Partridge.
Florence Converse: Photo by G. Walden Smith.
Jeannette Marks: Photo by Katharine McClellan. Courtesy of the Mount Holyoke College Archives, Mount Holyoke College.
Gail Laughlin: Photo by C. W. Hearn.
Webb House residents: Photo by Partridge.

Photo Credits

Little House residents: Photo by Nicolas.
Students leaving for vacation: Photo by World Wide Photos.
Vida Scudder: Photo by Sue Page.
Mary Case: Photo by Bachrach.
Ellen Hayes: Photo by Gertrude Richards.

Index